Florida

ATLANTIC

OCEAN

Waycross
Savannah
St Simons Island
Brunswick
Homerville
Cumberland Island
Boulogne
Fargo
Canova
Fernandina Beach
White Springs
Jacksonville Beach
City
Jacksonville
Starke
St Augustine
Waldo
Chiefland
Gainesville
Williston
Ocala
DAYTONA BEACH TO JACKSONVILLE
Ormond Beach
Daytona Beach
De Land
New Smyrna Beach
Canaveral Nat'l Seashore
WALT DISNEY WORLD RESORT
Titusville
Kennedy Space Center
ETERSBURG TO CEDAR KEY
wildlife Refuge
Cape
CENTRAL FLORIDA
Orlando
Kissimmee
St Cloud
THE SPACE COAST
ORLANDO AND ITS OTHER WORLDS
TAMPA
Bartow
Melbourne
Tampa Bay
Sebring
Sebastian
Vero Beach
GULF COAST
Myakka River State Park
Fort Drum
Fort Pierce
Sarasota
Port Saint Lucie
SARASOTA TO NAPLES
THE PALM BEACHES
Stuart
Venice
Lake Okeechobee
Jupiter
Port Charlotte
North Palm Beach
Cape Coral
Palm Beach Shores
West Palm Beach
Sanibel Island
Fort Myers
Belle Glade
Palm Beach
Delray Beach
FORT LAUDERDALE
Naples
Collier-Seminole St. P.
Big Cypress
Boynton Beach
Pompano Beach
Marco Island
THE EVERGLADES
ort Lauderdale
Hollywood
MIAMI BEACH
Ten Thousand Islands
the Everglades
Kendall
Perrine
METROPOLITAN MIAMI
Miami Beach
SOUTH FLORIDA
Homestead
Cutler
Cape Sable
Key Largo
Bay
FLORIDA KEYS
Pine Islands
Tortugas
Marquesas Keys
Key West
Marathon
Florida Keys
KEY WEST

Grand Bahama Island
Freeport
BAHAMAS
Straits of Florida

INSIGHT ◉ GUIDES

FLORIDA

C334214899

◉ Walking Eye App

YOUR FREE DESTINATION CONTENT AND EBOOK AVAILABLE THROUGH THE WALKING EYE APP

Your guide now includes a free eBook and destination content for your chosen destination, all for the same great price as before. Simply download the Walking Eye App from the App Store or Google Play to access your free eBook and destination content.

HOW THE WALKING EYE APP WORKS

Through the Walking Eye App, you can purchase a range of eBooks and destination content. However, when you buy this book, you can download the corresponding eBook and destination content for free. Just see below in the grey panels where to find your free content and then scan the QR code at the bottom of this page.

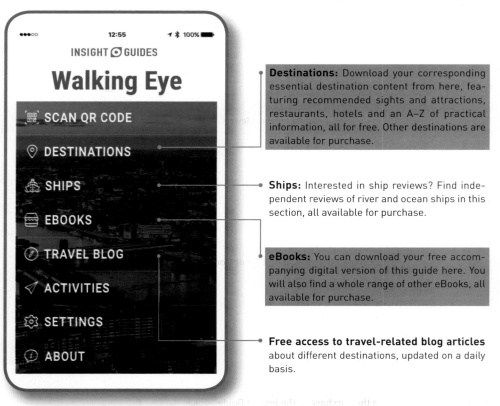

Destinations: Download your corresponding essential destination content from here, featuring recommended sights and attractions, restaurants, hotels and an A–Z of practical information, all for free. Other destinations are available for purchase.

Ships: Interested in ship reviews? Find independent reviews of river and ocean ships in this section, all available for purchase.

eBooks: You can download your free accompanying digital version of this guide here. You will also find a whole range of other eBooks, all available for purchase.

Free access to travel-related blog articles about different destinations, updated on a daily basis.

HOW THE DESTINATION CONTENT WORKS

Each destination includes a short introduction, an A–Z of practical information and recommended points of interest, split into 4 different categories:
- Highlights
- Accommodation
- Eating out
- What to do

You can view the location of every point of interest and save it by adding it to your Favourites. In the 'Around Me' section you can view all the points of interest within 5km.

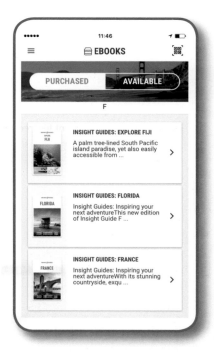

HOW THE EBOOKS WORK

The eBooks are provided in EPUB file format. Please note that you will need an eBook reader installed on your device to open the file. Many devices come with this as standard, but you may still need to install one manually from Google Play.

The eBook content is identical to the content in the printed guide.

HOW TO DOWNLOAD THE WALKING EYE APP

1. Download the Walking Eye App from the App Store or Google Play.
2. Open the app and select the scanning function from the main menu.
3. Scan the QR code on this page – you will then be asked a security question to verify ownership of the book.
4. Once this has been verified, you will see your eBook and destination content in the purchased ebook and destination sections, where you will be able to download them.

Other destination apps and eBooks are available for purchase separately or are free with the purchase of the Insight Guide book.

CONTENTS

Travel Tips

TRANSPORTATION

A – Z

FURTHER READING

Maps

Inside front cover Florida
Inside back cover theme parks

LEGEND
𝒫 Insight on
◉ Photo Story

THE BEST OF FLORIDA: TOP ATTRACTIONS

△ **Key West**. The Conch Republic, Margaritaville, Mañanaland – call it what you like, Key West is always up for a party. Perched at the end of the Florida Keys, the southernmost city is a hub of colorful nonconformity where free spirits find refuge from the mainstream and the rest of us can drop in for a couple of drinks. See page 153.

△ **Theme parks**. Disney, Universal, SeaWorld, Legoland, and Busch Gardens operate no less than 10 theme parks in Florida. At the center of the theme-park galaxy is Orlando, home of Walt Disney World Resort, which claims more than 50 million visitors each year. See pages 209 and 231.

▽ **Everglades National Park**. Encompassing more than 1.5 million acres (607,028 hectares) of subtropical wilderness, this national park sustains hundreds of plant and animal species, including endangered Florida panthers and West Indian manatees. See page 129.

△ **The Panhandle**. Had enough of the crowds in central Florida? The Panhandle, aka Northwest Florida, has miles of undeveloped beaches and quiet seaside towns to explore at your leisure. See page 311.

△ **Daytona 500**. NASCAR's most prestigious race (and one of the country's biggest sporting events) this is a blistering, 500-mile (800km) contest of driving skill and mechanical prowess. See page 189.

△ **South Beach**. The buff, bronze, and beautiful people gather at the red-hot nightclubs and glorious Art Deco hotels of this exotic neighborhood. See page 117.

▷ **The Dalí Museum**. Let your imagination run wild at this famous museum in St Petersburg, one of the country's finest museums dedicated to a single artist. See page 268.

◁ **Beautiful beaches**. White sugar sand and warm azure waters are the key ingredients of Florida's beaches. With miles and miles of coastline, there's a beach for every taste and occasion. See page 274.

◁ **Kennedy Space Center**. History and science are brought vividly to life at this fascinating complex where you can explore the past, present, and future endeavors of space exploration. See page 183.

▷ **The John and Mable Ringling Museum of Art**. A palazzo packed with priceless European art, this art gallery is a tribute to the man known for creating the "Greatest Show on Earth." See page 280.

THE BEST OF FLORIDA: EDITOR'S CHOICE

Mako – Orlando's super-fast shark-themed roller coaster.

BEST THRILL RIDES

Cobra's Curse. Busch Garden's popular roller coaster lifts you up 70ft (21 meters), only to hurl you toward snake fangs. See page 262.

Mako. Even sharks aren't scary compared to the fastest, longest, tallest ride in town. See page 236.

Avatar Flight of Passage. Soar through magical landscapes on the back of a banshee in this immersive 3-D experience. See page 224

Race Through New York Starring Jimmy Fallon. Why visit NYC when you can fly over its star attractions in this exciting ride? It's Manhattan like you've never seen it. See page 233.

Caladesi Island State Park.

BEST BEACHES

Bill Baggs Cape Florida State Park. Regularly rated as one of the best in the US, this pristine beach on Key Biscayne soothes the weary soul. See page 125.

Bradenton Beach. At the south end of Anna Maria Key, Bradenton has walkable streets and beaches that attract nesting sea turtles in summer. See page 277.

Caladesi Island State Park. Florida's No. 1 white-sand beach is a boat-in-only experience with a mangrove kayak trail. See page 265.

Sanibel Island. Do the "Sanibel Stoop" to collect lovely shells washed up on the shores of this beautifully preserved island. See page 283.

BEST OF THE OUTDOORS

Anhinga and Gumbo Limbo Trails, Everglades National Park. Explore the trails for a nose-to-nose encounter with a rambunctious alligator and spy the red-peeling gumbo limbo, aka the "tourist tree." See page 134.

J.N. "Ding" Darling National Wildlife Refuge. Early mornings in the colder winter months bring thousands of birds to this refuge. It's a rare opportunity to see roseate spoonbills, heron, pelicans, ibis, and anhinga birds. See page 284.

John Pennekamp Coral Reef State Park. The only living coral reef in the continental US reveals its riot of color to snorkelers, scuba divers, and those who take the glass-bottom boat tour. See page 144.

Merritt Island National Wildlife Refuge. See manatees and sea turtles in the shadow of Kennedy Space Center. See page 186.

Myakka River State Park. A former ranch, Florida's largest state park offers rustic cabins, campsites, hiking, and horseback riding. See page 281.

Calle Ocho street party.

RAISE A GLASS IN CELEBRATION

Calle Ocho. The largest Hispanic heritage festival in the Southeast is a sizzling, salsa-fueled street party. See page 107.

Ocala Rodeo. Forget about the long lines at the theme parks and hearken back to the good old days when the only thing treated like cattle in Florida was, well,

cattle. See page 302.

St George Island Mullet Toss. This beach party gives new meaning to the term "flying fish." See page 314.

Sunset Celebration at Mallory Square. Why applaud a sunset? In Key West the sun doesn't just set, it goes down in a blaze of glory. See page 155.

MUST-SEE MUSEUMS

Florida Museum of Natural History. It's a light, bright, kid-friendly museum with well-interpreted exhibits on Florida's life zones and native cultures, plus an awesome butterfly pavilion. See page 299.

The Dalí Museum. The

location is almost as bizarre as the large-scale psycho-drama paintings, but early Impressionist-inspired works show a more sensitive side of the surrealist master Salvador Dalí. See page 268.

Norton Museum of Art. French Impressionists, Post-Impressionists, and modern American masters put the Norton on a par with institutions many times its size. See page 176.

Vizcaya. With 70 rooms of European antiques, Vizcaya is a rare example of the opulent life. See page 114.

Opulent Vizcaya.

Anna Maria Pier, Manatee County.

Airboating in the Everglades.

Ocean Drive, Miami.

The Dalí Museum.

LET THE SUN SHINE

Florida's population has doubled in the past 30 years and it keeps growing. There are plenty of reasons for the Sunshine State's enduring popularity.

A mouthwatering plate of crabs.

From Tennessee Williams to Ernest Hemingway, some of America's greatest artists have found a land of refuge and adventure, whether fleeting or long-term, along the lovely coasts and inland forests of Florida. The image of the Sunshine State as a place where dreams come true has lost none of its appeal, and about 1,000 newcomers arrive every day on its sunny shores. People often joke that most of Florida's inhabitants were born elsewhere – anywhere from upstate New York to Cuba.

Travelers regard Florida as an unbeatable vacation destination – and with good reason. Nature has played a major role, providing everything from the tropical Keys, verdant inland forests, and wild Everglades to miles of shimmering beaches. And when nature isn't enough, man-made attractions fill the gap in fast-paced cities such as Orlando, theme park capital of the world; and Miami, where the ice-cream-colored buildings (restored to their 1930s Art Deco glory) provide the backdrop for posing and partying in trendy South Beach.

It is simple to get around Florida if you're comfortable behind the wheel, with rental cars easy to come by and reasonably priced. Accommodations are also plentiful, ranging from affordable roadside motels to quaint bed-and-breakfasts and lavish beachside resorts. The weather is unlikely to disappoint, though be aware that summers can be oppressively hot and humid with frequent thunderstorms that may interrupt outdoor pursuits.

The ethos of Florida is perhaps best embodied by Walt Disney, who settled in similarly sunny California but had a soft spot in his heart for the home of his eye-popping Disney World. As Walt himself once put it, "wholesome pleasure, sport, and recreation" should be as important as work to the United States' national character. In Florida, land of expansive vistas and heart-racing adventure, Disney found the perfect embodiment of his vision. Visitors are unlikely to be disappointed.

The beach at Taylor State Park, Key West.

Florida farmer and his mustang.

THE FLORIDIAN PEOPLE

A state with a singular identity to outsiders contains cultural multitudes, from Cuban-Americans to northern Jews to descendants of the German and Irish workers who fueled 19th-century immigration.

For many Americans, even many of those who live and vacation in Florida, the state and its people have a reputation for eccentricity, a quirkiness belied by the overwhelming popularity of carbon-copy suburban housing and manicured lawns. A quote summing up the colorful characters of the Sunshine State is often attributed to *Miami Herald* journalist and best-selling author Carl Hiaasen: "There's nothing wrong with Florida that a Category 6 hurricane can't cure."

But the real Floridians carry identities much deeper than their popular caricatures. An array of ethnic and national influences have dovetailed within the boundaries of one southeast peninsula to create a thoroughly modern melting pot, where no-nonsense Manhattanites break *pan Cubano* (Cuban bread) with neighbors steeped in Greek, Caribbean, French-Canadian, and African-American cultures. Visitors may only have the time to encounter one of these many threads in the Floridian tapestry, but their intermingling is constantly driving the state's sense of itself and its unique attitude towards life.

In short, the demographics of Florida may say one thing – about 78 percent white, 25 percent Hispanic, and 17 percent black, according to the most recent US census tallies – but the state's day-to-day reality tells a much more compelling, if occasionally unsettled, saga of different peoples living together.

DRIVERS AND SHOPPERS

The popular image of Florida tends to resemble quintessential 21st-century America, with strip malls and gated communities reinforcing conformity and convenience. That stereotype manages to be at once valid and inadequate in

Mallory Square, Key West.

its depiction of Floridian lifestyles; locals take to their cars for a quarter-mile trip to a chain store, but they also frequent walkable beachside boardwalks and ethnic restaurants that tend to lie hidden between the big box stores.

People come to Florida not only for vacation, but also to live. For the third most-populated state in the nation, Florida has a significant number of non-native residents, making the state a lively melting pot of cultures.

The economic value of tourism is embraced, with residents often taking pride in welcoming visitors as well as steering their own out-of-town friends and family to a favorite spot. Driving an hour or more to the *right* restaurant or the *best* spot to sunbathe is a common practice in a place where theme parks have made waiting in long lines less stressful than they might be elsewhere.

Floridians rarely consider their state part of the American South, despite its location, but many residents display a self-deprecating awareness of their pop-cultural role as the United States' dumb blonde. From the hanging chad scandal that held up the 2000 election to the growing popularity of weird "Flori-duh" news from the state's ample police blotters, Floridians often hide a more complex sense of self behind their sunny weather and shiny sport-utility vehicles. Perhaps the best

A portrait of John and Mable Ringling painted on the ceiling at their Sarasota mansion.

way to understand the local character, then, is to delve more deeply into the state's past.

A STRUGGLE FOR CONTROL

In the three centuries before Florida signed on as the 27th American state, three European nations jockeyed for influence over a wild region already tamed and beloved by many American Indian tribes. After the Spanish nobleman Juan Ponce de León came French Huguenots, such as Jacques Le Moyne, who put down roots in the north before battling their rivals for control over what is now the city of Jacksonville.

Florida ultimately fell to the British in the 1760s, only to be returned to Spain for about 30

years after the American colonies won their war for independence from the Crown. Today that long-ago quest for dominance plays out both in obvious and subtle ways.

The French impact on the state manifests in a long-thriving Francophone community, driven in recent years by French-Canadians and epitomized by the newspaper *Le Soleil de Floride* (established in 1983), as well as French colonial architecture still found in many cities. Spanish traditions, though subtle, were woven into the culture through the descendants of the original Spanish settlements. Much of the state's architecture and urban design owes a debt to the Spanish colonial style.

The British role in the state's evolution is also subtle, shadowing other diverse American enclaves where ancestors from Britain have smoothly integrated into the population. The Irish have maintained a strong hold on their rituals, with several Floridian cities hosting Irish music and dance festivals, as well as theater groups and restaurant-pubs that bring a strong touch of Emerald Isle to the Sunshine State.

HISPANIC HERITAGE

Florida is one of only nine American states with more than 1 million Hispanic residents, and it is also home to more than half the Cuban population in the US – and the number has surged since new rules came into place in 2015. The role of immigration in shaping Floridian culture cannot be overstated. This is a place where people choose to live, not simply because they were born here. A combination of celebration and tension has greeted new arrivals over the past century.

Latin Americans have been vibrant players in Florida since its earliest days, but the influx of Cuban expatriates that came after Fidel Castro took control of the island in 1959 helped shape much of the state's current identity. South Florida, in particular, was soon dotted with Cuban-American communities that brought their own religious rituals, cuisine, and political clout to a place with a complicated background. Not only did Florida pass between French, Spanish, and British control before joining the United States, it was also a part of the Confederacy during the Civil War, and the racist attitudes of some white Floridians persist to this day.

Although the Sunshine State has a reputation for easy living, the reality is that this is a place where many people have come together. What resulted has been a constantly changing experiment in coexistence, as Floridian newspapers indelicately referred to Cuban and Haitian "boat people" landing ashore in Miami, even as their already-arrived friends and family members were driving economic growth that benefited the state. With Nicaraguans, Venezuelans, Brazilians, and other Latino arrivals joining the tide by the late 1980s, the state legislature began a long debate over immigration that continues to this day.

While older Cubans tend to vote Republican espresso or munching on fried plantains and guava *pastelito* pastries. At night, the hypnotic rhythms of Mexican *salsa*, Puerto Rican *reggaeton* and Dominican *bachata* music are commonly spun on both nightclub dance floors and mainstream radio stations, particularly in the southern part of the state. In recent years, a thriving subgenre of Latin-southern fusion-style hip-hop, whose leading artists include Trina, Trick Daddy, Flo-Rida, and Rick Ross, has taken hold in Miami.

Perhaps the best example of Florida's complex relationship with its Hispanic residents can

Fine dining at St. Armands Circle in Sarasota.

(due to a long-standing conservative stance on cultural issues and stringent anti-communism ideals stoked by Castro), their American-born offspring are veering left. The rise of anti-immigrant sentiment among Conservatives has left Hispanic Floridians to beat back a tide of discrimination. Latino advocates and business leaders view a healthy immigrant population as an essential part of the state's culture, often butting heads with politicians who aim to crack down on undocumented arrivals by passing strong identity-verification laws.

On the lighter side, many Hispanic habits have become ingrained in Floridian culture, regardless of ethnic or cultural identity. On a lazy Sunday, you can find many locals sipping tiny cups of Cuban

⊙ ON THE PAGE AND SCREEN

The Floridian ethos is memorably recaptured by a slew of classic books, from the 1920s drama of Zora Neale Hurston's *Their Eyes Were Watching God* to the environmental thrillers of Carl Hiaasen. For a moving take on the state, try *Key Largo*, a 1948 film noir set in the southernmost islands, or *Edward Scissorhands*, a locally shot fable that sends up the suburbanites. Miami-set movies deserve a category of their own, particularly *The Birdcage*, a South Beach tale that helped push drag-queens into the mainstream. Or watch Will Smith's sun-drenched action flick *Bad Boys*. The quality may vary, but the imagery of the city makes a perfect introduction to its charms.

be found in the bilingual signs that direct drivers to major landmarks – despite the fact that English was named the official language of the state more than 20 years ago. Florida is one of 31 states that have declared English the official language, although the United States as a whole has persisted in not doing so.

NATIVE AMERICAN INFLUENCE

Florida's first people were tragically decimated by violence and communicable disease brought to their doorstep by European settlers. Luckily,

Pest control officers regularly trap alligators in suburban swimming pools.

their cultures have survived and their people play a central role in the state's story.

The Seminole Indians, also known as the Creeks before coming to Florida, maintain six reservations in Florida as well as a thriving business network that, according to its website, pays $3.5 million in federal taxes and directs $24 million elsewhere in the state's economy through casinos, a museum, a swamp safari, and other enterprises. The Seminole name is attached to everything from the sports team at a state university to one of its most populous counties, and its annual powwow draws significant crowds to Tampa. As the Seminole are proud of noting, theirs was the only tribe to never sign a peace treaty with the US government.

The Miccosukee tribe, which grew out of the Seminole tradition, maintains a strong presence in Florida. Operating everything from gas stations to a lavish country club as well as four reservations, Miccosukee members have developed their own educational curriculum to keep their traditions alive and remind locals that their history in the state predates Christopher Columbus.

Older tribes in the state include the Calusa, Ocale, and Apalachee. Over the course of several centuries, beginning with the arrival of Spanish conquistadors in the early 16th century, these tribal people intermingled and traded with the Europeans, and helped shape many of the sights currently seen in the state. It was these people who helped plant the first corn crops in Florida and carved out some of its still-vibrant recreational trails.

RETIREE REVIVAL

Only in Florida could you find a city-within-a-city where children are not permitted to stay for more than three weeks at a time. But The Villages, located an hour north of Orlando and christened "Disney World for retirees" by America's National Public Radio, is only the largest (population 157,000 and growing) of multiple planned communities in the state where senior citizens and their cultural trends are dominant.

More than 19 percent of Floridians are 65 and older, making the state a popular home for senior citizens. Indeed, most Americans either have an elderly relative living in the state or know someone who does. Many restaurants in areas popular with retirees are crowded with early-bird dinner patrons before 6pm, and shuffleboard and mah-jongg games are a common sight in residential developments, although Baby Boomer retirees favor pickleball and Zumba.

Yet Florida is also an excellent example of how retirees can be participatory members of their state. Its 55-and-over residents are strong players in the AARP (American Association of Retired Persons), the advocacy outlet for older Americans, making the group's Florida chapter a major player in both local and national politics. Particularly as the baby boomer generation swells the ranks of American seniors, retired Floridians are anything but leisurely in their pursuit of financial, health-care, and Social Security reforms.

THE AFRICAN-AMERICAN COMMUNITY

Florida was known for cultivating accomplished and self-sufficient majority-black communities even as other southern states struggled to put the ugly legacy of slavery behind them. One of the biggest symbols of the African-American role in Floridian development is Eatonville, the nation's first formally incorporated city led and

Today the state continues to rack up African-American cultural and academic achievement, sending several black representatives to Congress and electing its first black lieutenant governor, Jennifer Carroll, in 2010. But the legacy of urban blight and racial inequality still holds back the state's African-Americans, many of whom tend to be relegated by economic need to neighborhoods where education and health care are of poorer quality. Tension between African-Americans and the law remains a source of unrest, as shown by the reaction to the 2012 fatal

The golf course at the Gasparilla Club has amazing ocean views.

populated by black Americans. Now an Orlando suburb, the town is the self-identified hometown of writer Zora Neale Hurston, one of a handful of immortal black female writers, and remains a dearly held part of African-American history.

The same year that Eatonville was formed also saw Florida Agricultural & Mechanical University founded in Tallahassee for the express purpose of educating African-Americans. Today, A&M, as it is called, joins American Beach (on Amelia Island near Jacksonville) and other Florida sites as a reminder of the issues surrounding integration and civil rights in the state. St Augustine is also on the list of African-American landmarks, having hosted the first homestead for freed blacks in the state under the name of Fort Mose in the 1730s.

shooting of teenager Trayvon Martin by George Zimmerman in a Sanford gated community.

FLORIDA'S CHOSEN

Of the 7.2 million Jewish-Americans in the US, more than 9 percent of them call Florida home, and the state has the highest number of Jewish residents behind California and New York. Florida's population is 3.2 percent Jewish, making the state a potent locus for Jewish cultural and spiritual development.

The Jewish influence on American arts and politics grew in leaps and bounds during the mid- to late 20th century, but the religion was alive and well in Florida nearly two centuries earlier. The state's first acknowledged Jewish settlement was begun near Pensacola in 1763, though the oldest recorded Jewish congregation did not spring up in the Jacksonville area until 1876.

The real boom time for Floridian Jews began after World War II, when an influx drove the population from an estimated 25,000 to more than 175,000. The spike in Jewish residents also brought a notable number of unique sects within the religion to the state's sunny confines, including adherents from Cuba, Brazil, and Morocco.

Today parts of Florida – primarily South Florida – are home to an abundance of Jewish syna-

Walking the dog on Duval Street in Key West.

gogues, bagel shops, and community centers where major holidays from Passover to Purim are celebrated. Jewish residents are an active force in local politics, helping propel more than 15 of their own to the mayoralty of Miami Beach. Meanwhile, the religion's effect on the Floridian identity has been exponentially increased by pop-cultural touchstones such as the Boca Raton retirement home where Jerry Seinfeld's parents lived in his eponymous sitcom.

THE SNOWBIRDS

Just as some types of birds fly south for the winter, so do seasonal migrants flock to Florida during the colder months. Florida is hardly the only destination for snowbirds (and

"snowflakes", who travel back and forth), but it has acquired the biggest reputation for temporary residents, perhaps because of its friendliness towards retirees and its ample supply of mobile-home campgrounds, a popular vehicle of choice for middle-class permanent vacationers.

There are few reliable estimates of the current number of Floridian snowbirds, due to their constant mobility, although The Palm Beach Post counts a-month-or-longer seasonal residents at nearly 1 million statewide.

Far from dying out, the temporary migrant appears to be adapting, with fewer retirees and more working transients, both wealthy and working-class. The older, retired snowbird is more common in south Florida, with *The Palm Beach Post* reporting that the county gains 145,000 residents during "season," an 11 percent increase. Working snowbirds can be found anywhere in the state where openings exist in the service sector – such as theme parks, which happily dole out seasonal hours.

ASIAN-AMERICANS

While they are far from the most visible constituency in Florida, there are more than a half-million Chinese, Japanese, Korean, Filipino, Vietnamese, and other Asian immigrants residing here. This makes the state the ninth most popular destination for Asian-Americans. The state's native Asian population grew by 72 percent between 2000 and 2010 and is projected to top 1.8 million by 2050, according to the Asian-American Federation of Florida.

⊘ AMERICAN PARADISE

Florida is the de facto vacation destination for many Americans, and there is no shortage of bold-faced names who consider it a second (or even first) home. Madonna owned a lavish Miami home and frequented the city during the 1990s, and she has been joined in her Florida favoritism at various times by Sylvester Stallone, Rosie O'Donnell, P. Diddy, and Tiger Woods. Sports stars Michael Jordan, Shaquille O'Neal, Tiger Woods and Serena Williams all have homes in Palm Beach, as does President Donald Trump who frequently hosts global dignitaries at his flashy Palm Beach mansion and club Mar-a-Lago.

Sadly, Asian-Americans' most vocal recent emergence in Florida society ended in defeat. A 2008 ballot initiative would have eliminated language in the state constitution that prevented "aliens ineligible for citizenship" from owning property, a measure approved in 1926 amid a cloud of racial discrimination against Japanese immigrants. But conservative political groups outgunned Asian-American groups in a public relations battle over the initiative, recasting the anti-Asian-American language as a beneficial modern move against illegal immigration, and the social force exerted by the largest city in the state is greater than any single group, and visitors should not think that Miami is synonymous with Latino. The city takes pride in its diversity, and while one group may speak the loudest, all are given a hearing.

As Miami modernizes and incorporates ever more diverse influences, the broader state is guaranteed to follow suit – putting the neon-lit city at the leading edge of Florida's socio-economic evolution. Where the people of Miami lead, the state tends to follow.

Pirates storm the city of Tampa during the annual Gasparilla Invasion.

the technically irrelevant but historically offensive statute remains intact.

MIAMI VICE AND SPICE

Florida's biggest and most famous city looms larger than life over its people, serving as the launch pad for much of its major social trends, from immigration to suburban sprawl, as well as its artistic personality. The 1980s TV show *Miami Vice* spawned a culinary festival titled Miami Spice, with both monikers channeling the city's indigenous multicultural energy into a cosmopolitan image for the rest of the state and the world.

The metropolitan area of Miami, often referred to by its county name of Miami-Dade, has a population that is largely Hispanic. But

⊘ VIETNAMESE IMMIGRANTS

The Vietnamese population in Florida more than doubled between 1990 and 2000. Today the cultural traditions of Southeast Asia are a particularly strong presence in the Vietnamese district of Orlando, located in the Mills 50 neighborhood, and can also be felt and tasted in popular restaurants in Miami and Tampa.

The best time to experience a taste of Saigon in central Florida is during the winter Tet holiday, which is marked by a two-day festival of food, music, dancing, and a beauty pageant. Tet celebrates the Vietnamese Lunar New Year and is held at the Central Florida Fairgrounds.

DECISIVE DATES

c.8000 BC
Nomadic tribes reach the Florida peninsula and begin to settle the land a few thousand years later.

AD 300–1000
More than 10,000 Native Americans live in the Florida region when the Spanish arrive.

1513
Two decades after Columbus's voyage, Spanish conquistador Ponce de León is the first European to set foot on the peninsula, near present-day St Augustine. He later returns to Florida with settlers, but abandons his expedition.

1562
The French arrive in Florida to challenge the Spanish, who then strengthen their hold, founding their first permanent settlement three years later.

1586
A British attack on St Augustine triggers centuries of dispute between Britain, France, and Spain, and America.

1763
The English receive Florida from Spain in exchange for Cuba. Twenty years later, the territory is returned to Spain.

1803
The Spanish cede Florida's Panhandle to Napoleon, who soon sells the region to the United States.

1817–18
Pressure from settlers results in violence with Indian tribes and leads to the outbreak of the First Seminole War. Andrew Jackson overcomes Seminole resistance, then sets about taking control of Florida on behalf of the US government. He becomes Florida's first governor, and later US president.

1824
The newly founded town of Tallahassee is declared the capital of the Florida Territory.

1835–42
Seminole leader Osceola launches a campaign against the US Army which ends when most Indians surrender and are deported.

1845
Florida becomes the 27th state of the Union.

1861
Florida secedes from the Union and joins the Confederate States in the Civil War.

1868
Following a revolt against Spain in Cuba, the first wave of Cubans arrives in Florida.

1883
The great railroad era begins. Settlers head south.

1898
Revolution erupts in Cuba; the US joins in to drive Spain off the island.

1912
Completion of the final section of the East Coast Railroad to Key West, prompting the first property boom of the 20th century and raising the state's population to one million people.

1926–28
Two powerful hurricanes strike Miami, killing more than 2,000 people.

1930s–40s
Miami Beach's Art Deco hotels are built and tourism thrives in South Florida. During World War II Florida is used as a training ground for soldiers.

An impression of Florida Indians in 1564 by Jacques le Moyne.

1949

A military missile test site is established at Florida's Cape Canaveral.

1959

Fidel Castro leads a communist revolution in Cuba, setting off a long-term migration of thousands of Cubans who flee his regime. More *emigrés* from Central and South America follow.

1960s

The first rockets soar from Cape Canaveral at the start of the space race; the first moonshot is launched from Florida.

1970s

An economic recession badly hurts Florida, though cheer still reigns when Walt Disney World – the state's first major theme park – opens near Orlando.

1980s

The campaign to restore the Art Deco district of Miami Beach launches the area's renaissance.

1981

The Space Shuttle *Columbia* is launched from Kennedy Space Center, the beginning of the successful shuttle program.

1984

The influential TV series *Miami Vice* premieres, changing the public image of the city.

1992

Andrew, the biggest hurricane for decades, devastates southeast Florida.

1997

Designer Gianni Versace is shot and killed in South Beach.

2000

Florida is at the center of the infamous hanging chads controversy during the presidential campaign between Al Gore and George W. Bush.

2004

Four hurricanes pummel the coastline over a 48-day period, breaking a record set in 1964.

Art Deco buildings in Miami's South Beach.

The final launch of the space shuttle Atlantis on July 8, 2011.

2010

The Wizarding World of Harry Potter opens at Universal Orlando.

2011

NASA's space shuttle program comes to an end; all five shuttles are retired to museum around the country. *Atlantis*, the last shuttle to be launched, remains at Kennedy Space Center.

2013

Celebrations of the 500th anniversary of the arrival in Florida of Ponce de León.

2015

Disney World celebrates its 60th anniversary.

2016

Fifty people killed in shooting at Pulse, a gay nightclub in Orlando.

2017

Palm Beach makes national headlines as President Donald Trump spends most weekends at his home there, Mar-a-Lago, creating traffic and havoc. Irma, a Category 5 hurricane, causes widespread flooding and damage, particularly in the Florida Keys.

An Indian leader of the upper St John's River.

EARLY FLORIDA

Indigenous people thrived on local plenty from both land and sea long before the European invaders arrived and altered the course of history.

Florida's first inhabitants were Paleo-Indians fleeing the frozen north during the most recent Ice Age, when the Florida peninsula was a dry desert with a landmass twice the size of what it is today. Hunters were attracted by the warm climate and abundant game, including now-extinct ground sloths, mastodons, camels, and giant bison. Paleo-era remains have been uncovered at Silver Springs and other central Florida water sources.

ANCIENT HUNTERS

By 6000 BC, these first Floridians had coalesced into hunter-gatherers associated with particular territories, where they hunted otters, rats, squirrels, turtles, alligators, and opossums; they also fished in lakes, and gathered cactus fruit and other delicacies. Early Archaic people invented tools made from animal teeth and bone fastened to wooden handles. They ceremonially interred their dead wrapped in woven palmettos.

Calusa Indians inhabited Florida's Gulf coast.

A sinkhole in Dade County contains evidence of human habitation dating back about 10,000 years. Found at the site were the bones of extinct Ice Age mammals as well as stone tools and human remains.

The swampy land preserved the corpses so well that archaeologists excavating Windover Ponder near Titusville were able to extract human brain DNA – a first on the continent.

These early people consumed oysters and conchs in coastal areas as well as mussels and snails at freshwater sites, and used large shells

as tools for fashioning dugout canoes. The shell mounds were a distinguishing feature of their camps and can still be seen beside inland rivers and at the mouths of estuaries.

As early as 1500 BC, Archaic people were making the first ceramics in North America, which they strengthened with the fibers from Spanish moss and palmetto. They grew corn and squash and traded with other tribes from Alabama and Georgia. People living along the St John's River created distinctive effigy pots, stamped with corncob patterns.

Archaeologists are particularly fascinated by the more than 14,000 burial mounds, probably influenced by the Hopewell cultures of Ohio and Illinois, found throughout Florida. They occur in Matecumbe in the Keys, Bear Lake in the Everglades, Safety Harbor on the Gulf, and at dozens of sites in the Panhandle, and have yielded insight into religious rituals among these ancient people.

By the time Spanish conquistador Juan Ponce de León landed at Cape Canaveral in 1513, more than 150,000 Indians were living on the peninsula. The eastern Panhandle was the province of the Apalachee. Their neighbors in the western Panhandle were the Pensacola, Apalachicola, and Chtot. The Mayaimi people lived on the

in villages of palm-thatched huts. Chiefs and female nobles were lavishly tattooed and wore feather capes, shell beads, and metal belts. Males wore breechcloths of deerskin, while women dressed in skirts of Spanish moss so tightly woven it shone like silk.

THE SEMINOLE

By the early 1700s, Florida's Indian population was drastically reduced by warfare and European diseases. Between 1613 and 1617, half of the 16,000 converted Indians in Spanish missions in

A colorful diorama at the South Florida Museum depicts a Paleo-Indian man hunting an ancient bison.

shores of Lake Okeechobee. Modern-day Miami and Palm Beach were home to the Tequesta. Southwestern Florida was the territory of the fierce Calusa, whose shell-tipped arrows took Ponce de León's life in 1521. The largest group called themselves the Timucua. A related tribe called the Tocobaga lived in the Tampa Bay area.

CHIEFS AND NOBLES

The first European to document Florida's Indian culture was Frenchman Jacques Le Moyne. He made watercolors of Indians after surviving the 1565 massacre at Fort Caroline on the St John's River by Spanish conquistador Pedro Menendez de Aviles. Le Moyne's drawings show a tall, handsome people ruled by chiefs and nobles

northern Florida had died of infectious diseases. British colonists raiding from the coast of Carolina seized 1,000 Apalachee between 1702 and 1704, emptying villages in the north.

In Georgia, the Creek Indians had formed an uneasy alliance with the British, bartering animal skins and furs for guns. When that alliance collapsed, Spain seized the opportunity to invite the Creeks into depopulated areas of northern Florida. Sometime between 1716 and 1767, the Creeks began colonizing former Apalachee towns, spreading into the center of the state, where they took over former Timucuan farmlands, re-established trading networks, and lived alongside escaped slaves who had been granted sanctuary by the Spanish since 1693.

In Florida, the powerful Creek Indians transformed themselves into a new people: the Seminole. Their name was derived from the Spanish word *cimarron*, meaning "wild and unruly." Always great traders, the Seminole traveled as far as Cuba in dugout canoes and bartered with ships sailing along the Atlantic Coast. They hunted deer and other game in forested islands in the Everglades and grew corn, rice, watermelons, peaches, potatoes, and pumpkins.

In 1764, Spain gave up Florida to the British, and many Indians and black people left with

Osceola, a Seminole war leader.

the Spanish for Cuba rather than risk being forced into slavery on British plantations. The Georgia Creeks and Florida Seminole fared better. They used their alliance with the British to continue trading through the powerful Panton, Leslie & Company, owned by Scotsman William Panton, a friend of Alexander McGillivray, the half-English headman of the Creek Confederacy.

By the time Florida was returned to Spain by the American government in 1783, much of the land was settled by the Seminole and Spanish cattle ranchers and farmers. Many black people chose to live just outside Seminole villages, where they enjoyed the protection of their Indian neighbors in exchange for labor and goods.

THE LONG WAR

American ire over Spain's sanctuary policy for runaway slaves led to clashes along the Florida-Georgia border between 1785 and 1821. In 1818, Andrew Jackson, who would become Florida's first territorial governor under US rule, instigated the First Seminole War in Florida. His ruthless pursuit of Indian removal and extermination led the Seminole people to call him Sharp Knife.

After spending $20 million to fight a long and difficult Second Seminole War between 1835 and 1842, the US government coerced 3,824 Seminole Indians and runaway black slaves onto reservations west of the Mississippi. They abandoned the forts they had built, leaving only citizen-soldiers to defend new settlements like Orlando and Tampa. Skirmishes between settlers and the Seminole led to the Third Seminole War, which lasted from 1855 to 1858. At its close, the last Seminole holdouts, led by Chief Billy Bowlegs, were rounded up and sent to reservations in the Everglades and near Tampa Bay, where their descendants live today.

During this time, Florida's Seminole people proved themselves to be brave, implacable foes, well suited to guerrilla warfare in the swamps. The era's best-known Indian leader, Osceola, born Billy Powell in 1804 to an English father and Creek mother in Alabama, was neither Seminole nor a chief. But after moving with his mother to Florida early in the Second Seminole War, he grew to prominence as a war leader of ruthless daring. In 1837 he was captured under a white flag of truce by US Major General Thomas Jessup, a treacherous action that made Osceola a legend in the public's imagination.

Also legendary was Coacoochee, son of Miccosukee chief Philip and nephew of Micanopy, head of the Alachua Seminole near modern Gainesville. Coacoochee united these two main groups of Florida Indians and fought tirelessly during the Second Seminole War. But in 1842, he acknowledged defeat, telling his captors: "The white men are as thick as the leaves in the hammock; they come upon us thicker every year. They may shoot us, drive our women and children night and day; they may chain our hands and feet, but the red man's heart will always be free."

NEW SPAIN

The first of the Iberian explorers arrived in 1513, thirsty for a taste of magical waters, before conquistadors and other treasure seekers began looking for their own place in the sun.

Florida's calendar of official holidays salutes such notables as social reformers Martin Luther King Jr and Susan B. Anthony, Confederate leaders Robert E. Lee and Jefferson Davis, and of course Presidents Washington and Lincoln. And then there's Pascua Florida Day.

That occasion, known also as Florida State Day, is observed annually on April 2, and reminds us of how much of Florida's cultural and political history was built and shaped by early European explorers. The Spanish foundation was developed over three centuries of contact and conflict, adventure and achievement. The conquistadors mixed and matched their Spanish heritage with Native American and Anglo-American influences, as well as their English, French, and Dutch rivals. These interactions were rarely peaceable, and left an indelible mark that has been a part of making the state the multi-ethnic, constantly changing land it is today.

Juan Ponce de León, European explorer.

Juan Ponce de León called the Florida Keys "Los Mártires" because the low rocky islands reminded him of a line of martyred men.

LAND OF FLOWERS

The first stirrings of Spanish involvement in Florida came on March 27, 1513. On that date, crew members on the ship bearing Spanish explorer Juan Ponce de León spotted land that at first was mistaken for an island but turned out to be a peninsula, thick with vegetation. Ponce de León christened it La Florida because he and his men landed there during Eastertime, or Pascua Florida – the Feast of Flowers (a term still used for Easter Sunday in the Spanish-speaking world). The name stuck, and the La Florida moniker was initially applied to all Spanish holdings on the North American continent.

Some scholars believe that Ponce de León may have been preceded to Florida by earlier European pathfinders. One such explorer might have been John Cabot, who had voyaged to Labrador and northern locales years earlier, while Portuguese mariners had begun thrusting into the Atlantic nearly a full century before de León set sail. Still, credit has traditionally been given to de León.

SOLDIER OF FORTUNE

Who was this reputed discoverer of Florida, the state that would someday be represented by the

27th star emblazoned on the American flag? Ponce de León may have been the illegitimate son, born in 1460 of a Seville nobleman. As a young man, he fought the Moors as they made their last stand at Granada. He took part in the second of Christopher Columbus' voyages to the New World, and he became the first governor of Puerto Rico in 1509.

Said to be a frequent rival of Columbus' son, de León was given an opportunity by Spain's King Ferdinand I to become governor of a fabled island called Bimini, reputed to be a paradise flowing with waters that could perpetuate youthful vigor.

unknown shore was sighted. The expedition made landfall several days later, near the site that would become the first permanent settlement in the continental United States – St Augustine – and a river now known as the St John's.

AN UNFRIENDLY PEOPLE

Ponce de León's expedition ventured north to the mouth of the St John's River and south to the Florida Keys. After rounding the Keys, de León sailed up the west coast, possibly as far as Pensacola Bay. It became apparent to him that he had found

Jacques le Moyne's drawing depicts indigenous Indians at prayer.

The adventurer (then in his fifties) and his expedition set forth on March 3, 1513, to find what later lore labeled the Fountain of Youth. Bimini and that magically regenerative fountain would prove elusive, but Ponce de León made his fortune nonetheless.

Promised virtual ownership of the fabled island and anything else he might discover (including gold or other precious metals), the explorer and his crew poked about in the Bahamas for 25 days aboard the *Santa Maria de la Consolación* and the *Santiago*. There was no trace of Bimini, but they did locate the Bahama Channel, a short cut to the Caribbean from the Atlantic Ocean. Ponce de León and his crew celebrated Pascua Florida aboard ship. Six days later, on April 2, an

⊙ WHO'S FIRST?

Some believe that John Cabot, a Genoa-born mapmaker, beat Ponce de León to Florida. Cabot made several voyages to Labrador and other northern points shortly after Columbus' voyage of 1492. He won the praise of Henry VII, King of England, who commissioned him to chart the newfound lands. This he did although he only set foot ashore once. Cabot and his son Sebastian then sailed into Spanish territory in 1498. Here Cabot didn't come ashore, but shortly after their voyages, maps showing Florida were circulated in Europe. It is believed that Cabot perished when his ship was lost at sea on a subsequent voyage.

more than a mythical island. He made at least one more stop at Charlotte Harbor, once called Bahía Juan Ponce, near the modern city of Fort Myers. There he encountered Florida's native inhabitants. They were tall and powerful – and intensely hostile.

Ponce de León returned to Puerto Rico to plot his conquest of La Florida, but it wasn't until 1521 that he managed to scrape together two ships, 200 men, 50 horses, and all the equipment he needed. The king commissioned him and a contingent of missionary priests to settle the "island of Florida," taking care to treat the

Despite heavy losses, the Indians never retreated. An arrow hewn from swamp reed tore into Ponce de León's flesh. Six of his men, wounded, collapsed along with him. Survivors managed to get de León and the others into a boat. They reached Cuba, where de León died. Puerto Rico became the final resting place for this Spanish adventurer.

THE CONQUISTADORS

Three major expeditions and several smaller ones followed Ponce de León into La Florida during the next 40 years, seeking to tame the

An illustration depicting Juan Ponce de León and his men under attack.

Indians well, "seeking in every possible way to convert them to our Holy Catholic faith."

The explorer's put ashore near Charlotte Harbor, an event Catholic scholars consider the first authenticated instance of priests landing on the soil of the future United States. Unfortunately for the ill-fated entourage, their collective prayers proved fruitless. While laying foundations for the first shelters of the settlement, de León's men were surprised by a group of Calusas or Mayaimis, who attacked with a barrage of stones and arrows. The newcomers vainly tried to lead a counterattack; the men fought pitched battles with daggers, but blood quickly stained the newly consecrated soil. By some accounts, the Spanish even set snarling dogs on their enemies.

⊘ BAD TIDINGS

The initial hostile encounter between Ponce de León and the native people has led some historians to suspect that earlier contacts may have taken place between European colonizers and the Indians. Some historians speculate that slave hunters from Spanish settlements in the West Indies had previously sailed to Florida on raiding expeditions to capture and enslave local people. Reports from the explorers which maintain that Indians shouted Spanish words at the astonished navigators lend credence to that theory. Others believe that Indians in colonized islands had somehow sent their Florida neighbors word of their own harsh treatment at the hands of the Spanish colonizers.

hostile new land and its inhabitants. All failed, and about 2,000 Spaniards and an untold number of Native Americans lost their lives.

One such expedition was led by Pánfilo de Narváez, who waded ashore at Tampa Bay with about 400 men on Good Friday in 1528. A red-bearded soldier, Narváez earned his fearsome reputation when he lost an argument (and an eye) to Hernando Cortéz in Mexico. He firmly warned the Indians that if they did not obey him, and thus the king of Spain and the pope, "I will take your goods, doing you all the evil

dwindling party arrived in the Panhandle land of Apalachee exhausted and starving. The ships never showed up. Narváez and his men were forced to construct six makeshift vessels in which they set off for Mexico.

Alas, the ships vanished, and Narváez was never heard from again. Years later, four survivors of the expedition turned up in Mexico with an amazing story. Led by Alvar Nuñez Cabeza de Vaca, they survived a shipwreck, and wandered in the American Southwest for eight years before finally finding their way to Mexico.

Hernando de Soto.

A reconstruction of Spanish Mission San Luis de Apalachee, built in 1633.

and injury that I may be able... and I declare to you that the deaths and damages that arise therefrom, will be your fault and not that of His Majesty, nor mine, nor of these cavaliers who came with me." The Indians told Narváez exactly what he wanted to hear: there existed a land to the north called Apalachee, where they would find the treasure sought by every self-respecting conquistador: gold. Pánfilo de Narváez set out for Apalachee on foot, ordering his ships to rendezvous with him there. He found tall forests of longleaf pine, vast plains of cabbage palm, and sparkling springs and rivers, but no gold.

As Narváez pushed north, Indian raids and swarms of mosquitos took their toll. His

DE SOTO'S CAVALIERS

Hernando de Soto, the conquistador *par excellence* of his time, led a more ambitious assault on Florida, with only slightly better results than Narváez. In an 1836 narrative *Notices of Florida and the Campaigns*, M.M. Cohen described the escapades of the adventurous 36-year-old as "poetry put in action; it was the knight errantry of the Old World carried into the depths of the American wilderness ..."

De Soto landed at Tampa Bay in May 1539 with an army of 1,000 knights and fortune-hunters. They killed and enslaved Indians and penetrated the thick brush of the interior. Puzzled by the absence of gold and magnificent cities such as those he had seen in Peru and Mexico, De Soto pushed on through the Panhandle to Georgia and North Carolina before turning west to Alabama to continue his search. Three years and thousands of miles after his arrival in North America, De Soto died of a fever. His men submerged his body in the Mississippi River. Most of his conquistadors returned to Spain empty-handed.

Unfortunately, the precise details of De Soto's historic expedition died along with him. As Garcilaso Inca de la Vega, the son of a Spanish nobleman and a Peruvian Inca princess, wrote in his 1609 *History of the Conquest of Florida*, "the Spaniards did not think so much of learning the situation of places, as of hunting for gold and silver in Florida."

One lasting legend came from De Soto's venture, however. Near Tampa Bay, the conquistadors curiously scrutinized one Indian who greeted their arrival in fluent Spanish. Under his facepaint, the man turned out to be Juan Ortiz, a soldier who had landed with Narváez and survived capture in a remarkable manner. Garcilaso described Ortiz' ordeal at the hands of a Timucuan chief – or cacique – named Harriga: "He ate and slept very little, and was tormented ... he began to run at sunrise, and did not stop till night; and even during the dining of the cacique they would not suffer him to interrupt his course, so that at the end of the day he was in a pitiable condition ... The wife and daughters of Harriga, touched with compassion, then threw some clothes upon him, and assisted him so opportunely that they prevented him from dying."

Ortiz finally escaped with the aid of the chief's eldest daughter. Many years later, upon reading of the adventures of Ortiz, a biographer of Captain John Smith borrowed the scenario for his own subject and an Indian girl named Pocahontas. Smith then perpetuated the plagiarism by putting it into his own history.

Tristan de Luna y Arellano, a rich Spanish nobleman, was the next man to try and conquer Florida. He was undismayed by the previous failures and undeterred by the slaying of three missionaries by Indians at Tampa Bay in 1549. Ten years later, his party of more than 1,500 tried to establish a settlement on Pensacola Bay. Devastated by a hurricane, desperate for food, and disillusioned by Luna's quixotic leadership, the Spaniards abandoned the attempt in 1561.

A FOOTHOLD IN FLORIDA

Emboldened by Spain's preoccupation with pirates and its inability to colonize La Florida, a Frenchman named Jean Ribaut captained the effort to establish a settlement on St John's River in 1562. Ribaut constructed an arrowhead-shaped fort, Caroline, near modern-day Jacksonville.

That move intensified Spain's own efforts to gain a foothold on the land, but they also wanted to expel the French trespassers. A great armada under the command of Pedro Menéndez de Avilés established a site at a promising spot on the east

An engraving by Theodore DeBry.

coast, south of the French outpost, from which to mount its defense. The chosen day was August 28, 1565, the Feast of St Augustine. On September 8, Pedro Menéndez formally broke ground for a settlement that still bears the name of that patron saint. It was the first permanent settlement and is still the oldest continuous settlement, on United States soil, founded more than 50 years before the Pilgrims landed at Plymouth Rock in New England.

Well aware that Menéndez planned to attack, Jean Ribaut rushed back to Fort Caroline, assembled his forces, and tried to surprise the Spanish. But nature played a role in molding Florida's destiny. A hurricane grounded the French ships before they reached St Augustine. Meanwhile, Menéndez marched up the coast and seized the French fort, killing all the residents except Catholics, women, and children. On the way back to St Augustine, he encountered remnants of Jean Ribaut's assault party and had all but 16 of the 150 men put to death, including Ribaut, who was beheaded. The location of that bloody meeting became known as Matanzas – in Spanish, the place of slaughter.

With the French out of the way, Menéndez tried to guarantee Spain's Florida claims by befriending various Indian tribes, aiding Jesuit mission development, and trying to colonize other parts of the peninsula. Of the settlements,

paynted cunyngly with sondry collours, and the fore parte of there bodye and armes paynted with pretye devised workes of azure, redd, and black, so well and so properly don as the best paynter of Europe could not amend yt. The wemen have there bodies covered with a certen herbe like onto moste, whereof the cedertrees and all other trees be alwaies covered. The men for pleasure do always tryme themselves therwith, after sundry fasshions. They be of tawny colour, hawke nosed and of a pleasaunt countenaunce. The women be well favored and modest and will not suffer that one approche them

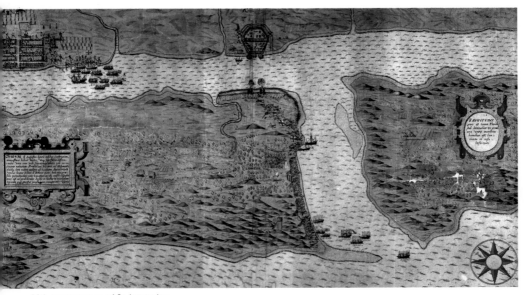

16th-century map of St Augustine.

only St Augustine would survive. England's Sir Francis Drake leveled the city in 1585, and another hurricane flooded the colony in 1599. Despite everything, St Augustine has survived for more than 400 years.

A PORTRAIT OF THE NATIVE AMERICAN

Although they were unsuccessful in their efforts to settle the land, Ribaut and his mapmaker, Jacques le Moyne, provided a meticulous word-and-picture portrait of the tribes they encountered in Florida. Ribaut wrote graphically in 1563: "The most parte of them cover their raynes and pryvie partes with faire hartes skins,

to nere, but we were not in theire howses, for we sawe none at that tyme."

Garcilaso de la Vega also provided insights into the customs and lifestyle of the Florida Indians. He noted many similarities in customs to the Incas, especially in their practice of putting their temples on artificial mounds mounted by wooden stairways: "The people of Florida are idolaters, and have the sun and moon for divinities, which they adore without offering them either prayers or sacrifices... [They have temples, but they make use of them only to inter those who die, and to shut up their treasures. They erect also at ... these temples, in the form of a trophy, the spoils of their enemies."

Contact with Europeans nearly destroyed the Indians. Some fell victim to diseases like chickenpox, measles, and colds, while slave traders spirited away as many as 12,000 people to a life of servitude. Many of those who resisted the European invasion died defending land their tribes had occupied for 10,000 years.

COMING OF THE SEMINOLE

Historians estimate that by the mid-16th century, the Indian population had dwindled to less than a quarter of its original size of about 25,000 people. Both Jesuit and Franciscan missionaries labored in Florida's humid conditions in their thick woolen robes, winning converts among the people of northern Florida with a string of about 50 missions in the 17th century. But British raiders leveled nearly everything at the turn of the 18th century, driving the few remaining Timucuans and Apalachees farther south. Spaniards took the last remaining 200 Indians to Cuba with them when they handed Florida over to the British in 1763. By that time, the Oconee Creeks had migrated into the peninsula from Georgia. In Florida, they would become known as the Seminole.

Timucua hunters used camouflage to stalk deer.

⊙ LE MOYNE'S VIEW OF FLORIDA

Jacques le Moyne described the customs of the Indians with both pictures and words. He wrote, for example, that the east-coast groups were generally more hospitable than those on Florida's west coast. He said that they cultivated fields of beans and maize which they stored in granaries; that they worshiped the sun and scalped and mutilated their enemies. He also praised the Indians' success in hunting deer by skillfully disguising themselves in deerskins and antlers. "I do not believe," he wrote, "that any European could do it as well."

He vividly portrayed the heavily tattooed chiefs and queens, who grew their fingernails long and sharpened them to points, and who painted the skin around their mouths blue. He said their striking attire included deerskin capes, belts made of Spanish moss, and earrings fashioned from fish-bladders inflated and dyed red.

Describing their social institutions, Le Moyne also said that the Florida Indians practiced what could be thought of as a form of representative parliamentarianism: "The chief and his nobles are accustomed during certain days of the year to meet early every morning... If any question of importance is to be discussed, the chief calls upon his *laüas* (that is, his priests) and upon the elders one at a time to deliver their opinions."

Billy Bowlegs, leader of the Seminole people during the Third Seminole War.

TURF WARS

Spain loses its grip, Native Americans are elbowed aside, and the United States takes control, only to plunge headlong into a military conflagration that tears the nation apart.

Although the Spanish presence in Florida was long in years, it was limited in scope, and was largely precarious, sporadic, and fragmented. For one thing, the peninsula lacked the precious metals (found in places like Mexico and Peru) that glittered like gold in Spanish eyes.

What mostly kept the Iberian occupiers hanging on to their peninsular possession for so long was the region's strategic location. For the conquerors of New Spain, the Straits of Florida represented a vital corridor through which their ships, laden with riches, could travel back to the homeland. For such treasures, the occupiers could put up with the persistent hostility exhibited by Native Americans, who were none too happy with the Spaniards' presence.

BRITAIN'S TERRITORIAL AMBITIONS

Despite years of occupation, Spain only managed to settle St Augustine and Pensacola, and to establish a small garrison at St Marks in the Panhandle. To the north, the British colonies cast a covetous eye on Florida, prompting Spanish authorities to build Castillo de San Marcos to defend St Augustine.

The castle's mass of earthworks and cannon repelled repeated assaults by the British, including a major attack by General James Edward Oglethorpe in 1742. As it turned out, England acquired Florida with the pen rather than the sword in 1763, via the first Treaty of Paris. Britain captured Cuba during the Seven Years War (known in America as the French and Indian War) and agreed to return Havana to Spanish control in exchange for Florida.

Remnants of the Spanish settlements quickly evaporated. The Creek tribes of

A member of the Confederate 1st Florida Cavalry.

Alabama and Georgia, who were generally on friendly terms with the British, increased their migration southward. Slicing the territory into East Florida (from the Atlantic coast to the Apalachicola River in the Panhandle) and West Florida (from the Apalachicola to the Mississippi River) made British administration easier, and the Brits virtually transformed the new territory into their 14th and 15th American colonies.

Spain had always operated from its base in Havana, but under Redcoat rule, Florida began to develop ties with the rest of the North American continent. New plantations of indigo, rice, and citrus, a subsequent increase in the slave trade from Africa and the West Indies, and a wave of new immigrants with Cork and Cockney accents marked British rule in frontier Florida.

BREAKING AWAY

The rumblings in the northern colonies that foreshadowed trouble never reached so far south. British subjects in Florida remained loyal to London when rebellion-minded American colonists turned their backs on King George III and declared independence on July 4, 1776. Angry residents of St Augustine even strung up effigies of John Hancock and John Adams and burned them.

Capitalizing on Britain's preoccupation with fighting the American Revolution, Spain recaptured Pensacola and regained control of all West Florida. East Florida remained Tory territory, its citizens donning red woolen coats and brandishing muskets to beat back three incursions by American Whigs from the North.

Then, 20 years after acquiring Florida, the British gave it back to Spain in 1783 under the

A depiction of Fort Brooke at Tampa Bay, 1835.

⊘ CROSSING CULTURES

Turmoil between the various ethnic groups and political powers that inhabited Florida in the late 18th and early 19th centuries gave rise to a host of colorful characters who were adept at forging links between cultures. Take, for example, Alexander McGillivray, the son of a Scotsman and a woman of Creek and French blood, who is remembered for his diplomatic skill. He cultivated a working relationship between Florida's Spanish governors, English traders, the US Army, and a confederation he organized among 45,000 Indians of several tribes. The alliance endured until his death in 1793.

William Augustus Bowles had no Indian blood, but he lived among the Creeks and married an Indian woman after emigrating from England. When the Spanish returned to power, he contacted McGillivray and offered to supply the Creeks with weapons to wage war against the Georgians. His adventures included an attack on the St Marks garrison near Tallahassee before the Spaniards captured him and sent him to Havana, where he died.

Zephaniah Kingsley was a flamboyant Scot who made his fortune from the slave trade. He imported thousands of people from Africa and the West Indies in the early 1800s, trained them in the servile arts, and then resold them for a vast profit. He became a legend by defending the slave system, even marrying one of his servants and raising the children as his heirs.

terms of the Second Treaty of Paris. That the territory resisted falling into the American column was small consolation.

A CULTURAL STEW

At the time of the American Revolution, Florida sheltered a wide cross section of the world's people. There were Africans and West Indians, English and Spanish, Germans and Greeks, Sicilians and Minorcans, and Creek and Choctaw Indians. All put down roots that flourished in the bright glare of Florida's sunshine.

United States soldiers setting fire to an Indian camp.

The second Spanish occupation of Florida fared little better than the first. British, black, and Indian refugees from the newly formed United States continued to trickle southward. Georgians stirred up trouble along the northern border, forcing Spain to withdraw to the 31st parallel, the modern-day border between Florida and Georgia.

CHANGING HANDS

In 1800, Spain ceded the Louisiana Territory to France, which in turn sold the territory to the US. The US then extended its claim in 1813 to Mobile in Alabama, which, at the time, was Florida's western boundary. Americans in West Florida instigated a movement for

independence. So, in yet another twist, the British (with whom the Spanish were allied in the War of 1812) sent troops to Pensacola to reinforce Spain's claim.

This sparked concern about the return of the Redcoats. Tennessee's Andrew Jackson, nicknamed "Old Hickory" because of his stern reputation, took it upon himself to stop the British rebuilding their forces in Florida. He used a Creek Indian uprising in Alabama as a pretext for advancing toward Florida. He defeated the Indians at the Battle of

Andrew Jackson.

⊘ SHIFTING FORTUNES

The story behind the Adams-Onís Treaty of 1819 is the shifting fortunes of national power – Spain in decline, the US in flower. The treaty reconfigured the geographical dividing line in North America between the two domains, with Florida as a chief bargaining chip, and it drew on diplomatic precedents dating as far back as the papal bull of 1493 that granted Spain colonial rights in northwestern America. For Spain, the slate was wiped clean of $5 million in debt, while the US got Florida. The treaty was ironed out in 1819 in Washington, DC, by John Quincy Adams, the American Secretary of State, and Luis de Onís, the Spanish foreign minister. It went into effect in 1821.

Horseshoe Bend, and then marched on Pensacola and drove out the British.

A subsequent skirmish between Americans and Indians sparked the First Seminole War (1817–18). Spain accepted an offer by the US to cancel $5 million in debts to Washington in exchange for ownership of the entire peninsula. Jackson returned to Pensacola in 1821. There, on July 17, he witnessed the raising of the Stars and Stripes over the Spanish capital. Old Hickory became Florida's first American governor.

associated with the Creek nation, started in the 1700s. The Creek took over the deserted farmlands left behind by the devastated local tribes and hunted in the forests where their ancestors had pursued game. These new Indians collectively came to be known as Se-mi-no-lee, meaning wild ones. Some spoke variations of the Hitchiti language, while others spoke Nuskogee.

As white settlers and Indians trickled into the new territory, Florida's population practically doubled, from 34,370 in 1830 to 66,500

The Seminole attack a US blockhouse on the Withlacoochee River in 1835.

THE ROAD TO CONFLICT

Andrew Jackson remained governor for only three months before returning to Washington, where later he would exercise influence over the new territory directly from the White House. The officials he left behind soon realized that the distance between Pensacola and St Augustine was too great to manage the territory effectively, so they consolidated the government in a village of Talasi Indians, and thus Tallahassee became the territory of Florida's capital in 1823.

Settlers pushed aside the Indians when founding Tallahassee, as so often happened when land was seized for farming. The migration of Indian tribes, who were mostly

in 1845. Jackson's initial clash with the Seminoles proved to be a taste of bloodier days ahead. Pressure mounted for the government to remove Florida's native people to reservations in the West.

REMOVAL AND RETALIATION

In 1823, Seminole tribes massed at Moultrie Creek near St Augustine. Led by Neamathla, chief of a group called Miccosukees, the Indians agreed to a compromise with the American government. Thirty-two chiefs signed a treaty calling for them to move their people and their black slaves to a 4-million-acre (1.6-million-hectare) reserve in west-central Florida, in return for payment for abandoned lands and financial aid to help them live on the new lands. Neither side abided by the provisions of the agreement. The Seminole found the land unsuitable for agriculture and migrated there slowly, if at all. Drought conditions aggravated food shortages, and the US government reneged on payments. In 1830, Congress passed a removal act requiring all Indians to be sent West.

The two sides met again at Payne's Landing on the Oklawaha River running through the rugged Green Swamp of central Florida.

their Florida lands. He managed to get the "X" of Micanopy, the chief of the nation, but few others. Florida tradition holds that an indignant young brave named Osceola plunged his knife into the document and cried, "The only treaty I will ever make is this!" With that act, Osceola became a hero. Though his great-grandfather was a Scotsman, Osceola publicly disavowed his white ancestry and fervently pursued the Creek culture. Historian Marjory Stoneman Douglas considered Osceola "unquestionably the greatest Floridian of his day."

Dogs were used to hunt Indians during the Second Seminole War.

This time, US officials managed to coax only seven chiefs into signing a new agreement, which canceled the Moultrie Creek Treaty and required the Seminole to move to reservations in the Arkansas Territory (part of present-day Oklahoma). Most of the Seminole nation reacted angrily when the seven chiefs returned from a visit to the new reservations and reported that they had been coerced into agreeing to the move. But President Jackson issued an edict to the Seminole in which he warned: "I tell you that you must go and that you will go."

Flanked by 10 companies of soldiers, General Duncan L. Clinch ordered Seminole chiefs at Fort King, near modern Ocala, to sign away

Inspired by Osceola's act of defiance at Fort King, the Seminole rebelled. A party of warriors ambushed Major Francis Langhorne Dade while he was en route from Fort Brooke (at Tampa Bay) to Fort King. The Indians killed Dade with their first bullet and massacred all but three of his 111 men.

THE CAPTURE OF OSCEOLA

The murder of Dade and his men touched off the Second Seminole War (1835–42), a bloody struggle in which the outmanned but determined Seminole fought the better-armed soldiers to a stalemate. The Indians used the wilderness of the Green Swamp to their advantage, striking at American settlements, then melting into the marshes. The war cost the US $40 million and nearly 1,500 dead. The settlers soon built defensive forts like Lauderdale, Jupiter, Myers, and Pierce.

Deception contributed to the defeat of the Seminoles. In 1837, Osceola rode into St Augustine under a white flag of truce sent to him by General Thomas S. Jessup. The general then violated his own flag by arresting Osceola. He imprisoned the now legendary warrior, his wives, children, and 116 others at Fort Moultrie in Charleston.

after promising to meet with them for truce discussions. General Zachary Taylor didn't pull any underhanded punches, however, when he defeated a party of Seminole braves on the Kissimmee River in the last major battle of the war. The army rounded up Seminole men, women, and children and in 1842 forced 3,000 of them to march west of the Mississippi River on what has become known as the Trail of Tears.

THE RETURN OF WAR

Some Seminole Indians managed to avoid

US troops in battle.

Railroad and hotel baron Henry Morrison Flagler.

Suffering from malaria and a broken spirit, Osceola died just a year after his capture. The attending doctor cut off his head, supposedly in retribution for an incident in which Osceola had severed his brother-in-law's head early in the war. The doctor's great-granddaughter recalled that he hung Osceola's head on a bedpost in the room of his three little boys whenever they misbehaved. Osceola's head was passed around as a curiosity, and was even exhibited at circus sideshows. Eventually it was given to the Surgical and Pathological Museum in New York City, where it was destroyed by a fire in 1866.

Osceola's death broke the spirit of the Seminoles. Jessup continued his trickery, capturing another 400 Indians as well as Chief Alligator

deportation by disappearing into the Everglades. There, under Chief Billy Bowlegs, they regrouped, and in 1855 massacred a camp of surveyors whom they considered trespassers. That ignited the Third Seminole War (1855–58). Soldiers and settlers hunted the Seminole like dogs for the next three years; they offered huge rewards for the capture of Indians. Chief Bowlegs surrendered with a group of warriors in 1858 and was sent West. Others stubbornly refused to leave and were able to evade capture. The Floridians eventually gave up the search, enabling about 300 Seminole people to remain beyond the impenetrable sawgrass rivers of the Everglades and, thus, in safety.

FROM STATEHOOD TO CIVIL WAR

After two decades of politicking, Florida became an American state on March 3, 1845, but the romance ended just 16 years later. A man's wealth in Florida was measured by the number of slaves he owned. Influential planters and landowners opposed the abolition of slavery and convinced their legislators to secede from the Union on January 10, 1861. Florida joined forces with the Confederate States and went to war against the North.

The Civil War proved particularly disastrous for Florida. The state had only barely recovered

of Fernandina Beach, at one time a haven for slave-smuggling after the United States banned the practice, fell to the Union in 1861.

Florida's Confederate soldiers fought back valiantly. Their biggest battle occurred on February 20, 1864, when 5,000 soldiers wearing Confederate gray marched against 5,000 soldiers in Union blue. They clashed at Olustee, east of Lake City. The Floridians suffered nearly 100 men killed and over 800 wounded, but the survivors held their ground. They stopped the advance of the Union army, which suffered twice as many casualties.

Confederate soldiers successfully repelled Union troops at the Battle of Olustee in 1864.

from the Seminole Wars, which had stunted its growth for decades. Agriculture had just begun making an impact with multiplying acres of cotton, indigo, rice, sugar, and tobacco. The rugged interior of the state began to open up in 1861, when the railroad sliced through the forests of scrub and pine and linked Tallahassee to Cedar Key on the Gulf Coast.

Such progress, modest as it was, was stunted by the Civil War. Florida mustered its minuscule population and even smaller budget to join the Confederate cause. Its participation in the war was both brief and limited, but devastating nonetheless. Union forces invaded the busy northeastern port of Jacksonville four times. They seized most of Florida's forts. The town

Dr John Gorrie of Apalachicola in the Panhandle changed the course of domestic life in 1848 when he invented an ice machine, the forerunner of modern refrigerators and air conditioners.

The Cradle and Grave Company, consisting of teenagers and old men, mostly died in a Panhandle battle, but the Baby Corp, mainly schoolboys, bravely turned back Union soldiers (who were wearing hats inscribed "To Tallahassee or Hell") at a natural bridge over the St Marks River on March 5, 1865. Union soldiers never reached Florida's capital city, but this was a hollow triumph for the Floridians. Only a month later, General Robert E. Lee surrendered and the bloody Civil War was over.

RECONSTRUCTION

The Civil War cost Florida about 5,000 lives and $20 million in damage to its smoldering cities. The anti-slavery novel *Uncle Tom's Cabin*, published in 1852 and written by Harriet Beecher Stowe (who would spend her later years in a

Among those attracted to the Sunshine State were developers, agriculturalists, and inventors. Swampland in the Caloosahatchee and Kissimmee valleys was drained, clearing the rivers for navigation and making the land solid enough for settlement and farming. Cubans followed Vicente Martínez Ybor to Tampa in the 1880s to roll tobacco, helping to make the name of the city synonymous with cigars. On the state's east coast, a Chinese immigrant, Lue Gim Gong, developed a frostproof

The Ponce de León was one of several hotels built to lure tourists from the North to Florida.

cottage in Mandarin on the St John's River near Jacksonville), inspired abolitionists, but hooded Ku Klux Klansmen continued to oppress the black population. Until the Civil Rights Act of 1964, black people in most of Florida and throughout the South still rode in the back of the bus and used segregated facilities.

The American flag flew over Tallahassee again on May 30, 1865. Political and economic reconstruction got off to a hesitant start. Florida remained a wild frontier where the strong and the armed prevailed. Still, the sun began to lure northerners to the warm shores in ever-larger numbers. Florida's population nearly doubled in the two decades immediately after 1860, from 140,000 to 270,000.

orange that began to flourish along the Indian River, laying the basis for Florida's citrus industry.

RAILROADS AND TOURISTS

The far-sightedness of two men of that period laid the groundwork for the boom that occurred in the 20th century. They were Henry Morrison Flagler (1830–1913), one of the founders of Standard Oil, and Henry B. Plant (1819–99). The latter constructed the Atlantic Coastline Railroad that linked Richmond, Virginia with Tampa. At the end of the line, Plant built the luxurious Tampa Bay Hotel, complete with minarets that still dominate the skyline. Tourists arrived, and Plant then offered the option of continuing by steamer from Tampa to Cuba.

Flagler's Florida East Coast Railroad had an even bigger impact on the state's growth. Beginning in 1885, he sank about $50 million into a series of hotels at locations connected by his railroad line, from the posh Ponce de León Hotel in St Augustine to the Ormond north of Daytona Beach. In 1894, his line abruptly ended on a desolate slip of land by the sea. Flagler dubbed the area Palm Beach and erected the Breakers Hotel.

Mrs Julia D. Tuttle, a wealthy refugee from Cleveland, Ohio, managed to convince Flagler to extend his railroad farther south to a strip of scrub on Biscayne Bay in 1896. Thus Miami came into being. Flagler laid tracks all the way along the Florida Keys to Key West by 1912, a year before his death. Wherever Flagler went, more hotels were sure to follow. And in their wake came a flood of tourists and immigrants. Florida's boom time had finally come.

☉ TOUTING THE SUNSHINE STATE

American affluence was on the rise after the Civil War, in that period generally known as the Gilded Age. Pleasure-seekers began widening their gaze beyond such standard enticements as Newport and Saratoga Springs, becoming attracted in particular in the latter part of the 19th century by Florida's natural beauty and mild climate. Luring them on was a growing number of descriptive guides touting the charms of the Sunshine State and various of its locales. One of the earliest was by no less a literary superstar than Harriet Beecher Stowe, author of *Uncle Tom's Cabin*, the blockbuster novel that helped trigger the Civil War. Her guide, *Palmetto-Leaves*, published in Boston in 1873, glowingly evoked the sunshine springs and green forests of the northeastern Florida region where she would spend her winters in the 1870s and 1880s. One of its chapters was entitled "Buying Land in Florida."

Singling out just two others in this early manifestation of the travelogue genre, George M. Barbour's *Florida for Tourists, Invalids, and Settlers* was first published in 1884, while the poet-critic Sidney Lanier's *Florida: Its Scenery, Climate and History* appeared even earlier, in 1875. Florida, in Lanier's florid prose, represented "an indefinite enlargement of many people's pleasures" as opposed to "that universal killing ague of modern life – the fever of the unrest of trade throbbing through the long chill of a seven-months' winter."

An Art Deco building in South Beach.

MODERN TIMES

They came from near and far in the 20th century, fun-seekers and refugees seeking new lives in a Sunshine State that was undergoing its own form of extreme makeover.

Up and down Florida's coasts, cities sprang up toward the end of the 19th century along the railroad tracks laid by entrepreneurs Plant and Flagler. The state's growth was stimulated by the Spanish-American War of 1898, a situation quite different from past occasions when conflict tended to depress economic activity.

Florida's role in the war grew out of the cigar factories and Spanish cafés of the community founded by Vicente Martínez Ybor in Tampa in the 1880s. Cuban immigrants cheered on efforts by their compatriots back home to free the island of Spanish control. Huge crowds turned out in Tampa to hear Cuban freedom fighter José Martí plead for contributions to the cause, which was so popular that a rising political star named Napoleon Bonaparte Broward achieved notoriety for surreptitiously supplying weapons and ammunition to Cuban rebels before the United States officially entered the war. Soon after, Broward became one of Florida's most progressive governors.

The sinking of the battleship USS *Maine* in Havana's harbor on February 15, 1898 gave America an excuse to join the revolutionaries in the war against Spain that broke out at the end of April. American troops poured into Florida, setting up tent cities while waiting to sail to Cuba.

The wreck of the USS Maine was raised in 1912 to clear Havana's harbor.

> When John Ringling was first buying land around Sarasota, he managed to acquire 66,000 acres (26,700 hectares) during a game of poker.

GOOD TIMES

Tampa became a command post for the military. Theodore Roosevelt stormed into town with his Rough Riders en route to glory at San Juan Hill near the Cuban city of Santiago. Red Cross founder Clara Barton established a hospital in Tampa, while a young British journalist named Winston Churchill checked into the Tampa Bay Hotel to report a bloody good story. At the very place where it began its conquest, Spain was being driven from the New World.

After the conflict, the victorious Americans returned to points north with accounts of their exploits – and glowing depictions of Tampa, Miami, Key West, and other Florida ports and their attractive ambience. Some returned home only long enough to gather up their belongings, and perhaps a few friends and intimates, before heading back to Florida. By 1920 the Sunshine State's first major boom was under way.

Many of the characters who wheeled-and-dealed in real estate were interested only in fast fortunes, and they plundered Florida much as the Spanish and British had done earlier. Others came, made money, stayed, and became state leaders. Walter Fuller was one such man; he carved up St Petersburg, a sun-kissed Gulf Coast city founded by Russian railroad czar Peter Demens. In his book *This Was Florida's Boom*, Fuller tells how he paid $50,000 for land

city of Sarasota, while Dave Davis dredged up islands that became enclaves for Tampa's elite.

ONWARD AND DOWNWARD

In 1926, a cold winter slowed spiraling prices. Then a hurricane whipped across the peninsula, killing hundreds and destroying some of the flimsy housing developments. This brought the madness to a hasty end. The Wall Street crash of 1929 and the Great Depression soon followed. Overnight, as it were, Davis and Fuller and dozens of other millionaires became paupers. Still,

New roads and bridges, such as the Gandy Bridge across Tampa Bay, encouraged development.

he resold for $270,000, a vast sum at the time.

Fast-talking salesmen sold swamp-like tracts at auction. Even the golden-tongued William Jennings Bryan (a perennial presidential wannabe) got into the act, peddling real estate at George Merrick's development in Coral Gables. That site was the nation's first planned community, replete with regal entrance gates, pools, hotels, golf courses, zoned business districts, and alluring lots on palm-lined boulevards and canals.

Carl Fisher dredged sand from the bottom of Biscayne Bay and transformed tangles of mangroves off the coast of Miami into a beach. In 1925 alone, 481 hotels and apartment buildings rose in Miami Beach. Over on Florida's west coast, circus tycoon John Ringling created the

the groundwork was laid. When Florida's growth resumed, happy days returned.

Between 1920 and 1940, the state's population doubled to nearly two million. By the start of World War II, tourists numbering upward of 2.5 million came to visit annually – a phenomenal figure. Florida's population was also growing increasingly urban. By 1940, more than 55 percent of the people were living in towns and cities, compared to only 37 percent in 1920. Tampa attracted industry; Miami drew the sun-worshipers. More hotel rooms were built in Greater Miami between 1945 and 1954 than in the rest of the state combined.

Pari-mutuel betting on greyhounds and horses was legalized in 1931, bringing in additional revenues for the state's coffers – and an incentive for organized-crime rings to enter the field. Members of the syndicate shuttled between profitable rackets in Miami. The notorious mobster Al "Scarface" Capone found the location so convenient that he moved into a fortified estate on Palm Island near Miami Beach.

SPACE AGE

Florida's greatest contribution to the future began to take shape after World War II, when the War Department started testing missiles at Cape Canaveral. Florida was host to the world's first scheduled airline service – a short hop between St Petersburg and Tampa – and in 1959 the first domestic jet flights in the US were launched. By that time, Cape Canaveral was well on its way to becoming the site of Kennedy Space Center. The last steps Neil Armstrong took on Earth before his giant step on the moon in 1969 were made on the sandy soil of Florida.

Some well-known personalities brought a measure of fame to the state during the 1960s. Jackie Gleason's hit television show enhanced Miami Beach's renown, this time under the rubric of "sun and fun capital of the world." Tennessee Williams, author of such major dramatic works as *The Glass Menagerie* and *A Streetcar Named Desire*, made Key West his winter home; he died there in 1983.

THE NEW FLORIDIANS

Florida's reputation as a haven for refugees was heightened by the Cuban revolution engineered by Fidel Castro and his socialist compatriots in 1959. It sent a wave of anti-Castro and anti-communist Cubans to Florida shores throughout the 1960s. During the 1970s a slow but steady exodus continued, and in 1980 another big influx of Cubans landed in the Key West region as part of the so-called Mariel boatlift. Most of those 125,000 refugees eventually made their way to the Miami area where an immigrant network was in place.

The 1980s also brought to South Florida some 75,000 Nicaraguans fleeing their country and its communist regime, and about 125,000 Haitians. In addition, the 1980s saw sharp increases in population in Palm Beach County, the Orlando area, and the Gulf Coast, as many Northerners streamed into the state in search of the Sun Belt lifestyle. Many of the nation's largest companies moved their headquarters south to Florida, and the international banking industry bloomed,

particularly in Miami, well situated for trading with Latin America and the Caribbean. For Florida, it was an invigorating period of steady growth.

Unhappily, growth came as well from opportunists dealing in extra-legal and plainly illicit pursuits. With revenue from drug sales, the so-called Cocaine Cowboys pumped billions of dollars into Florida's economy but left a trail of crime and violence.

Miami continues to lead the nation in its diversity. According to the 2010 Brookings report, the Miami-Sort-Lauderdale-Pompano Beach area led

Cuban refugees arrive in Florida during the 1980 Mariel boatlift.

⊘ BUILDING AMBITION

Architecture is indicative of a state's ability to take setbacks in its stride. After a 1935 hurricane shredded the railroad through the Keys, engineers transformed it into the Overseas Highway, which still takes visitors on an exciting drive through the Florida Keys. Miami Beach, which sprouted Art Deco hotels in the 1930s and '40s, was one of few cities to undergo a building boom during the Depression. Construction of Florida Southern College, designed by Frank Lloyd Wright, began in 1938 and is a fitting monument to Wright's originality. It is the largest collection of Wright architecture on one sight anywhere in the world.

the nation by having 38.8 percent of its residents born in another country. Statewide, the number of immigrants in Florida rose from 1.5 million in 1990 to 3.4 million in 2012, according to the Pew Charitable Trusts. The vast majority (more than 3 million) came from Latin America including South and Central America, Mexico, and the Caribbean, says the Migration Policy Institute. The remainder are, in order, from Asia, Europe, Canada and other "Northern America" locales, Africa, and Oceania.

Along with the influx of immigrants and relocated Northerners, the 1980s brought pop-cul-

total number of annual tourists was estimated at 50 million to 80 million, with roughly a quarter of them coming from overseas. Above all, it was the arrival of entertainment magnate Walt Disney and his theme parks, the first of which opened in 1971, that decisively transformed tourism in the state.

Theme parks and other forms of wholesome family entertainment have proliferated in Orlando and now attract far more tourists than the magnificent beaches that line much of the coast. As cruise lines add ever-bigger ships, Florida benefits, as many of those ocean liners

Playing with the tigers at Busch Gardens Tampa Bay.

ture fame to the southern regions of the state. The slick, action-packed television series *Miami Vice*, first broadcast in 1984, transformed the international image of Miami from retirement haven to sleek and sexy paradise. Syndicated in more than 130 countries, *Miami Vice* glamorized the city's crime-ridden reputation and made tropical mayhem a fashionable trend.

A FLOOD OF TOURISTS

As the 1990s began, Florida was growing rapidly. The influx of newcomers included Europeans, South Americans, and Japanese, who saw Florida as one great sunny investment opportunity. Tourism, the golden egg for the Sunshine State's economy, continued to grow at astonishing rates. The

dock in the state ports. Port Miami alone had 4.8 million cruise passengers pass through in 2016. The Space Coast's Port Canaveral and Fort Lauderdale's Port Everglades together saw another 7.5 million. As a result, the cruise ship terminals are upgraded regularly to meet growing demand.

After years of development, Florida has at last learned the importance of preserving its natural heritage. The state has numerous parks and preserves, from the vast Everglades National Park to small recreation areas tucked in among the urban sprawl.

The battle over offshore oil drilling is argued throughout Florida, where concerns over the threats posted by coastal rigs to tourism and the environment were exacerbated by the 2010 oil spill in the Gulf waters of nearby Louisiana. Floridians can be bitterly divided on the question of whether the state should chase the economic benefits of oil exploration despite the risk of an environmental and economic calamity, but for now the inland waters remain as pristine as ever.

MAKING HEADLINES

Florida today ranks third in population in the Union, a number that neared 21 million in 2016. If it is not lacking in people, it is also not lacking in headline-making notoriety.

In 1994, images of Cubans arriving in Florida aboard home-made rafts made headlines around the world. Tensions inevitably resulted as the state struggled to cope with the influx. In 2000 the world's media focused on the plight of a 6-year-old Cuban boy named Elian Gonzalez, who survived a harrowing voyage in a small boat and an inner tube across the Florida Straits before being rescued; his mother and ten others perished in the attempt. Following a protracted legal tug-of-war between his American and Cuban relatives, Elian returned with his father to Cuba and remained there. Today Miami's sizeable and powerful Cuban population continues to disagree on how to deal with their homeland. The older generation tends to want to ice out all relations, while younger Cubans encourage building on the fledgling relationship begun by President Barack Obama while he was in office.

There was widespread grief on February 1, 2003, when seven astronauts aboard the *Columbia* space shuttle died when it disintegrated during re-entry into the Earth's atmosphere. The disaster did not stop Florida's dedication to space travel. NASA and private companies work hand in hand on the Space Coast to develop ways to visit the moon, the International Space Station, and Mars.

The grandest controversy of all was the legal struggle waged to decide the victor in the 2000 presidential campaign between George W. Bush, the Republican governor of Texas, and Al Gore, the Democratic vice president. The tally in the contest for Florida's 25 electoral votes was exceedingly close, and the legal jockeying by cadres of high-powered attorneys that resulted over the issue of a recount was unprecedented. Florida remains a swing state, with jurisdictions, even single neighborhoods, deeply divided during national elections. Presidential candidates campaign here frequently, hoping to swing the state's crucial electoral votes their way.

Orlando hit the headlines in 2016, when a security guard named Omar Mateen from the Space Coast went into the gay-oriented Pulse nightclub, and during three hours of terror killed 49 people and wounded another 53. It was the largest non-military-related mass shooting in US history at that time, tragically superseded by the Las Vegas Strip shooting a year later.

Hurricane Andrew devastated South Florida in 1992.

⦿ A CHECKERED LEGACY

The Seminole influence on Floridian culture lives on in the mascot of Florida State University's American football team, named Chief Osceola after the 19th-century tribal leader. The school's use of Indian imagery and native names rankles many living Native Americans, and the issue is often debated. In 2005 the National Collegiate Athletic Association took up the case; ultimately the sporting officials decided to allow FSU to continue using the Seminole mascot, with involvement from local tribes. Today, Seminole women design and create the authentic regalia worn by the chief during football games.

The Walt Disney Theater at the Dr. Phillips Center for the Performing Arts.

A replica of Michelangelo's David at the Ringling Museum of Art in Sarasota.

THE CULTURAL LANDSCAPE

Florida is sometimes comically dismissed as the "land of the newlyweds and the nearly dead," but the influx of newcomers has created a lively market for both the visual and the performing arts.

Like its history, the development of Florida's cultural character unfolded in a distinctly different pattern than the rest of the American South. During its initial period of Spanish rule, Florida was held primarily for strategic reasons and was sparsely colonized, with only a few Spanish residents. Consequently, the long colonial period left a scant legacy of Hispanic culture.

During the British occupation, an influx of other European emigrants flowed in, primarily from Italy and Greece. A Greek Orthodox shrine in St Augustine serves as a vivid reminder of the religion and culture of these early arrivals.

Although most American Indians in Florida were either killed by war or disease, or forced to march West on the Trail of Tears, a few hardy souls remained hidden in the Everglades. These Seminole Indians, with their sub-tribe the Miccosukee, continue to practice their traditional crafts and rituals, as evidenced at the Miccosukee Cultural Center in the Everglades, along the Tamiami Trail, and at the annual Seminole tribal fair in Hollywood.

Young Shepherdess by William Bouguereau at the Appleton Museum of Art.

The top American states feeding Florida's population boom are New York, New Jersey, Ohio, Michigan, and Illinois. Some might say that Yankees have remade South Florida in the image of the Northeast.

SLOW START

When Florida became a state in 1845, nearly half of its population of 60,000 were black slaves working on cotton and sugar plantations, and maintained a culture steeped in West African traditions of music and storytelling. Among white settlers – most of whom came to Florida from Georgia and the Carolinas – a folk culture akin to that of the southern Appalachians predominated. There were only 140,000 Floridians (nearly half of them slaves) at the time of the Civil War. Any cultural awakening in the state would clearly have to wait for a significant increase in population, and for the growth of cities.

The population increase began with the discovery of Florida as a winter retreat for northerners, beginning with the arrival of railroads along the state's east coast in the 1880s. The 1920s saw the state's year-round numbers begin to climb; wealthy winter sojourners (known as snowbirds) such as circus king John Ringling gave a tremendous boost to the Florida arts scene. Ringling, who built his Venetian-inspired fantasy home, Cà d'Zan, in Sarasota, opened the John and Mable Ringling Museum of Art in the west-coast city in 1931. Another overwintering businessman, James Deering, created Miami's lavish Vizcaya estate.

SUDDEN SHIFT

In the first half of the 20th century, Florida's cultural atmosphere reflected a mix of white,

The Cummer Museum of Art in Jacksonville

Southern farmers and black, former slaves. Also in the mix were émigrés from the North, and local island populations. The political sea change that overtook Cuba in 1959 following the socialist revolution led by Fidel Castro, brought the arts and traditions of Florida's island neighbor into the mainstream. The great migration of Cubans – abetted by a smaller influx of Haitians, Dominicans, and people from other Caribbean nations – made a Latin American capital of Miami and transformed the cultural flavor of all but the northernmost portions of the peninsula.

For a sample of the Cuban performing-arts scene, take in one of the programs offered by IFÉ-IlÉ Afro-Cuban Dance and Music, a Miami-based organization that presents traditional and contemporary dances, concerts, and poetry readings (in Spanish), and sponsors a dance and music festival each July. There's also a Cuban-American Heritage Festival in Key West each June.

You don't have to visit Florida in the warmer months to enjoy the biggest of all Cuban celebrations: Miami's Calle Ocho (Eighth Street) Festival, held in March, draws 1 million visitors to a bash that concludes with a massive block party featuring 30 music stages. If March is too far off, head to Calle Ocho on the last Friday of each month, when the Viernes Culturales street party rollicks with music, dancing, and street performers. Miami's Haitian community, too, highlights its music and dance traditions with the annual Compas Festival, held in Bayfront Park each May.

VISUAL ARTS

The visual and performing-arts scene in Florida revolves around various venues, museums and festivals scattered among a half-dozen or so important population centers. In metropolitan Miami Beach, the Bass Museum of Art supplements its post-Renaissance European painting and sculpture with a strong Caribbean and Latin American presence, and Wolfsonian-Florida International University showcases decorative arts, architecture, and graphic design. But the biggest fine arts presence in the area is the ever-changing canvas of the Art Basel festival, an exhibition held every December that draws some of the world's finest galleries and dealers to chic shows and sleek parties.

Fort Lauderdale has a more low-key arts scene, with several up-and-coming contemporary galleries in the Las Olas neighborhood and a more traditional European and American focus at the city's NSU Art Museum. Jacksonville has a thriving arts culture of its own, shaped by students at the local University of North Florida, as well as Art Walk and First Friday events in a core crop of downtown studios.

Orlando boasts several respectable art museums, showcasing everything from pre-Columbian American art to the American Hudson River School of landscape painting to the entire Louis Comfort Tiffany chapel designed for the 1893 Chicago World Columbian Exposition.

The town best known for Mickey Mouse also showcases more refined modern art at three publicly owned galleries, two of which are inside City Hall.

Over on the west coast, St Petersburg has built a thriving local community around its world-famous museum dedicated to Spanish surrealist Salvador Dalí. Besides more established museums downtown, St Pete's Warehouse Arts District has a growing number of less polished arts venues. Among a slew of funky downtown spots, the ARTpool Gallery and Vintage Boutique offers upstart creatives a chance to showcase their fine and decorative artwork. The Chihuly Collection transports locals and tourists to the colorful, madcap oeuvre of glass artist Dale Chihuly. In Tampa, three museums opened in 2010 alone – the Tampa Museum of Art, Tampa Bay History Center, and Glazer's Children's Museum.

Sarasota has more of a quietly creative energy, thanks to the largesse of museum-endowing snowbird John Ringling, whose Ringling Museum of Art and Ringling College spawned no fewer than nine promising academic galleries for emerging contemporary art, led by the Selby. Off campus, the Art Uptown is the only formal co-operative gallery in Florida, giving artists a chance to share the spotlight.

PERFORMING ARTS

For classical music, the most important Miami area institutions are the Miami Symphony Orchestra, which performs at the Adrienne Arsht Center – Knight Concert Hall, and the Fillmore Miami Beach at The Jackie Gleason Theatre ; Florida Grand Opera, based at the Carnival Center for the Performing Arts (also with performances in Fort Lauderdale); the Miami Lyric Opera, offering performances at the South Miami Dade Cultural Arts Center; and Michael Tilson Thomas' New World Symphony, which bills itself as the "only full-time orchestral academy" in America. New World is based at the New World Center, designed by renowned architect Frank Gehry.

Works of modern masters are the highlight of the collection at the Boca Raton Museum of Art.

The Miami City Ballet makes its local home in the state's biggest metropolis, but also takes its ultra-modern twists on Twyla Tharp and other master choreographers north to Broward and Palm Beach counties, and the International Ballet Festival of Miami takes to the road in late summer.

Further north on the "Cultural Coast," the Sarasota Ballet stages a sampling of classics every season. Also in Sarasota, the Sarasota Orchestra gives one hundred classical, pop, and family-oriented performances each year. The Sarasota Opera, housed in a renovated 1926 venue, performs traditional selections such as *Madama Butterfly*, and modern tales such as *The*

⊙ CHORAL CAPITAL

Residents of Palm Beach have a special love for choral music. Many fine choral groups flourish near the city, including the Master Chorale of South Florida; the Masterworks Chorus of the Palm Beaches; Ebony Chorale of the Palm Beaches; the Choral Society of the Palm Beaches; the Boca Raton Singers; Palm Beach Opera's chorus; and Voices of Pride. Performing at venues throughout Florida's east coast, these polished vocalists offer a repertory ranging from classical oratorios to Gilbert and Sullivan, and from spirituals to show tunes. A favorite performance is the Masterworks Chorus's annual rendition of Handel's *Messiah*, held in December at the Royal Poinciana Chapel.

Crucible. Visiting groups perform at Sarasota's Van Wezel Performing Arts Hall.

In the Fort Lauderdale and Palm Beach areas, the Symphony of the Americas focuses on diversity in its concert selections while the Palm Beach Symphony takes a more classical approach. Fort Lauderdale's Broward Center for the Performing Arts, anchoring the city's Riverwalk Arts and Entertainment District, hosts national touring Broadway productions as well as concerts, comedy, classic performances, and dance productions.

performances a year. Clearwater's Ruth Eckerd Hall, with more than 2,000 seats plus the 250-seat Murray Theatre, hosts concerts and theatrical productions.

In Central Florida, the shining new jewel of downtown is the Dr. Phillips Center for the Performing Arts, a modern two-theater venue hosting a variety of performances indoors and out, among them traveling Broadway shows. A third theater, Steinmetz Hall, with 1,700 seats plus a cabaret-style gathering space called The Green Room, is under construction. The

The sculpture garden at the Ringling Museum.

Northeastern Florida's classical music scene revolves around the Jacksonville Symphony Orchestra. The 65-year-old ensemble, and its affiliated Youth Orchestra, perform in an acoustic gem, the Robert E. Jacoby Symphony Hall at the Times-Union Center for the Performing Arts.

The Straz Center for the Performing Arts, the largest center of its kind south of Washington, DC's Kennedy Center, is a complex of five theaters that serve as home to the Tampa Bay Symphony and Opera Tampa. Also on the state's west coast, the Naples Philharmonic performs at the city's Artis—Naples, a venue for both performing and visual arts that hosts more than 450 concerts and

Orlando Philharmonic Orchestra, Orlando Ballet, Dr. Phillips Center Jazz Orchestra, and Orlando Opera, among others, will all be based here.

STAGE TO SCREEN

Miami is the live theater capital of Florida, with dozens of stages large and small, as well as several locally based drama companies. Among them are the Actors' Playhouse at the Miracle Theatre in Coral Gables, offering professionally staged theater for children and adults, and City Theater, specializing in new, shorter drama – 10-minute plays. For Spanish-language performances, try the Teatro de Bellas Artes, in Miami's Little Havana neighborhood, where drama, comedy, and musical performances fit the bill. Foreign movie buffs shouldn't miss the Miami Film Festival every March, not to mention the dozen-plus smaller retrospectives that often bring new flicks from overseas.

Further south, the intimate Red Barn Theatre on Key West's lively Duval Street puts on a half-dozen shows between December and March, while the Tennessee Williams Theatre takes in more mainstream, crowd-pleasing productions. Key West also has its own opera theater, which plays host to musical shows and the South Florida Symphony Orchestra.

The unquestioned star of Sarasota's theater scene is the Asolo Repertory Theatre, where new standards such as the musical *Beatsville* are paired with reboots of *Ragtime* and *Evita*. Other local theater venues include The Players Centre of the Performing Arts, a recently relocated community group staging comedy acts and dramas; and the Venice Theater, 20 miles (32km) south of Sarasota in Venice, with a varied and ambitious schedule of comedy, drama, and musicals. The Sarasota Film Festival is a draw in its own right for top-drawer independent titles, such as the Oscar-nominated documentary *Gasland*.

In the Palm Beach area, the Dramaworks company mingles historically inspired dramas with musicals and established comedies. With three indoor theaters and an outdoor venue, the Raymond F. Kravis Center for the Performing Arts is the region's crown jewel. Kravis' Rinker Playhouse houses the independent MNM Productions featuring local talent. Other theaters include the Maltz Jupiter Theatre, winner of many Carbonell awards; The Wick, known for comedies and musicals – and also a costume museum; and Theatre Lab at Florida Atlantic University's Boca Raton campus, focusing on new plays. Chamber music takes center stage at The Core Ensemble, choosing non-traditional venues. The Palm Beach International Film Festival draws behind-the-camera talent to Palm Beach in spring and the Fort Lauderdale International Film Festival does so in the fall. The Donald M. Ephraim Palm Beach Jewish Film Festival features about three dozen films each winter.

Orlando and environs are richly endowed with live theater organizations. The Orlando Repertory Theatre presents an ambitious program of family-friendly plays; the Orlando Shakespeare Theater mounts 10 productions each year, including several of the Bard's works. The downtown Mad Cow Theatre presents stagings of classic and modern dramas in addition to a cabaret festival in May. The Orlando Film Festival, usually held in November, distinguishes itself by helping cultivate live comic talent as well as screen whizzes.

Alternative transportation in Key West.

⊘ SOUTHERN SYMPHONY

The South Florida Symphony Orchestra was founded by Sebrina Maria Alfonso, a fifth-generation "Conch" of Cuban ancestry, who serves as its conductor and music director. Each year, she assembles a group of up to 70 musicians who can commit to performing in Key West during the orchestra's four-concert winter series, which is supplemented by free outdoor concerts, children's programs, master classes, and a popular annual Christmas season revival of Menotti's *Amahl and the Night Visitors*. The Key West Symphony players all have careers with other orchestras, but enjoy bringing classical music to this arts-loving town in the Keys.

EXTREME WEATHER

Florida does nothing by halves. Famously, it boasts more sun than most corners of the United States, but it also has more than its fair share of rain and thunderstorms.

In her book *Cross Creek*, Marjorie Kinnan Rawlings says that in Florida the seasons "move in and out like nuns in soft clothing, making no rustle in their passing." It is hard to tell spring from summer, and fall slips into winter almost without notice. Temperatures drop in winter but rarely approach freezing; the coldest temperature ever recorded was a frosty –2°F (–19°C) in Tallahassee in 1899. It is rare, but not unheard of, for snow to fall in Florida, typically in the northern or Panhandle regions. Accumulation of more than a few inches is unusual.

Florida has the advantage of being sunny all year round. The Sunshine State isn't merely a catchy slogan dreamed up to lure tourists, but an official name that demonstrates the importance of the sun in raising billions of dollars for Florida by attracting tourists, baseball squads, and fashion photographers, who revel in the fact that in winter their models can pose in next to nothing against a blue sky while most of the nation is bundled up in sweaters. Many crops, including vegetables and fruit from oranges to mangoes, thrive in the warm and wet climate. Since more than half of the country's citrus crop is grown in Florida, farmers anxiously monitor the weather throughout the growing season.

Although Florida is known for sunshine, the state is also a place of extremes. Florida is wetter than anywhere else in the US. More than half the average total rainfall is recorded from June to September, when the state can be subjected to as much rainfall as some European cities get in a whole year. Key West is the driest city in the state and it still gets 40in (100cm) of rain annually.

Waves crash over the seawall at Fort Lauderdale in the aftermath of Hurricane Sandy.

Florida is the lightning capital of the US. Each year a handful of people are killed by lightning strikes in the state. The number of injuries caused is higher than those caused by all other risky weather events combined. The lightning belt extends from Jacksonville to Fort Myers, with one community within the Fort Myers area averaging 200 flashes per square mile each year.

In the sultry summer months, Miami Beach's famous Art Deco thermometer simply cannot cope.

A satellite image of Hurricane Frances, which struck Florida in September, 2004.

The Development of a Hurricane

A tropical storm is called a hurricane when its wind speed exceeds 74mph (119kmh). The hurricane is then classified from 1 to 5 according to the Saffir-Simpson Scale, which measures the wind speed and expected flooding. Category 5 is the worst, with winds of more than 155mph (249kmh).

Many of the hurricanes that hit Florida develop off the coast of Africa and move across the Atlantic. Several factors contribute to the formation of a hurricane, above all heat and wind. The key ingredient is the heat of the summer sun, which warms the surface of the ocean enough for water to evaporate. As the warm air rises, it condenses into thunderclouds, which are sent spinning by the rotation of the Earth. The hurricane moves forward at 7–30mph (11–48kmh) and can measure hundreds of miles across.

The National Hurricane Center in Miami tracks a hurricane's progress using radar and satellites. Pilots, known as Hurricane Hunters, also fly in and out of the storm in order to gather data. Warning of the severity of a hurricane can greatly reduce the damage done if the storm eventually makes landfall. While the winds can be devastating, most damage and deaths are caused by flooding from the storm surge – a wall of water that can reach a height of 20ft (6 meters).

Snow is so rare that merely a touch of it can cripple Florida. The highest recorded snowfall in the state was on March 6, 1954, when 4in (10cm) of the white stuff fell in Santa Rosa County near Pensacola. Frost and flurries are more common than actual flakes.

The Gulf Coast between St Pete Beach and Clearwater Beach enjoys an average of 363 sunny days a year. From 1967 to 1969 an amazing 768 consecutive days of sunshine were recorded here, so be sure to pack a hat and sun screen.

All along the Gulf Coast, official evacuation routes head north and west, while on the Atlantic coast, the routes head inland to the west. In 2017, Hurricane Irma prompted the largest evacuation in US history as hundreds of thousands of Floridians fled north.

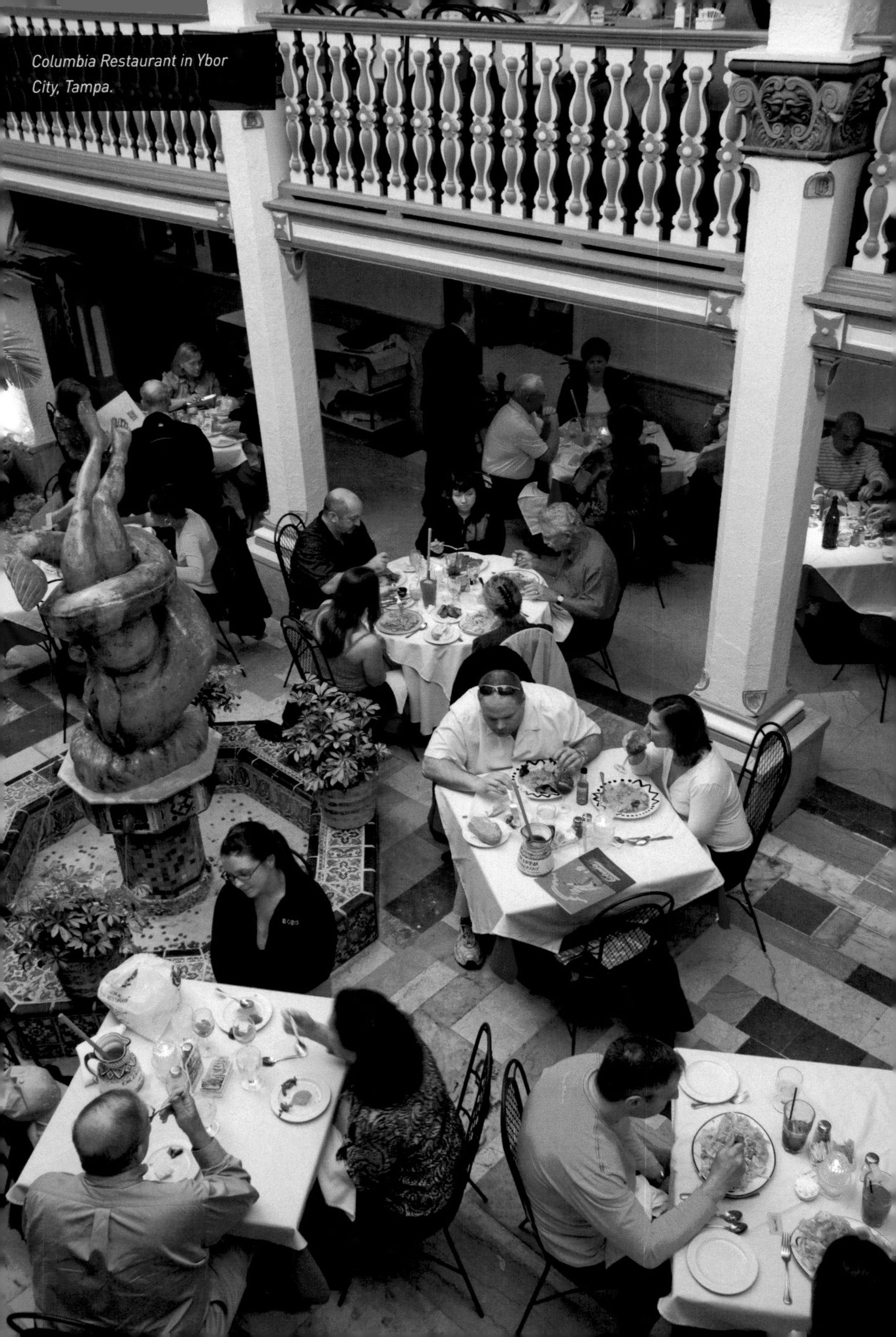

Columbia Restaurant in Ybor City, Tampa.

FLORIDA CUISINE

It's not all shrimp, alligator tail steak, and Key lime pie; the state's multi-ethnic population is reflected in its cuisine, and the strong Caribbean influence can add a tangy flavor when least expected.

For centuries, Florida cooks have charted a varied culinary course, drawing upon a bounty of local ingredients and a broad range of regional and international influences. There's no single Florida cuisine, but rather a panoply of Southern, Anglo, Caribbean, and Latin American trends that enliven an ever-changing food culture, one of the most exciting in the US.

> Florida's early explorers dined on boar, venison, and even bear, which the native people sometimes bartered with the settlers. The Indians also simmered turtle, duck eggs, frog legs, eels, and alligator in herbs.

In the beginning, Floridians – Indians and Europeans alike – dined off the peninsula's abundance drawn from land and sea. One passionate chronicler of old Floridian cuisine was the late Marjorie Kinnan Rawlings, Pulitzer-Prize-winning author of *The Yearling*, whose books *Cross Creek* and *Cross Creek Cookery* documented her life and kitchen adventures in her adopted home of Cross Creek, a tiny village in the northern part of the state where she lived in the 1930s and '40s. In *Cross Creek Cookery*, Rawlings set down her recipes for old-time dishes such as hush puppies, pecan pie, cream of peanut soup, and the more exotic coot surprise and alligator tail steak. One of Rawlings' favorite dishes was turtle eggs (not from sea turtles), whose "fine and distinct flavor" she praised, noting that "a dozen turtle eggs, with plain bread and butter and a glass of ale, make all I ask of a light luncheon or supper." Diners

A taste of lobster from Caretta on the Gulf at the Sandpearl Resort in Clearwater Beach.

can try many of these Cracker specialties at the Yearling Restaurant not far from Rawlings' one-time home.

HOTEL FARE

Many of these dishes are representative of the coastal South. Before it was discovered by winter-weary northerners, Florida was much more a typical Southern state than it is today, and Southern culinary folkways were predominant. When the outsiders did arrive, their tastes ran to the conventionally substantial hotel menus of the era. The table d'hôte offerings at the big Atlantic coast hotels might have been perked up with fresh local orange juice and locally caught seafood, but they were essentially what a traveler might expect at chic hostelries from Philadelphia to Boston.

When Miami began to attract vacationers and retirees from the North, one of the greatest culinary influences became the Jewish delicatessen found in New York. In Miami Beach, you'll never look far for a pastrami on rye. In Florida's cities and resorts, as in any cosmopolitan environment, Italian, French, Chinese, Thai, and a host of other international dining choices are always available.

Key lime pie is a classic Florida Keys dessert.

FLORIDA ORANGES

Despite rivers, lakes, and offshore waters that teemed with fish and shellfish, the food that first drew the attention of the outside world to Florida was the orange. Oranges are not native to Florida; they were first brought to the peninsula by the Spanish explorers Ponce de León and Hernando de Soto and soon grew wild.

The orange industry in Florida got its start as early as the 1770s. A century later, thousands of acres of groves had been planted, and Florida oranges were heading north by train just as the tourists were traveling south. The region around the Indian River (which is not a river but a saltwater lagoon 120 miles/190km long and seldom more than 2 miles/3km wide) became a prime growing area. Indian River is also famous for its grapefruit, a citrus family member that originated in the West Indies and was first planted in Florida in 1823. Shipments of grapefruit didn't reach the northeastern US until the 1880s, when Americans began to develop a taste for their tart, juicy flesh.

KEY LIME AND CONCH

One Florida crop that is indelibly linked with one of the state's most distinctive regions is, ironically, no longer grown commercially here: the Key lime. This small, yellowish lime is known to most visitors as the main ingredient in Key lime pie. Even in the Keys, when you order a slice of Key lime pie you'll be savoring fruit grown in Mexico – unless you've lucked into a mom-and-pop bakery or coffee shop that has a Key lime tree or two in the back yard. Like the Keys' pygmy deer (which are emphatically not on any menus), Key limes are far more famous than they are abundant.

Any mention of Keys cuisine brings to mind another of the islands' iconic dishes: conch (pronounced *konk*). Conch is so indelibly linked with the culinary traditions of Key West that its native-born residents call themselves conchs, but the mollusk itself, at least as far as local tables go, is a native no longer. Restrictions on harvesting the now-depleted shellfish in Florida waters mean that all conch served in the state are imported from the Bahamas. When you do order conch, it's the queen conch that you will be served. Its flesh, which is similar to that of calamari, is most frequently prepared in one of four ways: as conch salad, sort of a *ceviche* with a hot pepper kick; in a chowder, either tomato or cream-based; as cracked conch, strips that have been tenderized by pounding and lightly breaded or battered and fried; and in conch fritters, the best of which have a high ratio of conch to batter and have been fried at just the right temperature to avoid greasiness. There are some terrific conch fritters served by street vendors in Mallory Square, Key West, around the time when the inevitable tourist throng applauds the sunset.

FRESH SEAFOOD

Florida waters still yield a delicious array of seafood. Key West pink shrimp are a succulent alternative to the farm-raised supermarket variety, especially when tossed with pasta or fried and tucked into that New Orleans import, the po'boy sandwich. Stone crabs (there's a famous and eponymous restaurant in Miami Beach that built its reputation on them) are unique among sustainable shellfish resources in that their big, sweet claws (where all the meat is) grow back after they are removed and the crab is returned to the sea. Claws, however, don't figure at all as part of the lobsters harvested in South Florida waters. These are a different species from the cold-water specimens in New England. More properly called spiny lobster or langouste, they aren't armed with fat pincers but instead are

nearly all tail meat. They're most often served broiled; just make sure they don't spend too much time under the flame, which can make the flesh dry.

Finned fish commonly found on Florida menus include members of the snapper clan – yellowtail, hog, and mutton snapper are predominant – as well as mahi-mahi, the name given to the fish once commonly known as dolphin but rechristened to avoid confusion with the beloved mammal. Grouper turns up on quite a few Florida restaurant tables as well. Like conch, it's a

Fresh local shrimp.

Florida stone crab.

⊘ OYSTER BAR

Apalachicola Bay, one of the world's richest estuarine systems, is known for its oysters. At one time, it provided Florida with 90 percent of its annual oyster catch. Over-harvesting has seen stocks plummet, but the oysters that remain are still a treasure. Oyster farmers, poised on small boats, use tongs fashioned from two giant rakes to pincer their crop, which is cultivated in carefully selected water (neither too salty nor too fresh) in nurseries known as oyster bars. They can be harvested year-round, but the catch tends to be smaller during summer. The bay is also home to numerous species of birds, mammals and fish, and has the highest density of amphibians and reptiles in North America.

versatile and delectable ocean denizen that's a dietary mainstay of the nearby Bahamas, but fishing pressure on grouper has caused a worrisome decline in stocks, so it's best to save this fish for the occasional meal. The state's more innovative chefs are turning to fish that were formally shunned, such as lionfish – which is both invasive and prolific, sheepshead, trigger, porgy, bluefish, tripletail, and wreckfish, to give the more familiar fish time to repopulate.

A TASTE OF THE ISLANDS

By far the biggest news on the Florida food scene over the past few decades has been the impact made by the variegated cuisines of Latin America. Given the close proximity of Floridian the peninsula to the West Indies (Grand Bahama Island is a scant 60 miles/95km from Florida, Cuba only 90 miles/140km), it would seem to have been natural for Bahamian and Caribbean influences to have shown up earlier. But for centuries, mainland American tastes prevailed, and foreign flavors intruded mainly in Key West. One very old neighborhood in that city has long been imbued with the tastes of its Bahamian-descended inhabitants and their way with conch, grouper, pork, chicken, and the ubiquitous side dish of pigeon peas with rice.

During the late 19th century Cuban cigar makers began migrating to Key West, and they brought with them the harbingers of the cuisine that has since become part of the cultural signature of all of South Florida, especially Miami and its Little Havana neighborhood. The recipes the Cubans brought with them included *ropa vieja* (old clothes), a long-simmered stew of shredded beef; the slow-roasted pork called *lechon*; plantains fried in butter until they caramelize; and *picadillo*, a mélange of ground meat and potatoes seasoned with onions, tomatoes, pimientos,

Pasta with shrimp and mussels at a Naples restaurant.

⦵ SUSTAINABLE SEAFOOD

Given the extensive variety of seafood on Florida menus, it's a good idea to be aware of which species are relatively abundant and which have been negatively affected by fishing pressure. Grouper is a long-lived species that is particularly vulnerable to overfishing, and management of the fishery has been spotty. Orange roughy is another species with a long reproductive cycle – they don't mature until 20 years old – and their stocks have been significantly depleted by trawler fishing, which also damages their deep-water spawning habitat.

Among the least threatened commercially caught fish is mahi-mahi, which reproduces quickly and can sustain high fishing pressure, especially when the method used is trolling, as opposed to longline fishing. Albacore, yellowfin, mullet, pompano, and skipjack tuna stocks also stand up to commercial harvest, as long as proper methods are used, although longline and purse-seine fishing for tuna takes a heavy toll and causes the collateral destruction of sharks. Sustainable shellfish include Florida hard clams, which are farmed commercially off Brevard County on the Atlantic and along the Gulf Coast. They grow to maturity in suspended nets, which eliminates the need for harmful dredging, and do not require feeding with fishmeal or other potential pollutants, as the mollusks filter nutrients from seawater. For more information, visit www.seafood watch.org or http://smartcatch.fish.

green olives, and capers. Black beans and rice are a universal accompaniment, and a mainstay throughout the day is strong Cuban coffee, usually well sweetened and served in the morning with hot milk as *café con leche*. The one Cuban dish nearly every visitor can find, even without seeking out a Cuban restaurant, is the sandwich Cubano, stuffed with ham, roast pork, cheese, and pickles, served hot from a press. The *medianoche* version (named for its popularity as a midnight snack) is usually made with a sweeter variety of the thin-crusted Cuban bread that has

From Jamaica come spicy meat pasties (sometimes called turnovers) and jerk chicken and pork, the time-honored street foods of Kingston and Montego Bay, along with curried goat, chicken, and shrimp. The tamarind and ginger native to the island season many Jamaican dishes, and cassava bread is always a favorite.

Haitians, one of the most recent émigré groups, carried with them their fondness for fish boiled with lime juice, onion and garlic, and hot pepper. Highly seasoned beef patties and corn fritters are also reminders of the creole cuisine of their homeland.

The hearty Dominican stew called sancocho includes chicken, beef, plantains, yucca, and naranja agria (very sour oranges).

a soft, flaky inside. Tampa's version includes salami, and aficionados from the two cities battle over whose version is made as it should be.

ISLAND FLAVORS

Other kinds of Caribbean cuisine have followed the waves of immigrants that have come to Florida. A sizable Dominican community brought *pastelitos*, turnovers filled with meat or cheese; the hearty stew called *sancocho*, made with chicken or beef melded with the flavors of green plantains and any combination of cassava (yucca), the similar but creamier yautia, and potatoes, and invariably served with rice; and fish poached in coconut milk. *Buñuelos*, sweet donuts, are a popular accompaniment to coffee.

Florida's chefs experiment with all of these traditions, adding local produce and seafood to create a fusion all their own. The wonderful thing about the dishes of Florida is that they haven't supplanted each other either through the passing of time or the arrival of ethnic newcomers. The flavors of Florida exist side by side, admittedly more traditionally Southern in the north and Latin in the South, but always in close enough proximity so that a single sojourn in the state can supply a visitor with savory memories of Dixie barbecue, luminously fresh shellfish, a hefty *medianoche* sandwich consumed in the wee hours ... and that sack of oranges, so juicy that they should have been sold with a roll of paper towels.

The Incredible Hulk roller coaster, at Universal's Islands of Adventure, with Marvel Super Heroes aboard.

THE BUSINESS OF PLEASURE

It takes a heap of manpower and a lot of logistics to keep Florida's theme parks up and running and ahead of the competition.

Each evening, after approximately 150,000 guests exit through the turnstiles at Walt Disney World, the park's night crew swings into action. More than 25,000 people work until morning to refresh the cobwebs and "antique" grime in the Magic Kingdom's Haunted Mansion, mowing more than 2,000 acres (810 hectares) of grass, and distributing tons of food to more than 2,000 animals at Animal Kingdom, for starters. This crew is about half of the "cast" of 70,000 people hired by America's largest single-site employer to help keep Disney World "the happiest place on earth" – and perhaps the best maintained, as well.

Every day dozens upon dozens of pairs of sunglasses are turned into the Lost and Found at the Magic Kingdom. That's a few million pairs since the park opened in 1971.

The Magic Kingdom's Fantasy Parade at Walt Disney World.

For Disney World, Mickey and the gang are big business: the estimated more than 53 million people (that's roughly the population of Texas) who pass through its theme park gates every year will spend considerably more than $100 each on tickets, meals, refreshments, and souvenirs. It's no wonder so much hard work goes into ensuring that everyone has fun.

The folks at Disney produce and package pleasure. They provide a controlled, safe, and clean environment staffed by cast members (the Disney term for employees) who are always neat and well-groomed, and who never sport long nails, or visible tattoos or body piercings. They buff and polish a place where youngsters can frolic and parents can relive their childhood

fantasies alongside Cinderella, Peter Pan, and a host of cartoon characters that by now seem part of the American family. The cast does all these tasks well: Walt Disney World is the most visited vacation destination on earth.

DAY-TO-DAY DISNEY

Disney World functions well because it was planned that way from the beginning. When Walt and his brother Roy began scouting sites for an East Coast theme park, they wanted to avoid the mistakes they'd made in building Disneyland in California. One mistake was not purchasing a piece of land large enough to accommodate a self-contained vacation resort that could offer visitors everything they would want or need, so that they wouldn't have to go off-property to spend their money. Under a blind trust, Disney purchased 27,300 acres (11,000 hectares) of rural central Florida for an average of $200 an acre. Although it was mostly swamp, the 43-sq-mile (111-sq-km) parcel – a piece of land twice the size of Manhattan – would allow Disney to create a buffer large enough to keep competition at bay.

A HOME OF ITS OWN

Equally important was having the authority to develop and manage the property as Disney

Toon Lagoon, Universal's Islands of Adventure.

saw fit. The Florida legislature knew that the park would be profitable for the state, and thus approved a bill granting Disney permission to establish the Reedy Creek Improvement District, an area some have dubbed the Florida Vatican. The legislation gave Disney the authority to develop and manage every aspect of its property, including decisions about zoning, taxes, and even building an airport or nuclear power plant (should the need arise).

From the outset, Disney's plan was to retain complete control of the environment. With an initial investment of $400 million, the company built a plant that generates a significant percentage of the electricity needed to operate the park. In 2016, Reedy Creek worked with Duke

Energy to build a 22-acre (9-hectare) solar farm – shaped like Mickey's head – that provides additional energy to the complex.

Disney also set up its own waste disposal system, which now handles a daily load of tons upon tons of trash – much of it generated at the park's restaurants. The heart of the disposal system is a giant underground vacuum that sucks refuse from points scattered throughout the park and moves it at 60mph (97kmh) through tubes leading to a central repository, where it is compacted and transported to a landfill. Enormous amounts of material, including 6,500lbs (3,000kg) of aluminum cans, are processed each day at the park's recycling center. Disney's buses run on a diesel fuel made from vegetable oil.

When the Magic Kingdom was in its planning stage, designers came up with an elegant way to hide from guests the day-to-day operations necessary to run the park. They built a 2.8-mile (4.5km) utility corridor, or "utilidor," with 15ft (5-meter) -high tunnels at ground level, covered it with 8 million cubic yards (6 million cubic meters) of soil dug to create the Seven Seas Lagoon, and built the park over it. The utilidor houses the park's computer operations, offices, make-up operations, and costuming rooms. Color-coded connecting corridors permit Mickey and the gang a quick and easy way to suit up and scoot to different parts of the park.

VYING FOR DOLLARS

The Orlando Convention and Visitors Bureau estimates that more than 68 million people visit the destination annually. The hundreds of area hotels (with a combined total of more than 120,000 rooms) plus more than 20,000 vacation homes, restaurants, stores, and attractions all want a share of the money these visitors will spend, and most of them pool a portion of their advertising budgets to get it. Theme parks, including Universal Orlando, SeaWorld, and Gatorland, offer discounts in a myriad of free coupon books and through programs including the DEALS page on Visit Orlando's website, run by the Convention and Visitors Bureau.

Disney managers have taken a different route. Not only do they decline to advertise cooperatively with other businesses, they've pursued a policy of building attractions in an attempt to monopolize tourist dollars: hence the additions of Pandora – The World of Avatar (to compete with Wizarding World of Harry Potter) and Animal Kingdom (to draw clientele from Busch Gardens and SeaWorld). The expansion of Disney Springs to compete with Universal's CityWalk and downtown Orlando's Church Street Station was so effective that the latter has had sputters and starts for more than two decades.

Disney does offer discounts – generally on multiday packages, low-season rates, Florida-resident passes, and the Tables in Wonderland dining program, as well as in cooperation with the American Automobile Association (AAA). In an unusual move for a company that retains iron-fisted control over its marketing, the company has entered a distribution agreement with Travelocity.com, giving the travel website the authority to book theme park tickets, onsite hotels, and cruises for its customers.

DISNEY WORLD, HERE I COME

The Travelocity deal may well be an acknowledgment of the fact that there is more competition than ever for tourist dollars, and Disney is aggressively protective of its market share. Competition may also be the reason that Orlando theme parks, and Disney in particular, have stepped up their advertising campaigns.

Few sloganeering efforts have been as effective as the two-decade project that finds celebrity athletes gazing into a TV camera at the moment of their greatest victories and uttering the five words that confirm their status as superstars: "I'm going to Disney World." The catchphrase is the foundation of the successful "What's Next" campaign, designed to present Disney World as the place for people to go when they're celebrating.

STAYING ON TOP

Despite the growth of competing attractions, Disney World remains the 800lb gorilla of Orlando theme parks, outdistancing its nearest competitor by more than four times. In 2016, more than 53 million people paid admission to Disney World's four major theme parks, according to the TEA-AECOM Theme Index by the Themed Entertainment Association and AECOM. 19.4 million went to Universal Orlando, and 4.4 million flocked to SeaWorld Orlando. That's not counting the folks who visit the theme park complexes to attend conferences, frolic in water parks, play golf, eat at celebrity-chef restaurants, shop, see shows, or simply lounge in a nice hotel. But management knows that to stay on top, the parks have to continue to meet – better yet, to exceed – the expectations of its guests, 74 percent of whom are repeat customers. So in a business climate in which fuel costs rise and fall, the economy is often threatening to plummet, and competitors are getting savvier with their own attractions and technologies, quality must be maintained and image

Fish and chips at Disney's Downtown.

burnished even more aggressively. It's no wonder over-the-top new attractions open within the parks every year.

All three Orlando theme park complexes are aggressively trying to outdo one another wow-wise. At Disney, Animal Kingdom's Avatar Flight of Passage virtually brings riders through sweeping natural landscapes with scents and other senses-openers via 3-D virtual reality screen. Meanwhile Universal invites guests on a similar voyage – but over the top of the New York City skyline – with Jimmy Fallon's guidance in a wild, nearly joyful, sweep of the urban empire. And SeaWorld, in addition to opening thrilling new coasters, has revamped its Kraken to have a blow-your-mind interactive 3-D experience.

ON THE EDGE

The words most often used to compare Universal with Disney are "hipper," "edgier"... and "newer" – but that's far from the truth, considering Disney's expanded Fantasyland and Disney Springs complex, its new Pandora land, and upcoming expansions including a high-tech Star Wars complex under construction at Disney's Hollywood Studios. Both Universal and Disney complexes combine old and new, kiddie and cutting edge. At Disney, you can have a hokey holiday listening to a calm, pun-filled presentation made its Disney equivalent, Buzz Lightyear, feel almost quaint by comparison – although Disney then upped the game with the 3-D shooter Toy Story Mania. Terminator 2: 3-D, which combines live action with a 3-D movie, is a wild and violent extravaganza that assaults the senses with explosions, gunfire, billowing smoke, and ear-splitting volume. This is emphatically not the sort of show you want a young child to experience, especially those who may not fully understand the difference between playacting and real life. But kids may

A dolphin display at SeaWorld.

at the Magic Kingdom's Jungle Cruise, or you can fly a banshee over an otherworldly expanse. At Universal, you can bring the tots to watch the purple dinosaur Barney sing, or come face to face with a 3-story-tall gorilla that breathes in your face. True, there's no Disney equivalent to Universal's Simpson's line-up, including a thriller aptly called the Twirl 'n' Hurl. But then again little girls have forever-memories after being transformed into princesses at the glitzy Bibbidi-Bobbidi Boutique.

Because it's not as concerned with overall family image, Universal's rides and attractions tend to be more hair-raising. Even a fairly mild ride like Men in Black: Alien Attack, a ride-through, interactive shooting gallery, enjoy the fire and tricks at Indiana Jones Stunt Spectacular, which teaches how movies make action happen.

MAGICAL THRILLS

Universal's Islands of Adventure park lays to rest any debate as to which Orlando park offers the best thrill rides – although SeaWorld is aggressively marking its territory in this arena with a slew of a high-thrill attractions. In addition to gut-twisting roller-coasters like the Incredible Hulk and Dragon Challenge, there are innovative 3-D and simulator rides like Skull Island: Reign of Kong, the Amazing Adventures of Spider-Man, and the Simpsons Ride.

Perhaps the brightest jewel in Universal's crown, however, is the new Wizarding World of Harry Potter, a two-part re-creation of the famous young fictional hero's magical domain. The Hogsmeade section is in Islands of Adventure, the Diagon Alley neighborhood in Universal Studios Orlando. With certain tickets, you can ride the entertaining Hogwarts Express between the two; at the station, be sure to seek out Platform 9¾, where regular folks seemingly walk through a wall. At both sections, kids can pop into the same shops where Harry and his magic-loving friends bought their brooms, wands, and other gear (a canny merchandising crossover) while chowing down on food themed to J.K. Rowling's popular books (butterbeer, anyone?) and riding two types of Potter roller-coasters.

Although SeaWorld has been rated the world's best marine life park, management realized that it would have to introduce several thrill rides to keep attendance figures up. Its response to the challenge was Kraken, at the time the tallest, fastest, and steepest

The Blue Man Group plays at Universal Orlando.

Park maps are available at the gate to help you find your way.

☉ MOB MANAGEMENT: FOLLOW THE WIENIE

Crowd control designed to keep guests docile, mannerly, and patient in lengthy queues starts at Walt Disney World before visitors even enter the park. It begins as cars funnel into lanes at parking toll booths and drivers thread their way through the cones to assigned spaces. It continues as visitors listen to a barrage of instructions on the tram ride to the ticket booth, pass through security, and, finally, clear a park virtual turnstile.

Inside, guests are moved along with what the Disney people call wienies – or, more often, visual magnets: lures like Cinderella's Castle and Big Thunder Mountain that draw them from one spot to another. As Walt said, "you've got to have a wienie at the end of every street." Other controls include peppy music to keep guests moving and a flow-through ride protocol, whereby passengers enter on one side and leave on another, reducing loading time.

Many attractions have hidden lines: no one is waiting outside, but once inside, guests are channeled into winding corridors and wend slowly toward the loading zone. Because the scenery changes as they move, they sense progress. A variation is the pre-show – usually presented on video screens – that keeps guests entertained and fills them in on the ride's story line. In essence, the line becomes an extension of the ride – yet another Disney innovation. Disney also invites guests to book FastPass+ access for select rides way in advance.

roller-coaster in the South – which in 2017 re-emerged with a high-tech enhancement. Also in SeaWorld is the hypercoaster Mako, billed as longer, taller, and faster than any other coaster in town; Manta, where you speed along stingray-style; and Journey to Atlantis, described as part water ride, part roller-coaster – a white-knuckle combination that includes two of the steepest, wettest, and fastest drops of any ride in the world. Its latest addition, Infinity Falls, replicates a wild rafting trip.

The Wizarding World of Harry Potter replicates many features found in the popular books.

SeaWorld and Universal have long served alcoholic beverages. Disney didn't until 1984, because Walt didn't feel that it was appropriate in a family environment. But now three parks serve it freely, and at the Magic Kingdom select table-service restaurants offer wine and beer with dinner. (The no-booze policy almost sank Disneyland Paris when it first opened: Parisians, incredulous that they couldn't have a glass of wine, boycotted the park until management gave in.)

THE WAR OF MORE

Every attraction in the Orlando area wages a daily battle for tourist dollars, but the big three are engaged in a "war of more." Universal's answer to Disney Springs, an entertainment complex anchored by Planet Hollywood, a theater hosting Cirque du Soleil, plus restaurants with big names attached to them and an array of designer duds, is CityWalk, a similar complex occupied by theme restaurants and hip nightclubs as well as high-profile live shows such as Blue Man Group.

SeaWorld, vying with Disney's Animal Kingdom to be the No. 1 park for live animal acts, has Discovery Cove, where visitors can swim with dolphins and snorkel through a coral reef. Animal Kingdom has added behind-the-scenes experiences including the thrilling Wild Africa Trek.

They've all gotten into the waterpark act. Disney has long had Typhoon Lagoon and Blizzard Beach. SeaWorld matched that with Aquatica, which puts a spin on the traditional panoply of flumes and slides by introducing dolphins and other sea creatures into the mix. In 2017, Universal re-entered the fray with a tropically themed watery playground called Volcano Bay. It's claim to fame: no waits for rides, and no need to carry tubes upstairs yourself. For a lower-key waterpark experience, take kids 12 and under to the Legoland Waterpark, adjacent to the Legoland Florida theme park.

Universal and Disney are also locked in a battle to keep tourists from leaving their properties. Guests who stay at one of Universal's resort hotels enjoy a variety of special privileges, including complimentary on-site transportation, priority restaurant seating, and, most important at a park where lines for major attractions can be up to 90 minutes long, express access on most rides. Not to be outdone, Disney offers similar perks to guests at its hotels, most notably its Extra Magic Hours program, which allows resort guests to enter a designated park an hour before the official opening time and stay as long as three hours after closing.

Each year the parks raise their admission fees: as of 2017, the average cost for a one-day visit to the big three parks was $99–119, depending on the season. So it's important for each of them to continue to make their customers believe they are the biggest and the best. That's only good business.

THRILL MACHINES

The coasters at Florida's biggest theme parks are faster, wilder, and more imaginative than ever before.

When you get right down to it, the 21-plus crowd doesn't really visit theme parks for the themes. Walt Disney World's animated characters are appealing, but many teens and adults traveling child-free much prefer the feeling of flying through space and plummeting earthwards with harrowing abandon. When we surrender ourselves to the untender mercies of the best thrill rides, we are craving a taste of real-life mortal danger, while knowing that the brakes will work just in the nick of time.

The marquee thrill rides at the big Florida parks are high-tech cousins to the wooden roller-coasters that marked many early 20th-century amusement parks, and they use the same tricks of physics and physiology to induce delightful terror. For those who like a little thrill but not the terror of a huge one, smaller coasters like Magic Kingdom's Seven Dwarfs Mine Train a dash of scary.

G-FORCE AND AIR TIME

The most exciting sensations on a roller-coaster are the result of shifting G-forces, which lessen and magnify the force of gravity upon the riders.

A force of 1G, at which a 170lb (77kg) man feels like he weighs 17lbs, is what we feel under normal circumstances. Double the G-force and gravity's apparent effect is doubled: in other words, our 170-pounder feels like he's packing 340lbs (154kg). Most American coasters exert forces under 3Gs. A scant few pin riders back into their seats with 5Gs.

The initial descent from the top of the lift hill lessens G-force. Whipping back uphill increases it, while sharp turns exert G-force in a lateral direction.

These external effects focus on the inner ear, a tiny but crucial component of our anatomies that contributes not only to exhilaration but to the disorientation that makes rapid, twisting rides unappealing for many theme-park patrons. The inner ear is our gyroscope, enabling us to walk upright, but it cannot keep up when circumstances are manipulated as quickly and unnaturally as they are on a coaster ride. The result is dizziness, compounded by the sloshing and squeezing of the stomach.

THE STEEL AGE

Coaster design was revolutionized by the 1959 introduction of the tubular steel track. Steel liberated

Born to Be Wild – Passengers on Universal Studios' Hollywood Rip Ride Rockit can choose their own personal song to listen to during the ride.

coaster cars from having to remain right side up and made possible rides with corkscrews, helixes, and other gravity-defying effects. Later came suspended coasters, in which seats hang from the tracks.

On inverted coasters, seats are suspended without hinges to allow passengers to turn upside down. Universal Orlando's Dragon Challenge adds a new wrinkle, as dual coasters careen towards each other at 60mph (96kmh) – only to loop out of the way at the very last moment. Conventional coasters with their wheels on the bottom can also turn upside down, as they do on Universal's Incredible Hulk.

KICK START

Explosive, high-speed new propulsion systems are replacing the old chain-lift approach to launching a coaster. Among the new methods are blasts of compressed air and a tire-driven launch, frequently tied into visuals that pop thanks to the use of 3-D glasses.

SPORTS AND OUTDOOR ACTIVITIES

In addition to baseball, football, and basketball, Florida hosts a variety of outdoor activities, including the rush of surfing and diving.

Florida can be a very dangerous place for sports-junkie gamblers. But once you see that the rush of a twenty-yard fall into cool blue water and a speeding ball across the net is just as thrilling, you won't need to pay much to have a good time.

SPEED DEMONS

On a crisp February day in 1959, a race was held at Daytona International Speedway, and the world of stock car racing changed forever. Since then, headlines in newspapers the world over have chronicled car racing in Florida, but no story has ever approached that first race at Daytona in significance. It was the race that took Florida stock car racing out of the proverbial backwoods and brought with it a following that had previously been reserved for classic American race cities like Indianapolis.

Not that stock car racing in Florida was new. William H.G. "Bill" France, seeking his fortune in the South years before, transformed a group of grease-covered speed demons into the National Association for Stock Car Auto Racing, now better known as NASCAR. If the popular open-wheel cars could have a showplace like the Indianapolis Speedway, France speculated, why couldn't stock cars have a similar showplace?

The Daytona International Speedway made its debut on that February day in 1959. Its "D"-shaped speedway and ultra-high banking turns were designed for blazing speeds, and first-day fans were left enthralled – stock car racing, born in the north Florida hill country decades before, came of age in Daytona.

Today, spectators are still enthralled by the course and even more enthralled by the speeds. The patch of land in suburban Daytona Beach has since become the second most famous

The Philadelphia Phillies play the Tampa Bay Rays during spring training in Clearwater.

racecourse in the United States, next to Indianapolis. Names like Richard Petty and Mario Andretti have established Daytona as one of the greatest fuel-guzzling, engine-blasting, high-excitement speedways in the world. It is estimated that 101,000 fans jam the speedway each February for the Daytona 500, its premier race.

Shortly after Daytona is the famous 12 Hours of Sebring endurance race at Sebring International Speedway about 80 miles (130km) south of Orlando. Sebring is known for its less-than-smooth track, but drivers seem to relish the rough and rugged conditions. For the 35,000 or so spectators who converge on this small Florida town each March, the 12 Hours – like the Daytona 500 – is a good excuse to throw a party. The land surrounding the course turns into a huge campground; during the race, it looks like a giant cookout.

TAKING A GAMBLE

If the incessant roar of engines isn't enough to sate a craving for a sports-induced high, Florida offers the intoxicating thrill of legalized gambling, although its popularity has declined somewhat. In the fiscal year 2015–16, more than 340,000 people attended jai alai, greyhound, and horse races in Florida, waging at least $800 million – half the amount bet a decade earlier. Generally, pari-mutuel sports attract two distinct types of fans: the serious player who approaches his or her wager of choice with a steadfast dedication and desire to win, and the casual gambler betting for fun rather than profit.

Florida is one of the few states in the US where you can wager on human beings – as long as they are playing jai alai. Florida has numerous jai alai arenas (known as frontons), including those in Ocala, Fort Pierce, Miami, and Orlando. The wagers common to other pari-mutuel sports hold for jai alai: win, place, show, quinela, perfecta, and trifecta. All apply to the athletes who play this (currently male-only) version of handball.

The sport of jai alai originated in the Basque country and reached the US in the early 20th century. It came via Cuba, so it is no surprise that Florida has more jai alai arenas than anywhere else in the country.

AND THEY'RE OFF!

Thoroughbred racing is a major force in the state's gambling industry, though legalized gambling on Indian reservations has certainly cut into the sport's revenue stream. Horse racing's high-society tradition is known throughout the world and earned it the sobriquet the "Sport of Kings." The Palm Beaches area has been a winter destination for the nation's best horses and jockeys for years; in a routine winter season, every important thoroughbred in training east of the Mississippi River is likely to be stabled somewhere in South Florida. Thoroughbred breeders have their own enclave in Ocala.

Years ago, prominent sports, entertainment, and political figures made South Florida's horse tracks a place to see and be seen. These days, those memories still have a hold over some of the more elaborate tracks, but for the most part the crowds are more pedestrian than genteel. Gulfstream Park, north of Miami Beach and once one of the state's premier racing venues, is now more urban and sits in the middle of a high-rise condo community. Tracks are situated in Wellington, Pompano Beach, and Tampa as well.

Jai alai has the added thrill of pari-mutuel betting.

Between October and April, South Florida is also the focal point of the nation's harness racing. The opening of Pompano Park in Pompano Beach in 1964 served as the catalyst for what has become an annual southern migration of big-name harness horsemen to Florida. Virtually all of the sport's superstars ship their stables to Pompano for winter racing. They also prepare young horses being developed for the next summer's races in the North.

DOG RACES

Along with horses, Florida's greyhound racing industry is without peer. The state is by far the most important greyhound area in the nation if for no other reason than sheer volume.

Annual paid attendance statewide is about 8 million people who wager, with zeal, some $200 million per year. Florida has nine tracks, where the sleek canines can be watched as they are lured by an artificial rabbit around the track to the cheers of the crowd. The modern version of greyhound racing is believed to have evolved from a coursing meet held in 1904 in North Dakota. Anthropologists claim that Cleopatra kept greyhounds, a trait she shared with most Egyptian royalty. In England, the sport reached its great popularity

The Daytona 500.

during the Tudor period, in the reign of Queen Elizabeth I, who inspired the slogan "Sport of Queens".

INTO THE DEEP

For those craving the intense thrills of scuba diving, companies such as Force E, with centers in Boca Raton, Pompano Beach, and Riviera Beach, and Depth Perception in the Tampa Bay area, are the best pathways to a safe and memorable undersea experience. You can expect to pay a premium for a single scuba run without certification, which requires the accompaniment of a trained diver, which makes investment in a training course a tempting choice for those planning on taking the plunge.

Snorkeling, scuba's less challenging cousin, is another popular sport along the state's long sapphire coasts. The Florida Keys offer an official Shipwreck Trail (http://floridakeys.noaa.gov/shipwrecktrail) of sunken wrecks, dating back to the early 18th century and fully available to navigate. On the Gulf Coast, fossilized shark teeth draw hordes of treasure-seekers to the waters off Venice Beach. The only prerequisite for snorkeling is a reliable boat captain, for which prices can vary depending on the city and season, and a sturdy mask to keep your view clear. Avoid paying to snorkel in Miami Beach, where the crowds leave little to gape at beneath the surface.

If staying reasonably dry sounds more appealing, Florida offers plenty of other water-focused sports to divert the athletic tourist. Parasailing, where a speeding boat pulls harnessed cruisers until they soar high in the air to dip and dive, can be tried on almost every large beach, but is particularly popular on Cocoa Beach, near Orlando, and Bradenton Beach, in the Sarasota Area. Paddleboarding is on offer at resorts on both coasts, often with a daily paddleboard yoga option. Beach volleyball is the pick-up game of choice along both coasts, and jet skis are commonly seen zipping across the horizon on sunny days, and can usually be rented for about $100 per hour.

TEEING OFF

The spectacular weather in Florida makes it a destination for golfers. Many fans of the sport consider it a must to play the greens of famous courses such as the TPC Sawgrass in Ponte Vedra Beach, home of the PGA tour's Players Championship. Sadly for enthusiasts, the number of golf courses in Florida has plummeted in recent years. Still the state has 1,100 courses, more than any other state in the nation.

Beyond the daunting challenges of world-class – four magnificent courses including as the Copperhead course at Innisbrook in the Tampa Bay area host PGA events every year – nearly every city in the Sunshine State beckons to casual golfers with affordable and reservable tee times. Not every course is open to the public, but most hotel concierges can provide a recommendation to a nearby 18-hole jaunt.

Between Tampa and Orlando, the remote Streamsong Resort has two courses carved out of former phosphate mines. The sleek, sophisticated, quiet hotel and spa housing the greens is just as unusual. Championsgate, south of Disney World, is another popular newcomer with two Greg Norman courses.

Classicists might prefer one of the few dozen courses along the Florida Historic Golf Trail, most built by the 1930s.

Prices for a golfing excursion can vary widely, from less than $40 for a garden-variety afternoon to more than $400 per night for a full-service experience.

CASTING A LINE

Visitors to the Sunshine State may not realize how all those tasty cuts of fish make it to their plates, but those with the yen to bait a hook can experience the satisfaction of catching their own dinner – for the species that the state does not subject to strict catch-and-release requirements, of course. Fishing must be done with a license, making a trustworthy captain just as important for this sport as it is for snorkeling or scuba diving.

Many of the state's prized saltwater gamefish, such as bonefish and red snapper, are subject to per-day limits that licensed fishermen know how to monitor. Freshwater gamefish, such as the striped bass and bluegill, are less strictly curtailed. The biggest charter fishing hotspots are Destin in the northern Panhandle, the Gulf Coast waters off Fort Myers, and the Keys, where fishermen exert an immutable pull on the culture.

⊘ PADDLING PARADISE

Florida's coastline is known for its underwater vistas, from coral reefs to schools of angelfish, but above the waterline the scenery is just as thrilling. Kayakers and canoers flock to the state's islands and inland trails, with the Everglades' Wilderness Waterway and Cape Romano, located off Marco Island near Naples on the Gulf Coast, ranking near the top. In the Panhandle, historic Milton, with its Blackwater River State Park, bills itself as the Canoe Capital of Florida. Canoes are also available at many parks in the south, where mangroves are popular for exploring, but not advisable for sea adventuring. To find a rental company, visit www.kayakonline.com/florida.html or www.visitflorida.com/kayaking.

GAME, SET, MATCH

Even before superstar coach Nick Bollettieri opened his famous tennis academy in the town of Bradenton, between Tampa and Sarasota on the Gulf Coast, Florida was a top destination for tennis. Thousands of fans and enthusiasts follow in the professionals' footsteps every day by taking to hotel and public courts with nothing but a racket and a will to win.

Bollettieri's academy, now IMG Academy, has become a leading destination for amateurs looking to take the leap to pro at the same spot where

College Match Day at the USTA National Campus.

Serena Williams, Jim Courier, Monica Seles, and Andre Agassi cut their teeth. It trains visitors and pros in other sports, too, including football, baseball, golf, lacrosse, soccer, and basketball. A new Performance & Sports Science Center houses the Gatorade Sports Science Institute.

Orlando is also home to the USTA National Campus at Lake Nona, a $60 million, 100-court complex that opened in 2017. It quickly became a mecca for pros and enthusiasts looking to compete or improve their game.

Beach volleyball is a growing sport in Florida, even where there is no beach. Inland in Lake County, west of Orlando, the Hickory Point Beach Sand Volleyball Complex has 21 courts. A 4,000-sq-ft (370-sq-meter), $2-million fieldhouse is on the horizon.

A Florida backroad.

Falcon 9 rocket launch, Cape Canavaral.

Smathers Beach, Key West.

INTRODUCTION

A detailed guide to the entire state, arranged by region, with all the main sites clearly cross-referenced by number to the maps.

The Incredible Hulk roller coaster at Universal's Islands of Adventure.

Balladeer Jimmy Buffett put his guitar-pickin' finger on a fundamental reason for Florida's popularity as a retreat for routine-weary travelers with his 1977 album, *Changes in Latitudes, Changes in Attitudes*. In fact, no other place in the continental United States lies on a latitude further south. Some folks have become so addicted to the tranquilizing effects of Florida's balmy climes, they return year after year for another dose – and now baby boomers can buy into retirement communities themed after his popular Margaritaville concept.

Nature laid the groundwork for this annual people invasion by providing the beaches and forests. Then entrepreneurs added hotels and theme parks. Now, it's a bit harder to find a gator farm or an orange grove – or at least a place to try deep-fried gator meat and freshly squeezed juice – but you'll find them if you look in rural areas.

Florida is much too big and diverse to swallow in one gulp. The following information is designed to help you find your way around the state in smaller sips.

South Florida is anchored by Metropolitan Miami and Miami Beach, with its famous Art Deco District and hip, edgy Wynwood. It extends west to take in the wild expanse of the Everglades and Big Cypress Swamp, then south to the Florida Keys.

The Atlantic Coast stretches from Fort Lauderdale, within easy reach of Miami, right up to Jacksonville in the far north – taking in en route tony Palm Beach, the Space Coast, Daytona Beach, and historic St Augustine.

Neon sign on Calle Ocho, Little Havana.

Central Florida revolves around Orlando and crowd-pulling attractions such as Walt Disney World Resort.

The Gulf Coast has Tampa-St Petersburg as its nucleus, with Marco Island at its southern end and Cedar Key at its northern tip. Sarasota, Naples, and Fort Myers are the other major cities in this region.

North Florida encompasses the Panhandle region (whose promoters prefer the name Northwest Florida) – anchored by Tallahassee, the state capital, in the east, and Pensacola in the far west. It also takes Gainesville, with its prestigious state university, and the "Forgotten Coast" of Florida's Big Bend region.

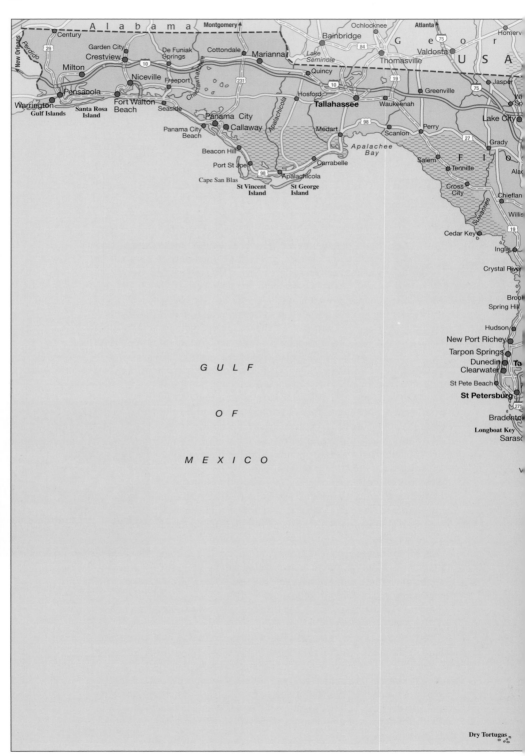

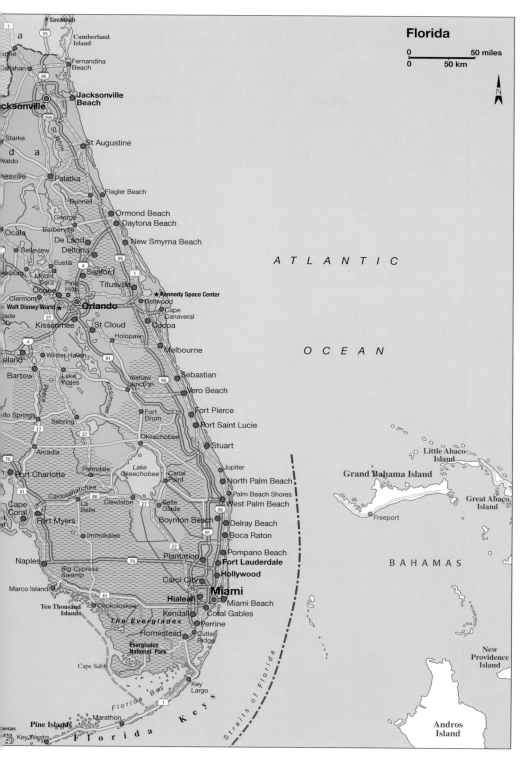

South Beach is a hub of sizzling nightlife and stylish shops.

SOUTHBEACH

↑ Post Office
↑ Española Way
← Police Station
← Old City Hall
← Flamingo Park
← Collins Avenue Shopping District
→ Ocean Drive

SOUTH FLORIDA

Miami offers urban thrills, with the Everglades just a short drive away and, to the south, the alluring, tropical Florida Keys.

Lounging on Smathers Beach in Key West.

South Florida is a region of extremes. In Miami you will find a great metropolis with a distinctly Caribbean flavor. In South Beach, the Art Deco architecture, chic shops, sizzling nightlife, and throngs of beautiful people (including quite a few actors and models) are the very height of celebrity chic. But equally compelling are the city's up-and-coming neighborhoods, such as the Design District, home to popular shops and bistros, and Wynwood, an arts center with murals on many buildings.

Beyond the skyscrapers of Miami are the swamps of the Everglades – an alligator-inhabited area of 1.4 million acres (565,000 hectares). This "river of grass" encompasses a fascinating blend of tropical and temperate environments, a laboratory where nature experiments with the ever-changing cycles of life and death.

Emblematic of Florida's physical and cultural connection to the Caribbean, the state's southern boundary doesn't come to an abrupt end, but trickles gently away in a necklace of coral and limestone islands known as the Keys. The archipelago stretches 180 miles (290km) from Miami's Biscayne Bay to the Dry Tortugas, just 86 miles (140km) north of Havana. The islands are sewn together by 113-mile (182km) -long US Highway 1, the Overseas Highway, stretching across 43 bridges from Key Largo to Key West.

The sunset reddens the horizon at Key Largo.

From the scuba culture of the Upper Keys to the bohemian counterculture of Key West, each island maintains its own identity. Visitors choose an island based on the activities on offer, ranging from sport fishing and diving to the chance to interact with dolphins or visit a tropical hardwood forest. Even the people differ from one key to the next: disillusioned Gold Coasters populate the upper islands, while people of the lower keys proudly call themselves Conchs and have removed themselves from the nine-to-five hustle. Mañanaland, Margaritaville, the American Riviera – the Keys have been called many things. Whatever the appellation, they are a place to take off your watch and kick back.

Miami Beach.

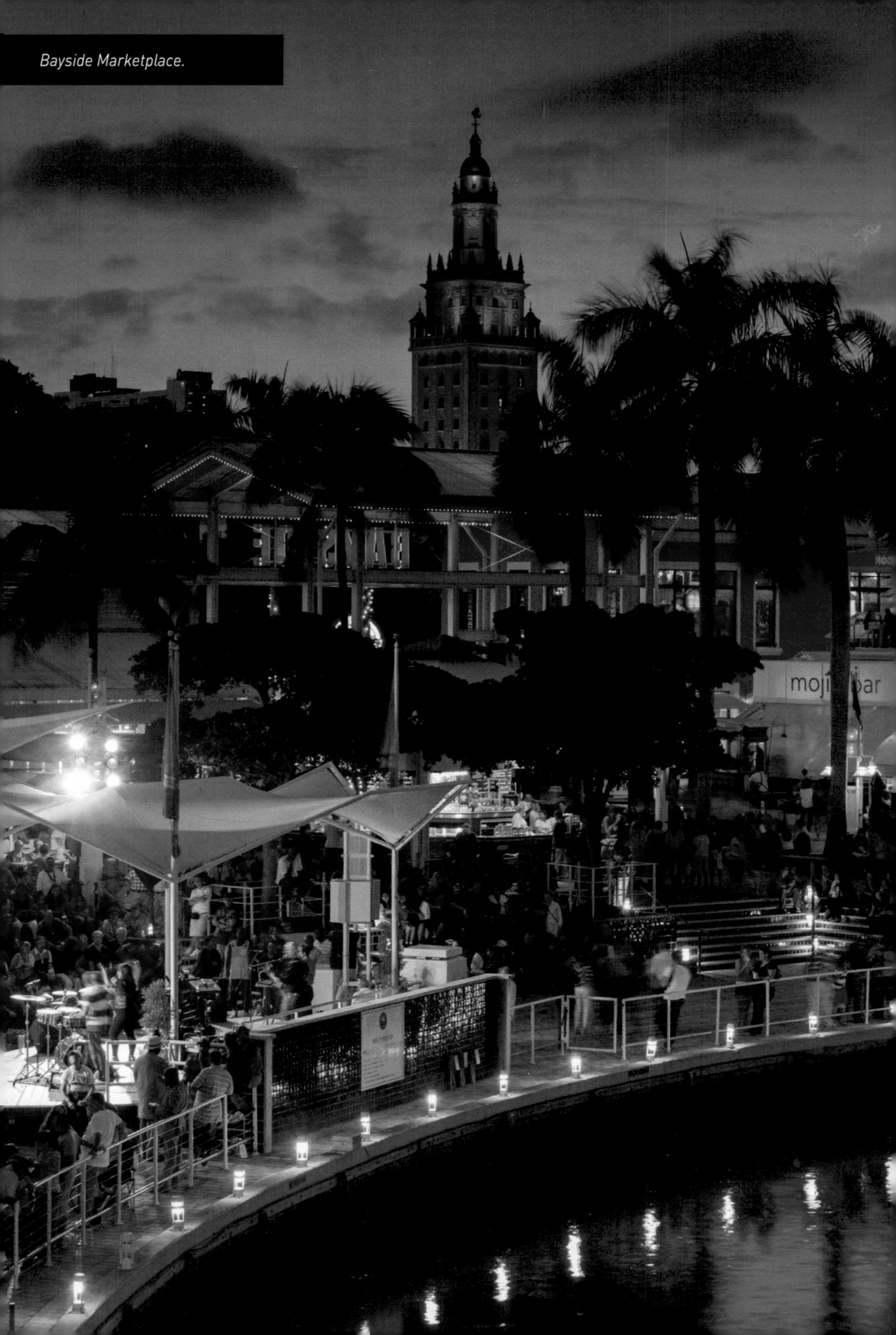

Bayside Marketplace.

METROPOLITAN MIAMI

South Florida's urban hub is a crossroads of Latin American, Caribbean, and Yankee cultures with a vibrant arts scene, great restaurants, and a distinctly tropical ambience.

Miami is the big dot on the Florida map. Brash, beautiful, exotic, and vibrant, it is the state's most complex and multifaceted city, large in size as well as personality. Made up of over 30 municipalities, Greater Miami is situated within Miami-Dade County and encompasses more than 500 sq miles (1,300 sq km) that contain a rich and diverse ethnic stew. About 60 percent of the area's population is foreign born, which means the city speaks with many accents – Spanish, French, Hebrew, Portuguese, Russian, Creole, and Jamaican, to name just a few.

With a population of more than 2.4 million, Greater Miami has its share of big-city problems, but it also has a stunningly beautiful natural landscape, a cutting-edge art community, the best Latin music this side of the Gulf Stream, and a restaurant scene that has most definitely come of age. Throughout its many incarnations of the past few decades – from Paradise Lost to the New Riviera – it has always fascinated visitors, and for good reason. It is full of energy yet laid-back and casual. It embraces all things shiny and new but remains a few steps behind other major American cities. It boasts of a world-class sophistication but is riddled with insecurities.

None of this is more apparent than in downtown Miami, where new

Palm trees ring the water's edge.

skyscrapers are being built seemingly everywhere. The building boom has created an urban core that's jam-packed with construction sites and road detours that will likely be around for a long time. This congested mess, however, has in no way dampened the excitement and enthusiasm that permeates the neighbourhood, which has the third-tallest skyline in the country.

DOWNTOWN

As it curves northward along Biscayne Bay, Brickell Avenue eases into

◎ Main Attractions

Bayside Marketplace
Arsht Center for the
  Performing Arts
Rubell Family Collection
MoCA
Ancient Spanish Monastery
Biltmore Hotel
Miracle Mile
Patricia and Phillip Frost
  Museum of Science
Vizcaya Museum and
  Gardens

Map on page 100

downtown Miami and is studded with futuristic buildings, many of which sparkle at night with colorful neon lights. Brickell crosses over the Miami River and becomes the major thoroughfare of **Biscayne Boulevard**. On the south bank of the Miami River and the east side of Brickell Avenue sits a controversial piece of land. Here, in 1989, construction workers unexpectedly uncovered a circle of stones that turned out to be the remnants of a Tequesta Indian settlement dating back more than a thousand years. After years of battles between historians and the developers who owned

the land, the neglected site – now deemed the Miami Circle – is slated to be turned into an urban park that will preserve the stones and contain an interpretive center placing them in their historic context.

BY THE BAY

Anchoring much of the downtown tourist traffic on Biscayne Boulevard is **Bayside Marketplace** ❶ (401 Biscayne Blvd; tel: 305-577-3344; www.baysidemarketplace.com; Mon–Thu 10am–10pm, Fri–Sat until 11pm, Sun 11am–9pm; free), a 16-acre (6-hectare) waterfront extravaganza

Metropolitan Miami

of more than 100 shops, restaurants, and attractions that often hosts free live concerts. Within walking distance of Bayside to the south is **Bayfront Park**, a verdant and peaceful waterfront public space.

At the southern end of the park is a memorial designed by the late Japanese sculptor Isamu Noguchi; it is dedicated to the crew who lost their lives aboard the space shuttle *Challenger* when it exploded over Florida in 1986. At night, Bayfront Park often puts on laser-light shows that throw beams of bright colors into the Miami night sky.

A few steps to the north of Bayside is the **American Airlines Arena**, home to the Miami Heat basketball team and a venue for major music events. Just beyond it is **Museum Park**, a lush greenway with a long baywalk that has the Pérez Art Museum and the Phillip and Patricia Frost Museum of Science.

Nearby is the entrance to the **Port of Miami**, a major marine commerce hub as well as the busiest port for cruise ships in the world, funneling over 4 million passengers a year to all points in the Caribbean.

Across the street is the **Freedom Tower ②**, one of the more significant historic buildings in the downtown area. Built in 1925, the peach-colored Mediterranean Revival building was the home of the now defunct *Miami News* and served as a processing center in the 1960s for Cuban immigrants who fled the communist takeover of their country, hence the name. Today, the perfectly preserved 17-story building regularly hosts art shows and cultural events.

ART AND CULTURE

Behind the Tower is a series of dense streets filled with electronic and jewelry shops, and the downtown campus of **Miami-Dade College**, site of the **Miami Book Fair International** held every November. Nearby on Flagler Street is the **Olympia Theater** (www.olympiatheater. org), a glorious Baroque-style theater that hosts the **Miami International Film Festival** each winter. Named for railroad magnate Henry Flagler, Flagler Street is one of the busiest thoroughfares in downtown, packed with small stores catering to shoppers who arrive in Miami with large empty suitcases.

At 101 W. Flagler is the **Metro-Dade Cultural Center Plaza ③**. A popular lunch site for downtown lawyers and office workers, the Plaza has an expansive tiled courtyard graced with flowing pools of water. It is also home to the **Miami-Dade Main Library** and the **HistoryMiami Museum ④** (tel: 305-375-1492; www. historymiami.org; Mon–Sat 10am–5pm, Sun noon–5pm), which maintains a permanent exhibit depicting 10,000 years of South Florida history.

The **Pérez Art Museum Miami** (1103 Biscayne Blvd; tel: 305-375-3000; www.pamm.org; Tue–Sun

The County Courthouse near the Metro-Dade Cultural Plaza.

A production of Puccini's Turandot at the Florida Grand Opera.

The Wynwood Walls build on Miami's dramatic traditions of street art.

10am–6pm, Thu until 9pm), where rotating exhibits range from American modern to European classical art. The **Phillip and Patricia Frost Museum of Science** ❺ (1101 Biscayne Blvd; tel: 305-434-9600; www.frost science.org; daily 10am–6pm) is dedicated to science exploration and the mysteries of outer space. This hands-on, family-friendly museum has two wings plus a three-level aquarium and a 250-seat planetarium that projects its show with 16-million-color 8K projection. The museum itself has experiential and interactive exhibits for exploring science, technology, engineering, and math.

Downtown's cultural hub, and a major element in the city's revitalization plan, centers around the **Arsht Center for the Performing Arts** ❻ (1350 Biscayne Blvd; tel: 305-949-6722; www.arshtcenter.com). The $461-million center, designed by César Pelli, was intended to elevate Miami's ranking among the world's great cities. Spectacularly beautiful, the venue includes a state-of-the-art concert hall and a separate ballet house that host major cultural events, including those of four resident companies – the **Concert Association of Florida**, **Florida Grand Opera**, **Miami City Ballet**, and **New World Symphony**. The smaller Black Box Theater is where more offbeat and intimate productions are held. On weekends, the center has free events on the plaza, such as flamenco dance classes, Caribbean steel bands, and Latin jazz ensembles.

THE UPPER EASTSIDE

Continuing north on Biscayne Boulevard, the urban atmosphere becomes grittier but also more interesting and artsy. In recent years this area has been tagged the Upper Eastside by hip young developers (many from New York) who see the neighborhood as an evolving work of art.

Also known as the **Biscayne Corridor**, this bustling area includes the neighborhood of **Buena Vista**, the **Wynwood Art District**, and the **Miami Design District**. A bohemian frontier,

it's where many enterprising artistic types have settled after fleeing the mainstreaming of South Beach in the last few years. Some are hard at work breathing new life into old MiMo (Miami Modern architecture) motels built in the 1950s or transforming shabby bungalows and small apartment buildings into hipster enclaves where emerging young artists in worn-out jeans mingle with interior decorators in designer clothes. With dozens of sleek Greenwich Village-like lofts popping up all over, it's a thriving area quickly rising in prominence in the international art world where intrepid visitors can view impressive private art collections during the day or dodge the lingering drug dealers late at night.

WYNWOOD

From 19th to 37th streets is the neighborhood of Wynwood (www.wynwood miami.com), where funky galleries are sandwiched between auto repair shops and trendy restaurants that also share the streets with two private collections: the **Rubell Family Collection ❼** (95 NW 29th St; tel: 305-573-6090; http://rfc.museum; Wed–Sat 10am–5.30pm, free tours at 3pm) and the **Margulies Collection ❽** (591 NW 27th St; tel: 305-576-1051; www.margulieswarehouse.com; Wed–Sat 11am–4pm, closed May–Oct). Housed in enormous warehouses, both collections contain a broad representation of contemporary art, sculpture, and photography.

The Rubell site is owned by New Yorkers Don and Mera Rubell, relatives of the late Steve Rubell, who owned the famous Studio 54 nightclub. Other respected art venues include the **Cisneros Fontanals Arts Foundation**, the **Fredric Snitzer Gallery**, the **Diana Lowenstein Gallery**, **Spinello Projects**, and the **Gary Nader Art Center**. On the second Saturday of the month, Wynwood hosts a Gallery Walk when art lovers stroll from gallery to gallery and enjoy complimentary wine, champagne, and hors d'œuvres.

DESIGN DISTRICT

Although the Wynwood Art District is the sassy new kid on the block,

An installation piece at the Rubell Family Collection.

A show opening at the Rubell Family Collection.

A mural adorns a brick building in Little Haiti.

it would not have been possible if it weren't for the more dignified **Design District** (www.miamidesigndistrict.net) a few blocks to the north. About 16 square blocks that run from NE 36th to NE 41st streets between NE 2nd and N Miami avenues, the Design District is a dense cluster of all things divine in the design world. In the 1920s the area was called Decorator's Row and has since gone through various periods of boom and bust. These days represent another boom period, and the compact village is once again an example of tropical splendor.

Easily explored in a few hours, it's full of high-end furniture importers, interior design showrooms, art galleries, and kitchen and garden boutiques. Anchoring the cluster is the historic **Moore Building** ❾ (4040 NE 2nd Ave), a gleaming white four-story gem that has an outdoor bamboo garden lounge and a nonprofit art gallery that consistently exhibits internationally acclaimed artists.

Ceramic saints and other figurines at a Little Haiti botanica.

Every December, **Design Miami**, the design offshoot of the phenomenally

successful Art Basel Miami Beach, is held adjacent to the Miami Beach Convention Center. During the event, the Moore Building and other venues in the Upper East Side have satellite art and design shows, parties, films, and seminars that complement the main schedule of events at the convention center.

Most shops in the Design District are open to the public Monday through Saturday from 11am to 5pm. As the area has grown in popularity, a few clever restaurants have shown up as well. One of the most renowned is **Michael's Genuine Food and Drink** (130 NE 40th St; tel: 305-573-5550; www.michaels genuine.com), an unpretentious but highly rated bistro.

LITTLE HAITI

One of the great things about Miami is its ethnic enclaves, and Little Haiti is no doubt among the more fascinating. Beginning a few blocks north of the Design District, it lies within the boundaries of 79th Street to the north, 46th Street to the south,

Biscayne Boulevard to the east, and I-95 to the west.

Little Haiti is a juxtaposition of immigrant optimism and inner-city decay, and it offers an intimate encounter with a rich Caribbean culture. Although perhaps not as economically successful as its Cuban-immigrant counterpart, Miami's Haitian community has prospered in the local arts scene and now plays an active role in city politics. Many Miami Haitians have moved into the middle-class suburbs, but the heart of the community is still in Little Haiti.

Here mom-and-pop grocery stores and small restaurants thrive as they cater to the community with heaping servings of *griot* (fried pork), *lambi* (stewed conch), and spicy oxtail stew. There are several small botanicas in the neighborhood, and they welcome visitors who want to sample or just look. Shops that specialize in religious paraphernalia and medicinal herbs for practitioners of the Afro-Caribbean religions of voodoo and Santeria, botanicas can be found in many other areas of Miami as well.

The **Notre Dame d'Haiti** Catholic Church ⑩ (130 NE 62nd St; tel: 305-751-6289) has long been an advocate of Haitian immigrant rights in Miami. It is also a great venue to meet local Haitians, especially on Sunday mornings when thousands come out for a Mass that blends traditional Catholicism with rhythmic Haitian music.

A few blocks away is **Libreri Mapou** (5919 NE 2nd Ave; tel: 305-757-9922), one of the few bookstores in Florida that specializes in Haitian Creole books and music. Owned by Haitian writer Jan Mapou, the bookstore also stocks Haitian arts and crafts and is a popular gathering place for Haitian writers and musicians.

NORTH MIAMI

About 2 miles (3km) to the north of Little Haiti is the city of North Miami (www.northmiamifl.gov), which has a Haitian-American mayor. A very diverse middle-class neighborhood, the city is also one of the area's up-and-coming arts districts. Most of the action here is around 125th Street, where there

The Museum of Contemporary Art is host to changing exhibits as well as films, musical performances, and artist workshops.

The Museum of Contemporary Art.

are several cafés, restaurants, and galleries that put on poetry readings and world music concerts. The big draw, however, is the **Museum of Contemporary Art North Miami** ⑪ (770 NE 125th St; tel: 305-893-6211; www.mocanomi.org; Tue–Fri and Sun 11am–5pm; Sat 1–9pm). Known for fresh contemporary art with lots of attitude, MoCA features rotating exhibits of local and internationally recognized artists. Its permanent collection includes works by Julian Schnabel, Louise Nevelson, and Yoko Ono. On the last Friday of each month is a free outdoor concert; the audience gathers on the grass with coolers full of wine and takes in the sounds of jazz, Latin, and folk music.

The other attraction in North Miami is the **Ancient Spanish Monastery** ⑫ (16711 W. Dixie Hwy; tel: 305-945-1461; www.spanishmonastery.com; Mon–Sat 10am–4.30pm, Sun 11am–4.30pm). Built in Segovia, Spain, in the 12th century, then dismantled and shipped to Florida in 1925, the monastery was rebuilt in 1952. Tucked behind stone walls with meandering tropical gardens, it's now a peaceful oasis within a busy neighborhood that is welcoming to visitors from all walks of life.

LITTLE HAVANA

Another ethnic enclave that offers an authentic experience is Little Havana, located in the south part of Miami-Dade County just to the west of downtown. It is here that the first wave of Cuban immigrants settled in the early 1960s; the cultural infusion is still apparent. While the Cuban population of Greater Miami – approximately a million people – has spread throughout every corner of the city, it is in Little Havana that the scent of Cuban coffee and the blare of salsa trumpets permeate the air, and heated arguments about a post-Castro Cuba can be overheard on almost every corner.

Although it is still a scruffy, lower-income neighborhood, Little Havana has gone upscale in some places with the addition of new art galleries, nightclubs, and restaurants that

A reconstructed cloister at the Ancient Spanish Monastery.

serve as the symbolic heart of the exile community. On the last Friday of the month, the place pulsates with **Viernes Culturales** (Cultural Fridays; http://viernesculturales.org), a street party of concerts, gallery openings, and historic walking tours of the neighborhood.

Most of the action takes place on **Calle Ocho** ⓭ (SW 8th St) between 14th and 27th avenues. This is also where the wildly flamboyant Latin street festival takes place each March.

But you don't need a festival to enjoy Calle Ocho, since the street bustles with action both day and night. At **Versailles Restaurant** (3555 SW 8th St; tel: 305-444-0240; www.versailles restaurant.com) the Cuban food is hearty and plentiful, and the clientele ranges from power brokers and politicians to poets and musicians. Always loud and very busy, it's perhaps the most famous Cuban restaurant in the US. Directly across the street is **La Carreta** (3632 SW 8th St; tel: 305-444-7501; www. lacarreta.com), another popular Cuban eatery, open 24 hours.

Heading eastward toward the Miami River, in the 1600 block of 8th Street, there are a few good finds, including; **Art District Cigars**, where visitors can choose from an extensive selection of stogies while taking in live Latin music; and **Molina Fine Art**, a gallery featuring vibrant paintings that reflect tales from Afro-Cuban folklore. Around the corner is the small **Bay of Pigs Museum** (1821 SW 9th St; tel: 305-649-4719; http://bay ofpigs2506.com; Mon–Sat 9am–4pm), a crowded collection of artifacts and memorabilia honoring Cuban exiles who died in the failed 1961 US invasion of Cuba.

JUST LIKE HOME

On the corner of 8th Street and 15th Avenue is **Domino Park** ⓮, also known as Máximo Gómez Park, a fenced-in courtyard where Cuban men gather for lively games of dominoes and talk about the good old days in Havana.

Next door to the park is **Little Havana To Go**, a playful souvenir

Cuban men often engage in spirited games of dominoes at Domino Park.

Street sculpture in Little Havana.

Miami's Miracle Mile is home to designer boutiques and upscale restaurants and cafés.

shop where visitors are treated to a complimentary *cafecito* and the shelves are brimming with all things Cuban – music, art, domino sets, cigars, and guayabera shirts. Across the street from the shop is the beautiful **Tower Theater**. Built as a movie palace in 1926, this perfectly restored Art Deco building is owned by the City of Miami and is host to film festivals, lectures, book signings, dance, and theatrical performances.

About two blocks away is **La Casa de los Trucos** (1343 8th St), a business originally founded in Cuba. Also known as House of Costumes, this neighborhood institution sells costumes, funny hats, masks, maracas, and magic tricks. In the area, the starstruck will enjoy the Calle Ocho Walk of Fame, which honors Cuban and Latin performers with in-ground stars.

At 1071 SW 8th Street is **El Titan de Bronze** (tel: 305-860-1412; Mon–Sat 9am–5pm), a corner shop where cigars are made by hand as they were in Cuba back in the day. You can watch the artisans rolls the tobacco,

The Biltmore Hotel.

get lessons about the different stogie styles, and, of course, buy a selection to bring home. Quality is serious business here: All rollers are of a Level 9 skill set, according to Cuban standards, and their work is inspected by a Master.

CORAL GABLES

To the south of Little Havana is a city where many affluent Cuban exiles moved after climbing the socio-economic ladder in Miami. Designed by developer George Merrick in the 1920s, Coral Gables is an enchanting city of Mediterranean-style architecture, ornate limestone arches, and a vibrant art and culture scene. With avenues named after cities in Spain and street signs on tiny white stones, it is not easy to navigate. But it has several landmark properties that are worth seeking out.

Surrounded by palatial mansions, the old **Biltmore Hotel** ⑮ (1200 Anastasia Ave; tel: 305-445-1926; www.biltmorehotel.com) was the grand dame of South Florida hotels in the

⊘ MAKING THE MIRACLE

Coral Gables' Miracle Mile is now known as a shopping destination, but its origins lie down a different path. It was the urban planning movement that first motivated George Merrick to craft one of the first planned communities during the booming 1920s. Long before the rise of the suburbs and the establishment of the interstate road system forced Americans into their cars, Merrick took pride in his vision of a district where every business was no further than a "two-block walk" away. Today the rise of crippling gridlock has made the Miracle Mile's pedestrian-friendly flavor a modern asset. Even the free circular trolley service is a throwback to Merrick's day, when electric trolleys roamed the Vizcaya-inspired streets of his city beautiful.

Roaring Twenties. Its swimming pool – billed as the largest in the US, was once the setting for elegant water ballets, and Johnny Weissmuller, star of Tarzan movies, set a world swimming record here in the 1930s. Today, with golf, tennis, and a spa, it is a playground for the international jet set and is often used for fashion shoots. The hotel offers free walking tours of the property on Sunday afternoons.

Within the hotel, the modern theater company **GableStage** (tel: 305-445-1119; www.gablestage.org; performances Thu–Sun evenings and Sun afternoons) is a rising player in the local arts scene. Its seasons are dominated by the type of witty, intellectual plays more commonly found in New York City, while tickets cost less than half of those on Broadway.

Another stunning swimming hole in Coral Gables is the **Venetian Pool** ⑯ (2701 DeSoto Blvd; tel: 305-460-5306; mid-Mar–mid-Sept Sat–Sun 10am–4.30pm, mid–end Mar Tue–Fri 10am–4.30pm, Apr–May Tue–Fri 11am–5.30pm, end May–mid-Aug Mon–Fri 11am–6.30pm, mid-Aug–mid-Sept Mon–Fri 11am–5.30pm; opening hours subject to change), a freshwater coral rock lagoon with caves and waterfalls amid lush tropical gardens. The pool is drained nightly and refilled in the morning with artesian well water. Its Venetian-style architecture and soft sandy beach provide a fine setting for an afternoon swim.

MIRACLE MILE

The commercial center of the Gables lies along and parallel to **Miracle Mile** ⑰, a visitor-friendly street filled with upscale boutiques, cafés, and restaurants. From several points on Miracle Mile, the **Coral Gables Trolley** offers free transportation throughout the business hub of the city every day to 10pm. A newer Grand Avenue loop hooks up to Downtown Coral Gables transfers and runs daily until 8pm.

The Trolley is also a convenient way to take in the **Gables Gallery Night** held on

Avid readers gather for books, author events, drinking, and dining at Books & Books.

The historic Venetian Pool is open to the public.

A classical sculpture at the Lowe Art Museum.

Schoolchildren take a tour of the Lowe Art Museum.

the first Friday of every month. Mostly specializing in fine Latin American art, there are many respected galleries in downtown Coral Gables such as **Virginia Miller Galleries**, **Americas Collection**, **The Orange Driftwood**, and **Cernuda Arte**. There are several modern luxury hotels in the downtown area, including the Hyatt Regency and Hotel Colonnade, but they can't compete with the charming Old World ambience of the historic **Hotel St Michel** (162 Alcazar Ave), which was built during the 1920s and includes an intimate Italian restaurant.

Within walking distance is Miami's literary epicenter, **Books & Books** (265 Aragon Ave; tel: 305-442-4408; www.booksandbooks.com; Sun–Thu 9am–11pm, Fri–Sat 9am–midnight). Housed in a stark white Mediterranean building with an inner courtyard, this is more than a bookstore. It's a full-service café that also offers live music and foreign films at night. Every night the store hosts readings by some of the world's most famous authors – Nobel laureates, Pulitzer Prize winners, politicians, presidents, talk-show hosts,

movie stars, and the like. It also presents many local authors and readings in both English and Spanish.

ART, HISTORY, NATURE

Toward the southeast of Coral Gables is the **University of Miami**, home of the **Lowe Art Museum** ⓲ (1301 Stanford Dr; tel: 305-284-3535; www.lowemuseum. org; Tue–Sat 10am–4pm, Sun noon–4pm). One of Miami's finest museums, the Lowe has a permanent collection of 19,000 objects that includes Renaissance and Baroque art; 19th- and 20th-century art; Egyptian, Greek, and Roman antiquities; Latin American and Asian collections; and Native American art and artifacts.

Continuing east, near Biscayne Bay, the attractions feature the handiwork of nature instead of people. **Matheson Hammock Park** ⓳ (9610 Old Cutler Road; daily sunrise–sunset) is a 630-acre (255-hectare) park with a marina, saltwater atoll pool, and small beach. Along with beautiful walkways and cycling trails through dense mangroves, Matheson Hammock has a

restaurant, picnic facilities, barbecues, and sailboat and kite-surfing rentals.

A little farther down the road is **Fairchild Tropical Botanic Garden** (10901 Old Cutler Rd; tel: 305-667-1651; www.fairchildgarden.org; daily 9.30am–4.30pm), the largest garden of its type in the continental US. Named for famed botanist David Fairchild, it has an outstanding collection of tropical flowering trees and more than 5,000 species of palms, ferns, and orchids. Many species in the park are rare and endangered; others are used for medicinal purposes and some for the making of perfume (the ylang-ylang tree blossoms are the primary ingredient of Chanel No. 5). Tram tours include a 40-minute narrated ride that is informative and fun. A virtual oasis in the middle of a big city, Fairchild also has several lakes that are a delight to the senses.

COCONUT GROVE

Next door to Coral Gables is the Miami neighborhood of **Coconut Grove**. Formerly an art colony and hippie hangout, the Grove (as locals call it) is one of Miami's oldest and most interesting neighborhoods. Built by Bahamian laborers about a century ago, it still has much of their laid-back attitude. At various times in its history it has claimed famous American writers, musicians, and artists as residents. Each July it hosts the **Goombay Festival**, a weekend street party that pays tribute to its Bahamian roots with live Junkanoo bands, conch fritter vendors, and dancing in the streets. The popular three-day Coconut Grove Art Festival (www.cgaf.com) takes place every February. With work by 360 internationally renowned artists on display this is great opportunity to buy jewelry, watercolors, glass art, or sculptures; some of what you pay supports the community's arts programs.

Under a dense canopy of green, the houses in the Grove run the gamut from palatial pink mansions to funky old Florida cottages. There is still a Saturday and Sunday morning **farmers' market** (Grand Ave and McDonald St), where locals gather to buy organic

Coconut Grove has a reputation for being an artsy, eclectic community.

Fairchild Tropical Botanic Garden.

fruits and vegetables as well as famous pies and fresh-squeezed juices. The main commercial activities center around Main Highway and Commodore Plaza, where on weekend nights the pedestrian traffic is heavy. Nearby is the old **Coconut Grove Playhouse**, a Mediterranean-style venue built in 1926 but currently out of commission due to financial woes. Fundraising and renovation plans are underway.

Across the street is the **Barnacle Historic State Park** ⑳ (3485 Main Hwy; tel: 305-442-6866; Fri–Mon 9am–5pm), home of the Miami pioneer Commodore Ralph Munroe (1851–1933), a boat-builder, mariner, botanist, and photographer. Built in 1891, the home overlooks Biscayne Bay and is filled with family heirlooms and antiques. It is totally secluded from traffic and other buildings. It's possible to sit on the home's wrap-around porch and imagine what life was like in South Florida before tourism took hold of the economy. Tours of the home and grounds are given at 10am, 11.30am, 1pm, and 2.30pm daily.

Special events at CocoWalk include fashion shows, live music, and ethnic festivals.

A few blocks away is **CocoWalk** ㉑ (3015 Grand Ave; www.cocowalk.net; Sun–Thu 10am–10pm, Fri–Sat 10am–11pm, bars open until 3am), a multistory shopping center and entertainment complex and the Grove's busiest attraction. Popular with college students on weekends, it has numerous bars and live bands playing.

Next door is the **Streets of Mayfair** (2911 Grand Ave; tel: 305-448-1700; Mon–Fri 11am–7pm, Thu until 8pm, Sun noon–5pm), another shopping venue, but this one anchored by the **Mayfair Hotel and Spa**, a tranquil and plush property with a soaring atrium, copper sculptures, and gushing fountains.

Near the entrance of CocoWalk, Grand Avenue connects with McFarlane Road, and this leads to S. Bayshore Drive. At McFarlane and Bayshore is **Peacock Park** ㉒, a large green playground that once contained South Florida's first hotel, the Bayview House (later renamed the Peacock Inn), built in 1883. Today the waterfront park is popular with Frisbee players and sunbathers, plus softball

and kickball teams, and it occasionally hosts an art festival.

Continuing north on Bayshore Drive is **Miami City Hall** ㉓, a beautifully preserved Art Deco building originally built to be a passenger terminal for Pan American Airways' seaplanes in 1934. Nearby is **Dinner Key Marina**, a popular mooring site filled with sailboats and yachts, as well as several landmark restaurants, including **Monty's Stone Crab**. Arriving by boat at these waterfront seafood spots is a popular and offbeat way for visitors to see the night skyline while making the most out of a day-long charter rental.

VIZCAYA

Tucked behind coral rock walls across the street from the science museum is Miami's grandest residence – **Vizcaya Museum & Gardens** ㉔ (3251 S Miami Ave; tel: 305-250-9133; www.vizcaya museum.org; Wed–Mon 9.30am–4.30pm; see page 114). Built between 1914 and 1916 for industrialist James Deering and intended to resemble an Italian Renaissance villa, Vizcaya required 10,000 laborers to complete. During its heyday it occupied 180 acres (70 hectares) and was a totally self-sufficient enclave with its own livestock and vegetable gardens.

Today, the opulent 70-room palace is a museum filled with European antiques, oriental carpets, tapestries, and fine art. Its Baroque and rococo interiors look exactly as they did when it was a private home. A few of the more dramatic rooms are the Tea House, inspired by French architecture; the Music Room, which contains an 18th-century harpsichord; and the Dining Room, which has the air of a Renaissance-era banqueting hall.

Docent-guided tours are offered all day long, and a special "Vizcaya by Moonlight" tour is offered one evening a month during the full moon from January to April. Surrounded by gardens and islands connected by footbridges, the mansion also has a coral rock grotto and swimming pool, dozens of outdoor sculptures, an orchid house, and a coral rock dock on Biscayne Bay complete with a vintage gondola.

The Vizcaya Museum and Gardens.

VIZCAYA

A bayfront villa set in formal gardens offers an evocative glimpse of bygone days and moonlit nights.

Inspired by the opulent country estates of the Veneto region of northern Italy, James Deering – a member of one of the wealthiest families in the US – set out to build a winter retreat in Miami. Constructed in 1916 on 180 acres (73 hectares) of spectacular bayfront, the house was designed to resemble an Italian Renaissance villa but also has Baroque, rococo, and neoclassical features. The estate's name is from the Basque word for "elevated place" and is also the name of a Basque province on the Bay of Biscay, which itself inspired the name of Miami's Biscayne Bay.

Deering, architect Burrall Hoffman Jr, and painter Paul Chafin inspired themselves by traveling to Italy to study architectural details. Along with imported doors, ceilings, and fireplaces, Florida limestone and native plants were employed to maintain a local ambience.

The house has 70 rooms and needed a staff of 30 during the four months the Deerings were in residence. Today, half of the rooms are open to public view. Every detail is exquisite, from the black-and-white marble tub to the gold-leaf cornices. Especially stunning is the swimming pool, extending from the sun-lit exterior to a grotto beneath the house, its ceiling adorned with shells and carved stone.

Sadly, Deering was able to enjoy the estate for less than a decade; he died in 1925. The family sold the estate to Dade County in 1952. In 1994 the Vizcaya estate was declared a National Historic Landmark.

The 17th-century statuary adorning the gardens includes mythological figures such as Neptune, Minerva, and Apollo.

The villa's south side faces the Italian Renaissance-style formal gardens, featuring elaborate stonework, pools, and greenery.

The Entrance Loggia's shaded vaults and marble surfaces invite visitors into the cool rooms within.

Vizcaya by Moonlight – spend an evening wandering among the sweetly scented gardens, guided by a knowledgable docent.

Vizcaya by Moonlight

"Miami by Moonlight" has long been a romantic angle for poets and songwriters to explore. Now visitors can enjoy "Vizcaya by Moonlight" tours, held once a month on the night of the full moon, and only in the more temperate season (January to April), weather permitting. The visit begins inside the palazzo itself, with a short talk on the gardens and statuary, including tips on the sights that are to be found throughout the moonlit grounds and what views to look out for along the way.

Programs begin at about 6.30pm and last around 90 minutes. The tour takes in Vizcaya's subtropical forest, proceeds toward the main house along a lit walkway lined with fountains and foliage, and includes live music, views of Biscayne Bay, and the gorgeous orchids in the David A. Klein Orchidarium on the north side of the main house. Vizcaya's café and gift shop remain open on these evenings.

Vizcaya is open every day (except Tuesday) from 9.30am to 4.30pm, and closes for Christmas and Thanksgiving. For information on tours, visit www.vizcaya.org or tel: 305-250-9133.

Deering named each guest room for the style in which it is decorated. The Cathay Bedroom is decorated with chinoiserie, popular in the 18th century.

Colombian landscape designer Diego Suarez spent seven years working on the grounds at Vizcaya.

The inlaid marble flooring in the Entrance Loggia catches the eye. The Loggia was originally open to the exterior.

Miami Beach from above.

MIAMI BEACH

Art Deco treasures; sizzling nightlife; a sun-kissed beach; and an endless parade of the rich, famous, and beautiful have transformed this once troubled strip into the American Riviera.

Miami Beach is a barrier island barely 15 miles (24km) long and a mile (1.7km) wide. Physically (and psychologically) distinct from its mainland big sister, it is a man-made paradise dedicated to the pursuit of pleasure.

Since it was incorporated as a city in 1917, countless people have come to its shores. They come to play, work, drink, dance, and run away from humdrum lives elsewhere. Although it has gone through several incarnations in its short lifetime – from elite playground of the rich in the 1940s and 1950s to the urban decay and rampant crime of the 1970s and then the hip New Riviera of the 1990s – Miami Beach continues to seduce visitors with its unique charms and glorious beach.

Today Miami Beach is a vibrant village filled with colorful characters who include American celebrities, vanguard artists, real-estate investors, wealthy South Americans, Caribbean immigrants, nouveau-riche Russians, fashion models, gays and lesbians, and world-weary New Yorkers. Spanish is the dominant cultural language of South Florida, making a basic phrasebook a helpful tool for chatting up locals, but those not conversationally fluent will find shopkeepers and locals more than willing to switch from their usual tongue to English.

Socializing on Ocean Drive.

SOBE AND ART DECO

At the southern tip of Miami Beach is the neighborhood of **South Beach**, or SoBe. When the Swinging Sixties came to an end, Miami Beach slipped into a period of decline that lasted for almost two decades. But then a few forward-thinking preservationists came to the rescue and spread the word that this thing called Art Deco was something worth saving. In 1979, the Miami Beach Art Deco National Historic District was founded, and things have been looking up ever since.

Main Attractions

South Beach
Jewish Museum of Florida
Ocean Drive
World Erotic Art Museum
Española Way
Lincoln Road
Fillmore Miami Beach
Holocaust Memorial
Bass Museum of Art
Bal Harbour

Map on page 118

Sunny Isles Beach
Golden Beach
HAULOVER
BEACH PARK
BAY HARBOR
ISLANDS
Broad Causeway
INDIAN
CREEK
VILLAGE
SURFSIDE
NORMANDY
SHORES
NORMANDY
J.F. Kennedy
Causeway
NORTH BAY
VILLAGE

Biscayne
Bay

NORTH
BEACH
RESORT
HISTORIC
DISTRICT

INDIAN
BEACH PARK
Russian &
Turkish Baths
Eden Roc Resort
Fontainebleau
Resort

Miami Beach
Visitors Center

FLAMINGO
PARK

LUMMUS
PARK

Art Deco
Welcome Center

SOUTH
BEACH

1 mile
0
0   1 km

Fontainebleau Resort,
Eden Roc

MUNICIPAL
GOLF COURSE

Lake
Pancoast

BAYSHORE
MUNICIPAL
GOLF COURSE

Miami City Ballet

COLLINS
PARK

The Bass **12**

Regional
Library

Holocaust
Memorial

BOTANICAL
GARDEN **11**

Convention
Center

Miami Beach
Visitors Center

Temple
Emanu El

The Raleigh

City
Hall

Fillmore **10**
Miami Beach

Delano Hotel

Lincoln
Theatre

Books & Books

Lincoln Road Mall **9** Lincoln Rd

Loew's Hotel

Regal
South
Beach
Cinema

Colony
Theater

ArtCenter
South Florida

Cameo
Theater

ART DECO
14th Pl.

Espanola **8** Way

Clay Hotel
& Hostel

Miami Beach
Post Office

FLAMINGO

NATIONAL

World Erotic **7**
Art Museum

Cavalier

Cardozo Hotel

Leslie
Carlyle
Tides Hotel

Memorial
Field

PARK

Old **6**
City Hall

HISTORIC

Wolfsonian **5**
FIU

Casa
Casuarina (former Versace Mansion)

Clevelander
Hotel

Art Deco
Welcome Center

Breakwater

Ocean Front Auditorium
Beach Patrol Headquarters

DISTRICT

The
Hotel

Pelican Café

Waldorf Towers Hotel

News Café

Colony Hotel

4 LUMMUS
PARK

Tap Tap

Miami Beach Drive (5th St)

3

2 Jewish Museum
of Florida-FIU

WASHINGTON

OCEAN/BEACH
PARK

PIER
PARK

Joe's Stone Crab
Restaurant

South Pointe
Tower

SOUTH POINTE
PARK

1

Miami Beach

BUOY

Star Island

E Star Island Dr

PARK

Miami Airport,
Jungle Island

Fisher Island
Ferry Terminal

US Coast
Guard Station

Miami
Beach
Marina

Terminal
Island

Causeway
Island

MacArthur Causeway

Main Channel

Port Blvd

Dodge
Island

Fisher Island

Fisher
Island Dr

University of Miami
Marine Laboratory

B i s c a y n e

B a y

A T L A N T I C

O C E A N

Government Cut

Pier

N

0   500 yds
0   500 m

Containing more than 800 Art Deco buildings constructed from 1923 to 1943, the Deco District is the first urban 20th-century historic district listed on the National Register of Historic Places. It has grown and prospered and served as the cornerstone of a new wave of preservation pride that has swept the entire island. Encompassing about 1 sq mile (2.5 sq km), it runs roughly from 5th to 23rd streets and Ocean Drive to Collins Avenue and Washington Avenue. The Art Deco Welcome Center at 10th Street and Ocean Drive is a good place to start exploring.

After driving across the MacArthur Causeway, the main thoroughfare to SoBe, the highway becomes 5th Street. Between Jefferson and Meridian on 5th is **Tap Tap** (819 5th St; tel: 305-672-2898; www.taptapmiamibeach.com), Miami Beach's best-known Haitian restaurant. Tap Tap also hosts live bands, author signings, and screenings of film documentaries with a socially conscious slant.

To the south of 5th Street is a neighborhood appropriately named **South of Fifth**, or SoFi, home to **South Pointe Park ❶**, a verdant 17-acre (7-hectare) playground with meandering walkways and great views of the Port of Miami. It is also one of the few vacant pieces of land on the island. A few blocks away is the **Jewish Museum of Florida – FIU ❷** (301 Washington Ave; tel: 305-672-5044; www.jewishmuseum.com; Tue–Sun 10am–5pm). Housed in two beautifully restored synagogues, the museum is full of artifacts that document the history of Jews throughout the state of Florida. The major permanent exhibit is MOSAIC: Jewish Life in Florida, with items dating back to 1763 and also featuring "Florida Jewish crackers" who ranched and farmed.

A few blocks away is the oldest restaurant on Miami Beach, **Joe's Stone Crab** (11 Washington Ave; tel: 305-673-0365; www.joesstonecrab.com), which has been serving the succulent crustaceans since 1913 and lists as a former

customer gangster Al Capone. Families visiting the beach may be diverted before exiting the Causeway, however, by the lush expanses of **Jungle Island** (1111 Parrot Jungle Trail; tel: 305-400-7000; www.jungleisland.com; daily 10am–5pm). Formerly known as the Parrot Jungle and first launched in the mid-1930s, this interactive zoological park lets visitors mingle with colorful monkeys and tropical birds. There is even a liger (a lion-tiger hybrid) named Hercules who calls the island home.

OCEAN DRIVE

Fifth Street ends at **Ocean Drive ❸**, the world-famous see-and-be-seen street where curvaceous Latin beauties and handsome bronzed hunks strut their stuff. Always busy, Ocean Drive is one of the prettiest streets in Miami Beach, filled with restored Art Deco hotels and dozens of outdoor bistros. **News Café**, on the corner of 8th Street, is as popular for its 24-hour people-watching potential as for its food and beverage.

Arguably the best way to get around is by Citibike, which has rental bicycle

A bar dancer at Mango's Tropical Café in South Beach.

Tap Tap restaurant is covered with colorful murals.

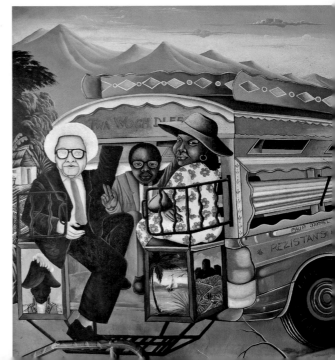

The World Erotic Art Museum.

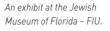

An exhibit at the Jewish Museum of Florida – FIU.

stations every few blocks. You'll pass fitness buffs walking, riding, and otherwise finessing their fit selves along the way.

Across the street is **Lummus Park ❹**, a hub of beach activity with a tree-lined promenade ideal for roller-bladers, a children's playground, and volleyball nets. Several unique lifeguard stands mark this part of the beach, each in a pseudo-Deco style; similar stands are now being installed further afield. In the next few blocks are some of the beach's great Art Deco darlings – the **Room Mate Waldorf Towers**, **Breakwater**, and **Clevelander** hotels, all preserved architectural gems. Locals refer to Lummus Park as "Muscle Beach," on account of the über-toned men and women who use its alfresco gym equipment. Fittingly, this is where Model Volleyball – yes, *that* kind of model – hosts its annual competition to the delight of ogling onlookers.

At 10th Street is the **Miami Beach Ocean Front Auditorium** (1001 Ocean Drive; www.mdpl.org), a public venue that hosts concerts and events. The complex includes a gift shop and the **Art Deco Welcome Center** (www.mdpl.org/welcome-center/; daily 10am–7pm), a nucleus of information on local architecture and history run by the Miami Design Preservation League, founded in 1976 to help preserve the region's built legacy.

At 1116 Ocean Drive is **The Villa Casa Casuarina** (http://nvmiamibeach.com), a strikingly beautiful Mediterranean Revival mansion surrounded by pine trees. Like Miami Beach itself, the property has undergone many metamorphoses. Designed to resemble Christopher Columbus's home in the Dominican Republic, it was originally built as an apartment house called Amsterdam Palace. In 1992 Gianni Versace bought the building and transformed it into a private Italian-style villa. Following Versace's death it was sold and re-opened as a boutique hotel.

A block away is **The Tides**, a hotel once owned by Island Records founder Chris Blackwell. Billed as the Diva of Ocean Drive, the Tides is a tower of luxury with a soothingly neutral palette that blends historic ambience with modern service – every guest is

⊘ WALKING TOURS

Covering the spectrum from flamingo pink to cool turquoise, with sculpted mermaids and neon lights thrown in for fun, tropical Art Deco architecture is a whimsical sight to behold. With its small scale and many nooks and crannies, the Art Deco District is best explored on foot.

The Miami Design Preservation League offers some of the best walking tours in Florida. Hosted by historians and architects, the 90-minute tours tell the story behind the style. Tours leave the **Art Deco Welcome Center** (1001 Ocean Drive) daily at 10.30am, with an additional 6.30pm tour on Thursday. Reservations are not required, but a hat and comfy shoes are suggested. Self-guided audio tours in five languages are also available daily from 9.30am to 5pm. For information, call 305-531-3484 or go to www.mdpl.org.

assigned a "personal assistant." In the next few blocks is a group of historic properties that were among the first to be restored in the late 1980s – the **Carlyle**, **Leslie**, and **Cavalier**.

WASHINGTON AVENUE

Two blocks to the west and running parallel to Ocean Drive is Washington Avenue, a less glamorous but more interesting street. While many great restaurants can be found here, there are also lots of tiny cafeterias, mom-and-pop grocery stores, tattoo parlors, and clothing boutiques selling garments that leave little to the imagination. Plenty of tourists can be found on Washington, but it is also where locals come for late-night snacks.

At 10th and Washington is the most impressive building on the street, the **Wolfsonian-Florida International University** ❺ (1001 Washington Ave; tel: 305-531-1001; www.wolfsonian.org; Mon–Tue, Thu, and Sat 10am–6pm, Fri until 9pm, Sun noon–6pm). Housed in a 1920s Mediterranean Revival structure that once served as a storage facility, the off-beat museum was founded by Mitchell "Micky" Wolfson Jr, heir to the Wometco movie theater chain, and contains a collection of decorative and propaganda arts from 1850 to 1950. Focusing on the social, political, and aesthetic significance of design, the eccentric collection includes bronze busts of Mussolini, posters, textiles, pulp periodicals, and furniture designed by Frank Lloyd Wright.

One block to the north is **Old City Hall** ❻, a beautiful Mediterranean Revival structure built to help the city revive from a devastating 1926 hurricane. It later became the first building in Miami Beach to be granted an historic designation and is now a community center for LGBT residents and visitors. Behind it is the **Miami Beach Police Station**, where officers gear up on bicycles for their daily patrols.

Nearby is the **World Erotic Art Museum** ❼ (1205 Washington Ave; tel: 305-532-9336; www.weam.com; Mon–Thu

11am–10pm, Fri–Sun 11am–midnight). Founded by Naomi Wilzig, a Jewish grandmother who amassed a 4,000-piece erotica collection, the museum holds a smoldering and informative display of sculptures, prints, and paintings.

Between 14th and 15th streets on Washington Avenue is the block-long **Española Way** ❽. A charming assortment of Spanish Mediterranean buildings, all painted bright pink and white, Espanola is one of the last bohemian sections of South Beach. Originally built to be an artist colony in the 1920s, it became a red-light district soon after and still retains a nonconformist spirit. It was here in the late 1930s that Desi Arnaz, Cuban singer and future husband of Lucille Ball, first performed in the US. With wrought-iron balconies and lots of outdoor tables, Española often hosts belly-dancing shows, Cuban jazz bands, and Haitian drummers.

LINCOLN ROAD

Once called the Fifth Avenue of the South, **Lincoln Road** ❾ (between 16th and 17th streets) is the prime artery for

A barista awaits the morning's customers at A La Folie Café on Española Way.

Jazzy art at an Ocean Drive gift shop.

⊙ Tip

The Miami Beach Trolley (www.miamibeachtrolley.com) provides free transportation from one end of the district to another. The trolleys travel in four loops: South Beach, Mid-Beach, Collins, and North Beach. They operate every 10 to 15 minutes from 6am to midnight, Sundays 8am to Midnight (except Alton-West, which always starts at 8am).

The Wolfsonian-Florida International University.

local street life in South Beach. Unlike the frenetic energy of Ocean Drive, Lincoln Road is more mellow and much easier to navigate. With roots that go back to the late 1920s, it is a storied place that was transformed into a pedestrian-only thoroughfare in the 1960s by modernist architect Morris Lapidus. Today it bustles with bars, restaurants, boutiques, galleries, coffee houses, jazz clubs, and theaters. Families with strollers, beautiful women walking their toy terriers, trendy artist types, and flamboyant drag queens all mingle here as one.

Much of Lincoln Road's revival goes back to 1984, when **ArtCenter South Florida** (924 Lincoln Rd; tel: 305-674-8278; www.artcentersf.org; Mon–Fri noon–6pm, Sat–Sun noon–8pm) first opened its doors. A nonprofit gallery with several working studios, it features three exhibition areas and regularly hosts cocktail parties and special arts events.

About two blocks away is the **Colony Theatre** (1040 Lincoln Rd; tel: 800-211-1414), an Art Deco jewel that was once a movie theater and is now a performing-arts venue. The New World Symphony is based in the **New World Center** on 17th Street, designed by renowned architect Frank Gehry and acoustician Yasuhisa Toyota.

At the western edge of Lincoln Road is the **Regal South Beach Cinema**, a modern multiscreen movie theater. Local residents regard the cinema as a much-needed addition but are less sanguine about nearby chain stores that lack the quirky character the beach prides itself on. One place that clings to the neighborhood's independent spirit is **Books & Books** (933 Lincoln Rd; tel: 305-532-3222; www.booksandbooks.com; daily 10am–11pm). Like its sister store in Coral Gables, Books & Books Miami Beach is more than a bookstore: it's a restaurant, café, and meeting place for local literati that often hosts readings by award-wining authors and special events supported by the arts community.

An ample stretch of Lincoln is transformed every Sunday into a popular farmers' market, where fresh organic fruit and home-made jellies can be purchased for an impromptu streetside picnic. In cooler months, the Antique & Collectible Market (www.lincolnroadmall.info/lincoln-road-antique-flea-market-sunday-schedule) pops up most weekends.

17TH STREET

To the north of Lincoln Road is **17th Street**, also known as Hank Meyer Boulevard – named for the publicist who convinced Jackie Gleason to move his show to Miami Beach in 1964. On the north side of the street is the **Fillmore Miami Beach ⑩** (1700 Washington Ave; tel: 305-673-7300, http://filmoremb.com), formerly the Jackie Gleason Theater of the Performing Arts. After the Arsht Center opened in downtown Miami, the old Gleason Theater underwent a renovation and now stages major rock, comedy, and pop performances. On the sidewalk along the south side of the theater is Miami Beach's version of the Walk of Fame, where handprints of famous inductees include Muhammad Ali, Ice Cube, and Ann-Margret.

On the west side of the theater is the **Miami Beach Convention Center** (www.miamibeachconvention.com), home to the December art extravaganza known as **Art Basel Miami Beach** (www.artbasel.com/miami-beach) as well as dozens of other trade shows and events. Nearby is the new **Miami Beach City Hall**, and a much welcomed patch of green, the **Miami Beach Botanical Garden** (2000 Convention Center Dr; tel: 305-673-7256; www.mbgarden.org; Tue–Sun 9am–5pm; free). Full of native plants and exotic orchids, this 2.6-acre (1-hectare) tropical garden offers classes and lectures and serves as the main environmental entity that encourages the densely built city of Miami Beach to "go green."

HOLOCAUST MEMORIAL

Until recent years, Miami Beach had one of the largest populations of Holocaust survivors in the US, so it made sense that the island would want to commission a testament to the tragedies of World War II. Designed by artist and sculptor Kenneth Treister, the **Holocaust Memorial** ⓫ (1933–1945 Meridian Ave; tel: 305-538-1663; http://holocaustmemorialmiamibeach.org; daily 9.30am–sunset; free) is a somber reminder of those who lost their lives in the Nazi death camps and to the survivors who went on to live heroic lives. The 42ft (13-meter) bronze sculpture is that of an outstretched hand reaching toward the heavens, with nearly 100 life-size artistic statues depicting families searching for help. The memorial also has a peaceful garden and plaza, a pictorial history of the Holocaust, and a granite wall inscribed with the names of thousands of victims. An app provides a walking tour in eight languages.

COLLINS PARK

In an effort to formally encourage a vibrant arts-and-culture scene in the Collins Park neighborhood, the Collins Park Arts District Overlay is an arts and culture hub between 20th and 23th streets, bordering the Dade Canal and Washington Avenue. At its heart are three components: headquarters of the Miami City Ballet; the Miami Beach Regional Library, a state-of-the-art facility and repository for books and artifacts on Miami Beach history; and **The Bass** ⓬ (2100 Collins Ave; tel: 305-673-7530; www.thebass.org; Wed–Mon 10am–5pm), a contemporary art gallery located in a 1930s Art Deco building designed by Russell Pancoast. Founded in 1964 through the donation of a private collection by John and Johanna Bass to the City of Miami Beach, it now has eight galleries featuring a mix of old masters and contemporary pieces.

MID-BEACH AND MIMO

North of the Bass Museum, the beach takes on a different tone and the buildings become taller, less Deco, and more futuristic in design. Stretching from 23rd to 63rd streets is an area known as **Mid-Beach**, which includes a few landmark

A bit mellower than Ocean Drive, Lincoln Road is nonetheless a colorful and lively place for shopping, dining, and strolling.

Biking past shops and restaurants on Española Way.

○ Tip

Gay and lesbian travelers can get information about accommodations, dining, events, and other services at The Hub of the LGBT Visitor Center (1130 Washington Ave; tel: 305-673-4440; Mon–Fri 9am–6pm, Sat–Sun 11am–4pm; www.gogay miami.com). The office, in the historic Old City Hall building, offers activities, programs, and services to the LGBT community.

properties. Built in 1954, the **Fontainebleau Resort** (4441 Collins Ave) was where the Kings of Cool – Frank Sinatra, Sammy Davis Jr, and Dean Martin – serenaded the crowds in the 1950s and 1960s. Ostentatious to the core, it was designed by the late Morris Lapidus, who today is considered the father of MiMo (Miami Modern) architecture.

Lapidus also designed its neighbor, the **Eden Roc** (4525 Collins Ave), the other grande dame of MiMo. Both are perfect examples of the over-the-top resort vernacular that came about during the unbridled American optimism of the 1950s. Both have also been renovated and expanded. For years MiMo buildings were considered tacky, an embarrassment to the aesthetically inclined, but after the millennium they were elevated to historic status and praised for their naive playfulness.

Common throughout Miami and Miami Beach, MiMo buildings are characterized by flamboyant angles and lines, accordion walls, cheese-hole masonry, massive columns, anodized aluminum, and terrazzo floors.

Shopping in Bal Harbour.

For visitors seeking an unusual afternoon, the **Russian & Turkish Baths** (5445 Collins Ave; tel: 305-867-8316; www.russianandturkishbaths.com) should get the blood going. Gender mingling is encouraged at this cavernous old-school steam and spa complex, located in the decidedly un-modern Castle Beach Club condo building. The "shvitz" room is a particular favorite, with buckets of cold water that provide relief from rocks that emit radiant, furnace-like heat.

NORTH BEACH

Once Collins Avenue passes north of 63rd Street, the neighborhood becomes **North Beach**, one of the more desirable residential areas. Formerly the realm of northern retirees, NoBe is now a hip and happening neighborhood full of young Brazilians, savvy Europeans, and other trendy newcomers. Full of MiMo architecture and a diverse group of good restaurants, it also has great beach access and an easy-going attitude.

To the west are the upscale resident islands of **Normandy Shores** and **Indian Creek**; to the north are the towns of **Surfside**, **Sunny Isles**, **Golden Beach**, and **Bal Harbour**, home of a famous upscale shopping center. **Bal Harbour Shops** (9700 Collins Ave; tel: 305-866-0311) houses luxury shops, from Bulgari and Gucci to Armani and Prada.

For a less expensive afternoon in the area, while away an hour at the **Old Spanish Monastery** (16711 West Dixie Hwy; tel: 305-945-1461; www.spanishmonastery.com), technically the "oldest building in the Western Hemisphere." This beautiful chapel was first built in the 12th century before being carefully deconstructed and shipped to Florida in the 1920s by William Randolph Hearst, the news baron who inspired the movie *Citizen Kane*. Time your visit right and take in an open-air concert at the **North Beach Bandshell** (www.northbeachband shell.com), a 1961 amphitheater with a big history, surrounded by domino and beach volleyball games.

KEY BISCAYNE

Just minutes from the hustle of Miami is an island getaway with golden beaches, secluded coves, plush resorts, and water sports.

A tiny barrier island just a few minutes from downtown Miami, Key Biscayne is an oasis of tranquility (famously, President Richard Nixon used it as a winter escape from his Washington woes in the 1970s). Although it has a sizable residential community, the island is also an exclusive tropical getaway that offers a serene alternative to Miami Beach with water sports, lovely beaches, a world-famous tennis center, and plush resorts.

After crossing the Rickenbacker Causeway Bridge over Biscayne Bay, the atmosphere quickly mellows. The first stop is **Virginia Key** where several outlets offer windsurfing and kiteboarding rentals on the calm bay waters. On the left side of the highway is a turn-off to **Virginia Key Beach Park**, a 2-mile (3km) stretch of sand that during segregation served as Miami's only "black beach." A dirt road nearby meanders down to **Jimbo's**, a quirky Old Florida eatery that has been serving smoked fish and cold beer since the 1950s.

AQUATIC THEME PARK

On the opposite side of the highway is the **Miami Seaquarium** (4400 Rickenbacker Causeway; tel: 305-361-5705; www.miamiseaquarium.com; daily 10am–6pm). Founded in 1955, the Seaquarium is a stellar marine research center as well as an aquatic theme park that features enormous tanks full of sharks, manatees, stingrays, alligators, and dolphins; exotic birds and wildlife; and spectacular water shows starring killer whales and sea lions. For an extra fee, the Seaquarium offers two-hour tours of the facilities that include a magical half-hour of swimming and playing with the resident dolphins.

Farther down the spine of the island is **Crandon Park Beach**, a public park complete with a soccer field and 18-hole public golf course. Considered one of Miami's most popular "party beaches," Crandon tends to be very busy on weekends. On the bay side nearby is the **Crandon Park Tennis Center** (tel:

305-446-2200), where top-ranked tennis pros compete each spring for prizes worth millions during the Sony Ericsson Open. Over 200,000 spectators turn out to watch such top-ranked players as Venus Williams and Roger Federer compete in the week-long event, and then partake in the after-hours parties.

Past the tennis center is the **Village of Key Biscayne**. With a population of about 10,000, the village is definitely for the well-heeled, and the tempo is slow and casual. Several bicycle rental shops make it easy for tourists to tour the island by bike.

At the far end of the island is **Bill Baggs Cape Florida State Park** (daily sunrise to sunset). Regularly rated as one of the best beaches in the US, Bill Baggs is a unique experience for a Miami-area beach – there are no lifeguards and no buildings within site of the sand. Dotted with endangered sea oats and towering Australian pine trees, the beach is broad and soft, and the water is deep close to shore. At the park's southern end is the **Cape Florida Lighthouse**. Built in 1825, it is one of the oldest structures in South Florida and the only lighthouse in the country to have been attacked by American Indians (Seminoles). Park rangers offer tours Thursday through Monday at 10am and 1pm. A few steps away is a restaurant with good seafood and frosty drinks. In the distance offshore are the few remaining stilt houses that comprised a once-vibrant community known as **Stiltsville**.

Crandon Park Beach.

📷 ART DECO: SOUTH BEACH STYLE

The exotic and colorful buildings on Ocean Drive are the product of Miami's unique interpretation of Art Deco style.

The splendid Art Deco buildings in Miami Beach were built to raise the spirits of Americans during the Great Depression. Many decades later, preservationists say that they are among the most architecturally significant structures in the US.

The roots of Art Deco go back to 1901, when the Société des Artistes Décorateurs was formed in Paris with the goal of merging the mass production of industrial technology with the decorative arts. It was proudly introduced to the world in 1925 at the Paris Exposition Internationale des Arts Décoratifs et Industriels Modernes. The nickname "Art Deco" gained currency only in 1966, when it was dreamed up for a retrospective of the 1925 Paris show. The Art Deco style was evocative of the new Machine Age, and was inspired by the aerodynamic designs of airplanes and cars; but it combined all kinds of influences, from the swirls of Art Nouveau to the hard lines of Cubism.

In the 1930s and '40s, hundreds of Deco structures were built in South Beach. Art Deco's stark, white exteriors were already well suited to Florida's hot climate, but architects in Miami soon developed their own style, later dubbed Tropical Deco. Many features, from window design to color choice, were inspired by South Florida's balmy weather and its seaside location. The more futuristic Art Deco style known as Streamline Moderne, which replaced some of the detail characteristic of traditional Art Deco with smoother lines and sweeping curves, was particularly popular in Miami.

Several elements of Art Deco, such as tube railings and porthole windows, were borrowed from the design of ocean liners.

The Colony Hotel graces Ocean Drive, in the heart of Miami's Art Deco district. More than 800 buildings in either Art Deco or Streamline Moderne style can be found in close proximity.

The Marlin Hotel on Collins Avenue is a classic Streamline Moderne building, and represents the design style that evolved from Art Deco. Notice the rounded corners and "eyebrows" – canopies which shade the windows against the sun. The long horizontal lines emphasize the aerodynamic design elements. The floral designs popular in Art Deco have been eliminated, leaving the lines of the building lean and sleek. Both Deco and Moderne roofs were typically flat, but often broken by a raised central parapet or pointed finial.

Barbara Capitman was instrumental in preserving Miami's Art Deco architecture.

The Fight To Save Miami Deco

The Art Deco hotels of South Beach provided a welcome refuge for visitors from all over the world, but by the 1960s the buildings had begun to decay. Several of the area's once-glamorous hotels became low-rent housing for the elderly, and much of the district became run-down.

In 1976, Barbara Capitman set up the Miami Design Preservation League to stop the demolition of the Art Deco buildings and to encourage their restoration. In 1979, 1 sq mile (2.5 sq km) of South Beach was listed in the National Registry of Historic Places. It was the first 20th-century district to receive such recognition.

In the 1980s, designer Leonard Horowitz endowed South Beach with a new color scheme, nicknamed Deco Dazzle, by painting many of the older buildings in bright and lively colors; originally most would have been painted white with color trim. Media interest in Miami's Art Deco enclave skyrocketed after South Beach became a favorite backdrop in the hit TV series *Miami Vice*. Fashion photographers such as Bruce Weber were drawn south to Florida for the gorgeous and colorful scenes.

The Art Deco architects in Miami tried out all kinds of new materials, including chrome, glass blocks, and terrazzo (a cheap, imitation marble). Stainless steel became a popular material, as did more exotic fabrics for furnishing coverings such as zebra and shark skin. Neon lighting was used for the first time in 1926, and is one of the most distinctive features of South Beach. While only a few colors were available when neon signage first became popular, nearly two dozen colors were available by the 1960s, and today there are more than 100 shades to choose from.

The Raleigh Hotel is considered an Art Deco masterpiece. The stones along the pool's edge emphasize its luxurious curls and curves, and complement the lush garden and ritzy bar nearby.

Kayakers near Everglades City.

THE EVERGLADES

A two-hour drive from Miami takes visitors to Florida's untamed heart – an ecological treasure rich in subtropical plants and animals.

It's an unseasonably warm, humid February morning in **Everglades City ❶**, the fishing village that serves as the gateway to the Ten Thousand Islands unit of **Everglades National Park** on the Gulf of Mexico. The sun is already glinting off the sapphire waters in front of the park's **Gulf Coast Visitor Center** (tel: 239-695-3311). At the dock, a narrated boat tour of scenic Chokoloskee Bay is just pulling out, while a seasonal park ranger gets ready to guide a paddling tour to Sandfly Island, a shell-mound island that was once home to Calusa Indians.

WATER WORLD

About a mile away, another kayaking trip is loading outside Ivey House, a popular eco-lodge. On the screened porch, a group of kayakers dressed in roll-down pants and shirts, closed-toe sneakers, and broad-brimmed hats lathers on sunscreen and insect repellent while listening to an orientation from the tour leader. They will drive by van north to the intersection of SR 29 and US 41, then another 6 miles (10km) east through Big Cypress National Preserve to the Turner River highway bridge. From this put-in, it's a leisurely southward paddle through the largest mangrove ecosystem in the US, a boggy place of tangled branch tunnels, estuary waters, and intimate wildlife viewing.

Day trips like these offer an enjoyable and safe introduction to the watery beauty of the **Ten Thousand Islands**, the Wild West frontier of the Everglades. The park's signature kayaking route, the 99-mile (160km) -long **Wilderness Waterway**, passes through the **Marjorie Stoneman Douglas Wilderness**, the largest wilderness east of the Mississippi, linking Ten Thousand Islands with Cape Sable and Florida Bay, the southernmost tip of the main park. You can do the challenging eight-day trip in either direction, beginning

Main Attractions
Everglades City
Flamingo
Ernest Coe Visitor Center
Shark Valley Visitor Center
Miccosukee Cultural Center
Ah-Tah-Thi-Ki Museum
Pa-Hay-Okee Overlook
Chokoloskee Island
Big Cypress National
    Preserve
Fakahatchee Strand
    Preserve State Park

Map on page 130

Shark Valley alligator.

Mosquitoes are abundant during the rainy season, from roughly June through October.

or ending at the old fishing village of **Flamingo** ❷ in Florida Bay.

The visitor center and marina at Florida Bay are relatively small; only basic facilities are available. Self-sufficient visitors may still enjoy outdoor activities like kayaking, boat tours, birding, ranger walks, and camping in the large, semi-developed beachfront campground (reservations strongly advised in high season; tel: 800-365-CAMP). Those unprepared for roughing it will want to base themselves elsewhere.

ORIENTATION

Hurricanes are a fact of life in South Florida. In the 1900s, killer hurricanes devastated Ten Thousand Islands, Lake Okeechobee, Homestead, and Flamingo. Overall, the loss of services at its major visitor hub has been a blessing in disguise for Everglades National Park. Many of the park's million annual visitors – most of whom arrive in Miami and devote a single day to the park before heading to the Florida Keys – explore farther afield and learn that the Everglades is much more than bogs,

birds, and bugs. It's actually a complex mosaic of nine ecosystems, comprising ponds, sloughs, sawgrass marshes, hardwood hammocks, and forested uplands essential to native wildlife, and covers all of South Florida from Biscayne Bay to the Gulf of Mexico.

The main part of the park is an hour south of Miami, off US 1. Hotels and restaurants are modest. One good choice for adventurous travelers is funky Everglades Hostel (www.evergladeshostel.com) in Florida City. It has dorms and private rooms, self-catering facilities, internet, and, like Ivey House (www.ivyhouse.com) in Everglades City, specializes in kayak tours of the park.

Park headquarters is next to **Ernest Coe Visitor Center** ❸ (tel: 305-242-7700; www.nps.gov/ever; daily 9am–5pm, from 8am in winter), just inside the park entrance. The visitor center is named for feisty landscape architect Ernest Coe who, starting in 1928, spearheaded the effort to get Everglades National Park authorized by Congress. It has exhibits, a film, a bookstore, and two campgrounds and trails at nearby Long

Everglades

0   20 miles
0   20 km

Pine Key. The two most popular trails in the park are 4 miles (6km) away at **Royal Palm Visitor Center** (exhibits, gift shop, ranger-led activities), the former state park that was the first piece of land acquired for the national park. The road to Flamingo is a 38-mile (61km) scenic drive that winds through the peaceful landscape.

The main entry to Everglades National Park along historic **Tamiami Trail** (US 41) is 30 miles (48km) west of Miami at **Shark Valley**. Biologically rich, Shark Valley is one of the three vital drainage areas for the Everglades and was added to the park in 1989. The unit's chief attractions are its proximity to US 41 and the accessible 15-mile (24km) loop road and side trails adjoining Shark River Slough. **Shark Valley Visitor Center ➍** (tel: 305-221-8776) is open daily and has ranger-led activities. You can walk or ride a bicycle or open-air tram on the paved loop year-round, although the wet season inundates many areas, making it hard to see the dispersed wildlife.

Close encounters with alligators and wading birds are guaranteed in the dry season, when animals concentrate in major sloughs. Alligators have an important role to play in the functioning of this ecosystem. Their thrashing creates wallows that fill with water used by other wildlife. A 50ft (15-meter) -high observation tower overlooks the River of Grass to give you great views.

MICCOSUKEE HERITAGE

Here you are in Florida's Indian Country. Airboat rides are available on the large reservation belonging to the Miccosukee Tribe (tel: 305-223-8380), whose private chickee-hut village compounds and tourist-oriented **Miccosukee Cultural Center** (www.micosukee.com/indian-village) ➎ adjoin Shark Valley on US 41. There are about 300-400 enrolled tribal members living on the reservation. Information is available at the tribal offices on the north side of US 41. The Miccosukee Tribe also runs a casino-hotel at the junction of US 41 and Krome Avenue (SR 997), the closest hotel to this part of the park, and has lands near the Big Cypress Seminole.

A park ranger offers advice to visitors at the Ernest F. Coe Visitor Center.

Visitors often see alligators up close in Shark Valley during the dry season.

☉ TRIBUTE IN ROCK

The Coral Castle Museum (28655 S. Dixie Hwy; tel: 305-248-6345; www.coral-castle.com; Sun–Thu 8am–6pm, Fri–Sat 8am–8pm) is not usually considered an Everglades tourist attraction, but this mind-boggling limestone palace in the nearby town of Homestead lures many visitors a half-hour south from downtown Miami.

The castle area, which features a sundial, rocking chairs, barbecue, and fountain all made of megalithic limestone (formed from coral) and held together solely by their own weight, is said to have been built by one man: a Latvian immigrant named Edward Leedskalnin, who spent 28 years designing and moving materials for a romantic tribute to Agnes Scuffs, the 16-year-old fiancée who broke his heart.

A photographer gets a close-up of the local birdlife.

Swamp safari, Big Cypress Seminole Indian Reservation.

The **Big Cypress Seminole Indian Reservation** (www.floridaseminoletourism.com) is a quiet, pastoral landscape reached from Exit 49 of I-75 (Alligator Alley) an hour from Fort Lauderdale. The Seminole are renowned for cattle ranching and maintain a big operation, along with a rodeo arena and rock mine. **Billie Swamp Safari** (www.billieswamp.com), within the reservation, offers airboat rides, swamp buggy tours, and wildlife shows (animal exhibits are free) plus the Swamp Water Café, all on a 2,200-acre (890-hectare) animal preserve.

By far the best interpretation of Seminole culture in Florida is available at the tribe's excellent **Ah-Tah-Thi-Ki Museum** ❻ (tel: 877-902-1113; www.ahtahthiki.com; daily 9am–5pm), an affiliate of the Smithsonian Institution. The museum has a film about Seminole history and interesting dioramas showing their distinctive chickee-hut architecture, distinctive colorful patchwork clothes, canoes, traditional foods, and seasonal ceremonies like the Green Corn Ceremony. Out back is a boardwalk trail with interpretive plaques about plants used for food and medicine. It ends at a replica Seminole Village.

RIVER OF GRASS

Exhibits at its three visitor centers tell the story of Everglades National Park. It's a long, complex, cautionary tale of what happens when a unique ecosystem is misunderstood, misappropriated, and misused by humans intent on their own agenda. The designation of the park was just the beginning; the ending is still to be decided (probably in court, if past battles are any indication).

Authorized in 1934 but only dedicated in 1947 after funds to purchase the land were approved, Everglades National Park is now recognized worldwide for its unique habitat. It protects the only subtropical preserve in North America and is a major edge place, where northern and southern flora and fauna species mingle. A large, flat prairie whose highest point is 8ft (2.5 meters) above sea level, at Chokoloskee Island, the park is, contrary to rumor, not a large, impenetrable

swamp. It is, as author, conservationist, and park champion Marjorie Stoneman Douglas famously observed, a "River of Grass" – at 50 miles (80km) wide, the largest continuous stand of seasonally inundated sawgrass prairie in North America.

Jeopardized by the rampant development surrounding it, today the Everglades is on life support. Its subtle beauty inspires visitors who take the time to get to know it, but the Everglades is most important as a sanctuary for wildlife. Living here are more than 400 species of birds, 125 species of fish, 60 species of reptiles and amphibians, 25 species of mammals, more than 120 species of trees, 1,000 species of seed-bearing plants, and 24 species of orchids, including the rare ghost orchid. The Everglades is the only place in the US where you'll find both crocodiles and alligators living side by side. Crocodiles (distinguished from alligators by a spade-shaped snout and two visible sets of teeth rather than one) are one of 14 endangered species protected here. Others are Florida panthers, West Indian manatees, Cable Sable sea sparrows, and wood storks.

TROUBLED WATERS

The headwaters of the Everglades are 80 miles (129km) to the north in the Kissimmee River Basin, now protected in the Nature Conservancy's Disney Wilderness. Disastrously channelized for ranching and agriculture, the Kissimmee River was once a wide, shallow river whose waters used to wend slowly south to Lake Okeechobee.

Surrounded by the massive 1930 Hoover Dike, which controls flooding and provides irrigation for agriculture, Lake Okeechobee, Florida's largest lake, is a dying ecosystem. The lake's historic role in the Everglades system was pivotal. Up to 60 inches (150cm) of summer rainfall caused it to seasonally overspill its margins, allowing floodwaters to slowly move south across the sawgrass prairie. This water nourished the wetlands and percolated through limestone into the Biscayne Aquifer, the main source of drinking water for South

> **⊙ Tip**
>
> For an entertaining and informative account of the politics of Everglades protection, read *The Swamp* by journalist Michael Grunwald.

Tourists snap photos on the Anhinga Trail.

A survivor of several hurricanes, historic Everglades City Hall remains a handsome local landmark.

The Gumbo Limbo Trail leads through a hammock of strangler figs, gumbo limbo trees, and royal palms.

Florida. It then exited the mainland via the huge mangrove swamps at the salty edge of the estuaries into Biscayne and Florida Bays and the Ten Thousand Islands region of the Gulf.

Fully 50 percent of the Everglades has been lost since the 1930s, along with 93 percent of its 2 million birds. Encroaching urban settlements, pollution by nitrate fertilizers from subsidized sugar-cane agriculture around Lake Okeechobee, subsequent invasion by exotic species, and habitat loss have been an ecological disaster.

In 2000, one of the world's largest environmental efforts, the Comprehensive Everglades Restoration Plan (https://evergladesrestoration.gov), was authorized by Congress. It is designed to return water to more natural patterns of quantity, timing, and distribution throughout the South Florida ecosystem, ultimately improving the state's ecosystem for 2.4 million acres (971,000 hectares). The South Florida Water Management District, together with the US Army Corps of Engineers, is working to mimic nature

with seasonal water releases south of Lake Okeechobee's agricultural areas. The effort will be given a huge boost thanks to the state's purchase of land back from the US Sugar Corporation.

THE MAIN PARK

The collision of urban environment and natural ecosystem is easy to appreciate when you visit the main park. Agricultural fields and tropical plant nurseries surround homely Homestead and Florida City, continuing all the way to the park entrance where, magically, human development disappears and the huge vistas of sawgrass prairie and tree hammocks take center stage all the way to Flamingo.

For many visitors, the highlights of a visit to the main park are the two easy trails at historic Royal Palm, east of the scenic drive. Nothing seems to perturb the lively shenanigans of alligators and anhingas and the silent predations of blue herons, snowy egrets, and other wildlife going about their lives in the Taylor Slough. The short **Anhinga Trail** lets you get astonishingly close

⊙ WATSON MURDERS

The most notorious outlaw of Ten Thousand Islands was Ed Watson, who moved to Chokoloskee in the early 1880s. Watson was suspected of murder in Florida and in the Oklahoma Territory. His luck ran out in Chokoloskee. First, he got into a fight with town patriarch Adolphus Santini and tried to slit his throat. Then two squatters turned up dead on his land. Three more corpses were found on his property, ostensibly murdered by a man named Cox. Watson threatened to kill the man, but the locals had had enough. A mob grabbed Watson and killed him. After this, the murders stopped, leading to the inevitable conclusion that Watson had been behind them all. The critically acclaimed book *Killing Mister Watson*, by Peter Matthiessen, fictionalizes the tale.

to wildlife. The **Gumbo Limbo Trail**, named for the tree with the red peeling bark known as "the tourist tree," loops through a hardwood hammock forest reshaped by Hurricane Andrew in 1992.

Heading south, the **Pineland Trail** leads through some of the most diverse pinelands in south Florida, ending at the campground at **Long Pine Key ❼**. The **Pa-hay-okee Overlook ❽** is a boardwalk trail that offers the best place in this part of the park to experience the more than 20 different grasses that compose the sawgrass prairie at the heart of the Everglades.

If you continue to Flamingo, you'll be rewarded by views of white and brown pelicans and other birds massing offshore on white sandbars in the turquoise waters of Florida Bay. Meander along the beach trail to get a closer look, or stand on the concrete breezeway at the **Flamingo Visitor Center** (tel: 239-695-2945; Nov–Apr daily 8am–4.30pm; call for opening hours at other times), binoculars in hand, and enjoy the tranquil beauty. Part of the Florida Keys is in the park, along with the Intracoastal Waterway. For more information, contact the Key Largo Ranger Station (tel: 305-852-0304).

TEN THOUSAND ISLANDS

Like Flamingo, Everglades City and **Chokoloskee Island ❾** are former fishing villages. Chokoloskee Island was settled by Europeans in the 1870s, although it had long been home to Calusa Indians. Smallwood Store (www.smallwoodstore.com), a stilted building with its own quay, is now a dusty family-run museum, open daily for a small fee. It belonged to Charles Smallwood, who ran a trading post in the Ten Thousand Islands region. Supplies were shipped from Key West, Fort Myers, or Tampa by boat; local sugar-cane syrup, fish, and produce were shipped in return.

In Everglades City, the Stone Crab Capital of Florida, early 20th-century homesteader George Storter was a merchant, as well as postmaster and a hotel owner. Hurricanes devastated Everglades City and Chokoloskee in 1909 and 1910, leveling all but the

An airboat operator guides visitors on a tour of the Everglades.

Sunset over Chokoloskee Bay.

⊙ Tip

If time permits, stop at Clyde Butcher's Big Cypress Gallery (52388 Tamiami Trail, Ochopee; tel: 239-695-2428). Butcher's gorgeous, large-format, black-and-white images of Big Cypress and the rest of the Everglades will haunt your dreams. Look for them on the walls of many hotels and other businesses throughout southwest Florida.

Several companies offer eco-tours, with an emphasis on low-impact modes of travel like canoes and kayaks that are excellent for spotting wildlife.

highest ground of the old Calusa shell mound, salting farm fields, and forcing many homesteaders to leave.

Tragedy gave entrepreneur Barron Collier an opening to buy southwest Florida on the cheap. Collier initially used Everglades City as his base for building the 1928 Tamiami Trail, later moving the county seat to Naples. The lodge that adjoins the bed-and-breakfast inn at Ivey House is Everglades City's oldest structure: a former boarding house for trail workers. Collier bought Storter's waterfront hotel to use as a hunting and fishing retreat. These activities, popular with residents and visitors, are still a draw at the hotel-restaurant-marina Rod and Gun Club (http://everglades-rodandgunclub.com).

BIG CYPRESS

Early in the history of Everglades National Park, it was clear that Big Cypress Basin, which receives much of the water flowing southwestward from Lake Okeechobee, warranted protection as a key element of the hydrologic system. The calls for action became urgent in the 1960s, when burgeoning land development and speculation schemes led to extensive logging and the partial draining of Big Cypress Swamp. In 1968 a proposed jetport on the swamp's eastern edge created a land rush and provoked massive opposition to development.

In 1974, a compromise between pro-development and pro-conservation groups was reached, when Congress authorized 720,000-acre (290,000-hectare) **Big Cypress National Preserve** ⑩. It was one of the first preserves to be managed by the National Park Service for multiple uses that include hunting, fishing, and off-road vehicles and airboats in addition to wildlife protection and low-impact activities like birding, hiking, and camping.

Oasis Visitor Center ⑪ (33100 Tamiami Trail East, Ochopee; tel: 239-695-1201; www.nps.gov/bicy; daily 9am–4.30pm) is exactly halfway between Naples and Miami, 5 miles (8km) east of SR 29, and has exhibits to help you plan a visit. All attractions are accessed

off the Tamiami Trail. There are four scenic drives (The Loop, Turner River Road, Wagonwheel Road, and Birdon Road) and developed **Monument Lake** and **Midway campgrounds** along US 41.

The 27-mile (43km) **Loop Drive**, beginning opposite the visitor center, is your best introduction to the beauty of Big Cypress. A gravel road travels among the glades (a term first used to describe the Everglades by an English surveyor in the 1700s). There are numerous openings in the forest that offer a peek at dwarf cypress trees (there are no "big cypress" – the name refers to the size of the forests) reflected in mirror-smooth brackish waters. Look for alligators, snowy egrets, and other bird rookeries. There are four small campgrounds, available on a first-come, first-served basis, with no water or usage fee.

A 6.5-mile (10km) one-way portion of the **Florida National Scenic Trail** begins near the entrance to the Loop. Passing through **Roberts Lake Strand**, it's a wonderful way to find solitude among the haunting cypress.

Remember: Outdoor activities are really only tolerable in the winter dry season, when temperatures average 75°F (25°C), humidity is generally low, and bugs are less pesky.

WEST TAMIAMI TRAIL

All along the Tamiami Trail are places to pull off and watch egrets, herons, ibis, anhingas, cormorants, and other birds fishing in the Tamiami Canal. West of Big Cypress are several enjoyable trails and campgrounds. **Kirby Storter Roadside Park** has a pleasant boardwalk trail among the dwarf cypress. **H.P. Williams Roadside Park**, on the north side of the road, adjoins the Turner River highway bridge and has picnic tables. The tiny roadside hamlet of **Ochopee** is famous for having the smallest post office in the country. Ochopee is one of the few places on US 41 with a restaurant, actually a roadside shack serving seafood on paper plates.

Just past the turn-off for SR 29 is **Big Cypress Bend**, a delightful boardwalk trail that offers a glimpse of Fakahatchee Strand Preserve **Fakahatchee**

Birdwatching on the Big Cypress Bend boardwalk.

The Ochopee Post Office is reputed to be the smallest in the US.

⊘ SAVING THE GLADES

About 30 percent of the Everglades has been lost due to human interference. Roads, canals, and dikes impede the water's normal flow, and much land has been drained for farming. The use by industrial agriculture of chemical fertilizers has taken a heavy toll as well. The campaign to save the Everglades took a step forward in 2010 when Governor Charlie Crist finalized the purchase of more than 70,000 acres (28,000 hectares) of land from the US Sugar Corporation before leaving office. The deal was originally expected to be at least double that size before political and bureaucratic pressures cut it down, but Crist's plan for the state to begin active conservation work still holds the promise of restoring the natural flow of water from Lake Okeechobee south across the Everglades.

Strand Preserve State Park (tel: 239-695-4593), dubbed the Amazon of North America. If you only have time to hike one trail on US 41, this is a great choice. Fakahatchee Strand is a productive bird rookery. It's also the only spot where you'll see stately royal palms growing alongside dwarf cypress in strands.

Fakahatchee Strand is most famous as the orchid and bromeliad capital of the US, with 44 native orchid species and 14 native bromeliad species, many epiphytes, or air plants, that grow on tree branches. Fakahatchee's orchids gained notoriety in the 1998 bestseller *The Orchid Thief*, author Susan Orlean's evocative account of the $10-billion illegal orchid trade. The exposé focused on orchid collector John Laroche, a horticulture consultant arrested for stealing rare ghost orchids in Fakahatchee Strand and propagating them for profit. The book was the source material for the 2002 movie *Adaptation*.

WILDLIFE AND WILDERNESS

If you have time, consider driving the **Jaynes Scenic Drive** north into the park, which takes you through open prairie that is home to Florida panthers and raptors like red-tailed hawks and vultures. Endangered panthers, which require several hundred square miles of habitat each, are almost never seen, although you may see their preferred prey, white-tailed deer. Naples Zoo, which has an excellent panther exhibit, works closely with Panther National Wildlife Refuge and Everglades National Park staff to radio-collar and track panther activity in the Everglades.

From Fakahatchee it's only 25 miles (40km) to Naples, a wonderful base for day trips. As you drive north you'll see the sparkling Gulf of Mexico. Ten Thousand Islands National Wildlife Refuge protects wildlife and is also a good place for kayaking. Another state park, Collier-Seminole State Park, sits at the turn-off for Marco Island across from Rookery Bay Estuarine Preserve. It has excellent camping, hiking, and picnicking. One of the walking dredgers used to drain the Tamiami Trail route is on display.

Elevated boardwalks allow hikers to view the watery sections of the park.

The Pineland Trail.

📷 EVERGLADES ECOLOGY

The "River of Grass" sustains a combination of tropical and temperate species found nowhere else in the United States.

The Everglades ecosystem is entirely dependent on the subtropical cycle of dry winters and wet summers. The fauna and flora of the region have adapted to these alternating seasons, often moving from one part of the Everglades to another according to the fluctuations in water level – the lifeblood of this vast and mysterious wilderness.

The larger Everglades ecology consists of a variety of smaller systems, each vital to the health of the overall ecosystem. The various habitats that make up the Everglades ecosystem include:

Hardwood hammocks: tree islands that stand above the high-water level and support mahogany, cabbage palms, and other trees, and also provide a refuge for mammals such as raccoons in the wet season.

Bayheads: small, shallow islands dominated by bay trees growing on rich, organic soil.

Willows: wispy vegetation that grows in the deep water near hammocks – generally in the shape of a donut with a gator hole at the center.

Sawgrass prairie: covering much of the Everglades, sawgrass grows on a thin layer of soil formed by decaying vegetation on the region's limestone base.

Freshwater sloughs: channels of freshwater that help plants and animals survive the harsh conditions of the dry season.

Cypress swamps: areas where the water is deepest and the layer of soil extremely thin. Cypress trees are among the few species that tolerate such water-logged conditions.

Coastal prairie: areas that contain salt-tolerant plants like cactus or saltwort.

The Florida panther is a subspecies of the cougar that has adapted to a subtropical climate. This shy cat lives in the most remote areas of the Everglades, particularly in Big Cypress Swamp. The panther is endangered: only 30 to 50 survive in the wild.

Alligators are vital to the ecology of the Everglades. During the wet season, they use their feet and snout to dig holes that store water during the dry months and serve as an oasis for many animals, including turtles and birds

Epiphytes, also known as air plants, are nonparasitic plants that grow on trees but get water and nutrients that run down the bark and gather in crooks and hollows. Among the most distinct epiphytes found in the Everglades are Spanish moss and orchids.

An aerial view of the Everglades.

Everglade Natives

A long list of animals calls the Everglades home, among them several important types of American wildlife:

Birds of prey: colorful and talkative red-shouldered hawks favor the sawgrass, while ospreys like to dive for their dinner in the mangroves and a small group of bald eagles, the iconic American bird, nest at their leisure.

Reptiles: more than 50 of these cold-blooded water-lovers dwell in the park, with the alligator and crocodile getting much of the spotlight; but lizards and snakes, from the endangered Eastern indigo to the invasive boa constrictor, also lurk in the dark.

Carnivorous mammals: harder to spot at times, these include the tree-climbing gray fox, the majestic bobcat, the playful river otter, and the Everglades mink, a semi-aquatic predator that is a skilled and athletic hunter.

Water-loving mammals: the pilot whale and the well-known bottlenose dolphin are the leaders of this pack, according to the US National Park Service.

Amphibians: jumping in and out of the water, this tiny, often camouflaged group includes the Florida chorus frog and the spadefoot toad.

The Seaside Seabird Sanctuary in Indian Shores is a wild bird hospital. Many birds are brought here to recover from illness or accident, and then returned to the wild.

One of the Everglades' most majestic birds is the great blue heron. It stands motionless in the water to catch its prey, spearing fish, amphibians and aquatic insects with lightning speed.

A great expanse of sawgrass, punctuated by tree islands known as "hammocks," is the classic Everglades landscape. Because hammocks are slightly elevated, the ground rarely floods and remains dry, while the air remains moist because it is protected from the sun by the tall, leafy trees that grow in the dry earth.

FLORIDA KEYS

A string of islands off the state's southern tip beckons travelers with beautiful beaches, crystal-clear waters, and some of Florida's best snorkeling and scuba diving.

The Florida Keys are a ragged skein of some 800 islands formed of ancient coral reefs transformed into limestone bedrock. Only about 80 of them have names. The 20-plus islands that lie in a direct line were strung together first by an improbable railroad in 1910. Following the railroad's destruction during the Labor Day Hurricane of 1935, the islands were connected by the southernmost portion of US 1, dubbed the **Overseas Highway**, a 125-mile (200km), 42-bridge exercise in forced linear travel. It is nearly 7 miles (11km) long, connecting the islands over the Atlantic Ocean, Florida Bay, and Gulf of Mexico in unalterable sequence. In 2009, Overseas Highway was designated an All-American Road by the National Scenic Byways program. The entire coastline – 2,800 sq nautical miles (9,603 sq km) – is a designated National Marine Sanctuary.

The road through the Keys may appear to be a tacky strip lined with seedy storefronts, billboards, and gas stations. In many places, that's exactly what it is – but stifle your disappointment. Like the Everglades, the Keys do not dazzle the casual tourist who stays behind the windshield. Park the car. Get on a bicycle or boat. Suck in the sweet, clean air. Gape at the immense canopy of sky and the mounds of whipped clouds. Can you see the curve of the earth in the distance, where the sea turns from aqua

John Pennekamp Coral Reef State Park.

to azure? Put on a mask, snorkel, and fins, or rent a rod and reel.

BISCAYNE NATIONAL PARK

Although not officially on the Keys, **Biscayne National Park ❶** (tel: 305-230-7275; www.nps.gov/bisc), a few miles east of **Homestead**, encompasses the northernmost portion of the region. Most of the park's 173,000 acres (70,000 hectares) are inaccessible by car. It's a watery world of coral reefs, mangrove shoreline, and tropical lagoons, inhabited by an astoundingly varied array of

Map on page 144

Main Attractions
Biscayne National Park
Key Largo
John Pennekamp Coral
  Reef State Park
Windley Key
Islamorada
Pigeon Key
Bahia Honda State Park
Big Pine Key

⊙ Tip

Addresses on the Keys are given as mile markers (MM). The markers begin just south of Florida City at MM 126 and end in Key West at MM 0. The Keys are divided into four sections: upper, MM 106–65; middle, MM 65–40; lower, MM 40–9; and Key West, MM 9–0. The designations B/S and O/S refer to bayside or oceanside locations.

creatures ranging from manatees and parrotfish to pelicans. At the **Dante Fascell Visitor Center** on Convoy Point, visitors can opt for Boca Chita Key boat tours, and sailing excursions with paddle boarding, snorkeling, and island visits. The center also offers films, interactive exhibits, and an art gallery aimed at introducing visitors to the sights and sounds of the world underwater.

ON TO THE KEYS

There are two ways to drive to the Keys from the mainland. The slower but more scenic route is US 1 south to Route 997 just beyond Florida City. A column of tall Australian pines graces the path to the Card Sound toll bridge. On either side of the bridge, clumps of red and black mangroves impersonate solid islands. The bridge ends on North Key Largo. A right on SR 905 leads through hammocks of Jamaica dogwood, loblolly, feathery lysiloma, and mahogany until the road runs directly back into US 1, the Overseas Highway.

The toll bridge and scenic detour can be avoided by continuing south on US 1 over Jewfish Creek. When US 1 eventually runs out, you've entered Key West.

KEY LARGO

Humphrey Bogart, Lauren Bacall, and Edward G. Robinson confronted a killer hurricane on **Key Largo** ➋ in the movie of the same name. All that remains of those nostalgic Bogie days is the Caribbean Club Bar (MM 104; http://caribbeanclubkl.com), where a few scenes are rumored to have been filmed, and the original *African Queen* (http://africanqueenflkeys.com), which has been fully restored and is now available for canal and dinner cruises.

The conch is queen of the Keys. Inside its shell – a familiar coffee-table ornament – the stalk-eyed blob is not among Earth's handsomest creatures. But if you can put the conch's looks out of your mind, conch fritters, chowder, or salad make a tasty meal with a spicy kick (although today most of the conch eaten in the US comes from the Bahamas). For a close-up look at queen or horseshoe conchs in their natural habitat, visit **John Pennekamp Coral Reef State Park** ➌ (MM 102.5; tel:

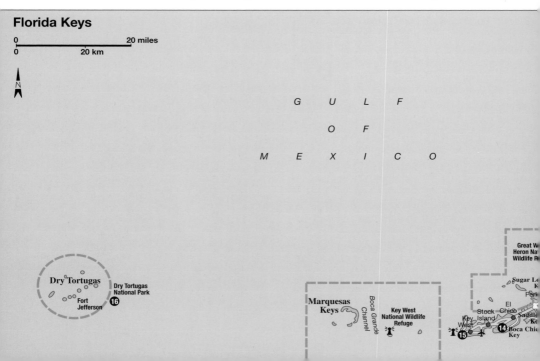

Florida Keys

0 — 20 miles
0 — 20 km

N

G   U   L   F

O   F

M   E   X   I   C   O

Dry Tortugas
Fort Jefferson
Dry Tortugas National Park ⑯

Marquesas Keys
Boca Grande Channel
Key West National Wildlife Refuge

Great W...
Heron Na...
Wildlife R...

Sugar L... K...
Per...

El Chico
Stock Island
Key West ⑮
Saddle...
**Boca Chic...
Key** ⑭

305-451-1202; www.pennekamppark.com; daily), the country's first undersea park. Together with the adjacent Florida Keys National Marine Sanctuary, the attraction covers about 178 sq miles (330 sq km) of coral reefs, seagrass beds, and mangrove swamps. The park extends 3 miles (5km) into the ocean and is about 25 miles (40km) long. The park offers glass-bottom boat rides, snorkeling tours, and kayak and paddleboard rentals. It also conducts scuba tours, ranging from a brief lesson followed by a non-certified dive that afternoon to four-day classes earning PADI open water certification. One of the highlights of a dive trip is a visit to **Key Largo Dry Rocks**, where the *Christ of the Deep*, a replica of Guido Galletti's statue *Christ of the Abyss* (in the Mediterranean Sea off Genoa, Italy) lies submerged in a natural valley surrounded by a coral reef in 21ft (7 meters) of water.

SWIM WITH DOLPHINS

The twin **Dolphins Plus** research and education centers (MM 102; tel: 866-860-7946; www.dolphinsplus.com; advance reservations) offer bottlenose dolphin swims and encounters. The friendly mammals can join visitors for a natural snorkel session, where any touching not instigated by the dolphin is prohibited, or a structured experience that includes a brief crash course in the species' anatomy and behavior. Dedicated dolphin-heads with $630 to spend can immerse themselves in the Marine Biologist for a Day program, where research is part of the experience.

At their adjoining facility disabled people participate in a five-day dolphin therapy program and visiting scientists apply to conduct their own on-site research, also provides the opportunity to swim and interact with dolphins in structured or unstructured swims. A special dolphin swim day is available for those fighting cancer, and the center's California sea lion even has an encounter day of his own that lets children high-five their new whiskered friend.

US 1 continues through Rock Harbor to **Tavernier ❹**, once the site of a huge wrecking fleet that cruised the reefs claiming salvage from grounded ships.

Feeding an ailing dolphin at the Dolphin Plus research and education center.

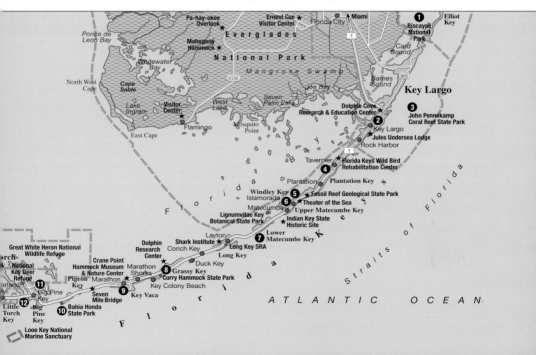

⊘ Tip

Some people refer to the Keys as a 126-mile (203km) traffic jam, which is at its worst on weekends. Try to plan your arrival and departure on a weekday.

Personal watercraft are available to rent throughout the Keys.

Today the nonprofit Florida Keys Wild Bird Rehabilitation Center (MM 93.6; tel: 305-852-4486; www.keepthemflying.org; daily) rescues and rehabilitates wild birds that have been injured by fish hooks, cars, and other human-related causes. The complex has two components: The Laura Quinn Wild Bird Sanctuary (93600 Overseas Hwy; daily sunrise to sunset), a refuge at which visitors can visit the permanent residents, and MissionWild Birds (92080 Overseas Hwy; Mon–Fri 9am–5pm), an educational hospital sharing information about migratory and wild native birds.

SOUTH TO THE PURPLE ISLES

Watch on the bay side for the **Rain Barrel Sculpture Gallery** (MM 86.7; tel: 305-852-8935; daily 9am–5pm), a unique artisans' village where sculptors of bronze and clay creations sell their wares. On **Windley Key** ❺ at the 125,000-year-old **Windley Key Fossil Reef Geological State Park** (MM 85; tel: 305-664-2540; www.floridastateparks.org/park/windley-key; visitor center: Thu–Mon 8am–5pm; seasonal tours Dec–Apr

Fri–Sun 10am and 2pm) visitors are offered a rare opportunity to view fossilized specimens of coral animals.

The 65-year-old landmark **Theater of the Sea** (MM 84.5; tel: 305-664-2431; www.theaterofthesea.com; reservation desk: daily 9.30am–3.30pm) is host to sea lion, dolphin, turtle, shark, and ray encounters, snorkel cruises, and a sunset eco-cruise. Reserve well in advance for dolphin encounters like swimming or painting with a dolphin. Younger children and those less comfortable in deep water can wade with the animals, or meet on land with one, for a lower price.

The realization that vast seas completely surround these small tufts of land sinks in as you cross the bridge over Whale Harbor to **Upper Matecumbe Key**. Polished fishing vessels lining the harbor trumpet the area's focus on sport fishing. The action revolves around **Islamorada** ❻ (pronounced *EYE-la-mo-RA-da*), which bills itself as the world's sport fishing capital. At the southern end of town, the **Hurricane Monument** (MM 81.6)

⊘ WRECKING CREW

It's difficult to imagine that overgrown Indian Key was once a bustling settlement. It was the home port of Jacob Housman, one of the Keys' most notorious "wreckers," who bought the property in 1831. In an age before lighthouses, he was one of a hearty breed of seagoing salvagers who sailed out to distressed ships that had foundered on coral reefs to rescue passengers, and then strip the vessels of anything valuable. Shipwreck salvaging was considered legal at that time. It also paid off. The disreputable Houseman's activities reaped him great success; he owned homes, warehouses, wharves, and more. Following an 1836 attempt to disengage Indian Key from Key West, he started losing his riches.

commemorates the 600 people who died in the Labor Day hurricane of 1935.

TARPONS, SPIDERS, DOLPHINS

Robbie's of Islamorada (MM 77.5; tel: 877-664-8498; www.robbies.com) on **Lower Matecumbe Key ❼** is the embarkation point for a visit to **Lignumvitae Key Botanical State Park**, accessible only by privately owned or charter boats (for reservations, tel: 305-664-2540; www.floridastateparks.org/park/lignumvitae-key; Thu–Mon 8am–5pm, guided tours Dec–Apr Fri–Sun 10am and 2pm). The tour includes a visit to the 1919 Matheson House and a stroll through a tropical forest. Rent a boat, kayak, paddleboard or Jet Ski at Robbie's and head out to **Indian Key**, an early wreckers' settlement.

From the Matecumbes, US 1 winds its way across increasingly breathtaking waterscapes to **Long Key State Park** (www.floridastateparks.org/park/long-key), with 60 oceanfront campsites, observation tower, boardwalk, and the Golden Orb Trail – named after the large

but harmless spiders that spin sturdy, ornate webs in the trees.

On **Grassy Key ❽**, Flipper is the most famous graduate of the **Dolphin Research Center** (MM 59; tel: 305-289-1121; www.dolphins.org; daily 9am–4.30pm), one of the oldest and most respected wildlife nonprofit organization in the region and a source of public education about the endangered local manatee population. This teaching and research facility offers narrated behavior sessions and swims with dolphins. Reservations can be made in advance online.

The center has no shortage of more frequently available shorter programming for those fascinated by its mission. Everything from T-shirts hand-painted by dolphins to Play with a Dolphin sessions is on hand, with prices varying depending on the experience. Guests with dreams of a future career can enroll in the Ultimate Trainer for a Day or a Researcher Experience program.

MARATHON

On the outskirts of **Marathon ❾**, the 1,000-acre (400-hectare) **Curry**

Sunbathing in Marathon.

Sunset provides a spectacular backdrop to an evening meal.

Tip

There are Chamber of Commerce information centers along US 1 that offer numerous money-saving coupons for many popular Keys attractions.

Hammock State Park (MM 56; tel: 305-289-2690; www.floridastateparks.org/park/curry-hammock; daily 8am–sunset) protects rockland hammocks, mangrove swamp, and seagrass beds. The park also offers cabins for rent, a rare local alternative to beachside tent camping.

Crane Point Hammock Museum & Nature Center (MM 50.5; tel: 305-743-3900; www.cranepoint.net; Mon–Sat 9am–5pm, Sun noon–5pm) offers a comprehensive overview of the Keys' history, wildlife, and ecology. Highlights include a wild bird center, a "creature feature" where snakes and hermit crabs roam, a century-old house, nature trails, and a simulated coral reef.

The Turtle Hospital (MM 48.5; tel: 305-743-2552; www.turtlehospital.org; daily 9am–6pm) in the center of town has an ambulance to transport sea turtles during rescues and releases. The facility – the only state-certified veterinary hospital in the world for sea turtles – has been looking after its patients for more than 30 years.

Guests who stay overnight at the adjacent Hidden Harbor Motel get a free tour of the hospital at 4pm, but others interested in watching the vets work up close can take a tour of the facility; all proceeds directly benefit the shelled residents. The hospital, which has tended and released more than 1,000 sea turtles since its 1986 opening, is largely donor-funded.

PIGEON KEY

Henry Flagler built housing on Pigeon Key to shelter the workers he brought to Florida to work on his Overseas Railroad (the nearby town earned its name when one of the workers referred to the project as a marathon). Several of the structures survive and are part of a tour that departs from the Pigeon Key Visitors Center (MM 47; tel: 305-743-5999; www.pigeonkey.net; departures at 10am, noon, and 2pm). A film tells the fascinating story of Mr. Flagler and Flagler's Folly, the railroad he built from Miami to Key West in spite of huge obstacles, and guided ferry tours are billed as a brief trip back to the early 20th century.

SEVEN MILE BRIDGE

The part of the highway that hops from Marathon to Big Pine Key is called the Seven Mile Bridge and spans the longest between-island stretch you can drive in the Keys. Just under 7 miles (11km), it runs over a channel between the Gulf of Mexico and the Straits of Florida. Paralleling it is the original bridge built for Flagler's railroad. The trains ran until the hurricane of 1935 ruined the roadbed and the Great Depression ruined the economy, making an automobile route the more practical alternative.

Just over the bridge is Bahia Honda State Park ⑩ (MM 37; tel: 305-872-3210; www.bahiahondapark.com; daily 8am–sunset), which has one of the best beaches in the Keys. You can rent a beach chair for the afternoon, camp out for a night, or explore the waters with rented dive equipment or a kayak. The highlight of a visit is a snorkeling tour out to Looe Key National Marine Sanctuary, whose 200-by-800-yd (182-by-731-meter)

Bahia Honda State Park.

stretch of reef is one of the world's most sensational aquatic showcases.

THE FINAL KEYS

Once past Bahia Honda State Park, you'll find **Big Pine Key** ⑪, which is second in size only to Key Largo. Big Pine Key is home to the **National Key Deer Refuge** (visitor center at 179 Key Deer Blvd; tel: 305-872-0774; http://fws. gov/nationalkeydeer; park: daily sunrise–sunset). The diminutive deer, a subspecies of the Virginia whitetail, grow to about 65lb/29kg (females) and 90lb/4kg (males). By the 1950s, poachers had reduced the population to a few dozen at most. Then the refuge was built, and in 1967 the deer was listed as an endangered species. Since then, their numbers have grown significantly. Turn right near MM 30 onto Key Deer Boulevard to the **Blue Hole**, a flooded quarry that attracts both deer and alligators.

Farther down US 1, the **Torch Keys** ⑫ are named after their flammable trees. A short distance off **Little Torch Key** is the secluded **Little Palm Island Resort and Spa**. Accessible by a ferry from Little Torch Key, the resort caters to an elite clientele, although the restaurant is open to the public.

Summerland Key offers scenic side roads, and **Cudjoe Key** has modern campsites for large trailers. On **Sugarloaf Key** ⑬, named for an Indian midden that looked like loaves of old-fashioned sugar, turn right just past MM 17 to view **Perky's bat tower**, built in 1929 as a boarding house for bats. The local businessman imported them in the hope they would swallow the island's mosquito problem, but once released from the tower, they never returned.

The **Saddlebunch Keys** are little more than a series of mangrove outcroppings. Big Coppit, Rockland, and East Rockland house the servicemen of the US Naval Air Station on **Boca Chica Key** ⑭. Stock Island serves as a suburb of Key West and is the home of the **Tennessee Williams Theatre** (tel: 305-295-7676; www.twstages.com). Before crossing the next bridge, prepare yourself for a very different world. You have literally reached the end of the road. This is Key West.

A two-man band keeps patrons entertained at a waterfront bar.

📷 FLORIDA'S CORAL REEF

Coral reefs have been described as underwater tropical forests. They teem with wildlife, from sea slugs to shoals of brilliantly colored fish.

The Florida Keys are fringed by the only true living coral reef in the continental US, stretching for more than 200 miles (320km) all the way from Miami to the Dry Tortugas. The reef is particularly rich in the Upper Keys, where it harbors around 500 species of fish and 50 types of coral.

A coral reef is an efficient and diverse habitat. Every source of nutrients is used and recycled through a variety of food chains. Each chain starts with algae, which is either loose in the water or living inside corals. Small fish graze on corals, and in turn they are preyed upon by large fish.

Inner or patch reefs develop in shallow waters and feature delicate corals and colorful residents such as angelfish, tang, and spiny lobster. Farther out is the main barrier reef, with larger stands of hardier coral, where predatory fish such as barracudas and sharks cruise around and moray eels lurk in caves.

Coral might look rock hard, but is fragile, and sensitive to the changes in conditions. Coral grows in shallow and clean salt water, where the temperature is at least 68°F (19°C). The water must also be low in nutrients; an excess of nutrients causes algae to flourish until it eventually smothers the coral.

Florida's reef has been under intense ecological pressure. The main threats are pollution (from agricultural run-off, oil, and sewage), overfishing, and tourism (the reef is damaged by clumsily driven boats and by careless divers who touch or step on it). A reef takes thousands of years to form, and new growth of coral cannot keep pace with rapid destruction.

Many types of fish like to hide in the nooks and crannies created by the coral, which also provides shaded areas for predators to lurk and wait for lunch to swim by.

The lionfish, with its distinctive stripey spines, is an invasive species that is harming much of the underwater ecology of Florida. The most unusual method of population control is Lionfish Derbies, held in Key Largo and three other parts of the state, where teams compete to catch the most lionfish, and then eat them for dinner.

The bigeye squirrelfish has a large eye and distinctively downturned mouth.

A polyp usually measures about a quarter of an inch (5mm) in diameter.

How Coral is Formed

Every coral is a colony of hundreds of soft-bodied animals called polyps. By extracting calcium from the sea water, each polyp constructs a skeleton of limestone that forms a protective casing; together these skeletons make up a coral. Most of the reef consists of the casings of dead polyps, which build up on top of one another over many thousands of years. Only the top surface of the reef is alive.

Until around 200 years ago, people commonly believed that polyps were plants. They are, in fact, related to jellyfish and sea anemones, and have tentacles, a mouth, and a stomach. During the daytime, the polyp extends its stinging tentacles around the mouth in order to catch phytoplankton in the surrounding sea water; they close again at night.

Most coral grows in partnership with algae, which exist inside them. Polyps get oxygen and nutrients from the algae and, in return, the algae extract carbon dioxide for photosynthesis. Algae also give coral its stunning array of colors.

The manner and rate at which a coral grows depends on the individual species and the health of the local water conditions.

Coral comes in many shapes and sizes, from the minute and pale to the large and color-ful, like this brilliant pink specimen. Scientists have predicted that nearly 50 percent of the world's coral will be extinct by the year 2030.

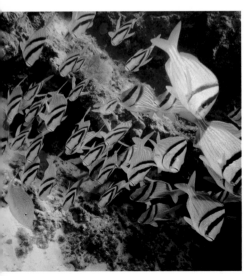

A school of anisotremus virginicus, also known by the common name of porkfish or paragrate grunt. The porkfish can produce a grunting sound by rubbing its teeth together.

A classic Conch house.

KEY WEST

At the state's southernmost tip is the Conch Republic, a place that draws freethinkers with a laid-back attitude and a penchant for good times.

The gateway to **Key West** – the southernmost point in the continental United States – is as prosaic as any in Florida. US 1 on the outskirts of town is littered with the detritus of modern life – an unbroken chain of shopping centers, hotels, car dealers, and fast-food restaurants. However, as you proceed south into the town center, the character changes: the American flavor of fast-food chains and strip malls evaporates into an ambience that's not quite Bahamian, not quite Cuban, and not quite nautical – just very Key West.

Here homes and businesses – some restored, some crumbling – meld in a collage of discordant color. The people who blend into this bizarre landscape are as incongruous as the palette: long-haired survivors of the hippie era, gay couples, leather-faced fishermen, jet-setters and yachters, and, of course, an enormous number of tourists. Only in Key West could so much that is so different seem so right.

THE EARLY DAYS

The character of Key West derives from its history as a haven for transients. Its proximity to the American mainland and the West Indies has introduced many different influences, but the city has transformed those influences into something totally its own.

Historic Whitehead Street.

The Calusa Indians managed to get to this speck 100 miles (160km) from the Florida peninsula, 90 miles (145km) from Cuba, and 66 miles (106km) north of the Tropic of Cancer. The Spanish were the first Europeans to explore the waters and build settlements here, but Indians and pirates made life dangerous. In fact, a young Spanish cavalryman, granted Key West by his governor in 1815, gladly sold it six years later for just $2,000 to Alabama businessman John Simonton. The settlement became part of the

Main Attractions
Fort Zachary Taylor
Little White House
Mallory Square
Audubon House and
    Tropical Gardens
Duval Street
Oldest House Museum
Sloppy Joe's
Hemingway Home and
    Museum
Southernmost Point
Key West Cemetery

Maps on pages
144, 154

US in 1821 when Florida was ceded by Spain. In 1845 the government began constructing a Naval Base (now called **Truman Annex**) and in 1866 completed **Fort Zachary Taylor** Ⓐ (Southard St; tel: 305-292-6713; www.floridastateparks.org/parks/fort-taylor; daily 8am–sunset, fort closes 5pm) to defend the coastline. The **East Martello Museum and Gallery** (3501 S. Roosevelt Blvd; tel: 305-296-3913; www.kwahs.com; daily 9.30am–4.30pm) was one of two towers that were begun – but never completed – and was meant to help defend the fort. Today it houses a museum of Civil War artifacts and local-history exhibits.

MIXED FORTUNES

For many years the business of wrecking – the salvaging of ships that foundered on treacherous offshore reefs – was a boon to the economy. By 1888 Key West was the largest city in Florida and had become the richest city per capita in the US, a distinction that lasted into the early 1900s. Towards the end of the 19th century, lighthouses reduced the need for wreckers, Cuban migrants had imported cigar-making along with their rich culture, and sponge fishermen also prospered.

Completion of the Overseas Railroad in 1912 added another dimension to the booming economy: tourism. Yet by 1930 Key West faced collapse. The stock market crash of 1929, coupled with the closing of the US naval station, disease in the sponge beds, and labor troubles that forced cigar makers to Tampa, began a decline that reached rock bottom with the destruction of the railroad in the 1935 hurricane.

World War II provided a catalyst when the Navy reclaimed their island facilities and President Harry S. Truman established his **Little White House** Ⓑ (111 Front St; tel: 305-294-9911; www.trumanlittlewhitehouse.com; daily 9am–4.30pm, tours every 20 minutes) on the base. The disastrous Bay of Pigs invasion followed by the Cuban Missile Crisis during John F. Kennedy's presidency brought another brief wave of military money. While not as visible as in the past, the Navy is still present in

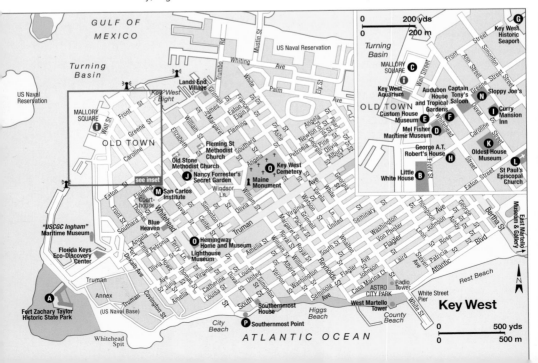

Key West

Key West, though tourism, shrimping, and restoration are major businesses.

GETTING ORIENTED

Old Town, the original part of the city, encompasses approximately 3,000 historic buildings, as well as Mallory Square and the Historic Seaport. There are two ways to get an overview of the island: the venerable **Conch Tour Train** (tel: 888-916-8687; www.conchtourtrain. com) and its newer clone, the **Old Town Trolley** (tel: 866-629-8777; www.historictours.com). The trolley allows riders to hop-on and hop-off at several spots along the route. Both leave every 30 minutes from different locations around town.

If Old Town is the heart of Key West, **Mallory Square** Ⓖ is its commercial soul. Throngs of visitors gather here every evening for the famous **Sunset Celebration**, because the sun doesn't just set here. On the contrary, the shiny orange orb gets an extraordinary send-off from an astonishing assortment of jugglers, fire-eaters, acrobats, and peddlers. The sunset teases the sky with a pink streak before torching it aflame in reds and oranges, eliciting standing ovations from the assembled crowd.

A word to the wise: Watch for the mega-cruise ships docking in the morning at Mallory Square, because tourist hordes will bum-rush the downtown area for the remainder of the day. It's best to avoid it if possible.

AROUND MALLORY SQUARE

Many of the main attractions are within walking distance of Mallory Square, and most of them tell a story about the area's rich history. The **Mel Fisher Maritime Museum** Ⓓ (200 Greene St; tel: 305-294-2633; www.melfisher. org; Mon–Fri 8.30am–5pm, Sat–Sun 9.30am–5pm) displays treasures from the Spanish ships *Nuestra Señora de Atocha* and *Santa Margarita*, which sank in the waters west of Key West during a fierce hurricane in 1622, as well as accounts of the hunt and dramatic salvage operation.

Pirate lore, Ernest Hemingway's bloodstained World War I uniform, and fanciful paintings by folk artist Mario

The Fort East Martello museum is housed in a structure built – but never used – as a defensive tower.

Music man in Mallory Square.

⊙ HARRY'S HIDEAWAY

There was once a famous part-time resident who loved this town even though he was the last person anyone would have diagnosed with Keys Disease. "I've a notion," he once remarked, "to move the capital to Key West and just stay." Harry S. Truman used to duck out of Washington whenever he could and settle in, loud Hawaiian shirts and all, at the former commandant's quarters at the Key West naval station. He brought plenty of work with him, but there was always time for fun. One of the highlights of a tour of the Little White House Museum is a poker table on the downstairs veranda, where Truman would stay up late with naval officers and civilian aides, playing hand after hand in a mellow matrix of bourbon, conversation, and cigar smoke. For lunch he would walk over to Pepe's on Caroline Street.

Crowds and entertainers gather for the daily Sunset Celebration in Mallory Square.

Sanchez are among the permanent exhibits at the **Custom House Museum** Ⓔ (281 Front St; tel: 305-295-6616; www.kwahs.com; daily 9.30am–4.30pm) in the 1891 Custom House.

John James Audubon (1785–1851) usually heads the lists of painters associated with Key West. In fact, the naturalist-artist spent only a short time here while sketching Florida's birds, but that tenuous connection with the city didn't stop entrepreneurs from renovating and reopening the 1830 house where he stayed. The **Audubon House and Tropical Gardens** Ⓕ (205 Whitehead St; tel: 305-294-2116; www.audubonhouse.com; daily 9.30am–5pm, last tour 4.15pm) showcases the artist's original of *Birds of America*.

HISTORIC SEAPORT

Once home to the island's shrimping fleet, the **Key West Historic Seaport** Ⓖ is now home port of most of the island's charter and touring boats, as well as the **Harborwalk** that connects a number of popular restaurants and bars, including **Turtle Kraals** and **Half Shell Raw Bar**. A visit to the city isn't complete without a voyage on its waters, and the **Key West Express** (tel: 888-539-2628; www.seakeywestexpress.com) sails from Key West to Fort Myers Beach and Marco Island.

OLD TOWN RAMBLE

Key Westers have long indulged an infatuation with restoring their homes, a hobby that has transformed the island into a live-in architectural museum, and the best way to savor Old Town is on foot.

Start on Caroline Street, with several fine old mansions. The **George A.T. Roberts House** Ⓗ at No. 313, with its spacious veranda and gingerbread trim, exemplifies Conch architecture. The **Curry Mansion Inn** Ⓘ at No. 511, which admits visitors (tel: 305-294-5349; www.currymansion.com), is also a guest house, as is the 1887 **Conch-style Cypress House Hotel** at No. 601 (tel: 305-294-5229; www.historickeywes-tinns.com).

Other highlights include **Nancy Forrester's Secret Garden** Ⓙ (518

Elizabeth St; tel: 305-294-0015; www. nancyforrester.com; daily 10am–3pm), a lush rainforest with orchids, palms, and tropical birds; writer Shel Silverstein's one-time Greek Revival home and studio on the 600 block of William Street; the Octagon House at 712 Eaton Street was once owned by famous clothing designer Calvin Klein; and poet Elizabeth Bishop's home at No. 624 White Street.

THE DUVAL CRAWL

Duval Street, which stretches from the Gulf to the Atlantic, has an iconic status in Key West. It's where the bars are – not all of them, but enough for a slow promenade down this bright, boisterous avenue where the music begins in the afternoon and continues into the wee hours at places like **Jimmy Buffett's Margaritaville** and the **Hog's Breath Saloon** (the address is technically on Front Street).

The lower end of Duval, toward Mallory Square, has a slew of souvenir shops selling lewd T-shirts and shot glasses. Wade past them to No. 322,

the **Oldest House Museum** Ⓚ (tel: 305-294-9501; www.oirf.org; daily except Sun and Wed 10am–4pm), the 1829 home of a sea captain who made his money from wrecking.

St Paul's Episcopal Church Ⓛ at No. 401 offers free organ and piano concerts on weekdays at noon. At No. 516 the **San Carlos Institute** Ⓜ (tel: 305-294-3887; Fri–Sun noon–6pm), a theater, museum, and cultural center, caters to the Cuban emigrant community.

PAPA'S PLACE

At the corner of Greene and Duval streets is one of Key West's most famous bars, **Sloppy Joe's** Ⓝ. Touted as one of Ernest Hemingway's favorite watering holes when he lived here from 1931 to 1940 with his wife Pauline, Joe's also plays host to the popular Hemingway Days, a July celebration of the author's persona. Purists will want to visit **Captain Tony's Saloon** (428 Greene St), the oldest licensed saloon in Florida. The interior, wallpapered in business cards and newspapers, will take you back to the time when

Colorful shops and cottages line the streets in Key West.

Audubon House.

The Hemingway Home is decorated with hunting trophies and other objects from the author's many adventures.

Sloppy Joe's, one of Ernest Hemingway's favorite bars, has been in business since 1933.

Hemingway relaxed with a drink after a hard day at the typewriter.

Hemingway would stroll down to the saloon from his home, now preserved as the **Hemingway Home and Museum** (907 Whitehead St; tel: 305-294-1136; www.hemingwayhome. com; daily 9am–5pm). His writing studio appears as it did when he worked there on such novels as *To Have and Have Not*. Descendants of his six-toed cats still have the run of the place and drink from a fountain that once served as the urinal at Captain Tony's.

THE SOUTHERN TIP

Across the road from Hemingway's house is the **Key West Lighthouse and Keeper's Quarters Museum** (938 Whitehead St; tel: 305-294-0012; www. kwahs.com; daily 9.30am–4.30pm). Built in 1847 and decommissioned in 1969, the lighthouse has been restored and visitors can climb the 88 steps for incredible views of the surrounding town.

A rather smaller beacon is the **Southernmost Point** , at the corner of Whitehead and South streets. While the town has lost its title as southernmost point in the US to a spot on the Big Island of Hawaii, this landmark is still 755 miles (1,215km) south of Los Angeles.

Nearby is the 1896 **Southernmost House** (1400 Duval St; tel: 305-296-3141; www.southernmosthouse.com; daily), an inn that exhibits documents, including autographs of George Washington and Thomas Jefferson, and memorabilia from former Key West residents Hemingway and Tennessee Williams (who lived at 1431 Duncan St).

BAHAMA VILLAGE

In **Bahama Village** on the western edge of Old Town, the city's Caribbean atmosphere is at its strongest, with modest, colorfully painted wooden houses, restaurants, and shops. On Thomas Street, Ernest Hemingway sometimes boxed at the **Blue Heaven** (729 Thomas St; tel: 305-296-8666; www.blueheavenkw.com) restaurant, back when it was a saloon with a reputation for roughness. If you like your

historical sites with a bit of swing, jazz trumpet legend Theodore "Fats" Navarro lived at No. 828.

KEY WEST CEMETERY

Even the 20-acre (8-hectare) **Key West Cemetery** Ⓠ (www.friendsofthekeywest cemetery.com), established in 1847, has fascinating sights. Among them is a statue of a lone sailor that commemorates the 252 men who died aboard the battleship USS *Maine*, which sank in Havana in 1898. Other famous epitaphs read "I told you I was sick" and "Devoted fan of singer Julio Iglesias." The unique nature of Key West's residents is apparent even after death. The cemetery has been the center of a controversy because of the local custom of recycling graves, although space is at a premium, since at least 100,000 people are buried here, when only 30,000 live on the island.

OFF KEY

Key West isn't the last of the Florida Keys. To reach the westernmost of the islands, you have to travel by boat or seaplane to the Dry Tortugas, 68 miles (109km) beyond Duval Street's last bar.

Romantic as it sounds today, the name merely told 16th-century mariners that the island was "dry," meaning there was no fresh water; *tortugas*, Spanish for turtles, meant there was no fresh meat. There wasn't much on the island until 1846. That was when the US government started laying bricks on the Tortugas' Garden Key to create the hexagonal Fort Jefferson – the "Gibraltar of the Gulf" – and provide a safe haven for American vessels pausing near the entrance to the Gulf of Mexico. Never completed, and abandoned by the Army in 1874, in 1992 the fort became **Dry Tortugas National Park** ⓰ (for ferry and seaplane information, tel: 888-382-7864; www.fortjefferson.com). Today, the appropriate line for the place might be "ye shall beat your swords into snorkels." The waters beneath the fort's walls are ideal for exploring the coral reefs that are one of the Keys' most famous attractions.

Key West Lighthouse and Keeper's Quarters museum.

Southernmost House.

Fishing on Amelia Island.

Nightly entertainment at the Trade Winds Lounge in St Augustine.

ATLANTIC COAST

The sunshine and beaches are a big attraction, but there are also fascinating historic sites, including the oldest continuously occupied city in the US.

Kitschy architectural detail at the Magic Beach Motel on Vilano Beach.

Driving Florida's Atlantic coast retraces the route that funneled early tourists toward the seaside playgrounds of Miami and Fort Lauderdale. Strung along the coast are dozens of towns, each with a distinct personality and its own slice of the tourism market.

Fort Lauderdale, on the southern end of the Gold Coast (which starts just north of Miami), was once known for hard-partying college students, but has worked hard to refashion itself into a family-friendly and less fast-paced sightseeing alternative. Palm Beach and Boca Raton, on the other hand, are favored by the upper crust, who inhabit lavish waterfront mansions and exclusive country clubs.

To the north is the Space Coast, site of the Kennedy Space Center. Nearby are the brackish lagoons and pristine beaches of Merritt Island National Wildlife Refuge and the old-time, seaside town of Cocoa Beach.

The pace quickens dramatically at Daytona Beach, which has tried to move away from its past as a spring break destination; it remains the proud home of the Daytona 500 and other auto races. Historic St Augustine, the oldest continuously inhabited city in the US, operates at a decidedly slower pace and contrasts sharply with Jacksonville, Florida's largest city, with a revitalized downtown, numerous museums, and an active port.

Motorists on the Atlantic coast have a choice of routes. A1A is slow and narrow but usually within tantalizing sight of the ocean; US 1 is somewhat

Kennedy Space Center Visitor Complex.

speedier but tends to be clogged with local traffic; and I-95 is, predictably, the fastest and least scenic but is still a sensible choice if you need to cover the greatest distance in the least time.

Las Olas Boulevard beach.

FORT LAUDERDALE

The party scene has mellowed and the town is cultivating a family-friendly image, but the Strip remains a popular destination for those in search of sun, surf, and sand.

It seems almost inconceivable that the beautiful beaches of **Fort Lauderdale** ❶ were a dismal swamp just a century ago. A wooden fort built here during the Seminole Wars rotted for two decades after troops left in 1857. The only significant development during this period was the construction of a House of Refuge for shipwrecked sailors. For the most part, it remained a waterlogged hideaway for escaped slaves and army deserters.

Henry Flagler's railroad changed everything. In 1911, the city was incorporated. The swampy coast kept construction off the beach, and, as a result, the sands were kept open to the public, and hotels and businesses were situated on the far side of Route A1A.

BEACH PARTY

Known as the **Strip**, the city's palm-lined, 2-mile (3km) beachfront was romanticized as a spring-break destination in the 1960 movie and song *Where the Boys Are*. For much of the 1970s, the Strip was the site of what seemed like one big drunken beach party. A crackdown in the 1980s put an end to the brawls and other disruptions. New bars that were not part of hotels were banned, as was public consumption of liquor. Arrests for violations were common. By 1990, many spring-break revelers decamped to

Daytona Beach, which has also since dissuaded the college crowd from descending en masse.

You'll find many more families, couples, and young professionals here these days. The once-notorious **Elbo Room** bar Ⓐ, made famous in the movie, is still open, but even the bartenders admit that it's not what it used to be. Although toned down, Fort Lauderdale still has a lively bar scene, with much of the action along Commercial and Las Olas boulevards and the banks of the Intracoastal Waterway.

Main Attractions

Bonnet House Museum and Gardens
Riverwalk Arts and Entertainment District
NSU Art Museum Fort Lauderdale
Museum of Discovery and Science
Flamingo Gardens
Boca Raton
Loxahatchee National Wildlife Refuge

Maps on pages 166, 168

Tropical blossom at Butterfly World.

THE WATERFRONT

Fort Lauderdale is heralded as the Yachting Capital of the World; more than 44,000 yachts are registered here. Many tie up at **Bahia Mar Yacht Basin ⓑ** at the southern end of town. Fans of John D. MacDonald's Travis McGee novels may recognize the marina as home of the fictional detective's houseboat, **The Busted Flush**.

Just to the north, the **International Swimming Hall of Fame ⓒ** (1 Hall of Fame Dr; tel: 954-462-6536; www.ishof. org; daily 9am–5pm), a showplace for water sports, houses two pools, a diving well, and a swimming flume, as well as Olympic memorabilia.

THE STRIP'S NORTHERN END

At the northern end of the beach, hidden behind seagrape trees, **Bonnet House Museum & Gardens ⓓ** (900 N. Birch Rd; tel: 954-563-5393; www.bonnethouse.org; guided tours Tue–Sun 9am–4pm) is perhaps the city's most curious sight. Built in 1920 by the late Evelyn and Frederick Bartletts, it is a lyrical mansion of artistic whimsy, decorated with unusual antiques and an odd collection of knick-knacks.

Descendants of Mrs. Bartlett's beloved Brazilian monkeys still inhabit the manicured grounds of the 35-acre (14 hectare) estate, now listed in the National Register of Historic Places.

Across the way, at the 180-acre (70-hectare) **Hugh Taylor Birch State Park ⓔ** (3109 E. Sunrise Blvd; tel: 954-564-4521; www.floridastateparks.org/park/ hugh-taylor-bird; daily 8am–sunset), visitors can swim, hike, and rent canoes to explore the watery lagoons.

THE VENICE OF AMERICA

When developer Charles Rodes was faced with transforming acres of mangrove swamp into real estate in the 1920s, he resorted to "finger-islanding" – dredging up a series of parallel canals and using the fill to create long peninsulas between them. Rodes dubbed his creation **The Isles ⓕ**, and Fort Lauderdale earned the nickname "Venice of America." The Isles have more than 300 miles (484km) of canals and inlets, and along their frontage ornate mansions sit cheek-by-jowl with tiny boxes awaiting the wrecking ball.

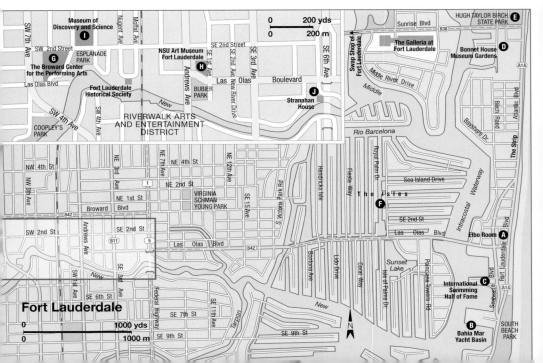

Numerous companies offer narrated tours of The Isles' "millionaire's row." The somewhat worn but serviceable **Jungle Queen** (tel: 954-462-5596; www.junglequeen.com), an old-fashioned riverboat, sails from a dock just off Seabreeze Boulevard, next to Bahia Mar. The *Carrie B* (Las Olas Blvd at SE 5th Ave; tel: 954-768-9920; www.carriebcruises.com), a replica 19th-century paddle-wheeler, offers 90-minute narrated cruises (11am, 1pm, and 3pm Oct–Apr daily, May–Sept Thu–Mon). Riders pay a one-time fare for unlimited trips aboard the **Water Taxi** (tel: 954-467-6677; www.watertaxi.com), which cruises the Fort Lauderdale, Hollywood, and New River waterways and includes stops at many downtown attractions.

RIVERWALK

Gas-lit Las Olas Boulevard, peppered with shops, restaurants, and galleries, is the major thoroughfare from the beach to downtown's **Riverwalk Arts and Entertainment District** (tel: 954-462-0222, 800-249-ARTS; www.riverwalkae.com). Many of the city's top cultural attractions are here, linked by a promenade along the New River. Close by is the **Las Olas Riverfront** (tel: 954-522-6556), where local restaurateurs are happy to serve docked boats at the marina and a Sunday jazz series brings harmonious horns to match the tropical breezes.

On the western end, **The Broward Center for the Performing Arts** ❻ (201 SW 5th Ave; tel: 954-462-0222; www.browardcenter.org) hosts a full roster of concerts, dance, opera, and ballet.

At the **NSU Art Museum Fort Lauderdale** ❽ (1 E. Las Olas Blvd; tel: 954-525-5500; www.nsuartmuseum.org; Tue–Sat 11am–5pm, first Thu of every month until 8pm, Sun noon–5pm) is an impressive collection that includes works by Picasso, Calder, Dalí, Warhol, and William Glackens. There's also an extensive exhibit of European Expressionists from the late 1940s and '50s, the so-called CoBrA works by artists from Copenhagen, Brussels, and Amsterdam.

Nearby, the **Museum of Discovery and Science** ❶ (401 SW 2nd St; tel: 954-467-6637; www.mods.org; Mon–Sat 10am–5pm, Sun noon–6pm), South

Tip

The Riverwalk Water Trolley (www.riverwalkwatertrolley.com; daily 11am–2pm and 4–11pm; free) will transport you up and down the Riverwalk. Water trolley times are available in the Sun Trolley Tracker App (www.suntrolley.com).

A Riverwalk restaurant.

The Museum of Discovery and Science features interactive exhibits designed to educate and entertain.

Florida's largest science museum, has more than 200 hands-on educational exhibits and the region's only IMAX3D/ PSE theater.

The **Fort Lauderdale Historical Society** (219 SW 2nd St; tel: 954-463-4431; www.oldfortlauderdale.org; Tue–Fri noon–4pm, Sat–Sun 9.30am–4pm), housed in the New River Inn, oversees several historic properties. At the promenade's eastern end is **Stranahan House** ❿ (Las Olas Blvd at 335 SE 6th Ave; tel: 954-524-4736; www.stranahanhouse. org; tours daily 1pm, 2pm, and 3pm), the restored turn-of-the-19th-century home of Fort Lauderdale pioneer Frank Stranahan, and Broward County's oldest

structure. Try the quaintly thrilling River Ghost tours on Sunday nights January through November.

Also along the Riverwalk is the Florida Grand Opera, the seventh oldest and 10th largest opera company in the US.

A SEA OF SLOTS

Numerous cruise ships with onboard casinos set sail from **Port Everglades** ➋ (www.porteverglades.net/cruising) in the southern part of the city.

JAI-ALAI, FISHING, BUTTERFLIES

Five miles (8km) south of Fort Lauderdale, in **Dania** ➌, is the **John U. Lloyd Beach State Park** ➍ (tel: 954-923-2833; daily 8am–sunset), with 310 acres (126 hectares) of barrier island and a stunning beach where boats of all sizes, as well as volleyballs and grills, can be rented for a small fee. It is also home to the **International Fishing Hall of Fame and Museum** (300 Gulf Stream Way; tel: 954-927-2628; www.igfa.org; Mon–Sat 10am–6pm, Sun noon–6pm), which calls itself the world's largest resource for sport fishing history. But most folks

Around Fort Lauderdale

0 ————— 5 miles
0 ————— 5 km

⊙ BLACK HISTORY

Fort Lauderdale's African American Research Library and Cultural Center (2650 Sistrunk Blvd; tel: 954-357-6282; Mon and Wed noon–8pm, Tue and Thu–Sun 10am–6pm) is one of the country's three such public research facilities, and the only one that includes Caribbean as well as African cultures. Today the local black population is growing rapidly, largely due to the arrival of Caribbean immigrants. But the area was not always so welcoming; segregation lasted well into the 1960s. Many citizens remember the days when they could swim only on holidays at John Lloyd State Park and had to attend segregated schools. Today immigrants from a host of nations are settling here, and the ethnic diversity is creating a cosmopolitan atmosphere unusual for a city of its size.

visit to catch the live sports action at **Dania Jai-Alai** (301 E. Dania Beach Blvd; tel: 954-920-1511; www.betdania.com). A blend of lacrosse and racquetball, played with a scooping basket called the *cesta*, jai-alai is a fast-paced treat.

Just to the west, in **Davie, Flamingo Gardens ❺** (3750 S. Flamingo Rd; tel: 954-473-2955; www.flamingogardens.org; daily 9.30am–5pm) encompasses an historic home, 60 acres (24 hectares) of rare plants, and a wildlife sanctuary with an expansive free-flying aviary of wading birds. The grounds are home to more than just feathered friends, with otters, panthers, and alligators.

HOLLYWOOD

Continue south to **Hollywood ❻**, which was founded by a Californian but bears no resemblance to its West Coast namesake. The major draw is the 2 mile (3km) oceanfront boardwalk – dubbed a "broadwalk" for its roomy width – and its entertainment complex of restaurants, bars, shops, and cinemas.

A stone's throw from the beach, **West Lake Park** (www.broward.org/parks/westlakepark) and its **Anne Kolb Nature Center** (751 Sheridan St; tel: 954-357-5161) offers a rare chance to hike or kayak through a preserved system of mangroves, imposing tropical trees that gather fresh water from the salty sea. Even paddling beginners will enjoy a trip through its secluded 3 miles (4.8km) of byways, but a $5 guided boat tour is available for those who prefer narration by an expert.

The **Seminole Hard Rock Hotel and Casino** (tel: 954-327-7625; www.seminolehardrockhollywood.com) offers 24-hour entertainment.

UP THE COAST

The beach drive north from Fort Lauderdale is particularly rewarding. The oceanfront strip of A1A through **Deerfield Beach ❼** is lined with small, moderately priced motels and inexpensive restaurants. From here the road brushes the shoreline Intracoastal Waterway.

Pompano Beach ❽ is yet another fun-in-the-sun resort area known for its beaches, water sports, and cultural offerings. The Ali Cultural Arts center, in an early 20th-century building, celebrates the area's African-American community through dance, theater, music, and poetry events. Jazz legends Cab Calloway and Louis Armstrong are among those who boarded in the structure years ago. Shoppers out for a bargain congregate at the massive **Festival Marketplace** (2900 W. Sample Rd; tel: 954-979-4555; www.festival. com; Mon–Fri 9.30am–5pm, Sat–Sun until 6pm), which has more than 500 vendors selling trinkets of all shapes, sizes, and colors.

At Coconut Creek's **Butterfly World** (3600 W. Sample Rd; tel: 954-977-4400, www.butterflyworld.com; Mon–Sat 9am–5pm, Sun 11am–5pm), visitors can view more than 20,000 butterflies representing some 50 species that fly freely in aviaries at the world's largest facility of its kind.

> ### ⦿ Tip
>
> Now that's a shopping experience. The 80-acre (32-hectare) Swap Shop of Fort Lauderdale (3291 W. Sunrise Blvd; tel: 954-791-7927; www.floridaswapshop.com) has stores, restaurants, and a 13-screen drive-in theater within its 180,000 sq ft (11,000 sq meters).

A game of jai-alai.

The Seminole Hard Rock Hotel and Casino.

BOCA RATON

Legend has it that when architect Addison Mizner arrived in **Boca Raton** in 1925, his dream for 356 prime acres (144 hectares) was an upscale resort with a fleet of gondolas romantically plying a canal through town. In truth, he built a road, and that's it, before leaving, bankrupt, the following year. Still, over time the locale's Cloister Inn blossomed into "the world's most architecturally beautiful playground," with miles of landscaped streets, golf courses, polo fields, elegant shopping vias, and luxurious mansions. Today this locale, Camino Real, remains a coveted neighborhood centered around what is now the **Boca Raton Resort** (tel: 561-447-3000). The **Boca Raton Historical Society & Museum** (tel: 561-395-6766; www.bocahistory.org; Mon–Fri 10am–4pm) houses its history museum in the historic Town Hall and offers seasonal guided tours of the resort and other points of interest.

The **Boca Raton Museum of Art** (501 Plaza Real, Mizner Park; tel: 561-392-2500; www.bocamuseum.org; Tue–Fri 10am–5pm, Thu until 8pm, Sat–Sun noon–5pm) exhibits works by artists ranging from Matisse and Modigliani to Warhol, as well as pre-Columbian and African art.

Also in Mizner Park is the **Cultural Center** (433 Plaza Real, Mizner Park; tel: 561-368-8445; www.miznerparkcac.org), where sopranos share the stage with lecturers at the annual Festival of the Arts every March. When rain makes indoor browsing preferable, many locals flock to the sprawling **Town Center** (600 Glades Rd, Boca Raton; tel: 561-368-6001).

Boca doesn't neglect nature; at one end of the oceanfront **Red Reef Park** lies the **Gumbo Limbo Nature Center** (1801 North Ocean Boulevard, Boca Raton; tel: 561-338-1473; www.gumbolimbo.org; Mon–Sat 9am–4pm, Sun noon–4pm; donation suggested), where injured sea turtles are nursed back to health and butterflies fly freely.

DELRAY BEACH

Delray Beach is an inexpensive alternative to the resorts to the north and south. A strip of Atlantic Avenue near the coast, along with the nearby Pineapple Grove district, is a lively hub of trendy restaurants and art galleries filled with a stylish young crowd. The nearby **Morikami Museum and Japanese Gardens** (4000 Morikami Park Rd; tel: 561-495-0233; www.morikami.org; Tue–Sun 10am–5pm) is a tribute to the culture of a colony of Japanese immigrants. With lush Zen gardens and rotating exhibits of sumptuous visual arts from the Japanese imperial era, the space has something for everyone.

It is well worth making the trip 10 miles (16km) inland to the **Arthur R. Marshall Loxahatchee National Wildlife Refuge** (tel: 561-734-8303; www.fws.gov/loxahatchee; refuge: daily sunrise–sunset, visitor center: daily 9am–4pm), which contains the most northerly part of the Everglades and cypress swamp. Wildlife ranges from alligators to a great variety of birds.

A peacock at Flamingo Gardens.

Kids learn about birds, bugs, and tropical plants at Butterfly World.

PALM BEACH

There are Mediterranean-style mansions, classy shops and restaurants, pristine nature preserves, and several fine cultural venues in and around this sanctuary for the super-rich.

The joke has it that Mother Nature would have built **Palm Beach** if she had enough money. Indeed, the sweet aroma of dollars permeates the entire length of the 4.5 mile (7km) island, a living tableau of over-the-top opulence. Fortunately, plans floated by locals over the years (including one requiring residents to have ID cards to enter) sank, and the roads into – and out of – one of the country's wealthiest towns are open to all.

You can leave plebian Florida – and enter Palm Beach – by proceeding north on Route A1A. You can't miss it. The garish shopping centers and neon hotel signs vanish. Clean, uncluttered streets take over. The structures behind the high walls of concrete and ficus hedges aren't museums; they're the trophy homes of the ultra-rich.

PALM BEACH TAKES ROOT

There seem to be various stories as to the origins of the city's signature palm trees. The most popular relates how a boatload of Spanish sailors on the *Providencia* transporting 100 cases of wine stumbled upon the barren strand in 1878. They sold their cargo, including 20,000 coconuts, to a shrewd islander for $20. The islander sold coconuts for less than a nickel to his neighbors. They planted them in the sand and, voilà, the beach got its palms.

In the 1890s, Henry Flagler visited the area. He liked it, built a winter home (Whitehall), and transformed Palm Beach into a personal playground for his wealthy, fun-loving friends. Astors and Vanderbilts and assorted dukes and duchesses followed Flagler into town. They stayed at Flagler's Royal Poinciana Hotel, one of the largest wooden buildings ever constructed and the largest resort hotel of its time. With more than a touch of the era's characteristic racism, black men once pedaled guests around the grounds

⊘ Main Attractions

The Breakers
Worth Avenue
The Society of the Four
  Arts
Flagler Museum
CityPlace
Norton Museum of Art
Lion Country Safari
Savannas Preserve State
  Park
Vero Beach
Sebastian Inlet State Park

📍 **Maps on pages 174, 178**

Worth Avenue, Palm Beach.

Tip

Take a walk on the wild side at Palm Beach Zoo (1301 Summit Blvd; tel: 561-533-0887; www.palmbeachzoo.org; daily 9am–5pm), just off I-95. The 23-acre (9-hectare) zoo is home to more than 550 animals, among them Malayan tigers, jaguars, panthers, and spider monkeys.

aboard "Afromobiles," and a feature attraction was Cakewalk Night, when black dancers competed for a big white cake, then entertained richly dressed guests with spirituals.

The hotel burned down several times and eventually was reborn as **The Breakers** Ⓐ (1 S. County Rd; tel: 561-655-6611; www.thebreakers.com), but its spirit carries on – fortunately, minus the Afromobiles and tasteless entertainment. Two championship golf courses, a 20,000-sq-ft (1,858-sq-meter) spa, and 10 tennis courts, in addition to a litany of high-end shops and a kids' camp program, make the beachfront resort a perennial favorite with visitors.

Palm Beach's transformation began when New York architect Addison Mizner came to visit in 1918. He stayed on, adding his ostentatious flourishes to existing Spanish structures, creating a fanciful yet functional self-contained world of spires, courtyards, plazas, and arcades that contribute greatly to the town's present-day charm and distinctive appearance. Visitors can see his designs along many of the manicured avenues.

THE SEASON

Unless you prefer to gape at empty mansions undergoing beauty treatments and garden manicures, visit during the social season – an indeterminate period of time that falls between Thanksgiving and Easter. That's when you'll glimpse the beautiful people who actually live in these palatial dwellings. The annual migration of the moneyed class ignites a round of galas, charity balls, and cocktail parties. People willing to pay $1,250 or more per plate can get invited to some of the prestigious balls.

TOURING THE TOWN

The centerpiece of downtown Palm Beach is **Worth Avenue** Ⓑ, the nation's only shopping district bordered by the Intracoastal and the Atlantic. It has been likened to London's Bond Street, Paris' Faubourg St Honoré, and Rome's Via Condotti. Here a multitude of art galleries, boutiques, antique shops, and jewelry stores – many housed in buildings designed by Mizner – open onto courtyards and winding vistas. Mizner's 1920s Town Hall and Casa de

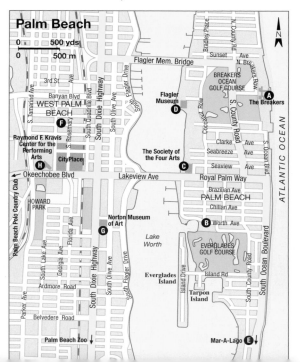

Leoni (450 Worth Ave), which hints at a Venetian Gothic influence, also exemplify his style. For those less eager to give the credit card a workout, a Palm Beach historian gives periodic historical walking tours; contact the Worth Avenue Association (tel: 561-659-6909; www.worth-avenue.com) for details.

The cultural hub of Palm Beach is **The Society of the Four Arts ⓒ** (2 Four Arts Plaza; tel: 561-655-7226; www.four arts.org; gallery: Mon–Sat 10am–5pm and Sun 1–5pm, gardens: daily 10am–5pm), a nonprofit cultural organization founded in 1936. The campus, on the Intracoastal Waterway, encompasses an art gallery, auditorium, two libraries, sculpture garden, and botanical garden.

Continue down Coconut Row to Whitehall, built in 1902 and now open to the public as the **Flagler Museum ⓓ** (1 Whitehall Way; tel: 561-655-2833; www.flaglermuseum.us; Tue–Sat 10am–5pm, Sun noon–5pm), the top attraction in Palm Beach. Flagler and his third wife, Mary Lily, lived in this great Beaux Arts mansion, dubbed the Taj Mahal of North America, for 11 years until Flagler's death in 1913. The rooms and most original furnishings have been restored. Highlights inside include the Grand Hall, with its painted ceiling and elegant staircase, the Music Room, the Drawing Room, and Flagler's private railroad car, on display in the Flagler Kenan Pavilion. Nearby is the Royal Poinciana Chapel, founded by Flagler in 1896, and Sea Gull Cottage, Flagler's first winter home in Palm Beach.

The Breakers has weathered booms, busts, and even two fires, but it remains one of the nation's first-class resorts. Stately Venetian arches lead into the lobby, comfortable sofas and Persian carpets line the rambling hallways, and the Circle Dining Room has a skylight, cathedral windows, and a bronze chandelier. The Flagler Steakhouse is one of the town's power restaurants.

Show up at least a half-hour before noon to get a courtyard table at the elegant **Café Boulud** (tel: 561-655-6060; www.cafeboulud.com/palmbeach) in the Brazilian Court Hotel. Younger heirs gravitate to **Ta-boo** (tel: 561-835-3500; www.taboorestaurant.com), right on the Avenue, and the cigar room at the **Leopard Lounge** at the Chesterfield Hotel (tel: 561-659-5800; www.chesterfieldpb.com). The Esplanade, at the eastern end, is a two-story clutch of shops surrounding a courtyard with another popular lunch spot, **Café L'Europe** (tel: 561-655-4020; www.cafeleurope.com).

MANSION ROW

Near an area known as Billionaire's Row, South Ocean Boulevard runs past the Moorish estate of late cereal heiress Marjorie Merriweather Post. Named **Mar-A-Lago ⓔ**, the National Historic Landmark is owned by entrepreneur, TV reality star, and US President Donald Trump, who bought the 17-acre (7-hectare) property in 1985, and after seven years turned it into a private club on the first floor, with his residence on the second floor. He opened membership to anyone who could afford the $150,000

Worth Avenue is the centerpiece of Palm Beach's upmarket shopping district.

With a staff of 1,800, the Breakers is kept tidy.

Formerly a church, the Harriet Himmel Theater is the centerpiece of CityPlace.

Bethesda-by-the-Sea Episcopal Church was built in 1925.

initiation fee and the annual dues. It was here, in 2004, that Trump married supermodel Melania Knauss. He still visits occasionally, security forces en masse, which causes massive traffic jams that unnerve the neighbors.

Nearby is El Mirasol, a home built by Mizner and formerly owned by Yoko Ono. Next door stands a house that once belonged to Woolworth Donahue, heir to the dime-store fortune.

On North Ocean Boulevard is the former estate of the Kennedys. The Kennedys began wintering there in 1935, and became known as the "Winter White House" in the 1960s when John F. Kennedy became US President, but John Ney wrote of a local prejudice against this neighboring "royal family," presumably because they were Catholic. It was here, in 1992, that Kennedy's nephew, William Kennedy Smith, was charged with raping a young woman he had met in a Palm Beach bar. After a televised trial, Smith was found not guilty.

For those seeking a less motorized look at all the hoopla, the 9-mile (14.5km) **Lake Trail**, nicknamed the "Trail of Conspicuous Consumption", offers stellar people- and mansion-watching.

THE SPORT OF KINGS

With champagne and canapés hawked from a canopied cart instead of hot dogs and beer, it's obvious that polo is not like a Sunday-afternoon baseball game. Palm Beach's pet sport is played at the nearby **Palm Beach Polo and Country Club** (11199 Polo Club Rd, West Palm Beach; http://palmbeachpolo. com) and Boca Raton's **Royal Palm Polo Sports Club** (2703 NW 71st Blvd; http:// royalpalmpolo.com). You must either be rich or have a wealthy sponsor to participate. But it costs little to watch from your car. More than 20 area polo fields host matches from October to July. In the spring, the **International Polo Club Palm Beach** (3667 120th Ave S, Wellington; www.ipc.coth.com) brings out a crowd of young swells for its popular Sunday brunch-and-polo events.

THE OTHER PALM BEACH

Across Lake Worth, the city of **West Palm Beach**  was conceived as a satellite by its rich patron, Flagler. It was reserved for servants, gardeners, and other workers who toiled to keep Palm Beach from crumbling while their employers partied, shopped, and played polo. In fact, parts of the city are not fancy at all. But **CityPlace**, an upscale shopping, dining, and entertainment complex, has changed the face of downtown. Centennial Square, at the top of Clematis Street and also known as Fountain Park, has a $2-million interactive fountain, with fountain shows daily at half-hour intervals.

One good reason to come to West Palm Beach is to visit the **Norton Museum of Art** (1451 S. Olive Ave; tel: 561-832-5196; www.norton.org; Tue–Wed and Fri–Sun noon–5pm, Thu noon–9pm). The museum is undergoing a major expansion program (due for completion in late 2018) and admission is free during construction.

Among its most vaunted possessions are works by Cézanne and Picasso, as well some by Georgia O'Keeffe, Edward Hopper, and Andy Warhol. Only a small portion of the collection is on view at this time.

The **Raymond F. Kravis Center for the Performing Arts** **H** (701 Okeechobee Blvd; tel: 561-832-7469; www.kravis.org) is a major venue for a wide variety of performing artists and groups, ranging from show business legends such as John Cleese and Itzhak Perlman to the latest Broadway hits like *Book of Mormon*.

PALM BEACH GARDENS

Much of Palm Beach County that surrounds Lake Okeechobee is used for sugar cane production; construction, real estate, and banking are other big industries. **Palm Beach Gardens** **2**, a burgeoning upscale suburb north of Palm Beach, is headquarters of the Professional Golfers Association (PGA), which has given its initials to one of that town's main thoroughfares. The PGA operates numerous championship golf courses and a Hall of Fame.

Twenty miles (32km) west of downtown West Palm Beach in the town of **Loxahatchee** is **Lion Country Safari** **3** (2003 Olion County Safari Rd; tel: 561-793-1084; www.lioncountrysafari.com; daily 9.30am–5.30pm), the area's top family attraction, where you can drive along 4 miles (6km) of jungle trails past nearly 1,000 roaming animals. The well-fed lions seem to have grown rather lazy, but it's thrilling to watch one lead a parade of cars or see a giraffe peering back at you; keep your windows closed. There are also safari boat rides, a petting and feeding area for small animals, and a reptile and dinosaur park.

JUPITER AND SINGER ISLAND

Route A1A curves back to the beach over Blue Heron Boulevard. You can follow it through the high-rises of **Singer Island** **4** (home of John D. MacArthur Beach, one of the state's best) all the way to **Jupiter** **5**. This town once was a terminal for the Celestial Railroad, which took its name from the stations it served – Juno, Neptune, Mars, and Venus, as well as Jupiter. Flagler's railroad bypassed

CityPlace has more than 75 shops and restaurants, plus nightclubs and a movie theater.

The Cuillo Centre for the Arts on Clematis Street is a performing-arts venue.

The Kravis Center encompasses a 2,200-seat concert hall, a playhouse, and an outdoor amphitheater.

this peninsula, so it remains less developed. Water-bound visitors seek out Blue Heron Bridge, under which a snorkeling and diving jaunt reaps spottings of warm- and cold-water species close to shore. Look for seahorses, octopi, sea robins, and batfish, among others.

Just off Route A1A, visitors can climb the 105 cast iron steps of the restored 1860 brick **Jupiter Inlet Lighthouse and Museum** (tel: 561-747-8380; www. jupiterlighthouse.org; 10am–5pm Jan–Apr daily, May–Dec Tue–Sun). The reward is a fabulous view of the Gulf Stream – a veritable river in the Atlantic Ocean. Cross the bridge to tour the museum's **Dubois Pioneer Home**, the oldest in Palm Beach County.

The mansions of Jupiter Island house millionaires who aren't fond of Palm Beach, and the owners are equally wary of tourists. You will find no hotels, convenience stores, or gas stations here. Police tend to pull over any vehicles that stray off public roads into the private drives. Still, it's worth a look. Turn off US 1 to SR 707 through an archway of overhanging trees.

INTO THE WILD

Just north of Jupiter off US 1 in **Hobe Sound**, **Jonathan Dickinson State Park** ❻ (tel: 772-546-2771; www.floridastate parks.org/parks/jonathan-dickinson; daily 8am–sunset) preserves the last wild river in southeast Florida. You can rent a canoe or kayak and paddle along the upper Loxahatchee River past alligators and rarities like bald eagles. The park – on World War II secret radar-training land – rolls through tall sand dunes that peak at Hobe Mountain, an 86ft (26-meter) sand pile with an observation deck. It is the highest point in South Florida.

The park encompasses the restored homestead of Trapper Nelson, a folk hero who opened a zoo where he wrestled alligators and devoured raw possum. After health officials closed the zoo, he retreated into isolation. When police found him dead, some suspected foul play because he had been holding up a multimillion-dollar land deal. The Trapper Nelson Interpretive Site is accessible only by boat with park staff.

Farther north, you cross the St Lucie Canal, which, together with the Caloosahatchee River, forms the Okeechobee Waterway linking the east and west coasts. It is used by thousands of craft annually. In **Stuart** ❼, naturalist Nancy Beaver offers two-hour trips into the Indian River Lagoon on **Sunshine Wildlife Tours** (her boat leaves from Pirate's Cove; tel: 772-219-0148; www.sunshinewildlifetours.com; departs 10.15am and 12.45pm Tue, Wed, and in season Sat). Bottlenose dolphins and manatees are often spotted from aboard the cruise, which includes a visit to Bird Island, one of the state's top bird rookeries.

ON THE BEACH

East of Stuart is **Jensen Beach**, where turtles are a big attraction. In May of each year, large loggerheads and green sea turtles crawl out of the ocean at night to lay eggs in the sand. Nearby, on the rocky shores of **Hutchinson Island** ❽, you'll find two fascinating properties owned by the Historical Society of Martin County (825 NE Ocean Blvd; tel: 772-225-1961; http://elliottmuseum.org; daily 10am–5pm). **The House of Refuge at Gilbert's Bar** is the last of 10 houses built more than a century ago for shipwrecked sailors and travelers, its ambience haunting enough to draw an honest-to-goodness paranormal investigation by the non-profit Florida Ghost Team. **The Elliot Museum**, named for inventor Harmon Elliot, contains all manner of wonderful things, from Elliot's inventions to a mini-circus.

Savannas Preserve State Park ❾ (tel: 772-398-2779; www.floridastateparks.org/park/savannas; daily 8am–sunset), a freshwater marsh that stretches for 10 miles (16km) to Fort Pierce, has habitats similar to those of the Everglades. The park's education center is in Port St Lucie. The drive up Route A1A to **Fort Pierce**, home to an experimental preserve for the imperiled ivory bush coral, is particularly scenic.

DRIFTWOOD AND DISNEY

Vero Beach ❿ has miles of lovely beaches, plus the Indian River Island Sanctuary, which can be reached by a footbridge at the end of Dahlia Lane. Another chief landmark is the rickety-looking **Driftwood Resort** (www.thedriftwood.com) on Ocean Drive. Eccentric entrepreneur Waldo Sexton fashioned it from just that. Visitors can snack in the dining room or stroll through this architectural jumble perched like a shipwreck at the tide line. So improbable is the construction, it looks as if a simple tug might bring the whole thing down. Yet it has withstood high waves and fierce hurricanes ever since the 1930s.

The **Ocean Grill** (1050 Sexton Plaza; tel: 772-231-5409; www.ocean-grill.com; lunch Mon–Sat, dinner nightly), also created by Sexton, is a short stroll up the beach. Its bar extends over the water, where windows mist with sea spray. There are several similarly named spots in the Palm Beach vicinity, but only Vero's version was built by Sexton and

The Norton Museum includes works by 19th and 20th century European and American artists.

converted into an officer's club during World War II.

Another major presence here is **Disney's Vero Beach Resort** (https://verobeach.disney.go.com), a sprawling, elegant complex with several restaurants, a lavish spa, and infectiously fun activities like a nightly singalong with s'mores.

Pelican Island National Wildlife Refuge (www.fws.gov/pelicanisland; daily 7.30am–sunset) is the oldest wildlife sanctuary in the US, established in 1905 by President Theodore Roosevelt to protect all manner of birds. Charter a boat for a close look, particularly if you are a knowledgeable birdwatcher, but obey signs warning you to "Stay off the island."

SEBASTIAN INLET

Thirteen miles (21km) north is **Sebastian** ⓫. **Sebastian Inlet State Park** (tel: 321-984-4852; www.floridastateparks.org/park/sebastian-inlet), on the ocean, is excellent for fishing and swimming. At the southern end of the park, the **McLarty Treasure**

Museum (daily 10am–4pm) is on the site of an old Spanish salvage camp. It deals mainly with the loss of a Spanish Plate Fleet during a hurricane in 1715. The displays include coins and jewelry. Archeologists believe an Indian mound nearby may contain the skeletal remains of some of Florida's first European settlers. Some claim that shipwreck survivors may have lived with the Ais tribe even before the founding of St Augustine in 1565.

Sebastian Inlet is unique on this side of the state because it offers decent surfing. Most non-wind enthusiasts hang out in the regions between Sebastian Inlet and Daytona Beach.

On Route 1, **Mel Fisher's Museum & Treasure Store** (1322 US Hwy 1; tel: 772-589-9875; www.melfisher.com; Oct–Aug Mon–Sat 10am–5pm, Sun noon–5pm), a northern franchise of a Key West staple, is a museum that exhibits the astounding finds that "The World's Greatest Treasure Hunter" and his crews salvaged from numerous sunken ships.

Aerial view of Jupiter and Hobe Sound.

LAKE OKEECHOBEE

Water-management schemes and agriculture have taken a heavy toll on lake, though restoration plans offer a glimmer of hope.

It was once a mythical lake, unknown to European settlers until 1837, when Colonel Zachary Taylor stumbled upon it during the Second Seminole War. People of the Mayaimi and Tequesta cultures, and later the Seminole, lived on its margins, paddling out on the lake to fish. At 730 sq miles (1,890 sq km), Lake Okeechobee (from the Seminole *oki chubi*, or "big water") is the largest lake in Florida. For 6,000 years it has been the canary in the coal mine for the ecological health of the Everglades.

The Kissimmee River fed the lake, flushing the central Florida prairie country through a broad, winding floodplain to the limestone basin that impounds the lake. During the wet season, the 20ft (3-meter) -deep lake self-regulated by spilling its banks, sending a sheet flow trickling into the sawgrass wetlands of the Everglades. During the dry season, the lake shrank, exposing littoral bulrush marshes that supported apple snails, the principal diet of birds called snail kites. Nature's polarities – large and small, fast and slow, wet and dry – were all embraced by the complex ecosystem. It was a marvel of natural engineering, unique in the world.

Starting with Howard Disston in 1881 and Governor Napoleon Broward in 1905, irrigation schemes designed to stoke new agricultural development began to drain the Everglades and tame Lake Okeechobee. Hurricanes in 1926 and 1928, which killed more than 2,500 people when a wall of water from Lake Okeechobee flooded towns, led to the creation of the 20ft (18-meter) -high Herbert Hoover Dike, part of the popular 1,400-mile (2,250km) Florida National Scenic Trail.

In 1948, Congress authorized the Central and South Florida Project, creating 1,800 miles (2,900km) of roads, canals, and levees designed to provide flood protection for urban and agricultural lands and preservation of fish and wildlife habitat. In 1971, the US Army Corps of Engineers channelized the Kissimmee River, opening up lands for ranching. On the south, sugar plantations pumped runoff into the lake to keep cane beds dry. Lake levels dropped to 12ft (4 meters).

ECOLOGICAL DISASTER

For the Everglades, it's been an ecological disaster. Fifty percent of the original wetlands are gone. Wading bird populations have been reduced by 90 percent. Fourteen animal species are listed as endangered. Lake Okeechobee has become a dumping ground, its bottom sediments overloaded with phosphates from agricultural runoff, arsenic, and pesticides that must be disposed of as hazardous waste. There has been an outcry on the tourist-dependent Gulf and Atlantic coasts as polluted freshwater releases into the Caloosahatchee and St Lucie estuaries have created red tides and disturbed the delicate ecosystem of oyster and crab hatcheries.

In 2016 $32 million a year was allotted to Everglades restoration as part of the Central Everglades Planning Project. The trimming of the state's once-grand plan to purchase land from US Sugar Corporation, the country's largest sugar producer, to restore the southward flow of water from the lake through the Everglades has renewed some alarm over the area's future. However, a Wildlife Refuge and Conservation Area, established in 2012 and since expanded, could help to preserve this unique habitat.

A sign on Lake Okeechobee.

A SpaceX Falcon 9 rocket lifts off from Cape Canaveral.

THE SPACE COAST

Kennedy Space Center, at the heart of NASA's launch pad to the heavens, tells the story of America's adventures in space.

The National Aeronautics and Space Administration (NASA) launch center is at the heart of the Space Coast, a 40-mile (65km) swath of land that stretches from its northern end in Titusville through Cocoa Beach and south to the Melbourne–Palm Bay area.

CENTER OF OPERATIONS

Cape Canaveral has long been the name of the peninsula that extends south from Merritt Island and east of the Banana River. (Its name was changed to Cape Kennedy after the president's 1963 assassination but was changed back to Canaveral in 1973.) It's the site of the Cape Canaveral Air Force Station, where the earliest experimental American military rockets were launched. **Kennedy Space Center ❶** (State Road 405, Merritt Island; tel: 855-433-4210; www.kennedyspacecenter.com; daily from 9am; center may be partially or completely closed on launch days), which includes the launch pads used for rocket launches, is on Merritt Island. It lies within the Merritt Island National Wildlife Refuge.

Although the space center is a government facility, the **Kennedy Space Center Visitor Complex** is operated by a private company without the benefit of taxpayer funds. The complex

sprawls across a landscaped campus, incorporating nearly a dozen buildings and several outdoor exhibits.

At first glance it appears small compared to the theme parks, but even with a full day you'll be hard pressed to fit everything in. In addition to the KSC Visitor Complex, a main component is the bus tour that takes you to assorted outlying sites. This alone takes at least an hour. A daily schedule that gives starting times for the various experiences and attractions is provided, along with a

Main Attractions

Kennedy Space Center
Astronaut Hall of Fame
Merritt Island National
 Wildlife Refuge
Black Point Wildlife Drive
Canaveral National
 Seashore
Cocoa Beach

Map on page 184

Photographers attend a rocket launch at Cape Canaveral.

Tip

The International Space Station travels around the Earth at 17,500mph (28,200kmh), which is 10 times faster than a speeding bullet.

map of the complex. Additional tours are available for a fee and best booked in advance as they often sell out (see the Tickets and Packages section of the website).

If you want an extra dose of education, rent a KSC SmartGuide for the day (charge). It provides maps, a customized audio tour, and fun facts in eight languages. If you're carrying a smartphone, you can also upgrade to the Space Visor, which provides virtual tours of restricted areas.

KENNEDY SPACE CENTER BUS TOURS

Tickets can be purchased or collected at the entrance. Visitors in possession of printed ticket can proceed to the turnstiles. Begin your visit by heading straight for the bus tours as the waits get longer and the sun hotter as the day grows older (last bus departs 2.5 hours before closing). The tour escorts, many of whom are retired NASA staff, give a running commentary, and point out the resident wildlife. Only about 10 percent of

the Kennedy Space Center's 140,000 acres (34,000 hectares) is used for the space program – the rest is a designated nature reserve. On the KSC bus tour, keep an eye out for alligators sunning beside the ponds. You may also see some of the reserve's 10,000 wild pigs. Drivers will point out enormous eagles' nests; some measure 7ft (2 meters) wide, weighing around 1,000lb (450kg), and have long-time residents.

The restricted areas you'll get to see change periodically, and more than one tour might be available per day, but all are fascinating. A frequent destination is the **Vehicle Assembly Building**, where rockets are put together. At 525ft (160 meters) tall, it is the largest single-story building in the world. Learn where NASA's Commercial Crew and Cargo partners such as SpaceX, Boeing, and United Launch Alliance (ULA) operate at this multi-user facility. You also might be shown the future mobile launcher of NASA's Space Launch System and the Launch Control Center.

The Rocket Garden.

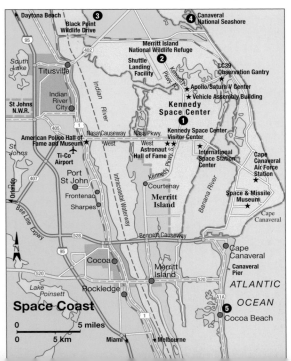

Space Coast

The **Apollo/Saturn V Center** allows you to walk around and under a fully restored Saturn V moon rocket, and watch a fascinating multimedia recreation of the first Saturn V manned mission launch.

KENNEDY SPACE CENTER VISITOR COMPLEX

Use the rest of your visit to explore the KSC Visitor Complex, organized into Mission Zones where attractions and tours are grouped by chronological era. To the left of the entrance is **Heroes & Legends**, featuring the US Astronaut Hall of Fame. The three-part exhibit about the early space pioneers uses cutting-edge technology to delve into astronauts' experiences. Nearby is the **Rocket Garden**, an impressive array of historic rockets from early space missions. Try and catch one of the enlightening 15-minute guided tours.

At **Journey to Mars: Explorers Wanted**, a guide with multimedia components, enlightens visitors about past and current Mars-related events. The IMAX 3-D Space Films are interesting, too, if you have time, as is Eyes on the Universe: NASA's Space Telescopes 3-D.

But make the Shuttle: A Ship Like No Other a priority. This super-interactive exhibit, in the far right of the complex, has 60 hands-on exhibits. You'll get to see the actual Atlantis shuttle, take an 8.5-minute ride that feels as if you're aboard, and then learn more through a choice of short entertaining films by astronauts.

If you want to view a rocket launch, packages are available from Kennedy Space Center – check the website for further details (www.kennedyspace-center.com). The KSC Visitor Complex offers the closest public viewing of rocket launches, with four possible viewing areas to choose from. Alternatively, you can view the launch from along US Highway 1 North, near Titusville, where you can see the launch pad across the Indian River.

BACK TO NATURE

In contrast to all this high-tech adventure are two nearby nature preserves. At the 140,000-acre (57,000-hectare)

There are lots of interactive exhibits at the Kennedy Space Center.

A Hubble photo of the Carina Nebula.

⦿ TURTLE WALKS

It's one of the most riveting beachside spectacles served up by nature: a 600lb (270kg) loggerhead sea turtle trudges ashore in the moonlight and, in a grueling act of devotion that lasts up to two hours, digs a sandy nest in which she lays as many as 100 eggs. Rear flippers working counterpoint to cover up her handiwork, then carving out a shallow, false nest to trick yolk-hungry predators, the turtle finally crawls back to the ocean. To see this, there's no better place than Canaveral National Seashore. After locating a female that has already begun laying and is not likely to be spooked, rangers escort small groups to witness the ritual. Tours start around 8pm and last until midnight. Reservations can be made in May or June by calling 386-428-3384, ext. 18.

Audiovisual displays, interactive exhibits, and numerous artifacts chronicle the development of the US space program.

Replica of the Hubble Space Telescope.

Merritt Island National Wildlife Refuge ② (PO Box 6504, Titusville; tel: 321-861-0667; www.fws.gov/merritt island; daily dawn–dusk, closed several days before launches), adjacent to Kennedy Space Center, endangered West Indian manatees loll peacefully in brackish lagoons, sea turtles waddle ashore to lay eggs on pristine beaches, and alligators bask in the sun on creek banks. The refuge lies along a migratory flyway, and the sky is filled in early spring with warblers and shorebirds while, on the ground, egrets and herons are in breeding plumage, wood storks and ospreys build nests, and bald eaglets test their wings.

The mild climate and varied environment of marshes, hardwood hammocks, pine forest, scrub, and coastal dunes sustain more than 500 species of wildlife, including more than 20 on the Endangered or Threatened Species List. This is one of the most important nesting areas in the country for loggerhead, green, and leatherback turtles. Much of the wildlife can

be spotted along the 7-mile (11km), one-way **Black Point Wildlife Drive ③**, a self-guided driving tour through salt- and freshwater marshes. The entrance is on SR 406, a mile east of the intersection with SR 402. Manatees, most prevalent in the spring and fall, can best be viewed from the observation area near Haulover Canal Bridge on SR 3.

The best time to visit the refuge is during the off-season, when wildlife populations are at their highest and mosquitoes, high temperatures, and thunderstorms are least likely to present a problem. The Visitor Information Center, 5 miles (8km) east of US 1 in Titusville on SR 402, has wildlife displays, educational resources, fishing information, and trail maps.

Nearby **Pelican Island National Wildlife Refuge** is accessible via a boardwalk over the ocean which offers stunning views of the island (tel: 772-562-3909; www.fws.gov/pelicanisland; daily 7.30am–sunset). This bird rookery – the nation's first National Wildlife Refuge – was established in 1903.

BEAUTY AND THE BEACH

Adjacent to the wildlife refuge is the 57,000-acre (23,000-hectare) **Canaveral National Seashore** ❹ (212 S. Washington Ave, Titusville; tel: 386-428-3384; www.nps.gov/cana/index.htm; daily 6am–6pm; visitor center daily 9am–5pm), whose miles of barrier dunes and sea-swept beaches are a haven for beachcombers and nature-lovers. Two of the beaches, **Apollo** and **Playalinda**, at the northern and southern tips of the park, have restrooms, boardwalks and, from May 30 to September 1, lifeguards. In between, the landscape remains untouched. Portions of the seashore may be closed before shuttle launches or when parking lots are full.

A word of note: Canaveral is the destination of choice for Florida's nude sunbathers, who are constantly at odds with local authorities. The legal wrangle over whether Florida's laws against public nudity can be enforced on federal land has been going on for years. If you want to chuck your clothes, you'll have plenty of company. But there's no guarantee that a deputy sheriff won't slink out of a palmetto thicket and slap you with a citation.

Those who prefer beaches in a more developed setting will find **Cocoa Beach** ❺ to their liking – an old-time seaside town with chain motels, restaurants, and souvenir shops, as well as first-rate beaches. The town's landmark is the Westgate Cocoa Beach Pier (www.cocoabeachpier.com), which juts 800ft (245 meters) out above the ocean from Meade Avenue. The arcade atop its rustic wooden pylons is lined with restaurants, bars, shops, and a fishing deck, with lifeguards on duty.

The biggest attraction in Cocoa Beach is the **Ron Jon Surf Shop** (4151 N. Atlantic Ave, Cocoa Beach; tel: 321-799-8888; www.ronjonsurfshop.com; daily 24 hours), a neon-lit palace devoted to bikinis, boogie boards, surfboards, and scuba gear. Famous surfers occasionally drop in for autograph sessions; scuba-diving and surfing lessons are also available.

Endeavour is seen after the rotating service structure is rolled back in preparation for the shuttle's final launch.

Lightner Museum.

DAYTONA BEACH TO JACKSONVILLE

From America's premier auto race to its oldest continuously inhabited city, Florida's northeast coast encompasses high-speed thrills, big-city attractions, and miles of beautiful beaches.

In 1903 automakers Alexander Winton and Ransom E. Olds, the father of the Oldsmobile, raced along the sands just north of **Daytona Beach** ❶ in the first official time trial in motor-sports history. In the 30-odd years that followed, 15 land-speed records were set on Daytona's 23 miles (37km) of hard-packed quartz sand, culminating with a 1935 run by English racer Sir Malcolm Campbell that clocked in at a stunning 276.82mph (445.49kmh). The National Association of Stock Car Auto Racing (NASCAR) was founded here in 1947. In 1959 NASCAR president William "Big Bill" Henry Getty France, once a beach stock-car driver, opened the Daytona International Speedway (1 Daytona Blvd, Daytona Beach; tel: 800-748-7867; www. daytonainternationalspeedway.com).

MOTOR CITY

These days NASCAR fans converge on Daytona in early February for a marathon of racing that culminates in the annual **Daytona 500**. Motorcycles take over several weeks later during **Bike Week**, which – along with **Biketoberfest** in October – is one of the world's largest motorcycle events. But Daytona offers plenty to entertain racing enthusiasts any time of year. Thirty- and 90-minute tours are often on offer.

Come into the city from I-95 along International Speedway Boulevard and

the storied raceway looms large to the right. A $400-million overhaul, completed in 2016, transformed the raceway into a high-tech stadium whose features include 60 luxury suites with trackside views and Wi-fi access throughout. Nearby, the **Motorsports Hall of Fame** Ⓐ (1801 W. International Speedway Blvd; tel: 386-681-6842; www.mshf.com; hours vary) is stocked with fanfare for the racing-crazed, with sections dedicated to stock cars, sports cars, open-wheel, drag racing, powerboating, motorcycles, land speed records and aviation.

◎ Main Attractions
Daytona 500 Experience
Main Street Pier
Museum of Arts and Sciences
Bulow Plantation Ruins
  Historic State Park
St Augustine
Castillo de San Marcos
Flagler College
Lightner Museum
MOCA Jacksonville
Neptune Beach
Amelia Island

◉ Maps on pages
190, 192, 194

At the Colonial Quarter.

Daytona Beach has over 23 miles (37km) of white sandy beaches.

Originally powered by a kerosene lamp, the Ponce de León light could be seen 20 miles (32km) out to sea.

Those with a low NASCAR tolerance will probably be satiated with a walk around the extensive welcome center and gift shop, but for a significant extra fee diehard fans can take three laps around the track riding shotgun with a professional driver, or driving a race-car on their own, at the Richard Petty Driving Experience. If you haven't had enough, head over to the **Living Legends of Auto Racing Museum** Ⓑ (2400 S. Ridgewood Ave; tel: 386-763-4483; www.livinglegendsofautoracing.com; Mon–Sat 10am–5pm; free) for more racing memorabilia, vintage autos, and photos.

BEACH BASICS, USA

Separated from the mainland by the Halifax River and reached via a series of high bridges, Daytona Beach's famous beachfront is anchored by the iconic **Main Street Pier** Ⓒ. It is one of four wooden piers on the East Coast, and, at 1,000ft (305 meters), is the longest one. It offers fantastic panoramic views, especially from The Roof bar on top. Summer concerts play in the historic oceanfront Bandshell.

This is the heart of the region's 23 miles (37km) of Atlantic beachline, a bounty for surfing, boogie boarding, and paddle boarding. Parts are crammed with hot dog vendors and water-sports rentals. Cars are allowed on certain strips of the beach, accessible (for a $10 fee) from designated ramps. But go easy on the gas pedal – the 10mph (16kmh) speed limit is strictly enforced.

Daytona Beach is festival-happy, bringing in hordes for more than 60 events a year, celebrating everything from manatees to chowder, Harlem dance to Greek culture.

BEYOND THE BEACH

Daytona Beach wasn't always full of fast cars and rowdy families. Glimpses of quieter days can be found at the city's excellent **Museum of Arts and Sciences** Ⓓ (352 S. Nova Rd, State Route 5A; tel: 386-255-0285; www.moas.org; Mon–Sat 10am–5pm, Sun 11am–5pm). Inside, the Prehistory of Florida Gallery tracks the story of the state's development from prehistory to modernity. The star of the exhibit – and a big hit with kids

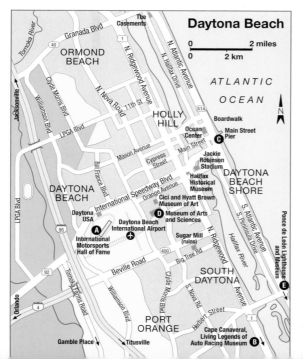

– is the 13ft (4-meter) -tall skeleton of a giant ground sloth. The largest and most complete ever discovered in North America, it was excavated in 1975 from a site known as the Daytona Bone Bed by a pair of amateur paleontologists. Allow at least half a day in order to see the Decorative Arts exhibit, the planetarium, and collections from Africa, Cuba, and elsewhere. Outside, an interpretive nature walk winds through the dense hardwood forest of pretty **Tuskawilla Preserve**.

On the same campus, the Cici and Hyatt Brown Museum of Art has more than 2,700 watercolor and oil paintings of Florida.

A few miles south of the Daytona Beach strip sits the meticulously restored **Ponce de León Lighthouse and Museum** Ⓔ (4931 S. Peninsula Dr; tel: 386-761-1821; www.ponceinlet.org; daily 10am–6pm, but closing times vary with seasons and events, see website for details). Completed in 1887, it is, at 175ft (53 meters), the tallest lighthouse in Florida, not to mention one of the best maintained in the country. The lighthouse keeper's residence and

other outbuildings are full of exhibits on Daytona Beach's maritime history and the development of lighthouse technology through the years.

ORMOND BEACH

As Route A1A North winds along the shore toward St Augustine it'll take you through the former "Millionaire's Colony" of **Ormond Beach** ❷, site of that legendary first time auto-racing trial in 1903. Originally home to Timucuan Indians, the area was colonized by the British in the 18th century. Settlers established vast indigo and rice plantations such as the 20,000-acre (8,000-hectare) Mount Oswald plantation, run by Scotsman Richard Oswald and now the site of **Tomoka State Park** ❸.

When Spain took control of Florida in the early 19th century, King Ferdinand offered land grants to planters living in the Bahamas. Ormond Beach is named for British sea captain James Ormond, who received a grant of 2,000 acres (800 hectares) to develop his plantation on the Halifax River. Other early settlers included Charles Bulow; the ruins

Stores on Main Street.

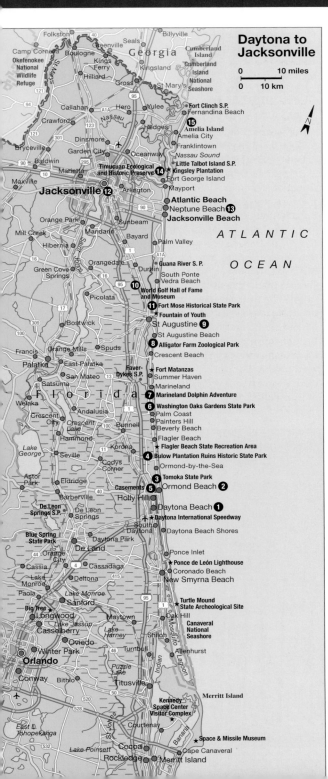

Daytona to Jacksonville

0   10 miles
0   10 km

of his vast plantation – destroyed in the Second Seminole Indian War – are preserved at **Bulow Plantation Ruins Historic State Park** ④ (3501 Old Kings Rd, Flagler Beach; tel: 386-517-2084; www.floridastateparks.org/park/bulow-plantation; Thu–Mon 9am–5pm) about 3 miles (5km) west of Flagler Beach.

Henry Flagler extended the Florida East Coast Railroad to Ormond Beach in the late 1800s, and by the turn of the last century the area was the summer playground for wealthy society folk with names like Astor and Vanderbilt, who stayed at the posh Ormond Hotel. Wealthy industrialists such as John D. Rockefeller made Florida their winter home. Rockefeller wintered for more than 20 years in Ormond Beach, where he was famous for his golf game and passing out dimes to his neighbors. When he died in 1937, at age 97, *The New York Times* noted that "his spare figure was a familiar sight" in the community. His home, the **Casements** ⑤, named for its many casement windows, is now a museum and cultural center (25 Riverside Dr; tel: 386-677-7005; www.thecasements.net; guided tours Mon–Fri and Sat am).

UP THE COAST ROAD

If you've got time en route to St Augustine, take a detour just north of Ormond Beach to drive the **Ormond Scenic Loop & Trail** (www.ormondscenicloopandtrail.com) – a scenic 30-mile (48km) stretch of road shaded by ancient live oaks and curtains of Spanish moss. Take Highbridge Road west from A1A, past tranquil salt marshes full of herons and egrets, to Walter Boardman Road, then head south on the Old Dixie Highway, which passes both Bulow Plantation Ruins State Park and **Bulow Creek State Park** – home of the towering, 400-year-old Fairchild Oak – before curving back toward Ormond Beach.

Back on the road to St Augustine, A1A passes through the quiet communities of **Flagler Beach**, **Painters Hill**, and **Palm**

Coast, home of **Washington Oaks Gardens State Park** 6 (6400 N. Oceanshore Blvd; tel: 386-446-6780; www.floridastateparks.org/park/washington-oaks; daily 8am–sunset), notable for its acres of formal gardens showcasing both indigenous and exotic flora.

Two miles (3km) north is **Marineland Dolphin Adventure** 7 (9600 Oceanshore Blvd; tel: 904-471-1111; www.marineland.net; daily 9am–4.30pm), the world's first oceanarium. Originally built as an underwater film studio, the facility, rebuilt and later sold, is now a place where kids and adults alike can interact and swim with 16 Atlantic bottlenose dolphins and learn about sea turtles, sand tiger sharks, and marine invertebrates.

For yet another close encounter with Florida wildlife, stop into the St Augustine at the **Alligator Farm Zoological Park** 8 (999 Anastasia Blvd; tel: 904-824-3337; www.alligatorfarm.com; daily 9am–5pm, until 6pm in summer). Opened in 1893, it houses every kind of crocodilian in the world. It also has a wading bird rookery that is open in spring and summer.

ST AUGUSTINE

Though Pensacola and Jacksonville can lay claim to European settlers before **St Augustine** 9 was established in 1565, both earlier colonies quickly fell victim to famine, plague, and war – making this pretty, historic city on Matanzas Bay the oldest continuously occupied settlement in the United States. First founded by the Spanish 42 years before the British staked a claim to Virginia's Jamestown, St Augustine endured thanks to a series of forts that helped the settlers defend against repeated attacks by Seminoles, pirates, and the British.

The last of these fortresses, **Castillo de San Marcos** F (1 S. Castillo Dr; tel: 904-829-6506; www.nps.gov/casa; daily 8.45am–5pm) still looms at the edge of the bay. Built of coquina, a limestone made from bits of cockle shell and sand that's indigenous to northern Florida, the Castillo withstood repeated bombardments thanks to the soft rock's unique ability to absorb cannon blasts. It was ceded to the British in 1763, returned to the Spanish in 1784, then turned over to the newly formed United States in 1821.

Castillo de San Marcos has stood guard over Matanzas Bay for more than three centuries.

Historic re-enactors prepare to fire a cannon from Castillo de San Marcos.

The Oldest Wooden School House is one of dozens of historic structures in St Augustine's colonial district.

A stained-glass panel in the Cathedral Basilica of St Augustine depicts scenes from the life of the city's patron saint.

It served as a Union prison (under the name Fort Marion) during the Civil War and was retired from active duty in 1900. Along with a reconstructed section of the defensive earthwork, the Castillo is now a national monument, at 245 years old the oldest masonry fortification in the United States.

St Augustine proudly celebrates its tempestuous history, noting that five flags have flown over the city: Spanish, British, Spanish again (under a new flag), Confederate, and US. Though there are many ways to explore the town – including trolley, horse-drawn carriage, and a plethora of ghost-themed excursions – a walk through downtown may give the best sense of the scope of its heritage.

THE OLD CITY

A short walk from the **Visitor Center G** at 10 S. Castillo Drive (www.citystaug. com; daily 8.30am–5.30pm) takes you past the crumbling Huguenot Cemetery to the gate of the colonial district, a pedestrian-friendly strip of historically significant buildings and exhibits interspersed with shops selling

everything from Spanish-inspired pottery to Thomas Kinkade paintings.

Just past the gate is the **Oldest Wooden Schoolhouse H** (14 St George St; tel: 888-653-7245; www.oldestwooden schoolhouse.com; daily), built in the early 18th century. Originally a bachelor's home, it was converted to a one-room school in 1788. Nearby is the **Colonial Quarter I** (33 St George St; tel: 904-825-2857; http://colonialquarter.com; daily 10am–5pm), a living-history museum where costumed guides lead visitors through the daily life of a typical 18th-century Spanish colonial village. Down this street, the reconstructed **Spanish Military Hospital Museum J** (3 Aviles St; tel: 904-342-7730; www.spanish militaryhospital.com; daily 10am–6pm) gives a glimpse of the grimmer side of colonial life.

At the south end of the district, the **Oldest House Museum Complex K** (14 St Francis St; tel: 904-824-2872; www.saintaugustinehistoricalsociety.org; daily 10am–5pm), operated by the St Augustine Historical Society, includes Florida's oldest surviving dwelling

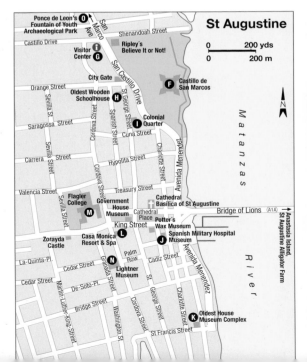

from the Spanish colonial period. The site has been occupied since the 1600s, but the current structure dates to the early 1700s. It combines British, Spanish, and American architectural influences, with thick coquina walls on the first floor and a second floor made of wood. Inside are antique furnishings and exhibits detailing the workings of a colonial household. The complex includes several other buildings full of exhibits on the cultural and military history of St Augustine and the state of Florida, plus a traditional garden, an 18th-century detached kitchen, and a museum shop.

HENRY FLAGLER'S HEYDAY

Head west up King Street to a trio of buildings built by railroad man Henry Flagler, a figure arguably as pivotal in Florida's development as the Spanish. All three were formerly luxury hotels, though only the crenellated **Casa Monica Resort & Spa** Ⓛ (95 Cordova St; tel: 904-827-1888; www.casamonica.com), built in 1888, still serves in that capacity.

The 400-room **Hotel Ponce de León**, a sparkling example of Spanish Renaissance architecture, is now the main residence hall for private **Flagler College** Ⓜ (Flagler's Legacy tours: 59 St George St; tel: 904-823-3378; http://legacy.flagler.edu; charge for tour), a four-year liberal arts school with a student body of about 2,500. Only part of the building is open to the public.

Across the street, what was once the Hotel Alcazar is now the **Lightner Museum** Ⓝ (75 King St; tel: 904-824-2874; www.lightnermuseum.org; daily 9am–5pm). Chicago publisher Otto Lightner bought the building in 1946 to house his impressive and eclectic collection of Gilded Age art and antiques, which includes everything from Tiffany glass and Art Nouveau furniture to mechanical musical instruments, needlework, buttons, and curiosities like a mummy and shrunken head. Be sure to check out the ceramic statuette of a newsboy in the stairs to the third-floor gallery: he's holding a copy of *Hobbies*, the magazine that made Lightner's fortune.

St George Street leads through the heart of the historic district in St Augustine.

Flagler College was formerly the Hotel Ponce de León.

Tiffany glass at the Lightner Museum.

Live oaks and Spanish moss form a canopy over a street near the Fountain of Youth.

HEADING NORTH

On the edge of town, San Marco Avenue, the road leading back to I-95, is lined with antique shops and trolley-tour outfits. A garish sign points the way to **Ponce de Leon's Fountain of Youth Archaeological Park** (11 Magnolia Ave; tel: 904-829-3168; www.fountain ofyouthflorida.com; daily 9am–5pm) a 15-acre (6-hectare) archeological park on the site of the Timucuan village where Ponce de León first claimed Florida for the Spanish Crown. It's free to drink from the titular natural spring.

There's not a lot on the interstate between St Augustine and Jacksonville save for outlet malls, with the exception of **World Golf Village**, with two championship golf courses and the **World Golf Hall of Fame** ⑩ (1 World Golf Pl, St Augustine; tel: 904-940-4133; www.worldgolfhalloffame.org; Mon–Sat 10am–6pm, Sun noon–6pm). Also in the complex are an IMAX theater, a PGA Tour Golf Academy, and a hotel.

Back on Route A1A, about 2 miles (3km) north of the city lies the site of Gracia Real de Santa Theresa de Mose, better known as **Fort Mose** (pronounced *mo-say*; www.fortmose.org), the first free community of former slaves in the United States. A century before the Emancipation Proclamation, enslaved African-Americans fleeing South Carolina plantations journeyed to this sanctuary where, if they pledged allegiance to the Spanish king and converted to Catholicism, they were guaranteed freedom. The fort had its own militia and served as the northernmost defense of St Augustine during the Revolutionary War. It was abandoned in 1763 and is now contained within **Fort Mose Historic State Park** ⑪ (15 Fort Mose Trail; tel: 904-823-2232; www.floridastateparks. org/park/fort-mose; daily 9am–5pm).

JACKSONVILLE

Sprawling across the St Johns River, **Jacksonville** ⑫ is an odd hybrid. It's not a mammoth tourist draw compared to its Florida kin nor is it a center of industry, but then again it is home to more Fortune 500 headquarters than any other urban center in the state. It is, however, Florida's most populous city and, thanks to its

consolidated city-county government, the largest city in terms of sheer land-mass in the United States. Founded in 1791 as Cowford – after the shallow, narrow part of the St Johns River across which farmers led cattle – it was later renamed for Old Hickory himself, Andrew Jackson, then governor of the Florida territory.

An important port for both Union and Confederate forces during the Civil War, the little city emerged relatively unscathed from that conflict, only to be essentially destroyed on May 3, 1901. The Great Fire of that year started in a mattress factory and razed more than 2,000 buildings over 146 city blocks, as devastating in scope as the Great Chicago Fire 30 years earlier. Legend has it that the glow from the inferno could be seen from as far away as Savannah, Georgia. Still, the city rebuilt quickly, as architects and designers flocked to town to make their mark.

Ten years later it was a major naval and shipping hub, while the extension of rail lines to the area made it, like St Augustine and Ormond Beach, a popular resort destination for moneyed Northerners. Drawn by the mild climate, the nascent movie industry moved in as well; by 1916 Jacksonville had more than 30 studios, making it the winter film capital of the world. It was also, perhaps most notably, a vital player in the development of an African-American film industry, thanks to directors like Richard Norman, whose Jacksonville-based Norman Studios produced a series of feature films depicting black characters as heroes and romantic leads at a time when parts for black actors were limited.

A Colonial cannon is on display at the Fountain of Youth.

Like many American cities, Jacksonville suffered in the latter part of the 20th century as sprawl decentralized the civic core and investment moved out of town. But today traffic over Jacksonville's magnificent bridges testifies to its continued vitality. The port remains a busy shipping center; a few miles north, at the mouth of the St Johns, massive aircraft carriers and other vessels dock at the **Mayport Naval Station**, outside the fishing village of Mayport. Thanks to some aggressive urban planning, parts of a once-distressed downtown have been

World Golf Village.

CUMBERLAND ISLAND

Just over the border in Georgia is an island frozen in time, where nature plays a dominant role and wild horses roam the beach.

Georgia's largest and southernmost barrier island, Cumberland Island captures the diversity of the coastal ecosystem in one package. Sand dunes and an uninterrupted stretch of beach line the eastern shore, where loggerhead turtles creep ashore to lay their eggs. Inland are quiet hardwood forests of oak and pine and freshwater ponds hospitable to gators; to the west, tidal marshes, harbor fiddler crabs and myriad birds. It's a peculiarly magical place, thanks to one simple fact: though humans have inhabited the island through the years, there have never been so many as to significantly alter or endanger the natural environment.

For centuries the island was a seasonal fishing destination for Timucuan Indians. Later, Spanish and then British settlers established military outposts. In the 18th century, Revolutionary War hero General Nathanael Green bought land on the island, and in time his widow and heirs built a mansion and named the estate Dungeness. By the mid-19th century, the island supported 15 plantations and small farms – and about 500 slaves.

Union troops held the island during the American Civil War, but after emancipation, times were tough. Farms failed and plantations shut down. Up on the north end of the island, a small settlement was the locus of a community of former slaves. The tiny, rustic First African Baptist Church – best known as the site of the 1996 wedding of John F. Kennedy, Jr, and Carolyn Bessette – still stands today.

Then, in the late 19th century, industrialist Thomas Carnegie, brother of Andrew, bought two defunct plantations, including Dungeness, and built an even grander home on the foundation of the old mansion. Thomas died in 1886, but his wife, Lucy, and their nine children remained on the vast estate, eventually building several additional houses on the island for the Carnegie daughters. With Vanderbilts and Duponts as their guests, they entertained in high Gilded Age style.

When Lucy Carnegie died in 1916, her will dictated that her horses be turned loose. Today about 200 wild horses, descendants of the Carnegie herd, roam the island freely. Visitors probably won't get close enough to see them, but they're often visible by boat as they amble down a deserted beach.

In the 1970s, a Hilton Head developer endeavored to turn land bought from the Carnegie heirs into a resort, complete with marina and golf course. Happily, those plans were abandoned, and most of Cumberland Island is now preserved in perpetuity as a National Seashore, though private citizens still have rights to some tracts of land, which are held in trust by the Park Service.

Island visitors are limited to 300 a day via a $20-per-person twice-daily ferry from the village of St Mary's, about an hour's drive from Jacksonville, with an extra daily departure from the island between March and October. Cars are forbidden to all but Park Service personnel and permanent residents. The exclusive Greyfield Inn is the only lodging on the island that doesn't require a tent. A day trip allows for about four hours of sightseeing – enough time to tour the otherworldly ruins of the Dungeness estate and walk a loop through the salt marshes and up the hard-packed beach of the Atlantic shore before ducking back through the mossy forest to the western shore and the ferry dock (island entry fee $4).

A wild horse grazes at Dungeness.

successfully refashioned as a tourist-friendly entertainment zone.

THE REBIRTH OF DOWNTOWN

The heart of rejuvenated Jacksonville is at 128 Forsyth Street, where you'll find the lavish **Florida Theatre**. Designed in high Moorish style to resemble a starlit courtyard, it opened in 1927 as a luxury vaudeville and movie palace and is, perhaps most famously, the site of Elvis Presley's first-ever concert appearance. Extensively rehabbed in the 1980s, it's now a cornerstone of the downtown arts renaissance; see www.floridatheatre.com for programming.

Also downtown are the **Museum of Science and History** (1025 Museum Circle; tel: 904-396-7062; www.themosh. org; Mon–Thu 10am–5pm, Fri until 8pm, Sat until 6pm, Sun noon–5pm), full of exhibits on Jacksonville's history and ecology, and the **Museum of Contemporary Art Jacksonville** (333 N. Laura St; tel: 904-366-6911; http:// mocajacksonville.unf.edu; Tue–Sat 11am–5pm, Thu until 9pm, Sun noon–5pm). Originally founded in 1924, "MOCA Jax"

moved to the Western Union Telegraph Building in 2003. Both the permanent collection and the changing exhibition galleries showcase a broad spectrum of work by contemporary artists.

The free "First Wednesday" art walk (http://jacksonvilleartwalk.com; first Wed of the month 5–9pm) is another popular way to take the measure of the city's art scene. The self-guided gallery hop encompasses a range of venues in more than 15 downtown blocks and includes local artists, brick-and-mortar businesses, and an arts marketplace. You can pick up a map of the 60-plus participating venues at The Jacksonville Landing or MOCA, or download it from the website.

The **LaVilla Museum** located in the Ritz Theater (829 N David St; tel: 904-807-2010; http://jaxevents.com/venues/ritz-theatre-and-museum) depicts the rich history of Jacksonville's African-American Heritage. Those with a sweet tooth will want to stop at **Sweet Pete's** (400 N Hogan St; tel: 904-376-7161; www.sweetpetescandy.com) near Hemming Park for housemade sea-salted

Andrew Jackson was the first US governor of Florida and Jacksonville's namesake.

Jacksonville Landing on the St Johns River.

A marble archer takes aim in the gardens of the Cummer Museum of Art.

The Cummer Museum of Art and its riverside gardens.

caramel, personalized chocolate bars, and candy apples.

A few other attractions lie north of downtown. The **Jacksonville Zoo and Gardens** (370 Zoo Pkwy; tel: 904-757-4463; www.jacksonvillezoo.org; daily 9am–6pm) has 2,000 animals, among them jaguars and anacondas that roam around faux Mayan temples. Tigers have their own land. More than 1,000 species of plants are on display. Nearby, the **Anheuser-Busch Brewery** (111 Busch Dr; tel: 904-696-8373, www.budweiser tours.com; Sept–May Thu–Tue 10am–4pm, June–Aug daily 10am–5pm) offers free tours – and complimentary samples – to those interested in learning where their Budweiser comes from. Those seeking a craft-beer scene will enjoy the Jax Ale Trail, featuring five microbreweries that have a joint "passport" and events.

INTO THE NEIGHBORHOODS

Across Main Street Bridge is the chic neighborhood of **San Marco**, whose business district was designed in the 1920s to mimic Venice's Piazza San Marco. At 1996 San Marco Boulevard,

the Art Deco **San Marco Theatre** (www.sanmarcotheatre.com) anchors an upscale commercial strip of boutiques, wine bars, cafés, and art galleries. Showing first-run movies and serving food and beer, it's a popular destination for young professionals and families.

Just southwest of downtown are genteel **Avondale** and **Riverside**, full of vintage 19th-century homes and soaring oaks and magnolias. One neighborhood landmark is the **Cummer Museum of Art & Gardens** (829 Riverside Ave; tel: 904-356-6857; www.cummermuseum. org; Tue 10am–9pm, Wed–Sat 10am–4pm, Sun noon–4pm; free Tue 4–9pm). Inside, 13 galleries showcase traveling and permanent exhibits covering an 8,000-year span of art history. Behind the museum, beautiful formal gardens – one Italian, one English – slope down to the St Johns River. The American Garden is called the Omsted Garden in tribute to its renowned designer, Frederick Omsted, who also masterminded New York City's Central Park.

Tourists seeking more pop thrills may want to make a pilgrimage to

⊘ AMERICAN BEACH

In 1935, at the height of Jim Crow, African-Americans were forbidden to use Florida's beaches. So it was a monumental day when businessman Abraham Lincoln Lewis, president of the Afro-American Life Insurance Company, bought 200 acres (80 acres) of Amelia Island and founded American Beach, the country's first African-American resort. In its heyday, middle-class black northerners traveled over 1,000 miles (1,600km) through the segregated South to vacation on Amelia Island. Black families thronged to the beach on weekends, and jazz greats like Louis Armstrong and Cab Calloway drew packed crowds. Today only 120 acres (49 hectares) remain, but its historic significance has been recognized. In 2002 American Beach was placed on the National Register of Historic Places.

Riverside's **Robert E. Lee High School**, whose strict former gym teacher, Leonard Skinner, unwittingly gave his name to Jacksonville's favorite sons, the rock band Lynyrd Skynyrd, thanks to his habit of suspending the band members for having long hair. After the grave of front man Ronnie Van Zant was vandalized in 2000, his remains were moved and interred in the family plot in Riverside Memorial Park Cemetery.

Riverside's historic **Five Points** district offers a cluster of hip restaurants and funky shops around the intersection of Park, Lomax, and Margaret streets. The center of young, artsy Jacksonville, Five Points is a great area for a leisurely afternoon of window-shopping. Check out the eclectic offerings in the 1928 **Park Arcade Building**, one of Jacksonville's earliest commercial structures and once home to Florida's first indoor-outdoor miniature golf course.

Built in the 1920s as an exclusive subdivision, adjacent Avondale is a bit more upscale. On the central strip of St Johns Avenue you'll find everything from Lilly Pulitzer boutiques to jazzy bistros.

Side streets offer blocks of beautifully restored Mediterranean Revival homes and an array of welcoming parks. Much of Riverside/Avondale was designated a historic district in 1997.

Jacksonville's southernmost neighborhood of **Mandarin** has a fascinating history all its own thanks in large part to the influence of Harriet Beecher Stowe, who wintered in the small farming community from 1867 through 1884. Following the success of *Uncle Tom's Cabin*, Stowe owed her publisher another book. Rather than write a second novel, she lovingly documented the landscape and culture of northern Florida in *Palmetto-Leaves*. The collection of sketches about fishing on the St Johns River and picnicking under live oaks laden with Spanish moss is considered some of the earliest (though unintentional) promotional writing about Florida and was instrumental in enticing tourists to the south. In 1872 Stowe helped found a racially integrated school in Mandarin; the building still stands today as home to the preservation-minded **Mandarin Community Club** at 12447 Mandarin

Fernandina Beach is a popular destination for charter fishing.

Amelia Island.

A friendly tavern in Fernandina Beach.

Powerboats and other pleasure craft berthed at a Fernandina Beach marina.

Road. Across the street a plaque marks the site of the former Stowe cottage.

BY THE SEA

The pretty shore communities of **Atlantic Beach** and **Neptune Beach** lie about 20 minutes due east of Jacksonville. While the white-sand beaches may not offer the hedonistic pleasures of Daytona Beach, the sand is softer, so no driving is allowed, and Jacksonville, lying north of Florida's tropical zone, actually has four seasons, so the water can be gray and choppy. – a boon if you want to try surfing.

Where Atlantic Avenue hits 1st Street and the beachfront, there's a strip of restaurants and shops. **Pete's Bar**, at 117 First Street, is a local landmark, popular for both the cheap beer and pool. Novelist John Grisham is a regular, and the watering hole features prominently in his novel *The Brethren*, set in and around Neptune Beach. A bit farther south, **Jacksonville Beach** offers a bikini-friendly strip of surf shops and bars popular with college students and others looking to party.

NORTH TO AMELIA ISLAND

Up A1A from Jacksonville's beaches are the resort communities of **Amelia Island** and **Fernandina Beach**. They're an easy day trip from downtown on the interstate or, if you're coming up the coast road, via the St Johns River Ferry (http://stjohnsriverferry.com) from Mayport to Fort George Island. The brief crossing costs $6 for cars and $1 for pedestrians, and boats run every 30 minutes.

A half mile from the ferry dock is the **Kingsley Plantation** (11676 Palmetto Ave; tel: 904-251-3537; www.nps.gov/timu; daily 9am–5pm) in the **Timucuan Ecological and Historic Preserve** , a 46,000-acre (18,600-hectare) expanse of woods and wetlands. Built in 1798, the plantation house is the oldest in the state. Merchant and planter Zephaniah Kingsley settled here in 1814 with his Senegalese wife, Anta Mdgingine Jia (or Anna, as she was known), whom he purchased as a slave in Cuba and consequently freed. Their vast estate produced cotton, indigo, and sugar cane and was home to 80 enslaved Africans

until 1837, when, faced with increasingly oppressive laws restricting the rights of persons of color, Kingsley moved his family and 50 freed slaves to Haiti. A self-guided tour of the restored grounds and buildings, which include both the large main house and the tiny slave quarters, offers a fascinating glimpse into an earlier way of life.

SEASIDE RESORTS

Just south of the Georgia border, A1A crosses the Intracoastal Waterway to beautiful **Amelia Island** ⑮ (www.amelia-island.com), 32 miles (51km) northeast of Jacksonville. Amelia is famed as a posh escape for the wealthy, who congregate at the exclusive **Omni Amelia Island Plantation Resort** and the lavish **Ritz-Carlton**. But the island has plenty to offer those outside the Forbes 500.

The quaint town of **Fernandina Beach**, on the island's northern tip, dates back to the 1850s. From the Victorian courthouse (now the post office) to the gracious frame homes bearing gingerbread balustrades, turrets, and gables, the town is a snapshot of another moment in time. In the late 19th century, Fernandina was a busy, affluent shipping port, and the state's first resort destination for the rich Yankees who later moved south to St Augustine, Ormond Beach, and beyond. A walking tour of the historic district's 40 blocks takes visitors past a fantastic array of Gothic, Queen Anne, and late Victorian architecture.

One building worth a particular look is the **Tabby House** at 27 S. Seventh Street. Made from a traditional cement mixture of crushed oyster shells called "tabby," the lacy, intricate Victorian home was designed by R.S. Schuyler and is now on the National Register of Historic Places.

The **Amelia Island Museum of History** (233 S. Third St; tel: 904-261-7378; www.ameliamuseum.org; Mon–Sat 10am–4pm, Sun 1–4pm), housed in the former Nassau County jail, offers a quick

and comprehensive overview of the area's evolution from Timucuan village to Spanish mission, Civil War port, and Victorian-era playground, and continues up to the modern day.

East of Fernandina Beach you'll find **Fort Clinch State Park** (2601 Atlantic Ave; tel: 904-277-7274; www.floridastateparks.org/park/fort-clinch; daily 8am–sunset). Construction of this fort at the mouth of the St Mary's River was begun in 1847 but was never completed. It served as a military post during the Civil War, the Spanish-American War, and World War I, and became one of the state's first parks in 1935.

Nowadays visitors can tour the remains of the barracks, preserved in their Civil War state, as well as hike, camp, and picnic on the dunes or along the freshwater ponds and salt marshes that provide a habitat for birds, turtles, alligators, and a multitude of other Florida wildlife. Across the sound you can see the heel of Georgia's Cumberland Island, a national seashore from top to toe.

Leave room for a sumptuous dessert at the Amelia Island Plantation Resort.

Segways are a fun and speedy way to explore Amelia Island.

Dudley Do-Right's Ripsaw Falls at Universal's Islands of Adventure.

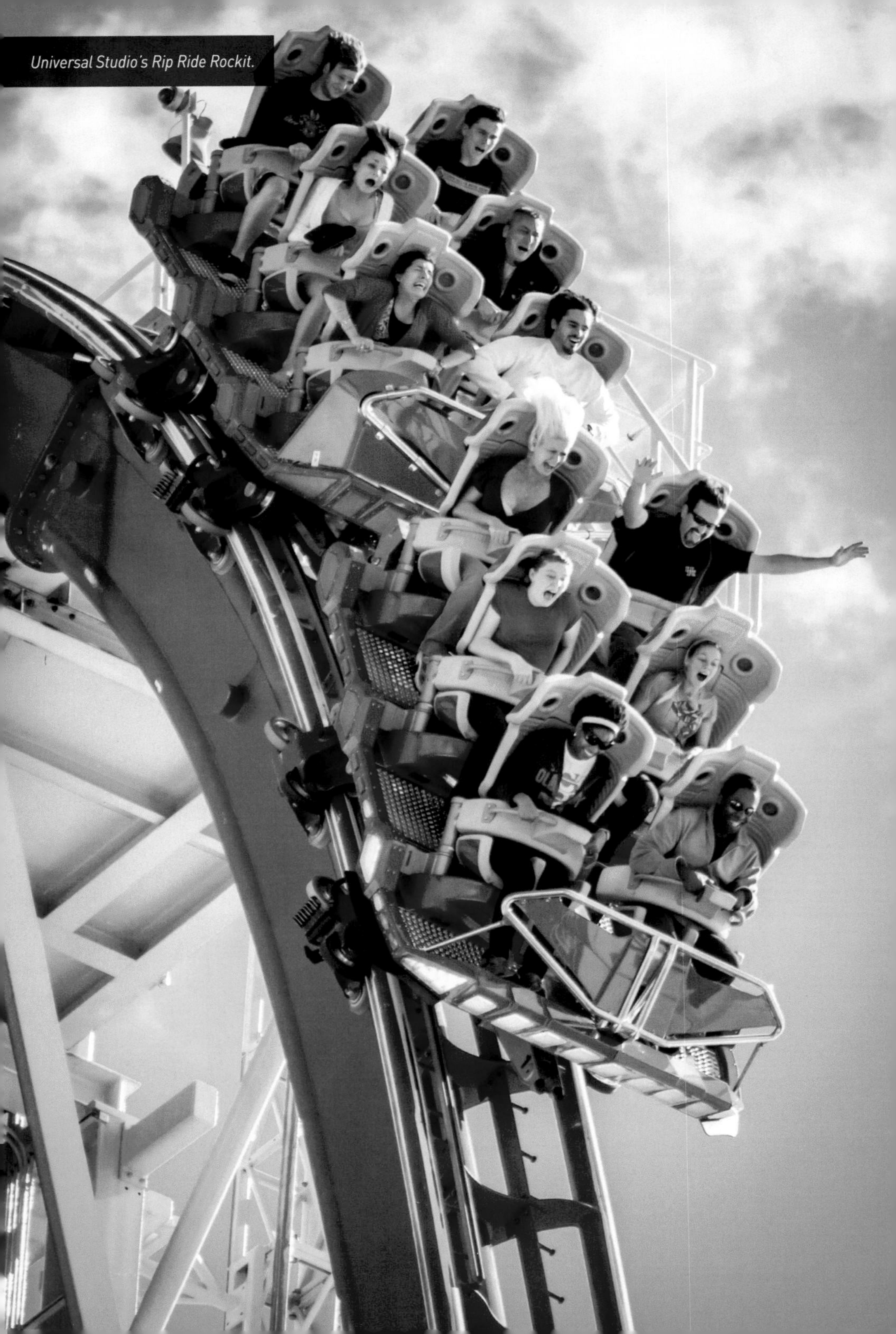

Universal Studio's Rip Ride Rockit.

CENTRAL FLORIDA

Theme parks are the order of the day, but there are also gardens, museums, and even a few nature preserves where you can escape the crowds.

Mennello Museum of American Folk Art.

The lake-studded, river-creased terrain of Central Florida has long lured tourists seeking an escape from reality. Initially they came to walk in gardens hung with Spanish moss and brimming with flowers, gaze at fish through crystalline spring water, and encounter birds, alligators, and other exotic wildlife. Then a famous mouse set up shop in the neighborhood. The resulting expansion of tourist attractions was unmatched in volume and variety and, despite the stunning white sands and aquamarine waters of the coast, visitors headed inland in droves. They flocked to Central Florida to experience self-contained pleasure domes that use technology to tease and tantalize the senses. Simple pleasures like fishing, swimming, and lazing in the sun have been elbowed aside by hi-tech engineers who can resurrect long-dead presidents and bring Harry Potter's world to life in stunning detail.

Inevitably, Walt Disney World Resort remains king of Central Florida's theme parks and thus merits a whole chapter to itself, beginning with a little background information and progressing through attraction-packed accounts of each of the Disney theme lands. The other major theme parks – Universal Orlando, SeaWorld Orlando, Legoland, and other more modest (though, in some cases, no less endearing) attractions – are covered in their own chapter.

MagicBands give fast access to attractions and hotel rooms at Walt Disney World.

Orlando is a thriving modern city with a huge number of hotels. Examples of Art Deco and Belle Epoque architecture survive among the high-rises and shopping centers, and suburban, well-off Winter Park is a pleasant place in which to touch base with reality. Art museums are one of Orlando's hidden secrets, too, as are impressive sports facilities for both playing and viewing, which just goes to show that Orlando can appeal to those interested in both high and low culture.

Big Thunder Mountain Railroad.

WALT DISNEY WORLD RESORT

Fantasy continues to thrive at this multifaceted, often magical, resort, just as Walt imagined. Disney World remains a magnet for millions of starry-eyed visitors, both young and old.

If you're under the impression that **Walt Disney World Resort** ❶ (www.disneyworld.com) is nothing but an overgrown amusement park, think again. Situated off Interstate 4 about 16 miles (26km) from downtown Orlando, Disney World is a city in its own right. Encompassed within its 47 sq miles (111 sq km) – an area twice the size of Manhattan – are four of the most elaborate theme parks ever constructed, as well as two water parks, an upmarket shopping, dining and entertainment district, four golf courses, two putt-putt options, two spas, an enormous sports complex, a wedding pavilion, a watersports center, 36 lodging facilities, and over 500 restaurants, cafés, and other eating and drinking options.

Disney World has its own police force, fire and sanitation departments, power plant, and water treatment facility, and an average daily population of more than 145,000 people – just counting theme park visitors, not those on site for spas, golf, or conferences, or the daily portion of 70,000 employees. It even has quasi-governmental status, thanks to a deal Walt Disney and brother Roy cut with the state of Florida creating the Reedy Creek Improvement District, a public corporation that gives the Disney company powers that are usually reserved to municipalities, such as issuing bonds, levying taxes, and establishing building codes. It can

even build an airport or a nuclear reactor, if the need arises.

The motivation behind Disney World's expansiveness is to provide an all-in-one vacation experience that induces visitors to stay longer and spend more. Indeed, many people find that one visit isn't nearly enough; they return year after year, with or without children, and never feel as if they've run out of things to do.

SURVIVAL STRATEGIES

For the uninitiated, visiting Disney World can be a bewildering experience; the

Main Attractions

Main Street, USA
Pirates of the Caribbean
Space Mountain
Mission: SPACE
World Showcase
Hollywood Studios
Kilimanjaro Safaris
Expedition Everest
Disney's Boardwalk
Typhoon Lagoon

Maps on pages 210, 212, 217

Mickey and friends at the Magic Kingdom.

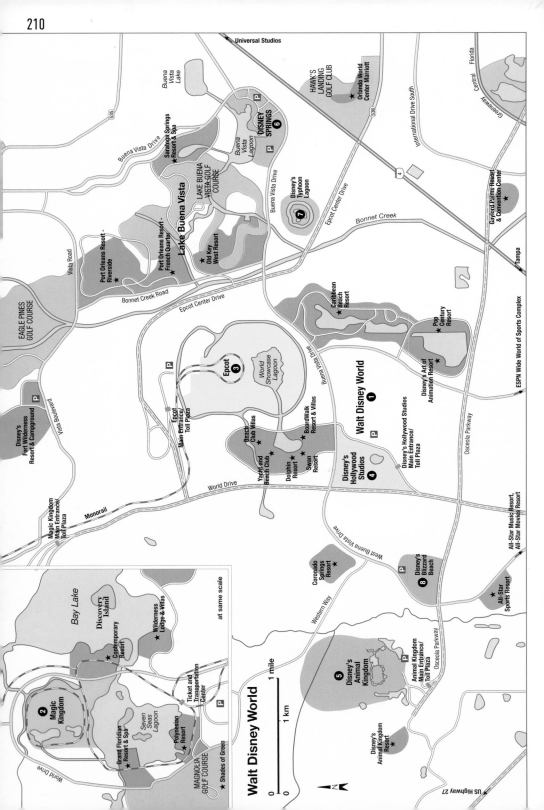

Walt Disney World

Walt Disney World ①
Magic Kingdom ②
Epcot ③
Disney's Hollywood Studios ④
Disney's Animal Kingdom ⑤
DISNEY SPRINGS ⑥
Disney's Typhoon Lagoon ⑦
Disney's Blizzard Beach ⑧

Universal Studios

Buena Vista Lake

HAWK'S LANDING GOLF CLUB
Orlando World Center Marriott

Saratoga Springs Resort & Spa
Buena Vista Drive
LAKE BUENA VISTA GOLF COURSE
Lake Buena Vista
Buena Vista Lagoon

Central Florida
Greenway

International Drive South

Port Orleans Resort - Riverside
Port Orleans Resort - French Quarter
Old Key West Resort

Buena Vista Drive
Disney's Typhoon Lagoon

Gaylord Palms Resort & Convention Center

Tampa

Vista Road
Bonnet Creek Road
Epcot Center Drive

EAGLE PINES GOLF COURSE

Epcot Center Drive
Bonnet Creek

Caribbean Beach Resort

Disney's Fort Wilderness Resort & Campground

Vista Boulevard

Epcot
World Showcase Lagoon

Epcot Main Entrance/ Toll Plaza

Buena Vista Drive

Pop Century Resort

Disney's Art of Animation Resort

ESPN Wide World of Sports Complex

Magic Kingdom Main Entrance/ Toll Plaza

Monorail

Beach Club Villas
Yacht and Beach Club
Dolphin Resort
Swan Resort
BoardWalk Resort & Villas

Walt Disney World ①

Disney's Hollywood Studios Main Entrance/ Toll Plaza

Disney's Hollywood Studios ④

World Drive

Osceola Parkway

All-Star Music Resort, All-Star Movies Resort

at same scale

Bay Lake
Discovery Island
Contemporary Resort
Wilderness Lodge & Villas

Magic Kingdom ②

Coronado Springs Resort

West Buena Vista Drive

Disney's Blizzard Beach ⑧

All-Star Sports Resort

Seven Seas Lagoon
Grand Floridian Resort & Spa
Polynesian Resort
Shades of Green

Ticket and Transportation Center

MAGNOLIA GOLF COURSE

World Drive

Western Way

Disney's Animal Kingdom ⑤

Animal Kingdom Main Entrance/ Toll Plaza

Osceola Parkway

Disney's Animal Kingdom

US Highway 27

1 mile
1 km
0

N

happiest place on Earth takes on a very different aspect when you're waiting in line, sweat trickling down your back, and your kids – exhausted from a day of overly ambitious touring – are whining like police sirens.

How do you prevent your dream vacation from degenerating into a nightmare? The first thing you need to know is that Disney World is not the kind of place that rewards spontaneity. Planning is essential, and reservations – for hotels, rental cars, and restaurants – are a must. Luckily, new technology allows you to secure your room, meals, and must-ride attraction spots months in advance via the My Disney Experience website and app.

Timing is equally important. The two biggest gripes tourists have about Disney World are the crowds and the prices. You can minimize both by traveling off-season, when the theme parks aren't quite so mobbed and hotels and airlines offer sizable discounts. Time of day is a consideration, too. In general, attendance at the theme parks peaks between the hours of 10am and 4pm.

The best strategy, therefore, is to arrive as early as possible, take a break in the afternoon for shopping and a sit-down meal (or, if you're staying at an on-site resort, sneak back to your hotel for a snooze and a swim), then pick up the trail in the late afternoon or evening.

As for getting around, a car is easiest but Disney provides alternatives. If you're staying in an official hotel, you can take a free Disney's Magical Express bus from the airport. Once on site, complimentary shuttles will transport you among hotels and attractions, and theme park parking will be free for you. For quicker transport, cleverly themed Minnie Vans will give you a $20 lift using the Lyft app on your smartphone. Anyone can hop on the monorail and boats connecting the Magic Kingdom hotels with that park, more boats along the Boardwalk run to and from Epcot and Disney's Hollywood Studios. Overhead trams will eventually let visitors move around via overhead gondolas on the Disney Skyliner which will connect Epcot and Disney's Hollywood Studios with at least four hotels.

⊘ Tip

FastPass allows guests to avoid long lines at some of Disney World's most popular attractions, and FastPass+ allows those staying in official resorts to reserve their time slots for a trio of rides per day three or even six months in advance. Tap your MagicBand on a reader, or insert your ticket in a FastPass machine, get a ride time, and return later with little or no waiting. The rules change periodically, so be aware that the FastPass system may only allow you to have one FastPass ticket at a time.

The Magic Kingdom's Splash Mountain.

⊘ BEHIND THE SCENES

If you're curious about those secret corridors under the Magic Kingdom, want to learn about the art and history of Disney animation, or yearn to swim with the fish in Epcot's Living Seas aquarium, sign up for one of the resort's Behind the Scenes tours, which grants you special access.

There are more than a dozen tours guided by enthusiastic cast members or experts. Among the most popular are the five-hour Keys to the Kingdom tour, limited to the Magic Kingdom; Backstage Magic, a day-long excursion through the Magic Kingdom, Disney-MGM Studios, and Epcot; Wild Africa Trek, which includes close-up animal spotting in the Animal Kingdom, plus thrills and an excellent meal; and Backstage Tales, which includes a visit to a wildlife housing area and veterinary hospital at Animal Kingdom. Most tours require participants to be at least 16 years old; however, Disney's Family Magic, a two-hour interactive exploration of the Magic Kingdom, is open to all ages.

Tours vary in price, frequency, and duration. Some require the purchase of separate park admission, and those lasting more than four hours can include lunch. All require an advance reservation. For information, visit www.disneyworld.com/events-tours or call 407-939-8687.

> **Tip**

Disney World Resort is very popular as a honeymoon destination, and you can get married here too – at the elegant Wedding Pavilion or elsewhere. No-frills ceremonies are available, but if you have the cash to spare, you can invite all your favorite Disney characters and have an elegant ceremony and reception.

Keep in mind that the gates at Disney World sometimes open 30 to 60 minutes earlier than the scheduled times via Extra Magic Hours (for guests who stay at Disney hotels). Granted, dragging yourself out of bed at 7am to get to the parks by 8am is hardly appealing, but you can often do more in the first couple of hours, when lines are short, temperatures are milder, and you're feeling fresh, than in the remainder of the day.

Attitude is a key element, too. Resist the temptation to be too ambitious. The tendency among most visitors is to squeeze as much as possible into the shortest period of time. This seems like sound economics: you paid a bundle to get in and now you want your money's worth. But before committing yourself to an elaborate touring plan, consider the hazards of trying to do too much. Unrealistic expectations will lead only to disappointment and exhaustion. Don't try to do everything in one day; pick three or four attractions must-see each day and fill in with other experiences if time allows. In addition, rushing from one attraction to another

Cinderella's Castle.

decreases your changes of discovering Disney's small pleasures – a butterfly garden, a character encounter, or a street performance, for example. Those surprises are filled with pixie dust.

MAGIC KINGDOM

The **Magic Kingdom ❷** (tel: 407-824-4321; www.disneyworld.com; daily, hours vary, see website for details) is Disney World's oldest park and the one closest to Walt's original vision of a "timeless land of enchantment." Over the years some attractions have changed or been updated. In fact, the Fantasyland portion has been vastly expanded in recent years. Still, this is, and always has been, a children's park. Painstaking detail, good humor, and whimsy with which Walt's vision is brought to life rarely disappoint even the most jaded traveler.

MAIN STREET

Setting the stage at the entrance to the park is **Main Street, USA**, a picture-perfect evocation of an American town. Although the corridor has no rides or shows, it enchants with more than a

Magic Kingdom

Seven Seas Lagoon

dozen shops and restaurants as well as a fleet of double-decker buses, horse-drawn trolleys, and old-fashioned fire trucks. The **City Hall** to the left has maps and information and can book meals. It also contains the park's Lost and Found office. At the top of Main Street, housed in a stately Victorian-style building near the entrance, is the **Walt Disney World Railroad**, which takes passengers on a 20-minute circuit around the park in vintage steam engines. To the right of the main entrance is the tucked-away **Town Square Theater**, which frequently has headliner Disney characters, most notably Mickey Mouse himself, available for photos and autographs.

Otherwise, Main Street is meant to be explored. In addition to the highly decorated souvenir shops there are such gems as the barber's shop with a barber-shop quartet and the **Main Street Watch-maker**, which sells timepieces featuring Disney characters. Main Street leads to a roundabout known as the Hub, beyond which is **Cinderella's Castle**, the visual anchor of the park and a Disney World icon second only to Mickey himself; the

Forecourt Stage is home uplifting musical productions such as **Mickey's Royal Friendship Faire**, an energetic and entertaining live show. Pathways radiate from this central plaza into five distinct zones, starting on the left (as you face Cinderella Castle) with **Adventureland**, a mélange of fantasy architecture and lush plantings meant to evoke exotic locales such as the South Seas and the Amazon. The attractions here are a mixed bag. **Pirates of the Caribbean** is the best of the lot – an audio-animatronic romp through the Spanish Main with rum-swilling buccaneers and lots of yo-ho-ho high spirits. This ride was updated to include Johnny Depp's character from the movie of the same name, which in a meta-twist was based on the original ride at Disneyland in California.

The other attractions in Adventure-land serve to entertain kids with time to spare. These include the **Magic Carpets of Aladdin**, a basic hub-and-spoke ride; the **Swiss Family Treehouse**, a free play area based on the Robinsons' fictional home; **The Enchanted Tiki Room**, a short show featuring animatronic birds

Main Street USA.

⏱ ON ARRIVAL

If you are not staying at a Disney Resort, allow plenty of time to, first, park your car and, second, to get from your car to the Magic Kingdom's entrance. Parking lot trams will drop you off at the Ticket and Transportation Center, where you can buy your ticket and then board a boat or the monorail to reach the main entrance. From here you must join the other people who have been directly deposited from their Disney Resort transportation. Other Disney parks operate similarly with trams delivering you from the parking lot, more or less, to the park's main entrance. Visitors staying with Disney enjoy an advantage as their transportation (monorail, bus, or boat) will bring them to the park's entrance from the front of their lodging. Resort guests can park at each theme park for free; for others, each car spot costs $20 per day.

(which provides a chance to cool off); and **Jungle Cruise**, a 10-minute boat ride featuring animatronic animals and a hokey narration. Check them out if lines are short; otherwise, stroll over to Frontierland, where the theme is the Old West and the rides are more interesting.

FRONTIER FANTASY

The two biggies at **Frontierland** are **Splash Mountain** and **Big Thunder Mountain Railroad**. The first is a log flume ride with a *Song of the South* theme and a drenching, five-story finale – enough to elicit screams without inducing real terror. The other is a roller-coaster in an elaborate red-rock setting. Scenes of ramshackle mining camps whiz by as your runaway train careens through canyons and caverns and over rickety bridges. Though this is hardly a kiddie ride, it's a piece of cake compared to the big coasters at other Orlando parks.

Opposite Big Thunder Mountain you can hitch a ride on one of the rafts that crosses the so-called Rivers of America (actually a circular lagoon) to **Tom Sawyer**

The Seven Dwarfs Mine Train.

Island, a refreshingly low-tech attraction where kids explore caves, trails, and a pioneer fort under their own steam.

Another big attraction in Frontierland is the **Country Bear Jamboree** – a 16-minute hillbilly revue starring a cast of animatronic bears. Though it's been a crowd-pleaser for nearly three decades, the cornball humor isn't everybody's cup of tea.

The Wild West melds into colonial America in **Liberty Square**. The most popular attraction here – and perhaps the best in the park – is the **Haunted Mansion**. Visitors board a "doom buggy" for a tour of the house, visiting a library full of "ghost writers," a haunted ballroom and, in a clever bit of "astral projection," an apparition that appears in your car. The holographic effects – cutting edge when the ride opened some 25 years ago – hold up pretty well. On the opposite side of Liberty Square, the **Hall of Presidents** is an animatronic show with a true-blue American theme. The high point is a roll call of all US presidents, followed by remarks by the current president and Abraham Lincoln.

If you're looking for a quick way to rest your feet, head over to the Liberty Square Riverboat, a vintage Victorian steamboat that tours the Rivers of America.

FOR THE YOUNGEST

Lined with fairytale castles, **Fantasyland** is intended for the preschool crowd. Kiddie rides such as **Dumbo the Flying Elephant** and **Cinderella's Golden Carousel** will be familiar to anyone who has been to a county fair, although Disney dresses them up beautifully. Dark rides like **Under the Sea – Journey of the Little Mermaid** recap Disney's most memorable films and songs.

Notable among the classic rides is the **Mad Tea Party** – what folks in the amusement-park biz call a "spin-and-barf" ride – which whirls you around in a teacup mounted on whirling discs. And then there's **It's a Small World**, the ride that Disney critics love to hate, featuring scores of animatronic dolls in folksy costumes singing a chirpy melody. Love it or hate it, you can't say you've experienced the Magic Kingdom without riding it at

least once. Across from here are two of Fantasyland's finest children's attractions. **Peter Pan's Flight** is a fantastic dark ride over the streets of London to Neverland. Your pirate ship flies past key scenes from the classic Disney film before touching down. **Mickey's PhilharMagic** plays on vintage films, incorporating countless songs and characters into a so-called 4-D movie aimed at young children. Meanwhile, **The Many Adventures of Winnie the Pooh** is a ride that is worth no one's time, as it feels in every way a poor imitation of the slow, child-friendly rides Disney normally does so well.

A rickety roller coaster similar to Big Thunder Mountain, the **Seven Dwarfs Mine Train** brings adventurous guests into the world of *Snow White and the Seven Dwarfs*. Riders in the mine cars pivot back and forth while also climbing up and zooming down amid a mine "where a million diamonds shine," in the end seeing the dwarfs' cottage with Snow White dancing inside. Ariel-lovestruck kids adore **Under the**

☉ Tip

The FastPasses for Space Mountain run out by midday, so get one early if you plan to ride it at all.

Dumbo the Flying Elephant.

☉ HOW TO CUT IN LINE

The biggest gripe people have about theme parks is the long lines. Both Disney and Universal have heard your grumbles and now offer programs that greatly reduce the amount of time you'll spend staring at the back of another person's head. The FastPass and FastPass+ systems allow you to collect a time slot for Disney's most popular attractions. As the day goes on, the time between ticket issue and your redemption window continues to grow. Some rides may run out of FastPass tickets before lunchtime. Magic Kingdom has also added boredom-killers to some lines. Children awaiting the Winnie the Pooh ride and the dual Dumbos can now play as they wait.

For the big thrill rides, Single Rider lines offer a wait nearly as short as the FastPass system, but your party will be split up.

Ice-cream stands and other food vendors are situated throughout the parks.

Fireworks light up the Magic Kingdom.

Sea – **Journey of The Little Mermaid**, a leisurely 5-minute tour through an underground cavern – you'll be in a pastel clamshell car – to watch Ariel and her nautical mates experience major moments of the movie's storyline to the soundtrack highlights.

Always a super-popular ride with an ultra-slow-moving line, **Dumbo the Flying Elephant** brings a duo of rides – both involving tethered airplane-like little elephants riding above Storybook Circus, one going clockwise, the other counter-clockwise. The Circus itself entertains those waiting for their turn with interactive gadgets under a "big top." Bring tots onto **The Barnstormer Featuring the Great Goofini**, a starter roller-coaster with smallish dips. **Princess Fairytale Hall** is the be-all-and-end-all character spot for the royalty-obsessed, and several princesses are always available for meet-and-greets in the regally appointed air-conditioned gathering space.

Unless you have a reservation for a meal at **Be Our Guest**, a spectacular French restaurant themed around the story *Beauty and the Beast*, stop in for a look-see at the magnificently adorned Beast's castle.

Wannabe knights and princesses (aged 3 to 12 years) can have their dreams come true at the **Bibbibidi Bobbidi Boutique**. Hair, make-up, nails, accessories, and maybe wardrobe (depending on the package you choose) will transform them into their favorite Disney hero or heroine.

TOMORROW'S WORLD

Wrap up your visit to the Magic Kingdom at **Tomorrowland**, a confection of chrome-and-neon architecture inspired by such disparate sources as H.G. Wells and Fritz Lang's *Metropolis*. **Space Mountain** is an indoor roller-coaster replete with whiz-bang visual effects, including scary stretches of inky darkness. The ride is bumpy enough to rattle your innards without the looping of the mega-coasters at other parks. A new Tron ride is being built next door. **Buzz Lightyear's Space Ranger Spin** is fun, too – a cross between a dark ride and a shooting

⊘ DISNEY'S HOMETOWN

Epcot was originally conceived by Walt Disney as an experiment in urban planning – an Experimental Prototype Community Of Tomorrow inhabited by real citizens. His father had helped build an exhibit at the 1893 World Columbian Exposition in Chicago, and Disney himself had been a long-time advocate of inner urban planning and city beautification projects. The plan was abandoned after Walt's death in favor of an unimaginative "world's fair," but the dream wasn't permanently forgotten. It was resurrected in 1994 in the form of Celebration, a town designed from the ground up by Disney "imagineers." Now with 7,500 residents (but no longer owned by Disney), the town has the manicured, spotless look of a theme park, featuring houses designed by some of the world's most notable architects. Despite Celebration's commercial success, the experiment hasn't all been smooth sailing. Some residents chafed at the restrictive bylaws, and the school's progressive agenda provoked the wrath of parents and county supervisors. So, is Disney's experiment in "new urbanism" a success? You can judge for yourself. Celebration is 5 miles (8km) south of Disney World near the intersection of US 192 and I-4. Special events include vintage car shows in March and September, a Sci-Fi Fourth of July, and events with bubble "snow" around the winter holidays. For information, call 407-566-1200 or visit www.celebration.fl.us.

arcade that lets you zap aliens with a laser gun while being whisked around an indoor track. Make **Monsters, Inc.** a priority. This laugh-out-loud funny 400-seat show features one-eyed Mike Wazowski as the MC of a comedy show that, using technology, involves audience interaction. Just hope you're not singled out to be "that guy."

At **Walt Disney's Carousel of Progress**, the audience sits in a rotating theater that chronicles the way technology has changed the lives of an animatronic family. Old folks seem to enjoy the show. Teens and young adults find it a snooze.

Hop aboard the **Astro Orbiter** and soar high above Tomorrowland. Afterward enjoy a relaxing ride on the **Tomorrowland Transit Authority PeopleMover**. This ten-minute eco-friendly tour guides you through Tomorrowland attractions including getting a look inside Space Mountain. **Stitch's Great Escape!** features the mischievous alien getting loose and treating the audience to some special sights, sounds, and smells.

PARADES, CONCERTS, AND FIREWORKS

No journey to the Magic Kingdom is complete without taking in one of the star-studded parades or shows, or seeing the night-time fireworks display. The **Festival of Fantasy Parade** (afternoons daily) is an uplifting extravaganza that brings the park to a standstill and is a big hit with young children who can't get enough of waving at famous characters. Without tots in tow, use this time to take advantage of short waiting times and take a couple of spins on Space Mountain. The **Happily Ever After** nighttime fireworks fest not only lights up the sky, but also involves laser projections on the castle – Quasimodo swinging from turrets, the *Toy Story* gang getting playful – as uplifting music (taped from a 75-piece orchestra) plays. To get the full effect you must have a clear view of the front of Cinderella's Castle. This makes the hub and the Plaza Restaurant very popular as showtime approaches. After the fireworks some nights, you can stay around for **Once Upon a Time**, recapping Disney stories with music and

Spaceship Earth looms over the entrance to Epcot.

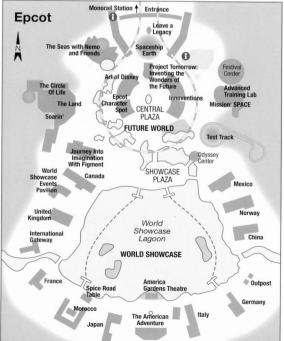

projections, and then the **Electrical Water Pageant**, a patriotic light show on the water. During the day, the **Move It! Shake It! Dance & Play It!** bop fest brings cheerfulness to a whole new level outside the castle.

EPCOT

Opened in 1982, Disney World's second theme park, **Epcot ❸** (daily, see www. disneyworld.com for details), is modeled loosely on a World's Fair. The park is laid out in two circular areas. The first, **Future World**, anchored by the monumental golf ball called **Spaceship Earth**, is devoted to science and technology. Its attractions are housed in pavilions that contain rides, shows, and exhibitions. Inside Spaceship Earth, for example, is a dark ride that transports passengers through a series of animatronic tableaux chronicling the history of communications from the Stone Age to the Space Age, with an interactive component.

To the left of Spaceship Earth (in the outer ring of World Showcase) is **Universe of Energy**. The main attraction here will soon be a Guardians of the Galaxy ride.

Another pavilion houses one of Epcot's most thrilling rides. Dubbed **Mission: SPACE**, it delivers an astronaut-like experience, simulating a rocket lift-off and the weightlessness of space. Disney hired NASA consultants to design the ride. It's so realistic that barf bags are available. A tamer version is available for those not wanting to experience the G-force of take-off. The newest component, the Green Mission, invites participants to tour Earth.

Next is **Test Track**, featuring six-person vehicles that undergo a series of tests – acceleration, road handling, suspension, crash – that simulate the course at a General Motors proving ground. From Test Track, it's a short walk to **Innoventions,** an exposition of new products.

On the opposite flank of Future World is a trio of pavilions, each worth a visit given enough time. **The Seas with Nemo & Friends** takes you down under in your ride vehicle – a clam mobile – and afterward you can join in **Turtle Talk with Crush**. The centerpiece is a saltwater

High-octane thrills at Test Track.

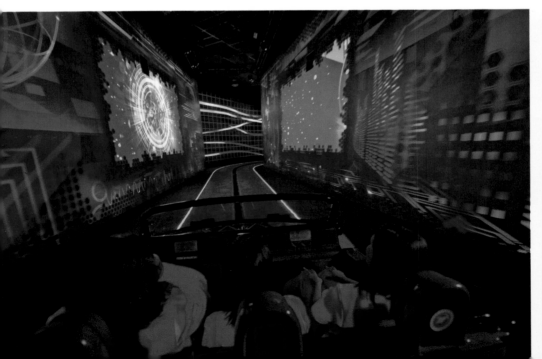

aquarium containing an artificial coral reef with tropical fish, sharks, sea turtles, and an occasional scuba diver. Dolphins and manatees have their own tanks, where visitors can get a close-up view.

LIFE AND LAND

The strongest environmental message – and probably the most popular ride – in the whole park is found inside **The Land** pavilion. The **Circle of Life** features characters from *The Lion King* who are persuaded by Simba to stop the needless destruction of their native habitat for a useless holiday resort (a paradoxical sentiment for Disney to endorse by anyone's standards). **Living with the Land** is a slow boat ride through different exhibits about agricultural production. You will see many of the crops grown here on the menu at the Garden Grill.

One unqualified success in The Land is **Soarin'**, a hang-gliding simulator that takes you over various sights of outstanding beauty of Earth. The show spans six continents and includes music and scents to honor create the feel of being in each place.

The big draw over at the **Imagination!** pavilion is a 3-D movie, **Captain EO**, which is a musical starring Michael Jackson and a cast of interstellar characters. The dark ride in this pavilion, called **Journey into Your Imagination with Figment**, is one of Epcot's misfires. Skip this pavilion on your first couple of visits.

WORLD SHOWCASE

Some children may consider World Showcase – a quick tour through 11 nations of the world – a bore, but most adults, at least those who like to shop, eat, or drink, will find it interesting. Each pavilion gives you the chance to experience a nation's consumables without actually visiting the country. As this half of Epcot usually stays open later than Future World, a couple could easily make a romantic, if early, night of it. In some ways it's better than Disney Springs, as the food is more ethnic and the atmosphere, especially at night, is less hectic.

Top of the romantic destination list would be **Mexico's** dimly lit **San Angel Inn Restaurante**, set under a re-created Mayan temple. The only ride in Mexico is

Moroccan-style dining at Spice Road Table.

⊘ Tip

A tip board at the corner of Hollywood and Sunset Boulevards lists the waiting times for all attractions at Hollywood Studios, although your My Disney Experience app has them too.

the **Gran Fiesta Tour Starring the Three Caballeros**, a mild dark ride featuring Donald Duck touring various Mexican landscapes. The main features of **Norway** are a re-created stave church and a Norwegian castle that houses the **Akershus Royal Banquet Hall**, hosting princess meals with quite good food all day long. The hit movie *Frozen* is featured in the **Frozen Ever After** attraction, with music from the movie and a chance to meet the characters. The fast food outlet has excellent quick meals.

China features one of the best shops in World Showcase, a well-decorated if culinarily simple restaurant in the **Nine Dragons**, and an enjoyable Circle-Vision (the screen wraps completely around the audience) film called **Reflections of China,** which is scheduled to be revved up a bit. Set in a re-created temple, it takes you from the Great Wall of China to Hong Kong and shows some of the most remarkable natural environments. There are no proper attractions at **Germany**, but with a year-round Oktoberfest atmosphere and several fine German beers on offer, no one ever

really seems to notice. The **Biergarten Restaurant** is the main attraction, but shops in half-timber houses also sell some fine Christmas ornaments and wooden toys for younger children. Designer labels, wines, and even ashtrays are for sale in the **Italy** pavilion, which is a collage of Venetian architecture that includes the Doge's Palace and the Campanile from St Mark's Square. Italian cuisine is served up in **Tutto Italia Ristorante** with excellent pizza at the neighboring Via Napoli.

PATRIOTIC FERVOR

Portraying one's own country in a theme park full of sweeping generalizations was always going to make interesting viewing for outsiders. No one will be surprised by the patriotic nature of the attractions, but the **Spirit of America Fife and Drum Corps**, the **Voices of Liberty**, and even the **American Adventure** film do their best to explain this patriotism to foreign guests. The film, which features an animatronic Ben Franklin and Mark Twain among others, does its best to provide a balanced

Sunset Boulevard.

view of American history by including the destruction of Native American cultures and the horrors of slavery. By the end, though, emotive patriotism replaces historical accuracy. Even more disappointing is that with America's rich culinary scope, from Cajun cornbread to New England clam chowder, Disney chose for the **Liberty Inn** to serve burgers and fries – although its barbecue pork sandwich does have a cult-like following.

Many people come to the **Japan** pavilion just to shop. There is a huge selection of smartly designed sushi plates and knives, silk garments, eccentric toys, and other delicate trinkets. Though the quick-service restaurants here serve fine sushi, the sushi and teppanyaki restaurants are a nice escape from the bustle outside. The **Morocco** pavilion has some of the finest faux architecture in World Showcase. You can even have a go at getting lost in the warren of shops selling Middle Eastern art and dress, including fine rugs and bronzework. The country's cuisine is summed up at **Restaurant Marrakesh**, which has a belly dancer, but foodies prefer the more creative Spice Road Table, with small plates and good wines, and even the counter-service Tangierine Café, with excellent Mediterranean platters.

It should be no surprise that you get two fine restaurants, **Les Chefs de France** and **Monsieur Paul**, and an accomplished patisserie in the France pavilion. Monsieur Paul is truly a special-occasion destination, so make reservations if you have the budget. There is also a fine wine shop and a delightful market selling soaps, cosmetics, and dinnerware. **Impressions de France** is a panoramic film shown throughout the day that takes you on a sweeping journey over the French countryside. An attraction featuring the clever mouse from *Ratatouille* is under development. Get your gourmandizing done before you leave France – fish and chips are the main grab-and-go fare in the **United Kingdom** pavilion. This little Britain has everything from Blighty, including a Beatles cover band at the **Rose and Crown Pub**, which serves excellent takes on traditional pub foods.

America's neighbor gets a more rugged display with mountainous terrain and the Circle-Vision Film, **O Canada!** The signature restaurant **Le Cellier Steakhouse** serves meals hearty enough for any lumberjack.

DISNEY'S HOLLYWOOD STUDIOS

Dedicated to the "Hollywood that never was and always will be," **Hollywood Studios** ❹ (daily, see www.disneyworld.com for details) is a park in transition. Originally an unabashed attempt to compete with Universal Studios Orlando, the park has some of Disney's best rides. Two new areas that promise to be wow-worthy are under construction – one a tribute to Star Wars, tentatively called **Star Wars: Galaxy's Edge**, the other an expansion of an already-popular tribute to the *Toy Story* franchise. For now, with many older rides gone, the park is one of the complex's weaker ones.

⊘ ESPN WIDE WORLD OF SPORTS COMPLEX

This vast complex on Victory Way near Hollywood Studios, just west of I-4, features a 7,500-seat baseball stadium, a 5,500-seat basketball fieldhouse, an indoor 8,000-seat multi-sport cheer and dance venue, 10 tennis courts, and facilities for about 30 other sports.

The complex hosts scores of amateur and professional events including the Atlanta Braves' spring training. The multi-sports venue features baseball, football, training programs for high school and college baseball, lacrosse, soccer, softball, and volleyball, as well as tournaments ranging from Little League baseball and inline hockey for kids to the US Men's World Cup Soccer Team. For a list of upcoming events, call 407-939-2040 or visit www.espnwwos.com/events. Admission is charged for premium events such as Invictus and Pro Bowl Week games.

For water sport fans, the Walt Disney World Resort has a web of waterways connecting its many lakes, large and small, and almost all the Disney resorts are on a lake or canal, with their own landing places or marinas. Dozens of different types of pleasure craft can be rented, even if you're not an experienced boat handler. Sailing conditions are best at two big lakes – Seven Seas Lagoon and Bay Lake at the Magic Kingdom Resorts. Sammy Duvall's Watersports Centre at the Contemporary resort offers water skiing, wakeboarding, tubing, and parasailing.

Epcot's Frozen Ever After transports visitors by boat to the Kingdom of Arendelle, where Olaf and friends perform songs from the hit movie.

The Tree of Life, situated at the heart of Disney's Animal Kingdom.

Upon entering the park, visitors are immediately transported back to the golden age of Hollywood. Lining either side of **Hollywood Boulevard** – the park's main staging area – are replicas of iconic Tinseltown buildings, most housing shops stocked with Disney merchandise. This is also the first place you'll encounter costumed characters, including actors playing stock Hollywood types (a struggling actress, an imperious director, and so forth) who do street skits.

Straight ahead, beyond the Center Stage, in a replica of Graumann's Chinese Theater, **The Great Movie Ride** sat majestically for years. Now the site will be turned into a lively attraction called **Mickey and Minnie's Runaway Railway**. The high-tech ride, with physical twists and turns, will seem like cartoon shorts during which riders enter the supersharp movie screen. The adventure will be 2.5-D, meaning super-clear without the need for 3-D glasses.

Hollywood iconography continues on **Sunset Boulevard**, which veers off to the right of the plaza. About halfway down, in a roofed amphitheater modeled after the Hollywood Bowl, is **Beauty and the Beast Live on Stage**. This condensed version of the Disney film is a big hit with children. It lacks the air conditioning of other live shows, but often fills up prior to showtimes.

THE BIG SHOW

A few steps away is the entrance to a second open-air venue, the Hollywood Hills Amphitheater. This is the site of **Fantasmic!**, Hollywood Studios' big finale, which plays nightly just before closing. The special-effects crew pulls out all the stops, dazzling the audience with lasers, fountains, and fireballs in a show that pits Mickey Mouse against Disney's nastiest villains.

The structure hulking over the end of Sunset Boulevard is the **Twilight Zone Tower of Terror**, housed in what appears to be an abandoned hotel. Inside, you're ushered into an elevator that hurtles through space – up, down, up, down – with a few pauses for creepy, heart-stopping views. This is decidedly not an experience for those with shaky stomachs or a fear of heights.

The excitement continues over at the **Rock 'n' Roller Coaster Starring Aerosmith**, an indoor coaster with enough twists to satisfy hard-core thrill-seekers. The launch is especially riveting, achieving a speed of 60mph (97kmh) in less than 3 seconds. A word of warning: This is not a ride for lightweights. If you thought Space Mountain was a challenge, this one will knock you for a loop.

AROUND ECHO LAKE

Return to the center plaza and explore the area to left around Echo Lake. The big draw here is the **Indiana Jones Epic Stunt Spectacular!**, starring stuntmen who re-enact scenes from *Raiders of the Lost Ark*, and then explain how the tricks are done. There are gunfights, fistfights, and other feats of derring-do, not to mention a couple of searing explosions.

An Imperial walker, one of those spacey war machines that sprang from the mind of George Lucas, stands in front of **Star Tours: The Adventures Continue**, the park's only simulator ride. Here you're ushered into a starspeeder for a madcap 3-D journey through the cosmos. The ride isn't particularly frightening, but it does give passengers a good shake.

Further on, you'll find Muppet Courtyard, identified by a Miss Piggy planter. Behind that is Jim Henson's **Muppet Vision 3-D**, a raucous 25-minute romp with Kermit, Piggy, and the rest of the muppet crew.

ANIMATION COURTYARD

At the end of Mickey Avenue in a little plaza called the Animation Courtyard are two kid-oriented favorites and a Star Wars attraction. **Voyage of the Little Mermaid** and **Disney Junior – Live on Stage!** – are sweet and schmaltzy, and intended for families with small children. At the **Star Wars Bay Launch**, fans of the science-fiction series can experience a variety of other-worldly fun like seeing artifacts and touring memorabilia galleries, and playing interactive video games. (At night, fans can watch the outdoor show **Star Wars: A Galactic Spectacular**, which involves projections onto the Chinese Theater.)

ANIMAL KINGDOM

Disney World's largest theme park, **Disney's Animal Kingdom** ❺ (daily, see www.disneyworld.com for details), is essentially a state-of-the-art zoo dressed up in extravagant style – although the Pandora – The World of Avatar land is like its own otherworldly tiny theme park. You realize you're in for something special the moment you walk through the front gates into an area known as **The Oasis** – a tropical garden laced with trails that lead past alcoves containing river otters, anteaters, sloths, and other small animals.

Emerging from The Oasis, you're greeted by a view of the **Tree of Life**, an artificial banyan-like tree that rises 14 stories above **Discovery Island**, set in a large lagoon connected by bridges to the park's four main zones. What looks at first like the tree's gnarled bark are actually carved animal figures – more than 300 in all – swirling around the trunk and limbs. Showing

Star Tours takes riders on a virtual adventure in space.

Elephant-spotting at Disney's Animal Kingdom.

A giraffe wanders the savanna at Animal Kingdom.

The Na'vi River Journey at Pandora – The World of Avatar.

in a theater in the base of the tree is a 3-D film, **It's Tough to be a Bug!**, based loosely on the Disney-Pixar movie *A Bug's Life*. The story involves seeing the world from an insect's point of view. You experience what it's like being on the receiving end of a fly swatter and encounter several noxious members of the insect family, including an acid-spraying termite and a stinkbug with, shall we say, a bad case of gas. After dark, the tree's exterior is a screen of sorts for **Tree of Life Awakening**, a jaw-dropper with high-definition animal images projected onto the trunk in spectacular detail.

Walking around Discovery Island in a clockwise direction, the first bridge on the left leads to **Pandora – The World of Avatar**. Based on the hit James Cameron movie, *Avatar*, this high-tech sci-fi immersion experience has one amazing ride, a simpler ride, scenery that literally glows after dark, and a gift shop stocked exclusively with merchandise that fits the theme. Go out of your way to experience **Avatar Flight of Passage**. It's kind of like Soarin' on

a motorbike – or rather a winged ban-shee – only, leaning forward, you fly over fantasmical landscapes, with aromas and sounds that make it feel as if you're really in this fictional world. It is arguably the best ride in Orlando right now. For a peaceful diversion, ride the **Na'vi River Journey**. It's an indoor boat ride with scenery like a bioluminescent forest and a look-see with a very impressive-looking Na'vi Shaman of Songs.

OUT OF AFRICA, INTO ASIA

Return to Discovery Island and cross the first bridge on your left to **Africa**, where you immediately find yourself amid a clutch of shops and restaurants called **Harambe**, modeled loosely on a real-life Kenyan village. Next to an enormous, artificial baobab tree is the entrance to the park's most popular attraction, **Kilimanjaro Safaris**. Here visitors board safari vehicles for a 20-minute ride across a re-created patch of African veldt. As you see lions, giraffes, zebras, and other wildlife, your driver will stop and point.

⊘ THE MOUSE AT SEA

Since its inception in 1998, Disney Cruise Lines has upgraded to a full-service cruise line. Its ships travel to various ports of call in the Caribbean, Alaska, Canada, Mexico, and Europe, as well as making a biannual transatlantic voyage. Shipboard amenities range from lavish stage shows, first-run movies, fitness rooms, spas, and a choice of swimming pools, plus adult-oriented nightspots. Passengers rotate among several theme restaurants. There are currently four Disney ships: Disney Magic, Disney Wonder, Disney Fantasy, and Disney Dream. On the Fantasy, Star Wars and Marvel Superhero areas are geared for children. Two new ships are under construction. In addition to the ships, Disney owns and operates its own island, Castaway Cay, which serves as a port of call for the cruise ships and is a unique Disney destination. Uniquely, the horns on Disney ships have been modified to play the first seven notes from When You Wish Upon a Star, in addition to the traditional horn.

Douglas Ward, author of the influential *Berlitz Complete Guide to Cruising and Cruise Ships*, describes the Disney ships as "a sea-going never-never land" providing "a highly programmed, strictly timed and regimented experience," although travelers are free to ignore the itinerary and relax. For information, call 800-951-3532, visit http://disney-cruiselinecom or contact a travel agent.

Instructional sheets help identify the animals, many of them not commonly seen in American zoos.

It's only a few steps from the safari exit to the **Pangani Forest Exploration Trail**, a nature walk where you can view endangered species like black-and-white colobus monkeys, as well as hippos, gorillas, and meerkats. A research center harbors a colony of naked mole rats and a cleverly disguised aviary. **Festival of the Lion King**, with thundering, infectious music and dancing, is worth your while, as is the nearby restaurant **Tiffins** and its adjacent **Nomad Lounge**, both offering table service, interesting foods, and adult libations.

If you're looking for a break from the crowds, you might consider a side trip to **Rafiki's Planet Watch**, an area for environmental education. The journey starts with a ride on the Wildlife Express, a replica of a vintage steam locomotive that passes through the not-terribly-scenic backstage area. At the end of the line is the **Conservation Station**, a veterinary facility with exhibits on conservation and animal care. Skip both if pressed for time.

Next door to Africa is **Asia**, a pastiche of thatched huts, stone spires, and palace walls inspired by the traditional architecture of Thailand, Nepal, and India. Asia encompasses four main attractions. To your left as you enter is the Caravan Stage, presenting **Flights of Wonder**, a 20-minute show featuring hawks, falcons, parrots, and more than a dozen other birds. Also here is **Kali River Rapids**, a whitewater ride with a jungle setting and an environmental message. The third stop in Asia is the **Maharajah Jungle Trek**, a nature walk with views of Bengal tigers, fruit bats, and exotic birds. Animal Kingdom's thrill ride, **Expedition Everest**, was the most expensive roller coaster in the world when it opened in 2006. It feels like a decrepit mountain train scaling its way up the side of the world's tallest peak, and includes a steep backward drop when you come to the end of the track. As if that weren't enough to frighten you, there is always the chance that the Yeti might surprise you as well.

Expedition Everest.

Return to Discovery Island and cross the first bridge on the left to **Dino-Land, USA**. You'll notice a carnival-like atmosphere here, injecting a welcome dose of humor into the straight-faced approach elsewhere in the park. Just past an elaborate kids' play area called **The Boneyard** you'll find signs to **Dino-saur**, DinoLand's thrill ride. The concept here is that you're a visitor at the Dino Institute, a facility dedicated to "Exploration, Excavation and Exultation" and, you soon learn, the developer of a time machine that is about to transport you back to the Age of Dinosaurs. Your mission: Save the last surviving *Iguanodon* before an asteroid collides with Earth. What follows is a jolting ride through a misty Jurassic forest that's being pelted by a barrage of meteors. Dinosaurs abound, of course, not the least of which is a *Carnotaurus*, a ferocious predator with razor-sharp teeth and a sour disposition. The experience is quite intense, so exercise discretion when visiting with young children.

Next on the agenda is **Chester & Hester's Dino-Rama**, a mini-carnival,

Disney Springs town center.

with midway games and a couple of amusement-park rides: **Primeval Whirl and TriceraTop Spin**. A large shop, **Chester & Hester's Dinosaur Treasures**, is packed to the rafters with dino-related toys and novelties – a good place to pick up gifts for the folks back home. **Finding Nemo – the Musical** is the Animal Kingdom's production, and it's poor. The technique of using live actors carrying puppets is confusing, and at times this seems more of a college theater workshop than the highly accomplished production that is the standard for Disney.

After dark, stay for **Rivers of Light**, an outdoor show that meshes light beams and music with animal folklore.

DISNEY SPRINGS

Disney Springs ➏ is an entertainment complex on Lake Buena Vista about a mile east of Epcot. It's divided into four sections – West Side, The Landing, Town Center, and Marketplace – and is intended mostly for an adult audience.

The **West Side** is in a period of transition, as original tenants like Disney-Quest, Le Cirque's La Nouba, and a four-part Wolfgang Puck restaurant complex prepare to close. Still, it has Pop Gallery for unusual home-decor items; Splitsville, a high-end bowling alley with billiards, sushi, and other non-traditional amenities; **Planet Hollywood Observatory**, a rounded multi-story restaurant with a Guy Fieri sandwich menu and a rounded high-resolution ceiling screen; a multiplex; and **Characters in Flight**, a tethered hot-air balloon ride. In between are a few more restaurants, including **Bongo's Cuban Café and House of Blues**. **Sosa Family Cigars**, an upscale cigar bar, is one of the few remaining places strictly targeting adults only. The cigar retailer offers a large variety of low- to high-end cigars.

To the right is **Town Center**, a posh alfresco shopping mall lined with designer stores ranging from **Tommy**

Bahama to **Vince Camuto**, plus a large Coca-Cola Store. Hungry shoppers can grab a bite at Disney-run fast-fooderies like **Amorette's Patisserie** and **The Daily Poutine**, but consider reserving a table at Rick Bayless' **Frontera Cocina**. You'll find destination-worthy "modern barbecue" at **The Polite Pig**, run by one the Orlando area's top restaurant families.

Parallel but closer to the water, **The Landing** is also filled with stores plus new restaurants. Seek out **Chef Art Smith's Homecomin' Kitchen** for Southern fare, **Morimoto Asia** for Asian in a glitzy setting, **STK Orlando** for steak and seasonal specialties indoors and out, and **The Boathouse** and **Paddlefish** for seafood.

Open for years yet still a favorite for its food, decor, and entertainment, **Raglan Road Irish Pub and Restaurant** straddles The Landing and Marketplace. With a kitchen steered by Irish celebrity chef Kevin Dundon, this oversized pub re-creates the atmosphere of Dublin's Temple Bar during a tour-group party; in other words it looks much like any other Irish pub in America, except for its girth. Many shades of stout and ale are on offer alongside a fine selection of whiskey, and live Irish folk music with dancing takes you through the night.

Many of these restaurants have take-out windows selling reasonably priced meals, mostly hand-helds like sandwiches and baps, plus specialty cocktails. For quick and sweet, head to **The Ganachery** for superb chocolates and **Vivoli il Gelato** for Italian-style ice cream.

Also in the West Side is a **Harley-Davidson** shop. The merchandise here is dominated by leather jackets, T-shirts, hats, and assorted knick-knacks plastered with the Harley logo, though actual motorcycles – most bristling with chrome and other custom adornments – are also on display.

If you're a surfer – or just want to look like one – make a point of checking out **Curl by Sammy Duvall**, a high-end surf shop with an extensive selection of surfer-dude clothing, gear, and accessories. There are even a few surfboards.

Disney's Wild Africa Trek is a guided expedition (extra charge) that allows visitors to get up-close to African animals, including hippos, giraffes, and crocodiles

The Village Causeway at Disney Springs.

Tip

You can sign up for a 150-minute surfing lesson at Typhoon Lagoon. Lessons are offered on certain days of the week before the park opens to the public. The fee is $165.

SHOPPING ZONE

Marketplace occupies the eastern portion of Downtown Disney and is devoted to shopping and eating. It is the most family-friendly, and in fact has several free and inexpensive diversions for little ones. In addition to the world's largest Disney store are shops carrying home furnishings, sporting gear, and toys. Far more interesting is the **Lego Imagination Center**, if only for the Lego sculptures displayed around the store. For eats, there's the **Ghirardelli Soda Fountain & Chocolate Shop**, the dinosaur-themed **T-Rex**, and a **Rainforest Cafe** ensconced in what appears to be a smoldering volcano.

DISNEY'S BOARDWALK

You'll find a smaller entertainment complex at the **Boardwalk**, where jugglers, magicians, and such do street shows for passersby and rental surreys offer a fun way to travel from hotel to hotel. Diners have a couple of good choices: the **Flying Fish** serves inventive, top-quality seafood in a fanciful high-end space, and **Trattoria al**

Forno specializes in Mediterranean cuisine, though sports fans may prefer the ESPN Club, a bar with almost 100 TV screens.

Drinkers can sample handcrafted suds at the **Big River Grille & Brewing Works** or join the singalong crowd at **Jellyrolls**, which features a raucous dueling pianos act. Dancers can boogie at the **Atlantic Dance Hall**, modeled after the classic dance halls of the 1930s and 40s.

DISNEY'S WATER PARKS

If you're reasonably spry, don't mind hordes of teens, and aren't self-conscious about being seen in a swimsuit, you'll have a blast flying down the various chutes or bobbing peacefully on one of the gentle river trips.

Disney World has two excellent water parks to choose from when you're sticky with sweat and ready for a good dousing. A good fit for teenagers and young adults is **Typhoon Lagoon ❼** (tel: 407-560-4141; daily 10am–5pm, extended hours summer and holidays). Here you'll find a selection of high-speed slides as well as an enormous surf pool, a snorkeling trail where you can swim through the water with tropical fish and harmless sharks, and a relaxing 45-minute lazy-river raft trip that takes you through rainforest grottoes and waterfalls. On its Miss Adventure Falls, guests, seated in rafts, are brought to the top on a conveyor belt.

Blizzard Beach ❽ (tel: 407-560-3400; daily 10am–5pm, extended hours summer and holidays) is Disney's largest water park and offers the scariest and hairiest rides, including Summit Plummet, which zips riders down a 350ft (107-meter) ramp at speeds close to 60mph (97kmh). There are at least a dozen other slides, as well Teamboat Springs, as the world's longest "family whitewater raft ride," in which five passengers bob through 1,200ft (360 meters) of standing waves and aggressive sprays.

Castaway Creek at Typhoon Lagoon.

ORLANDO AND ITS OTHER WORLDS

Beyond the gates of Disney is a wide array of destinations, ranging from elaborate theme parks and first-class museums to alligator farms and wilderness areas.

Walt Disney World Resort's chief competitor is Universal Orlando Resort (www.universalorlando.com), a complex of two theme parks, a water park, five hotels, and an entertainment district about 9 miles (15km) down I-4. Hipper than Mickey, with a knowing pop sensibility, Universal is especially appealing to teenagers and young adults who like big roller-coasters, loud music, and action movies. Use the Official Universal Orlando Resort App to help you buy tickets, get around, see wait times, and plan around shows.

ISLANDS OF ADVENTURE

Universal's flagship property is **Universal Studios Florida** ① (tel: 407-363-8000; www.universalorlando.com; daily, hours vary, see website for details), a theme park inspired by the art and science of Hollywood movies. Sprawling across more than 400 acres (160 hectares), the park is laid out in eight themed zones, each with its own rides and shows, arranged around a lagoon. As Universal likes to remind us, this is a working production facility: sections of the park double as movie sets.

Although it's at the far end of the park, consider making a beeline for the **Wizarding World of Harry Potter**. The bigdeal ride here is **Harry Potter and the Escape from Gringotts**. As you traverse through the tunnels below a bank, you'll

encounter dangers from the villainous Voldemort and troublesome trolls. 3-D touches bring extra life to an already big thrill. Find time for Diagon Alley's gift shops, where interactive wands, wizardly robes, and Quidditch equipment make great souvenirs. The Hogwarts Express (access via special two-park ticket) will bring you to a sister Harry Potter land at the Islands of Adventure theme park. Seek out Platform 9¾ so you can appear to walk through a wall. Whether you just want to take in the otherworldly British universe, and maybe sip a Tongue Tying

Main Attractions

Universal Studios
Islands of Adventure
Wizarding World of Harry
  Potter
CityWalk
SeaWorld
Aquatica
Loch Haven Park
Cornell Fine Arts Museum
Legoland

Map on page 232

Marvel Super Heroes.

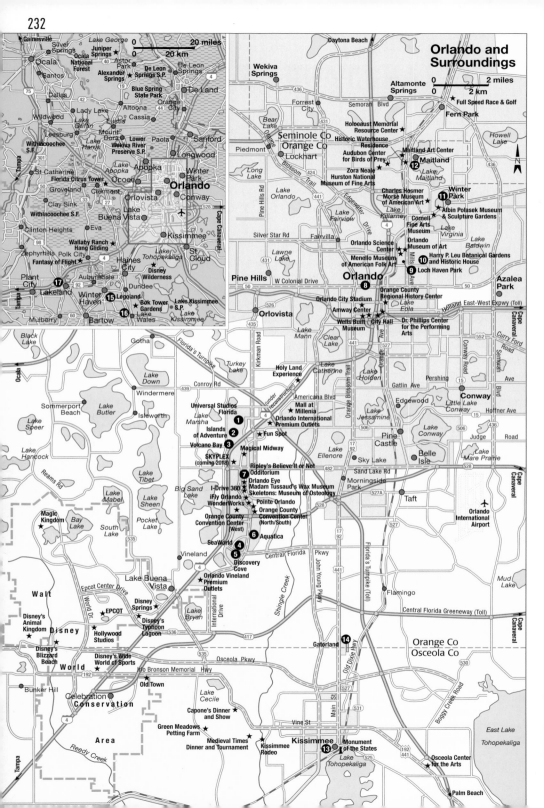

Lemon Squash with your cottage pie or toad in the hole at Leaky Cauldron, or are game for a full-on thrill ride, you will feel as if you are immersed in Harry Potter's world.

Beyond, one of Universal's biggest thrill rides is **Rip Ride Rockit**, dubbed the most personalized roller-coaster experience in the world. Built with its own on-board sound system, guests are able to choose the music they want to listen to during their roller-coaster experience. This 3,800ft (1,160-meter) coaster is what's called an X-car, and is the largest of its kind in the world. Each train has two cars with three rows, which hold six people in stadium-style seating. There's also **Race Through New York Starring Jimmy Fallon**, a ridiculously fun adventure through and over New York City, and **Transformers: The Ride – 3D**, a thriller involving Autobots and Deceptions. **Revenge of the Mummy**, an indoor roller-coaster that takes you on a three-minute ride through fireballs, with sharp twists and turns at high speed while trying to avoid capture by skeletal warriors. After a massive renovation, **The**

Incredible Hulk Coaster has returned, and with a monster-size energy. You'll twist upside down seven times and zoom at up to 67mph (108kmh). **Terminator 2 3-D** thrusts the audience into the action while resistance fighters John and Sarah Connor battle Skynet in an attempt to save the human race from annihilation. **Shrek 4-D** uses the same cinema technology, but is suitable for small children. In this movie Lord Farquaad returns to kidnap Princess Fiona. Shrek and Donkey have to embark on a journey to save her. **Fast & Furious: Supercharged**, based on Universal Pictures' highest grossing film franchise, is set to open in 2018.

On the light side, **Despicable Me Minion Mayhem** is a laugh-filled 3-D ride. **The Simpsons Ride**, with subtle humor, is a wild, virtual-reality journey through Krustyland, where the Simpson family tries to escape Sideshow Bob. The most nostalgic family ride is undoubtedly **ET Adventure**. This dark ride is a re-creation of the movie and is set in an area called **Woody Woodpecker's Kid Zone** devoted entirely to young children, which

⊘ Tip

One of Universal's best shows is the acclaimed Blue Man Group, although this is a touristy adaption compared to the clever original. You do not have to buy a theme park ticket to see this show. Tickets start at $60 for adults and $30 for children.

Partying with Elwood Blues on Delancey Street.

⊘ UNIVERSAL EXPRESS PASS

The Universal Express system allows visitors priority access to the most popular rides to avoid long lines. You have to pay for this privilege if you are not a guest at one of Universal Orlando's resorts. Prices start from $44.99 per person. The Tickets section of the Universal Studios website (www.universalorlando.com) displays a pricing key. The pass is only valid for one day at one park and is available as one express pass per ride, or unlimited all day. Though the cost can be steep, it's worth it. Guests do not need to wait for a time slot; just show up at the attraction and you'll be accommodated straight away. The Express Pass is not currently available in conjunction with the park's newest Harry Potter rides.

includes the **Woody's Nuthouse** Coaster, a kid-size roller-coaster that's fun for all ages. The water-soaked **Curious George Goes to Town** playground and ball factory is great for little ones. From there you can walk over to **Fievel's Playland** and see what the world looks like from a mouse's point of view. There are plenty of props for children to climb on. There are also two live shows: **A Day in the Park with Barney** and **Animal Actors on Location!**, a terrifically entertaining show which features many animal shelter rescues. **MEN IN BLACK: Alien Attack** is like playing a live action video game where your job is to take out the aliens.

The combination of humor and nostalgia is crucial to the success of shows like **Blues Brothers**. In **Fear Factor Live**, which is based on the hit reality show, audience members are selected at random to try hair-raising (and sometimes hare-brained) stunts. **Universal Horror Make-Up Show** lets you get a behind-the-scenes look at how Hollywood's best make-up artists create the life-like creatures you see in the movies and on television.

ISLANDS OF ADVENTURE

Universal's **Islands of Adventure ❷** (daily, hours vary, see www.universalorlando.com for details), isn't really made up of islands but rather of six elaborately-themed zones. Children's books, cartoons, and comic strips provide themes for rides, shops, and restaurants, and costumed characters such as Popeye, Bullwinkle, and Spider-Man make appearances. **Seuss Landing** was inspired by the beloved children's books of Theodor Seuss Geisel, also known as Dr. Seuss. On **The Cat in the Hat**, hop aboard your couch and take a trip through the pages of this childhood classic with the most mischievous cat around. **If I Ran the Zoo** is an interactive playground filled with characters from a variety of Dr. Seuss classics, while **Dr Seuss's ABC** guides children through the alphabet. **The High in the Sky Seuss Trolley Train Ride** takes you on a journey high above the **Seuss Landing** attractions.

The **Lost Continent** is divided into two sections: The first is an Arabian marketplace; the second is styled after the mythical Atlantis. **Jurassic Park** is a dinosaur-themed area based on Spielberg's 1993 film. On the **Jurassic Park River Adventure** you dodge amazingly life-like dinosaurs before taking a stomach-flipping, 85ft (26-meter) plummet. Afterward walk over to the **Jurassic Park Discovery Center** where guests learn how dinosaurs lived through a variety of interactive exhibits and displays.

The **Wizarding World of Harry Potter** is the park's megahit. Embark on an adventure in **Harry Potter and the Forbidden Journey,** where you fly above Hogwarts, escape a dragon attack, and get pulled into the middle of a Quidditch game. Gather your courage and climb aboard the **Dragon Challenge** and choose between riding a Hungarian Horntail or a Chinese Fireball dragon. The two intertwine on the tracks and are devilishly engineered for several near

The Incredible Hulk Coaster.

misses at speeds in excess of 55mph (90kmh). Before taking a training flight aboard **Flight of the Hippogriff**, visit the family-friendly roller-coaster **Care of Magical Creatures Grounds**. Next, pop in to **Olivanders** iconic wand shop and experience the magic of choosing the wand that's right for you. At the **Owl Post and Owlery Shop** guests can get an up-close look at a variety of owls, as well as mail letters to friends and family. **Zonko's** magic shop is filled with joke, magic, and novelty items. **Honey-dukes** candy shop is the perfect place to try chocolate frogs and every flavor Bertie-Bott ever made.

What makes the park extra special are the high-tech thrill rides. Expect to scream, or at least gasp, during **Skull Island: Reign of Kong**, where coming to face to face with a three-story-tall Kong – and oh yes, you'll hear him roar and feel his breath. **The Amazing Adventures of Spider-Man** combines simulator technology and 4-D visuals. Along the way you encounter a small army of evil-doers who send your tram into wild spins and lurches. The tour culminates in what feels like a headlong plunge into the city streets below, only to be saved at the last moment by Spider-Man.

If it's water action you're after, head to **Toon Lagoon** for **Dudley Do'Rights Ripsaw Falls.** Help Dudley save his love, Nell, before you take a jaw-dropping 75ft (23-meter) plunge. Embark on a white-water rapids adventure on **Popeye and Bluto's Bilge-Rat Barges**; be sure to bring a change of clothes. Kids will love exploring **Me Ship, the Olive**, where from a dry platform they can shoot water cannons on unsuspecting barge riders below.

In **Marvel Super Hero Island, The Incredible Hulk Coaster** catapults you up a tunnel with the same force as a fighter jet, before turning upside down seven times and plummeting back toward the ground. **Doctor Doom's FearFall** rockets riders 150ft (45 meters) into the sky.

CITYWALK

Before leaving Universal, drop in on **CityWalk**, where a dozen restaurants and nightclubs keep the party rolling long after the kids have gone to bed. The **Toothsome Chocolate Emporium & Savory Feast Kitchen** is a sweets fantasyland with a Steampunk, Wonka-like whimsy. It happens to serve decent sit-down meals, too. At **Cowfish**, burgers and sushi fill two different food craving needs – and mixes them together in certain dishes. TV chef **Emeril Lagasse** offers his Creole fare in a contemporary space with a serious wine list. **The Red Coconut Club** features signature Martinis, a happy hour, and live music daily, while at **Bob Marley: A Tribute to Freedom** reggae bands perform in an open-air courtyard that re-creates Marley's Jamaica home. Other nightspots include **Pat O'Brien's**, with its dueling pianos and world-famous Hurricane drink. **CityWalk** also features the world's largest **Hard Rock Cafe**, the theme-laden **Jimmy Buffet's Margaritaville**, and the chance to do karaoke with a live band and backing singers at the **Rising Star**.

Hogwarts Castle towers over the Wizarding World of Harry Potter.

⊘ Tip

SeaWorld's Dolphin Encounter program allows anyone to have a 3- to 5-minute encounter in a group of up to 10 people up-close with one of everyone's favorite creatures, with prices starting at $15. Other VIP programs give up-close looks at walruses, sea lions, and more.

VOLCANO BAY

In 2017, Universal opened **Volcano Bay** ❸, a 28-acre (11-hectare) Polynesia-themed water park with a huge peak at its center – and inside that 200ft (60-meter) volcano is the Krakatau Aqua Coaster. Besides the standard watery fun, this water park has a big selling point: Using new technology via Tapu Tapu bracelets that tell them when it's their turn to play, guests can try each ride without waiting in line, and, thanks to other technology, without hauling tubes up steps. Among the 18 calm and exciting challenges are a wave pool where the water surges in varying directions, twisting raft rides, three body slides, a saucer ride that zooms around curves, and a raft ride through darkness.

SEAWORLD, DISCOVERY COVE, AND AQUATICA

The other don't-miss theme park in Orlando is **SeaWorld** ❹ (tel: 407-351-3600; www.seaworld.com; daily, hours vary, see website for details). The world's largest marine park is the home of strutting penguins, prancing seals, and applause-hungry dolphins. In other popular shows include Clyde the otter and Seamore the sea lion cavort around a pirate ship, and familiar animals doing entertaining pet tricks. There are marine exhibits, including areas where you can touch the animals and a tunnel that leads you through a pool of sharks. To ease your way, use the SeaWorld Discovery Guide app, which does everything from help you find your car to see show times and the wait times for rides. Quick Queue, from $10 per day, lets you skip lines on the most popular rides.

SeaWorld has several big thrill rides, too. **Mako**, a "hypercoaster" billed as taller, longer, and faster than any other roller coaster in Orlando with a 200ft (60-meter) drop, nearly a mile of track, and speeds of up to 73mph (118kmh). In other words, thrills don't get much bigger than this. If you're a coaster-lover, you might want to make this your first SeaWorld stop. The more benign is **Journey to Atlantis**, a cross between a log flume and a roller-coaster. There's a story behind the ride involving the emergence of Atlantis, but with two 60ft (18-meter) plunges, several smaller dips, and a nonstop barrage of laser lights, you won't have a chance to follow along. Only hard-core thrill-seekers should consider riding **Kraken Unleashed**, a floorless roller-coaster with a drop of 144ft (44 meters), seven inversions, three subterranean passages, and a top speed of 65mph (105kmh). With the aid of virtual reality headsets, passengers are taken on a terrifying deep-sea journey.

Roller-coaster enthusiasts will not want to miss **Manta**. With its 3,359ft (1,024 meters) of track, it's a coaster that simulates the experience of flying. It has a drop of 140ft (43 meters), reaches speeds of nearly 60mph (96kmh), and is the second longest, tallest, and fastest coaster in the world. **Infinity Falls**, a whitewater

Universal's Volcano Bay.

rafting experience good for the whole family, is set to open in 2018.

While not necessarily scary like the others, take time for **Antarctica: Empire of the Penguin**. It brings you into the world of icy caves to see a penguin colony. Choose the mild or thrill-packed version of this exciting ride with a glacially impressive design. Afterward, walk around to visit with five species of penguin, 250 in all – including an underwater view – and watch more on the Penguin Cam. It's fun to watch the black-and-white creatures waddling over the ice, sliding down the snow mounds, diving, and swimming underwater at lightning speed.

Shamu Express is a junior-size coaster perfect for little ones. **The Sea Carousel** is a marine mammal themed merry-go-round ride. **The Flying Fiddler** is a free-fall children's ride. **Net Climb** is a great place to let the kids expend energy. It has a four-story climbing net, slides, and tire swings.

In recent years SeaWorld has revamped its shows. **Dolphin Days** shows Atlantic bottlenose dolphins at their entertaining best. In **Pets Ahoy!**, cats, dogs, and pot-belly pigs will have you laughing with their tricks.

The animal exhibits are the best part of the park. **Wild Arctic** is a flight simulator where guests can see walruses, beluga whales, and polar bears. At **Dolphin Nursery,** you can see baby and mother bottle-nosed dolphins. **Turtle Trek** gives you access to manatees and sea turtles while viewing a 3-D movie above and around you. Have you ever wondered what it felt like to touch a sting-ray? Visit **Stingray Lagoon**, where you can reach out and touch the rays. Pacific Point Preserve houses the seals and sea lions; **Shark Encounter** brings you through an 85ft (26-meter) tunnel to see sharks, barracuda, and venomous fish; and **Manatee Rehabilitation Area** keeps injured and rescued manatees.

Adjacent to SeaWorld is a very different theme park. SeaWorld calls it **Discovery Cove ❺**, and it's more akin to a tropical resort than an amusement park. For starters, admission is limited to 1,000 people per day, and

At Universal's Islands of Adventure Raptor Encounter, you can take a selfie with a velociraptor, if you dare.

Manta will get your feet wet at SeaWorld.

One of the thrilling tube rides at Aquatica.

An underwater viewing area gives visitors a unique perspective on one of SeaWorld's biggest stars.

guests pay a flat fee that includes just about everything they'll need – food, towels, snorkeling equipment, and more. What you get is the freedom to roam a beautifully landscaped 32-acre (13-hectare) property where you can snorkel around an artificial coral reef stocked with tropical fish, float down a tropical river, splash in waterfalls, or simply lounge beneath a palm tree on a perfect beach.

For most visitors, the highlight of Discovery Cove is an opportunity to swim with a dolphin. "Swim" may not be entirely accurate. What you do is interact with the animal under the watchful eye of a trainer, who teaches you hand signals that cue the dolphin to roll over, wave flippers, exchange kisses, and tow you along. The park also offers a swim-with-sharks opportunity, featuring a variety of species, as well as the chance to feed southern and cownose stingrays.

SeaWorld's third component is nearby **Aquatica ⑥**. This water park has some astounding elements, combining the traditional flume and tube rides with the sea life SeaWorld is famous for. The **Dolphin Plunge** is the most popular attraction. Its clear plastic slide dips through a pool inhabited by black-and-white Commerson's dolphins.

On **Ihu's Breakaway Falls**, riders face one another as they prepare to plummet 80ft (24 meters). **Taumata Racer** is an eight-lane racing slide with open and enclosed sections. **Whanau Way** is a four-slide tower offering four different speed experiences. **Omaka Rocka** features high-speed tubes and funnels that send riders forward and backward. Aquatica features two wave pools: **Cutback Cove** and **Big Surf Shores**. Then there's **Kata's Kookaburra Cove** and **Walkabout Waters**, which were designed with smaller children in mind. **Roa's Rapids** is a racing river action ride. **HooRoo Run** takes you through a thrilling six-story maze of tunnels with twists and turns. For something quieter, take a nice leisurely journey down **Loggerhead Lane**, a lazy river adventure, which takes you through the beautiful **Fish Grotto**.

I-DRIVE

Running alongside I-4 for about 10 miles (16km) between Disney World and downtown Orlando is **International Drive**, known as I-Drive, a tourist strip with hotels, restaurants, one-off thrill rides, shopping plazas, and, for lack of a better term, several "roadside attractions." Typical of this last category is **Ripley's Believe It or Not Odditorium** ❼ (8201 International Dr; tel: 407-354-0501; www.ripleys.com/orlando; daily 9am–midnight, last entry 11pm), a takeoff on Robert Ripley's books of oddities, with exhibits on such sideshow staples as two-headed calves and curiosities like a Rolls-Royce constructed of matchsticks.

Along the same lines is **Wonder-Works** (9067 International Dr; tel: 407-351-8800; www.wonderworksonline.com/orlando; daily 9am–midnight, last admission 10.30pm), although the emphasis here is on high-tech games and science-related exhibits. It's worth driving by just to see the extraordinary building, which looks like a neoclassical temple that's been turned upside-down. This is also home to the **Outta Control Magic and Comedy Dinnershow**. WonderWorks also runs the **Magical Midway** (7001 International Dr; tel: 407-370-5353; www.magicalmidway.com; daily noon–midnight). At **Pirate's Cove** (8501 International Dr; tel: 407-352-7378; www.piratescove.net/orlando; daily 9am–11.30pm), miniature golf fans have two courses to get their licks on the links. Captain Kidd's course is good for beginners while the more difficult Blackbeard's Challenge is popular among the more serious duffers. There is another location at 12545 SR 535 in Lake Buena Vista near Disney World Resort (tel: 407-827-1242).

Young families can spend hours at **Fun Spot Action Park** (5700 Fun Spot Way; tel: 407-363-3867; www.fun-spot.com; daily 10am or 2pm–midnight; with a sister location in Kissimmee).

Here you'll have old-fashioned fun with bumper cars and boats, go-karts, and all kinds of carnival rides, some of them thrillers.

International Drive is a prime area for shopping, too. **Pointe Orlando** (9101 International Dr; tel: 407-248-2838; www.pointeorlando.com; Mon–Sat noon–10pm, 9pm in summer, Sun noon–8pm, many restaurants and bars stay open later) is an attractive upscale retail complex with live entertainment, lots of lively bars and cafés, a mix of restaurants, the Main Event super-arcade with bowling and virtual reality games, and a 21-screen Cineplex that has an IMAX theater.

Down the road, **iDrive 360** (8375 International Dr; (https://i-drive360.com; 10am–2pm, individual establishments vary) packs in a slew of tourist attractions plus bars and restaurants. You'll first spot The Official Coca-Cola Orlando Eye, high-tech slow-moving ride with expansive views. Sharing the expansive complex are a **Madam Tussaud's** wax museum (www.madametussauds.com), the modern **SeaLife**

The quirky entrance to Ripley's Believe It or Not!

There is something for all ages at Ripley's Believe It or Not! on International Drive.

Aquarium (www2.visitsealife.com/orlando), with clever underwater areas designed for selfies; and **Skeletons: Animals Unveiled!** (http://skeletonmuseum.com), with the bones of more than 400 real animals. Bring kids to the **Sugar Factory** (https://sugarfactory.com) for oversized desserts. If you're all adult, opt for the Spanish fare at **Tapa Toro** (http://tapatoro.restaurant).

By 2018, you should be able to get a thrill from **Skyplex**, a 570ft (174-meter) vertical Polecoaster with a restaurant, lounge, and observation deck. Claims are that a sister ride, Skyfall, will have the world's longest single drop, plummeting from 460ft (140 meters) at 90mph (144.8kmh).

At the northern and southern tips of I-Drive are huge outlet malls with a welcome array of designer names. Across from the one at the very north and is an enormous once-traditional mall that is currently empty inside except for a multiplex movie theater where the reclining seats have comfy footrests, and glow-in-the-dark putt-putt. A few sizeable,

The indoor rope course at WonderWorks.

destination-worthy retailers found here, too: Sheplers Western Wear, Bass Pro Shops Outdoor World, and a Ron Jon Surf Shop.

I-Drive has the kinds of family attractions you'll find back home, but they are supersized, kept in excellent condition, and in many cases serve food and alcohol, which keeps parents happy while kids frolic. Among them are **Andretti Indoor Karting & Games** (9299 Universal Blvd, tel: 407-610-5020; Mon–Thu 11am–1am, Thu–Sat 11am–2am, Sun 11am–midnight), a $30-million spot that also has not only indoor go karts but also zip lines, a racing simulator, and rock climbing; **iFly Orlando** (8969 International Dr, tel: 407-337-4359; www.iflyworld.com/orlando), an indoor skydiving experience where you float on a column of air in a vertical wind tunnel; **I-Drive NASCAR Indoor Kart Racing** (www.idrivenascar.com); above-and-beyond laser tag at **Hard Knocks** (www.indoorwar.com); and several escape room facilities including **Escapology** (www.escapology.com).

DOWNTOWN ORLANDO

The downtown area of **Orlando** ❽ is a hub for business and the arts, with shops, galleries, and restaurants as well as gracious public spaces like **Lake Eola Park**, a 20-acre (8-hectare) oasis with an amphitheater, walking trails, and swan-shaped paddleboats. **Church Street Station**, an entertainment complex in a restored 19th-century train depot, is in the midst of a slow revival.

Orange Avenue, named for the city's most famous export product, lies a few blocks' west of Lake Eola Park and has become the main drag for downtown life. At its southern base is the **Grand Bohemian Hotel Orlando** (325 S. Orange Ave; tel: 407-313 9000; www.grandbohemianhotel. com), a top-class hotel that includes the **Boheme**, a well-adorned restaurant known for its business lunches and Sunday jazz brunch, and the **Grand Bohemian Gallery** (Grand Bohemian Hotel, 325 S. Orange Ave; tel: 407-581 4801; www.grandbohemi-angallery.com; Mon–Thu 10am–7pm, Fri–Sat 10am–8pm, Sun 10am–3pm; free), which features a fine collection of European and American art.

From Church Street to Washington Street, there is a medley of bars that would seem more appropriate on a college campus than in a business center. But there is culture here, too. At 29 S. Orange Avenue is the **CityArts Factory** (tel: 407-648 7060; www.cityartsfactory. com; gallery hours vary; free), housed in the old Philips Theater. This is the center for the Downtown Arts District and features a large exhibition space and several art galleries.

North of Central Boulevard is **Wall Street Plaza**, a bar and restaurant complex with happy-hour specials to lure office workers. Most nights feature live music. Walk through Wall Street Plaza to Heritage Square. In the stately 1927 Orange County Courthouse is the **Orange County Regional History Center** (65 E. Central Blvd; tel: 407-836-8500; www.thehistorycenter. org; Mon–Sat 10am–5pm, Sun noon–5pm). Here four floors of exhibits chronicle the history of central Florida.

> **⊙ Tip**
>
> Special events at Leu Gardens include summer jazz concerts and alfresco movie nights, plus free indoor storytimes for children.

Lake Eola.

Paintings at the Mennello Museum.

Changing exhibits focus on a variety of topics, ranging in recent years from the "rogues and rascals" of Florida's pioneer period to the area's rock 'n' roll history.

Ella Fitzgerald and Duke Ellington are just two of the luminaries who stayed at the Wells Built Hotel, erected in 1929 by William Monroe Wells, Orlando's first African-American physician. Opened as the **Wells' Built Museum of African American History and Culture** (511 W. South St; tel: 407-245 7535; Mon–Fri 9am–5pm), it houses exhibitions on life in the segregated South.

African-American culture is also the subject of the tiny **Zora Neale Hurston National Museum of Fine Arts** (227 E. Kennedy Blvd; tel: 407-647-3307; www. zoranealehurstonmuseum.com; Mon–Fri 9am–4pm, Sat 11am–1pm; free) in nearby Eatonville, the first black township in the United States, founded in 1887. Raised in Eatonville, Hurston later became a prominent figure in the Harlem Renaissance, authoring books such as *Their Eyes Were Watching God*

and *Of Men and Mules*. The gallery features work by African-American artists; an annual festival is held in Hurston's honor.

The ambitious new **Amway Center** arena (www.amwaycenter.com) attracts hordes for both sports and concerts, and the Orlando City Stadium (www. orlandocitysc.com/stadium) opened in 2017 as a home for the Orlando City Soccer and Orlando Pride soccer teams.

LOCH HAVEN PARK

Just north of downtown in lovely **Loch Haven Park** ❾ is a cluster of cultural institutions. The **Orlando Science Center** (777 E. Princeton St; tel: 407-514-2000; www.osc.org; hours vary seasonally) contains dozens of hands-on exhibits spread over four levels, plus a giant CineDome movie theater, a digital 3-D theater, and an observatory.

The exhibits appeal mainly to children of varying ages. Among the highlights are KidsTown, an 11,000-sq-ft (1,020-sq-meter) early childhood exhibit for children aged 7 and under. Its seven zones are packed

◎ DINNER THEATER

A unique entertainment option in Orlando is a night at one of its many dinner theater shows. These often cheesy affairs focus on big productions accompanied by standard fare. Some are most definitely better than others. **Caribbean Carnaval** (Loews Sapphire Falls Resort, 6601 Adventure Way; tel: 407-503-3463; www.caribbeancarnaval. eventbrite.com; Wed 7pm) is a festive weekly buffet enlivened by stilt walkers, acrobatic dancers, Caribbean music, and, for those who get in the spirit, limbo and a congo line. That complements the **Wantilan Luau**, held Saturday evenings in a sister Loews hotel at Universal Orlando (www. universalorlando.com).

The most classic – and perhaps most fun – dinner theater show is Disney World's **Hoop-Dee-Doo Musical Revue** (www.disneyworld.com), a funny, wholesome throwback with a fine all-American family-style dinner.

The **Medieval Times Dinner and Tournament** (4510 W. Irlo Bronson Hwy, Kissimmee; tel: 866-543-9637; www. medievaltimes.com/orlando), set in the 11th century, features a well-executed jousting tournament. Horses are chosen

from over 400 raised on a Texas ranch, where they return after a few pampered years in the spotlight.

Other theme dinners include **The Outta Control Magic Comedy Dinner Show** (9067 International Dr; tel: 407-351-8800; www.wonderworksonline.com/orlando), which offers hand-tossed pizza and unlimited beer, wine, and soda. Entertainment is a mixture of comedy, improv, and magic that promises to "tickle your funny bone every eight seconds."

Al Capone's Dinner and Show (4740 W Hwy 192; tel: 800-220-8428; www.alcapones.com) is a mob-like affair where guests give a secret password to enter the restaurant. You can partake in the American-Italian buffet while enjoying a musical show.

Other recommended shows include the **Sleuth's Mystery Dinner Show** (8267 International Dr; tel: 407-363-1985; www.sleuths.com), **Titanic Dinner Event** (7324 International Dr; tel: 407-248-1166; www.premierexhibitions. com), and **Pirate's Dinner Adventure** (6400 Carrier Dr; tel: 407-206-5102; www.piratesdinneradventure.com).

with interactive activities like water tables, a climbing structure, and a mini play orange grove. Elsewhere, hands-on science displays involving dinosaur fossils, earthquakes, aerodynamics, and engineering fascinate in halls like DinoDigs, Our Planet, and Kinetic Zone. The NatureWorks exhibit has a pond with turtles and alligators. The Crosby Observatory features a 10in refractor telescope for sky-watching.

On the other side of the park is the **Orlando Museum of Art** (2416 N. Mills Ave; tel: 407-896-4231; www.omart.org; Tue–Fri 10am–4pm, Sat–Sun noon–4pm), which stages 10 to 12 traveling exhibitions a year in addition to those from its permanent collection of Contemporary, American, African, and ancient pre-Columbian art, which includes works by Georgia O'Keeffe, John James Audubon, John Singer Sargent, and several American Impressionist painters.

A towering glass sculpture by Dale Chihuly stands in the atrium. Elsewhere are intriguing portraits in a variety of mediums, African Art with themed exhibitions ranging from textiles to vessels, and Art of the Ancient Americas with ceramic vessels and figures, gold jewelry, copper figurines, masks, and ritual objects from Central and South America dating back to 2000 BC. You'll also find American art from the 18th century to the present, including landscapes, portraits, and traditional and contemporary sculpture.

So-called "outsider art" is the focus of the **Mennello Museum of American Folk Art** (900 E. Princeton St; tel: 407-246-4278; www.mennellomuseum.com; Tue–Sat 10.30am–4.30pm, Sun noon–4.30pm), also in the park. In addition to visiting exhibitions, the museum shows works from its permanent collection, dedicated to the "primitive" paintings of Earl Cunningham, a self-taught artist, whose brightly colored canvases have been acquired by several major museums, including the Metropolitan Museum of Art and the Smithsonian Institution.

The Orlando Science Center is packed with hands-on exhibits about science and technology, as well as two movie theaters showing both educational and Hollywood movies.

An exhibit at the Cornell Fine Arts Museum.

The Charles Hosmer Morse Museum.

Alligator wrestling at Gatorland.

CENTER STAGE

Two of the area's best theaters are also in Loch Haven Park. The **Orlando Shakespeare Theater** (812 E. Rollins St; tel: 407-447-1700; www.orlando shakes.org) began in 1989 as a month-long festival and has since grown into a year-round theater; it has now partnered with the University of Central Florida. Its multiple theaters hold performances of not only the Bard's works but plenty of,pre-modern playwrights, too. It is exceptionally busy during the Orlando Fringe Festival (http://orlandofringe.org), where several productions, many wildly creative, are on at once. **The Rep** (1001 E. Princeton St; tel: 407-896-7365; www. orlandorep.com) pays special attention to providing affordable productions suitable for a younger audience by transferring classic fairy tales and children's books to the stage. In Downtown Orlando's pedestrian-friendly Church Street area, the **Mad Cow Theatre** (www.madcowtheatre.com) has two small theaters that entice theater-lovers with an eclectic mix of dramas and musicals, always with no bad seats to be had. An annual cabaret festival adds a lighter touch.

It's a short drive from Loch Haven Park to the **Harry P. Leu Botanical Gardens and Historic House** ⑩ (920 N. Forest Ave; tel: 407-246-2620; www.leugardens.org; daily 9am–5pm), where paths meander through 49 acres (20 hectares) of specialty gardens, including one of the largest collections of roses and camellias and areas devoted to palms, herbs, tropical plants, and wetlands. Short tours of the historic Leu House are offered throughout the day.

WINTER PARK

To the north of Orlando is **Winter Park** ⑪, an upscale suburb with a gracious, old-money atmosphere. Park Avenue is a good place for strolling when the tourist trails lose their charm; there is not a themed restaurant in sight, although a few low-key chains have snuck in. At the southern end of Park Avenue, on the trim Mediterranean-style campus of Rollins College, is the

Cornell Fine Arts Museum (1000 Holt Ave; tel: 407-646-2526; www.rollins.edu/cfam; Tue 10am–7pm, Wed–Fri 10am–4pm, Sat–Sun noon–5pm). Though quite small, it is one of the finest and oldest art museums in the Southeast. Each year, the Cornell stages six to eight exhibitions drawn from its holdings of more than 6,000 European and American works of art. The collection encompasses paintings, drawings, and sculpture from the 1450s to the 1990s. At the start of the school year, one gallery is dedicated to exhibiting work by contemporary local artists.

Also on campus are the Annie Russell Theatre and the Knowles Memorial Chapel, connected by a loggia. Both buildings were built in 1931–2 and feature on the US National Register of Historic Places.

Winter Park's other important museum is the **Charles Hosmer Morse Museum of American Art** (445 N. Park Ave; tel: 407-645-5311; www.morse museum.org; Tue–Sat 9.30am–4pm, until 8pm on Fri in winter, Sun 1–4pm), a few blocks away.

From lamps and leaded-glass windows to pottery, jewelry, paintings, and art glass, it contains the world's most comprehensive collection of works by Louis Comfort Tiffany (1848–1933). An expansive wing added in 2011 features exhibitions tied to Laurelton Hall, the late artist's Long Island, New York, home. Leaded glass windows, custom furnishings, and the architecture itself – plus the Fountain Court reception hall – are all on display.

Sculpture is the focus of the **Albin Polasek Museum and Sculpture Gardens** (633 Osceola Ave; tel: 407-647-6294; www.polasek.org; Tue–Sat 10am–4pm, Sun 1–4pm), a short walk from Rollins College. The collection is dominated by the figurative sculpture of Albin Polasek, the Czech-American artist who lived and worked here before his death in 1965. Works by Augustus Saint-Gaudens and others are also on display.

MAITLAND MUSEUMS

The vision of a single artist is in evidence a few miles north at the **Maitland**

The historic Waterhouse Residence and Carpentry Shop Museums.

⊘ DISCOUNT SHOPPING

Shopping in Orlando is dominated by enormous outlet malls. It's smart to plan for an entire day exploring these bargain retailers, and even smarter to purchase an additional suitcase for the trip back home. Many visitors can be found walking through the outlet malls towing rolling suitcases behind them. The two best are **Orlando International Prime Outlets** (4951 International Dr; tel: 407-352-9600), a sprawling open-air mall anchored by Last Call and Off Fifth, with about 200 outlet and factory stores including Vince, Ted Baker, and St. John, and **Orlando Vineland Premium Outlets** (8200 Vineland Ave; tel: 407-238-7787; www.premiumoutlets.com/outlet/orlando-vineland; Mon–Sat 10am–11pm, Sun 10am–9pm). Set around an interior open-air court, it features such designer names as Armani, Ralph Lauren, Salvatore Ferragamo, and Calvin Klein among its 110 stores, plus an Elie Tahari outlet and an outparcel with, among others, Tommy Bahama.

With so many supermalls in Orlando, it's easy to overlook the **Lake Buena Vista Factory Stores** (15657 State Road 535; tel: 407-238-9301; http://lbvfs.com) east of I-4, but it's small and therefore more manageable. The Gap and Reebok outlets offer some of the best discounts in Orlando. Eddie Bauer and Oshkosh B'Gosh are other options.

Orlando's most special mall (other than Disney Springs) is the **Mall at Millenia** (4200 Conroy Rd; www.mallatmillenia.com), which is anchored by luxury retailers Neiman Marcus and Bloomingdale's, plus Macy's. Its halls are rich with showrooms by renowned designers and upscale jewelers. Among the 150 other stores, though, are appealing chain stores with moderately priced merchandise.

The **Florida Mall** (8001 S. Orange Blossom Trail; www.simon.com/mall/the-florida-mall) is larger, with 250 specialty shops and department stores including its own Macy's plus Dillard's and value-priced anchors Sears and JCPenney. Its Crayola Experience, Build-a-Bear Workshop, American Girl, and M&M's World options make it appealing to families.

Art Center (231 W. Packwood Ave; tel: 407-539-2181; http://artandhistory.org/maitlandartcenter; Tue–Sun 11am–4pm) in suburban **Maitland** ⑫ Founded as an art colony in the 1930s by visionary artist and architect André Smith, the museum is designed in an idiosyncratic Aztec style on 6 acres (2.5 hectares). Still an active center, it offers instruction, concerts, and exhibitions.

When William H. Waterhouse settled in Maitland at the end of the 19th century, he was a pioneer. By the time he completed his home here, he had become one of the area's most in-demand builders. The **Historic Waterhouse Residence and Carpentry Shop Museums** (820 Lake Lily Dr; tel: 407-644-2451; http://artandhistory.org; Thu–Sun noon–4pm) have been fully restored to show how he and his family would have lived on the shores of Lake Lily. Waterhouse built this entire house himself using basic tools like those found in the carpentry shop. The house is viewed by tour only. There is also a self-guided tour through a traditional Victorian herb garden.

The Audubon Society of Florida's National Center for Birds of Prey.

Several hundred wounded eagles, hawks, ospreys, and other raptors are rescued and rehabilitated by the **Audubon of Florida's National Center for Birds of Prey** (1101 Audubon Way; tel: 407-644-0190; http://fl.audubon.org/audubon-center-birds-prey; Tue–Sun 10am–4pm) on Lake Sybelia. Although recuperating birds are kept in an isolated facility to minimize human contact, visitors can view many species that are too severely injured to be returned to the wild.

A somber experience awaits visitors at the small **Holocaust Memorial Resource and Education Center of Central Florida** (851 N. Maitland Ave; tel: 407-628-0555; www.holocaustedu.org; Mon–Thu 9am–4pm, Fri 9am–1pm, Sun 1–4pm; free). One room tells the history of the Holocaust with multimedia displays, another offers changing exhibits on various aspects of the Nazi extermination campaign.

KISSIMMEE

South of Orlando, a short drive from Disney World, is **Kissimmee** ⑬, a small town chock-full of chain motels, fast-food joints, and second-string attractions, most clustered around US 192, also known as Irlo Bronson Memorial Highway.

Before Disney there was **Gatorland** ⑭ (14501 Orange Blossom Trail; tel: 800-393-5297; www.gatorland.com; daily 10am–5pm), an old-fashioned tourist attraction that's managed to survive the development of modern theme parks by sticking with a simple formula: if one alligator is good, thousands are better. Visitors can view breeding pens and nurseries, stroll through a cypress swamp, see monkeys, snakes, and other exotic wildlife, and sample down-home delicacies like smoked gator ribs and deep-fried gator nuggets. Two shows keep visitors entertained: The Gator Jumparoo Show, in which alligators leap out of the water to snatch a chicken from a trainer's hand, and the Gator Wrestling Show, featuring a wrangler who manhandles one of the big reptiles. The Screamin' Gator Zip Line carries brave visitors along 1,200ft (367 meters) of zip lines, high above the resident crocs and alligators below. With separate ticketing, you can take a swamp buggy ride in a custom 12ft (3.7-meter) -high open-sided vehicle. The Stompin' Gator Off-Road Adventure promises a rough ride through the swap, replicating a real Cracker experience, plus a stop to feed the alligators.

In recent years, eco-tourism and facilities for athletic thrills have popped up around Kissimmee and its Osceola County environs. Among these are **Forever Florida** (www.foreverflorida.com), with nature tours and a fabulous variety of zip line runs; **Orlando Tree Trek** (www.orlandotreetrek.com), with adult and children's ropes courses; and **Wild Florida** (https://wildfloridairboats.com), with a gator and wildlife park. Sprawling resort complexes are home to golf courses with golf schools and high-tech learning facilities. Several vendors offer daybreak hot air balloon rides too. Visit www.experiencekissimmee.com for ideas.

LEGOLAND

Polk County has found new life in **Legoland Florida** ⑮ (One Legoland Way, Winter Haven; tel: 877-350-LEGO; http://florida.legoland.com; daily, hours vary, see website for details), the biggest Legoland ever built (by acreage). The park is home to more than 50 rides, shows, and attractions and features an amazing array of Lego creations. In **Duplo Village** little ones can experience the thrill of driving a car or flying a plane. In the **LEGO Kingdoms** take part in a **Royal Joust** while riding aboard Lego horses or take flight on **The Dragon**, an indoor/outdoor roller-coaster. **Imagination Zone** is all about letting your imagination and creativity take over. It is also home to the park's most impressive Lego statues, including a bust of Albert Einstein.

Characters from The Lego Movie: 4-D – A New Adventure at Legoland Florida.

At the heart of the park is **Miniland USA** with seven themed zones (California, Washington DC, New York, Las Vegas, Kennedy Space Center, Daytona and Florida). Pirate's Shores features a live action pirate stunt show. Thrill seekers shouldn't despair, because **LEGO Technic** has the Lego Technic Test Track, a powerful roller-coaster featuring life-size Lego Technic vehicles. In **LEGOLAND Water Park** ride wave racers while dodging water blasters. While inside the **Land of Adventure** climb aboard the **Coaster-saurus**, a junior coaster the little ones are sure to enjoy. **The Lost Kingdom Adventure** is a dark thrill ride, which means the ride is in the dark. Passengers fire lasers at targets while riding the all-terrain roller-coaster. **Pharaoh's Revenge** gives parents and children alike a chance to fire foam balls at their enemies. Afterwards see if you can find your way out of the maze and into the **Beetle Bounce**. In **LEGO City** there's something for everyone. At **Rescue Academy**, families pile into a fire truck and race to put out a blaze.

Driving School grants children ages 6 to 13 a real-life driving experience in a safe environment. The **Ford Junior Driving School** gives children ages 3 to 5 a chance to experience driving in a lesser capacity. There's also a Ford Driving School for 6–13-year-olds. **Flying School** is a steel, inverted coaster that lets children experience the feel of flight. Take some time and unwind with **The Big Test** an interactive, acrobatic show that playfully teaches about the responsibilities of fire safety in a fun and entertaining way. Wrap things up in the **LEGO Clubhouse**, which houses the world's first Massively Multi Online Game, or MMOG for short. In 2018, the force will awaken at **LEGO Star Wars Miniland**, including recreations of Kylo Ren, Finn, and other characters from the series' Episode VII movie.

If you're staying overnight, choose one of the two Lego-themed hotels right on the property. They'll be a highlight for your kids. Download the Quest to Legoland app for info on sites on your ride to the park. It's aimed at school-age kids.

The Safari Trek at Legoland Florida.

POLK COUNTY

Fantasy of Flight (1400 Broadway Blvd SE, Polk City; tel: 863-984-3500; www.fantasyofflight.com; sporadic openings Fri–Sun 11am–3pm) offers a trip down aviation's memory lane, featuring a small collection of owner Kermit Weeks' large inventory of vintage airplanes at any one time.

Wallaby Ranch Hang Gliding (1805 Deen Still Road; tel: 800-WALLABY; www.wallaby.com; daily) is the perfect option if you're looking for something out of the ordinary. Wallaby Ranch will send you up on a tandem flight with an instructor using a technique they call aero-towing. This means the hangglider is towed into the air with a specially designed ultra-light tow plane. Once you reach an altitude of 2,000ft (609 meters), your instructor releases the tow line. After a few minutes of instruction, you'll be in control.

Nature lovers should visit the Nature Conservancy's **Disney Wilderness Preserve** (2700 Scrub Jay Trail; tel: 407-935-0002; www.nature.org; daily 9am–4.30pm Nov–Mar, Mon–Fri Apr–Oct), a 12,000-acre (4,800-hectare) preserve with 7 miles (11km) of hiking trails through wetlands and pine flatwoods ecosystems. Guided walks and off-road tours are available.

SOUTH OF ORLANDO

Fifty-five miles (89km) southwest of downtown Orlando, **Lake Wales** ⓰, at 250ft (76 meters) above sea level, is one of the highest places in the state. The **Lake Wales Depot Museum and Cultural Center** (325 S. Scenic Highway; tel: 863-676-41759; www.cityoflakewales.com/439/depot-museum; Tue–Sat 9am–5pm) has displays related to Lake Wales' 1911 founding and 19th-century development. The downtown region is in the National Register of Historic Places. Even higher is the 205ft (62-meter) Singing Tower in **Bok Tower Gardens** (1151 Tower Blvd; tel: 863-676-1408; www.boktowergardens.org; daily 8am–6pm,

last admission 5pm), a special attraction just north of town. The National Historic Landmark, dating to 1929, has a 205ft (62-meter) tower housing a 60-bell carillon that plays music at least twice a day, plus magnificent gardens designed by Frederick Law Olmsted, Jr., of Central Park, NY, fame, and a 1930s mansion that is open for tours

Fifteen miles (24km) west of Lake Wales is **Bartow**, the center of an industry that has boosted the economy but taken a toll on the environment. SR 60 takes you past Bone Valley, heart of the phosphate mining industry. Florida produces nearly 60 percent of the US's phosphate, a key ingredient in fertilizer. Draglines often dig up fossils of mammoths and giant sharks.

AN UNEXPECTED GEM

Lakeland ⓱ is another blue-collar city. But if you're a Frank Lloyd Wright enthusiast then you'll want to see **Florida Southern College** (www.flsouthern.edu), where students study within the world's largest collection of buildings designed by Frank Lloyd Wright (1869–1959).

A significant percent of the world's orange juice starts off growing on a tree in Florida.

Despite the quick pace of growth in the Orlando area, there are still some natural spaces.

Maps available from the Sharp Family Tourism and Education Center (840 Johnson Ave, Lakeland; tel: 863-680-4597; daily 9.30am–4.30pm), and self-guided and in-depth tours are of these functional works of art – the oldest of which is the **Annie Pfeiffer Chapel** (111 Lake Hollingsworth Dr), built in 1938.

Explorations V Children's Museum (109 N. Kentucky Ave; tel: 863-687-3869; www.explorationsv.com; Mon–Sat 9am–5.30pm) features three floors filled with kid-powered exhibits. This hands-on, fully interactive museum lets children create their own news report, become a news anchor, or take the stage like a Broadway star.

ORLANDO NORTH

Seminole County (www.visitseminole.com), directly north of all things Orlando, bills itself as Orlando North and wants visitors to know about its nature offerings.

If you want some green to counter your theme park immersion, begin with a canoe or kayak rental along the Wekiwa River. One place to begin is **Wekiwa Springs State Park** (1800

Manatees in Blue Springs State Park.

Wekiwa Circle, Apopka; tel: 407-884-2008; www.floridastateparks.org/wekiwa springs; daily 8am–sunset). With enormous oak and cypress trees, this beautiful 7,800-acre (3,160-hectare) park is a gem for swimming in a natural spring or paddling along the Wekiwa River and Rock Springs Run. There are also hiking and biking trails.

For Old Florida fun, take an airboat ride along Lake Jessup with **Black Hammock Airboat Adventure** (2356 Black Hammock Fish Camp Rd, Oviedo; tel: 407-977-8235; www.blackhammockairboatrides.com; 9.30am–5.30pm). The lake is home to bald eagles, a host of birdlife, bobcats, turtles, and more than 10,000 alligators. If you don't spot one, you can see them in the live gator exhibit. Afterwards enjoy the views from the Lazy Gator Bar and Black Hammock Restaurant.

Visit **Blue Springs State Park** (2100 W. French Ave, Orange City; tel: 386-775-3663) November through March for a rare chance to see manatees in the wild. Set along the St. Johns River, this beautiful park contains large natural

springs which are a winter refuge for the manatee. A boardwalk with viewing platforms runs along the springs.

The **Geneva Wilderness Area** (www.seminolecountyfl.gov/parksrec/naturallands/geneva.aspx), with 180 acres (73 hectares) of mixed hardwood swamp, mesic flatwoods, and scrubby flatwoods, is excellent for light hikes. So is the adjacent **Little Big Econ State Forest** (www.freshfromflorida.com).

LAKE COUNTY

West of Orlando and north of Disney World, Lake County (www.visitlakefl.com) is evolving from a hilly citrus community to a sprawling suburb, but it has some noteworthy tourist stops. In the culture arena, look for the quirky **Presidents Hall of Fame** (http://presidentshalloffame.com), the **Lakeridge Winery** (www.lakeridgewinery.com), and the **Modernism Museum** (www.modernismmuseum.org), which shares its collection with the nearby restaurant **1921** (www.1921nva.com), owned by celebrity chef Norman Van Aken. Both are in scenic, lakefront **Mount Dora** (www.

visitmountdora.com), with small-time gallery hopping and boat tours among the ways to spend a few hours. On weekends, with live music and kiddie activities like pony rides, **Yalaha Bakery** (www.yalahabakery.com) is more an event than merely a lunch stop.

If you'd like to ride a seaplane, head your car to **Tavares** (www.tavares.org). It bills itself as America's Seaplane City, and that's because, on the shore of Lake Dora, its Seaplane Base and Marina is a hub for enthusiasts. Visitors can take a seaplane ride, splash in a seaplane-themed water park, or simply watch the vehicles fly in and out in large numbers. The Royal Palm Railway Experience, comprised of vintage 1950s train cars run on diesel, offers single-loop rides from Tavares to neighboring Eustis and Mount Dora. The ride has a theme tied into Warner Bros.

For more rugged adventures, make an appointment at **Revolution Off Road** (www.revolutionoffroad.com), where you can take a guided off-road ATV tour, ride an amphibious Mucky Duck vehicle, or try your hand at archery.

Seaplane on Lake Dora, Tavares.

A vintage train station is preserved at Heritage Village near Clearwater.

People and pelicans gather at Naples Pier.

GULF COAST

Beautiful beaches lure travelers to the west coast, but you'll also find vibrant urban neighborhoods, fine museums, an elaborate theme park, and, in a few quiet corners, a slice of Florida as it used to be.

Teeing off on Gasparilla Island near Fort Myers.

The Gulf of Mexico caresses the fine, bleached sand of Florida's western shores. Its warm waters undulate gently or, sometimes, not at all, often flat as a sheet of glass on humid summer days. Shells of every color and shape are washed up on the sands to the endless delight of beach-combing vacationers.

Such tranquil scenes stand in sharp contrast to the clamor on the shores. Newcomers and developers have laid siege to this once placid part of Florida. From the metropolitan Tampa–St Petersburg nucleus, one of the fastest-growing conurbations in the US, north to New Port Richey and south to Fort Myers, the Gulf Coast has begun to resemble the waterfront wall of windows characteristic of the Miami-to-Palm-Beach strip on the Atlantic Coast. Here you'll find retire-ment farms, condos, and mansions. With them have come massive malls, traffic jams, and urban sprawl.

And like the rest of Florida, the Gulf Coast is a place for indulging the imagination. The increas-ingly chic St Petersburg delves into the surreal at The Dalí, containing one of the most comprehensive collections of Dalí's work in the world, while the glit-tering domain of the circus is celebrated in Sarasota and Venice, where circus impresario John Ringling left a legacy of theaters, museums, schools for the performing arts, and festivals.

When it comes to theme parks, Busch Gardens Tampa Bay competes with the best of Orlando's attractions. A great swath of land has been turned into a miniature Africa, complete with big game and a jungle cruise.

Ringling Museum, Sarasota.

But the old Gulf Coast lingers in the fishing villages around Cedar Key and spots south of Naples, and Latino color still enlivens Tampa's Ybor City, founded by a wealthy Cuban tobacco merchant in the late 19th cen-tury and now, with its specialty shops, bars, and museum, a tribute to Florida's once thriving cigar industry. Art Deco, too, may still be encoun-tered in downtown Tampa, proving this architectural renaissance is not confined to sunny Miami Beach.

Downtown Tampa.

TAMPA

The largest city on the Gulf Coast has numerous cultural attractions, a historic Cuban neighborhood, and one of Florida's best theme parks.

History, as well as archeology, tells us Tampa's coastline has been inhabited for 12,000 years. Native cultures once called this area home, living off the land and sea until European settlers arrived and began colonizing the region. Spanish explorer Panfilo de Naravaez came here in search of gold and other wealth, but it was Henry B. Plant who truly put Tampa on the map and brought the area into the modern age when his railroad arrived in 1884. Yankee-born Plant made his fortune by consolidating the bankrupt railroads of the South after the Civil War. A self-made man who got his start delivering express packages, Plant also helped spearhead winter tourism in Florida.

A love of travel and foreign locale inspired the Moorish Revival design of the **Tampa Bay Hotel**, a national historic landmark now housing the Henry B. Plant Museum (see page 258). Constructed from reinforced concrete, the 6-acre (2-hectare) hotel building has six minarets, four cupolas, and three domes on the roof, totaling 13, the number of months in the Islamic calendar. One of six Florida hotels built by Plant, the 511-room Tampa Bay Hotel was the most modern resort of its day, with private baths, electric lighting, elevators, and telephones in every room. It had a beauty shop, barbershop, florist, grand salon, sanitarium, dining room, solarium, and ballroom with orchestra.

Immigrant Statue, Ybor City.

Landscaped grounds covering 150 acres (60 hectares) of waterfront included 21 buildings, an 18-hole golf course, tennis courts, croquet courts, a boathouse, stables, a racetrack, kennels, a bowling alley, a casino with a 1,500-seat auditorium, a swimming pool, even a zoo.

Set at the mouth of the Hillsborough River, Port Tampa Bay – the seventh largest in the US – is an industrial powerhouse, transporting more than 37 million tons of cargo annually, including phosphate from nearby mines, citrus, seafood, and petroleum products. The port

⊙ Main Attractions
Henry B. Plant Museum
Tampa Museum of Art
Tampa Bay History Center
Florida Aquarium
Ybor City
Busch Gardens
Museum of Science and Industry
Lowry Park Zoo

Maps on pages 258, 261

Old-time cigar shops are part of Ybor City's Cuban heritage.

hosts four cruise lines traveling routes to the Gulf of Mexico, the Caribbean, and Cuba. It is a short trip from attractions like Busch Gardens, the Lowry Park Zoo, the Museum of Science and Industry, Ybor City, and the Florida Aquarium.

Tampa's historic neighborhoods are experiencing a renaissance, driven by an influx of young, entrepreneurial residents. The spirit is breathing new life into once-moribund neighborhoods including downtown, the Cuban-influenced **Ybor City**, hipster havens Tampa Heights and Seminole Heights, and the bungalow-filled, historic upscale dining and shopping area of **Hyde Park/SoHo**. The TECO Historic Streetcar can carry you from downtown to Ybor City in a few minutes. The area's growing number of transportation options includes Coast Bike Share, ZipCar, and the Downtowner, a free electric shuttle service. You'll still need to hop on I-275 to visit Busch Gardens Tampa Bay, Tampa's Lowry Park Zoo, and the Museum of Science and Industry, but Tampa is a manageable destination, worthy of more than a quick stop en route to the Gulf beaches.

Tampa Bay has a growing hipster presence. It is home to two dozen craft breweries (and two food halls, with a third on the way). The area's first commercial brewery opened in Ybor City in 1897. Today, Cigar City Brewing (www.cigarcitybrewing.com) and Coppertail Brewing (www.coppertailbrewing.com) are destinations for aficionados. Cider and mead are also popular.

DOWNTOWN TAMPA

Symbolic of Tampa's ambitious revitalization project is the 2.4-mile (4km) **Riverwalk** (www.thetampariverwalk.com) cultural corridor completed in 2017 on the east bank of the Hillsborough River. In addition to the **Henry B. Plant Museum ❶** (401 W. Kennedy Blvd, Tampa; tel: 813-254-1891; www.plantmuseum.com; Tue–Sat 10am–5pm, Sun noon–5pm) are several other cultural institutions, including the five-theater **David A. Straz Jr Center for the Performing Arts ❷** (1010 North W.C. MacInnes Place; tel: 813-229-STAR; www.strazcenter.org), the largest theater complex south of Washington, DC. It is

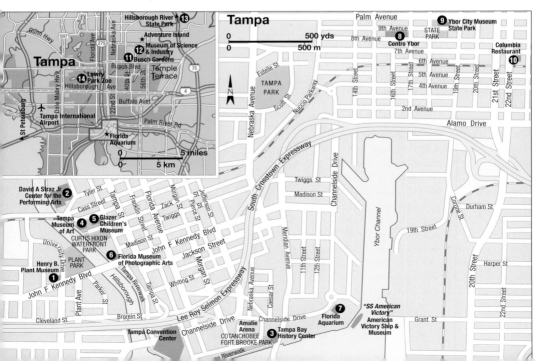

a major destination for theater productions, classical concerts, and the arts.

Anchoring the southern end, the **Tampa Bay History Center ❸** (801 Old Water St; tel: 813-228-0097; www.tampa bayhistorycenter.org; daily 10am–5pm) tells the story of Tampa from prehistoric times to the present. Tampa's strategic importance during a succession of wars is examined, starting with Fort Brooke (now no more than a historical marker), the 1824 military outpost used by the US Army during the Second and Third Seminole Wars (1835–55) and occupied by the Confederate Army during the Civil War. Tampa's important national role as a major mobilization point for US troops during the Spanish-American War in 1898 was reprised in World War II, when 15,000 servicemen were stationed at McDill Air Force Base.

The Riverwalk has yet more. **Tampa Museum of Art ❹** (120 W. Gasparilla Plaza; tel: 813-274-8130; www.tampamus eum.org; Mon–Thu 11am–7pm, Fri until 10pm, Sat–Sun 11am–5pm) is emerging as a state-of-the-art facility. The museum has a two-story atrium, stone floors, and a boxlike, cantilevered structure sheathed in a metal skin and programmable LED lighting that turns into a work of art itself after the sun goes down. TMA's wide-ranging art collection includes classical antiquities, regional contemporary art, and regular traveling exhibits.

The **Glazer Children's Museum ❺** (Glazer Children's Museum, 110 W Gasparilla Plaza; tel: 813-443-3861; https:// glazermuseum.org; Mon–Fri 10am–5pm, Sat 10am–6pm, Sun 1–6pm) is a draw for families. More than 170 interactive exhibits give little ones 10 and under the chance to learn, build, play, and experiment, and climb a 30ft (9-meter) climbing tower.

At the **Florida Museum of Photographic Arts ❻** (400 N. Ashley Dr, Cube 200; tel: 813-221-2222; http://fmopa.org; Mon–Thu 11am–6pm, Fri until 7pm, Sat–Sat noon–5pm), housed in a dramatic six-story cube, exhibits celebrate photography as an art form.

WATER WORLD

The largest visitor attraction within walking distance to the Tampa Riverwalk

Moorish domes cap the Henry B. Plant Museum – formerly the Tampa Bay Hotel – at the University of Tampa.

A shark prowls the waters of the Florida Aquarium.

⊘ GASPARILLA INVASION

Tampa's rites of spring occur every year when its businessmen and bigwigs don puffed-sleeved shirts and buckled boots and board the *José Gasparilla* for the annual Gasparilla Invasion. Pirates climb the three masts to the crow's nests, blast cannon, and set off for the mouth of the Hillsborough River flanked by hundreds of smaller craft with their own swashbuckling crews. Upon landing, pirates swarm the streets of downtown Tampa, where hundreds of thousands of spectators watch them lead the third-largest parade in the US. The first Gasparilla parade was held in 1904. It grew out of the Gulf Coast's reputation as a haunt for bloodthirsty buccaneers, particularly a legendary character named José Gaspar. Today, the annual invasion kicks off 10 weeks of festivals, parades, and parties know as Gasparilla Season.

is the soaring **Florida Aquarium**  (701 Channelside Dr; tel: 813-273-4000; www.flaquarium.org; daily 9.30am–5pm). This attractive aquarium is one of the best in the country. A carefully crafted interpretive theme tying together exhibits on three floors lets you follow a drop of Florida water from its source in one of the state's many springs to the sea, from its source on land and wetlands to the bay and, finally, the open sea.

Allow plenty of time to enjoy the many interactive exhibits, which include the Florida Wetlands Trail, Bay and Beaches, and the very popular Coral Reef, which is a 500,000-gallon (2-million-liter) replica of the Dry Tortugas in Key West. It is home to sea turtles, sand tiger sharks, and tropical fish. You can also get up-close views of ring-tailed lemurs in the Journey to Madagascar exhibit. Throughout the day, you can see divers in the Secret Sea Life Superhero exhibit give educational game show-style presentations about three oceanic species that the aquarium strives to protect. Add-on adventures include diving with the sharks (scuba certification is required),

Ybor City.

a Wild Dolphin Cruise on Tampa Bay, and close-ups with the penguins.

YBOR CITY

About the time Plant was building his rail system, steamship lines, and hotels, Vicente Martinez Ybor was planning to move his cigar factory from Key West. Just east of downtown, Cuban-influenced Ybor City grew to prominence as the Cigar Capital of the World. Cuban freedom fighter José Martí frequently made fiery speeches to build support for his 1890s revolution against Spain. A park in Ybor City honoring Martí remains property of the Cuban people and is open to visitors. Ybor City is now a popular shopping and nightclub district, bustling with activity into the wee hours. Its history and sites embrace the heritage of its Cuban, German, and Eastern European immigrants.

At one time Ybor City had 200 cigar factories, with hundreds of workers in each one. The original immigrant's backyard chickens have grown into a current population of wild chickens.

The red-brick buildings, wrought-iron balconies, and brick-lined streets survive, making it one of the most charming areas of the city. The cigar shops, still prominent here, have been joined by trendy shops and vintage clothing boutiques. After dark, Ybor City is Tampa's liveliest nightlife area.

The heart of the district along 7th Avenue – **La Setima** – is lined with bars, clubs, restaurants, cafés, and cigar bars, which come into their own after 5pm. **Centro Ybor**  has several good bars and cafés. Further along 7th Avenue is the beautiful tiled facade of the Columbia Restaurant, a local institution.

A Saturday market (www.ybormarket.com) takes place in Centennial Park at 9th Avenue and 19th Street. Opposite is the **Ybor City Museum State Park**  (1818 9th Avenue; tel: 813-247-6323; www.ybormuseum.org; Wed–Sun 9am–5pm), set in an old bakery dating from 1896. Here you can watch some of the last of the master cigar rollers at work, and take a walking tour of the district. Next door, several small cottages, or casitas, where the workers once lived provide a truly fascinating look into the life of the community. The historic streetcar travels along **Eighth Avenue** (putting riders one block from the main strip, known as La Setima), with shops selling hand-rolled cigars, vintage clothing, and strong *café con leche*. For lunch, sample a hot, pressed Cuban (a pork sandwich) at **La Tropicana**, considered the best in the city. Don't miss dinner at the landmark **Columbia Restaurant ⑩** (www.columbia restaurant.com) on the corner of 22nd Street. The family-run Columbia, built in 1905, is the real deal. Sit back and enjoy the flamenco show, strolling musicians, and the gracious black-jacketed waiters serving classic Spanish dishes like paella and garbanzo bean soup. There are other branches in the city, but none as authentic as the original.

WILD KINGDOM

Started in 1959 as a family zoo of exotic animals and tropical gardens for

visitors to the Anheuser-Busch Brewery, **Busch Gardens Tampa Bay ⑪** (10165 N. McKinley Dr, Tampa; tel: 813-884-4386; www.buschgardenstampa.com; daily 10am–6pm, but check website for changes) has matured into one of Florida's top theme parks. It combines the best of everything: a superb conservation zoo; professional concerts and seasonal shows; landscaped grounds; and rides, from super-soaking water rides to state-of-the-art roller-coasters, featuring gravity-defying inversions, barrel rolls, and intertwining tracks.

The park's 335 acres (136 hectares) include 10 distinct areas: Morocco, Crown Colony, Edge of Africa, Serengeti Plain, Egypt, Nairobi, Pantopia, Congo, Stanleyville, and Bird Gardens. Entering through Morocco, get an overview of the whole park by boarding the skyway ride, which begins at Crown Colony in the southeast and ends at Congo in the northwest. Or take a ride on the delightful miniature train, which puffs its way slowly around the 65-acre (26-hectare) Serengeti Plain on the park's east side, with stops at

Decorative lights illuminate Seventh Avenue near Centro Ybor.

Ybor City Museum.

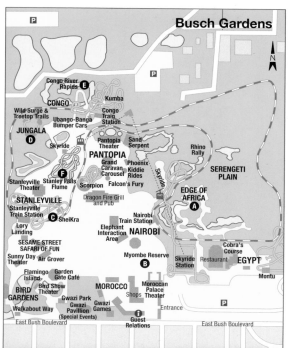

Tip

One day at Busch Gardens wasn't enough? Inquire about a free or discounted next-day ticket at Guest Relations before you leave the park.

Nairobi, Congo, and Stanleyville. The southwest corner, the original roadside attraction of tropical gardens, with flamingos, snakes, and exotic animals, is more slow-paced. It has toddler rides, bird shows, walk-through aviaries, and pleasantly shaded pathways.

Plan your visit to this huge park carefully and pace yourself: there are few short cuts between attractions, so you'll be on your feet for the better part of the day. A two-day pass lets you dedicate one day to learning about the 12,000 animals that live in naturalized environments in the park and another to enjoy the rides. Busch Gardens' rides load very quickly. Note that wildlife is more active in the cooler morning hours and the animals sleep in the afternoon.

AFRICAN SAFARI

The park's hottest tickets for animal-lovers are five daily **Serengeti Safaris** (limit 20 people, first-come, first-served) that start at Crown Colony and trek out onto the Serengeti Plain to view rhinos, zebras and giraffes. If you're keen, head there first and sign up for a tour.

If it's sold out, the next best thing is the **Edge of Africa** exhibit, which features nose-to-nose encounters with baboons, Nile crocs, hippos, a lion and lioness, hyenas, vultures, and meerkats. Rangers holding animal ambassadors, such as monkeys and snakes, stroll the park. They are trained wildlife biologists, and you'll learn a lot from them. Brass plaques have wildlife conservation messages that can be rubbed and collected in a free wildlife guide. Other displays mimic a biologist's field diary. Some of the best can be found in the entrancing **Myombe Reserve** gorilla exhibit in Nairobi, one of the most satisfying of Busch's animal exhibits.

WILD RIDE

It may seem odd to have rides in a wildlife park, but in the race for tourist dollars, Busch Gardens is determined to keep up with the other parks. Falcon's Fury, North America's tallest free-standing drop tower, stands at 335ft (102 meters) and takes riders soaring straight down at 60mph (97kmh). Florida's first triple launch coaster, Cheetah Hunt, launches riders on a 4,400ft (1,340-meter) sprint. **SheiKra**, North America's first dive coaster, is a floor-less monster that climbs 200ft (60 meters), then rockets 90 degrees down in a simultaneous loop and roll. More death-defying loops, dives, drops, and inversions are in store on the Kumba and Montu roller coasters at opposite ends of the park. The **Cobra's Curse** roller coaster puts a spin on family thrills with a 70ft (21-meter) vertical lift that brings you face-to-face with an 80ft (24-meter) snake king's fangs.

Jungala, in the Congo area, has a zip-line experience, a climbing area, a jungle village, and Bengal tigers, orangutans, and other residents of the former Claw Island. Congo also has the popular **Congo River Rapids**, which simulates a white-water ride, while next door in Stanleyville, the **Stanley Falls** flume ride guarantees a good drenching.

Falcon's Fury drop tower ride.

The **Sesame Street Safari of Fun** was designed just for the little tykes (under age five). It has play areas, junior rides, and shows. **Cheetah Hunt** is a 4,400ft (1,340-meter) -long coaster which reaches speeds of 60mph (96kmh) and runs through the Cheetah Run.

COOLING OFF

After a steamy day in the jungle, refresh yourself in the body flumes, lagoons, and waterfalls of **Adventure Island** (10001 McKinley Dr; tel: 888-800-5447; www.adventureisland.com; open seasonally). Another of Tampa's top attractions – the **Museum of Science and Industry** ⑫ (4801 E. Fowler Ave; tel: 813-987-6000; www.mosi.org; Mon–Fri 10am–5pm, Sat–Sun until 6pm) – is nearby. MOSI contains a vast array of lively science exhibits, a butterfly pavilion, a domed IMAX cinema, and hands-on contraptions that allow you to learn how your body works. One of the most popular attractions is Gulf Coast Hurricane, a re-created 75mph (120kmh) wind tunnel that pitches you right into the storm.

It's not all man-made hoopla. **Hillsborough River State Park** ⑬ (15402 US 301 N, Thonotosassa; tel: 813-987-6771www.floridastateparks.org/park/hillsborough-river; daily 8am–sunset), 15 miles (24km) from downtown, has a large campground and hiking trails and is a prime spot for canoeing. Tampa's **Lowry Park Zoo** ⑭ (1101 West Sligh Blvd; tel: 813-935-8552; www.lowryparkzoo.com; daily 9.30am–5pm) has wooden walkways that wind through 56 acres (23 hectares) and seven exhibit areas, including Asian Gardens and Primate World, a petting park, and a free-flight aviary. One highlight is the manatee hospital, where you can watch recuperating manatees swimming from above and below.

East of Tampa, **Giraffe Ranch** (38650 Mickler Dr, Dade City; tel: 813-482-3400; www.girafferanch.com; tours daily 11am and 2pm) is a fabulous non-touristy animal attraction run by a former zoo director with experience as an African safari guide. In a covered, open-sided tram – or on camelback, llamaback or Segway (which is incredibly fun) – a knowledgeable leader will bring you on an educational yet entertaining tour of the 47-acre (19-hectare) property. It's a working game farm and animal preserve with more than 400 animals of 70 species, among them ostriches, zebras, and giraffes, which you'll feed during your visit. Of special note are an endangered Kenyan antelope species called the eastern mountain bongo. Pay the extra fee to feed grapes to lemurs; the experience is worth the price. So is washing and feeding the rhino, and feeding otters or Bongo antelopes. A wallaby encounter is also fun.

A related property named **Safari Wilderness** (10850 Moore Rd, Lakeland; tel: 813-382-2130; www.safariwilderness.com) is closer to Lakeland. Here, you can take a truck tour or explore the savannah on horseback or camelback, or via kayak. A summertime sundown safari allows touring in cooler temperatures in warmer months. Kids love both parks, but so do adults traveling without little ones.

⊙ Tip

Canoe Escape (tel: 813-986-2067; www.canoeescape.com) organizes a variety of canoe trips through Hillsborough River State Park. Call for reservations.

Rhinos grazing at Busch Gardens.

The Don CeSar Hotel.

ST PETERSBURG TO CEDAR KEY

This city by the bay – home to The Dalí Museum and other cultural attractions – is a gateway to gorgeous beaches, unspoiled fishing villages, and crystal-clear rivers where manatees swim.

What makes the perfect beach? Florida geologist Dr Stephen Leatherman, also known as Dr Beach, thinks he can identify the best using criteria such as sand softness, number and size of waves, color and condition of water, presence of wildlife and pests, and human use and impacts.

When Dr Beach announces his annual list of Top Ten beaches, there are always a few Florida locations hovering near the top. **Fort De Soto Park** ❶, a huge county park, campground, and boat launch encompassing five barrier islands at the southern tip of the peninsula, is a former winner. So is **Caladesi Island State Park** ❷, a boat-in-only beach on an island north of Clearwater. **Clearwater Beach** ❸ is popular with many overseas visitors, and the Gulf of Mexico side of **St Petersburg** and the **Pinellas Peninsula** are perennial favorites.

Thousands of lodgings, from historic hotel resorts to vacation condos, along with neighborhood restaurants serving fresh grouper, stone crab, and other local seafood, crowd the seafront the length of Gulf Boulevard, the main thoroughfare. Each beach community is joined to the mainland by a causeway that crosses the tranquil Intracoastal Waterway. From here, you're just minutes from US 19, which links the 26 communities of the Pinellas Peninsula, and Interstate 275, linking Tampa and Sarasota via Tampa Bay bridges.

GULF SHORE

With record sunshine and turquoise waters lapping 35 miles (56km) of shoreline, the gulf is mesmerizing. Walk for miles on these super-clean beaches, swim or kayak in shallow gulf waters, go fishing and scuba diving, watch seabirds and other wildlife, take boat tours to undeveloped island refuges, or just soak up the sun. **Long Key**, at the south end, boasts **St Pete Beach** ❹, home

Main Attractions

Fort De Soto Park
Caladesi Island State Park
Clearwater Marine
  Aquarium
Wheedon Island Preserve
  Cultural and Natural
  History Center
Museum of Fine Arts
The Dalí Museum
Tarpon Springs
Cedar Key

**Maps on pages
266, 268**

Clearwater canine.

A pedicab trawls for passengers on the Clearwater beachfront.

to the bright pink historic Don CeSar Resort, and **Passe-a-Grill Beach**, with its low-rise historic district and quaint shops. On the quieter north end, the busy waterfront at **Clearwater ⑤** has kid-flavored distractions including **Captain Memo's Pirate Cruise** (25 Causeway Blvd, Dock 3; tel: 727-446-2587; www.captainmemo.com; daily), a two-hour cruise where parents relax while kids do educational activities.

Nestled in a residential waterfront neighborhood is **Clearwater Marine Aquarium** (249 Windward Passage; tel: 727-441-1790; www.seewinter.com; daily 9am–6pm), which quietly carries out award-winning work as a marine

rescue and release center. Enclosures hold recuperating sea turtles, otters, dolphins, and other sealife, all injured or impacted by human carelessness. CMA's star attraction is Winter, a bottle-nose dolphin who lost her tail to a crab trap. Winter was fitted with a prosthetic tail in early 2011, and is now learning to swim properly again. There are regular enrichment exercises with resident dolphins in the main pool and reserved times to feed a dolphin and have your photo taken (additional fee; visitors provide the camera). Multimedia presentations about CMA's work take place in an attractive circular theater.

Suncoast Seabird Sanctuary (18328 Gulf Blvd; tel: 727-391-6211; www.seabirdsanctuary.com; daily 8am–4pm; free) was founded by bird-lover Ralph Heath. Donations allow Heath to care for 500-plus injured and crippled cormorants, pelicans, sandpipers, white herons, and other seabirds.

Several miles inland, **Pinewood Cultural Park ⑥** (Walsingham Rd and 125th St North, Largo; www.pinewoodculturalpark.org) is home to two worthy attractions: the **Florida Botanical Gardens** (12520 Ulmerton Rd, tel: 727-582-2100; www.flbg.org; daily 7am–sunset), with 120 acres (48 hectares) of theme gardens and natural areas; and **Heritage Village** (11909 125th St N, tel: 727-582-2123; www.pinellascounty.org/heritage/; Wed–Sat 10am–4pm, Sun 1–4pm), a compound with vintage structures from the 1850s to the early 1900s.

ST PETERSBURG

St Petersburg ⑦ is beginning to overcome its reputation as a retirement haven. A regenerated waterfront, top museums, trend-forward restaurant, a major-league baseball team, year-round festivals, and activities geared to an outdoor lifestyle are attracting a stylish young demographic. Shuffleboard is even becoming popular with the hipsters, thanks, in part, to a free St Pete Shuffle every Friday night at the historic courts.

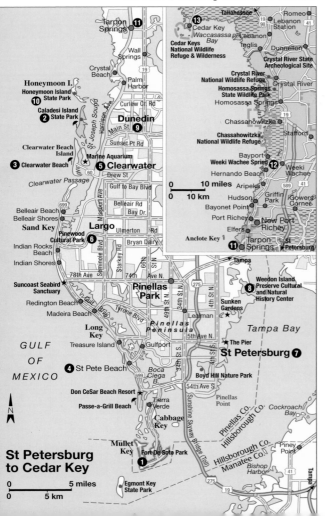

St Petersburg to Cedar Key

Tampa Bay was once home to the Tocobaga, Timucua, and Manasota people. Artifacts including shell mounds and an ancient dugout canoe have been excavated and are on display at the **Weedon Island Preserve Cultural and Natural History Center** ❽ (1800 Weedon Dr NE; tel: 727-453-6500; www. weedonislandcenter.org; daily sunrise til 15 minutes before sunset), a natural area of marshes and uplands crisscrossed by hiking trails on the Pinellas Peninsula. Spanish explorer Panfilo de Narvaez in 1528, followed by Hernando de Soto in 1539, named the peninsula Punta Pinal (or Point of Pines), which later became Pinellas. De Soto found the only mineral springs on the peninsula near a large Tocobaga village in Safety Harbor.

In 1875, 1,600 acres (650 hectares) of what would eventually become St Petersburg were purchased and settled by General John Williams of Detroit. Williams made a deal with exiled Russian nobleman Peter Demens to bring the railroad to Pinellas Peninsula. Demens overcame yellow fever and flooding to expand a short logging track on the peninsula into Henry Plant's Orange Belt Line, joining the gulf with citrus groves in Sanford in central Florida. The port prospered until the disastrous citrus freeze of 1894, when Plant bought the branch railroad for a song.

In 1914, St Petersburg again made transportation history when Tony Jannus piloted a flying airboat called the *Benoist* 21 miles (34km) over Tampa Bay, the world's first commercial flight.

ART AND HISTORY

Folksy **St Petersburg Museum of History** ❶ (335 2nd Ave NE; tel: 727-894-1052; http://historystpete.org; Mon–Sat 10am–5pm, Sun noon–5pm), though at the foot of the commercial pier complex, has exhibits on local history, including a full-scale replica of the *Benoist* airboat, plus the world's largest collection of autographed baseballs. The stirring story of St Petersburg's historic African-American community is well told at this museum, as well as at the nearby **Dr Carter G. Woodson Museum of African American History** ❷ (2240 9th Ave

A wildlife rehabilitator at the Suncoast Seabird Sanctuary introduces visitors to one of her patients – a double-crested cormorant.

Fort De Soto Park is often ranked as one of America's best beaches.

South; tel: 727-323-1104; www.woodson museum.org; Tue–Fri noon–5pm; free).

The elegant **Museum of Fine Arts**  (255 Beach Dr NE; tel: 727-96-2667; http://mfastpete.org; Mon–Wed and Fri–Sat 10am–5pm, Thu 10am–8pm, Sun noon–5pm) in downtown St Petersburg was founded by Margaret Acheson Stuart to house her private art collection, the museum has the atmosphere of a stately home showcasing family treasures. Monet, Morisot, Rodin, O'Keeffe, and Willem de Kooning are among the major artists represented here. There is an outstanding photography collection, and collections of pre-Columbian, Native American, African, Egyptian, Asian, and Greek and Roman art.

You can walk from here to the multi-part **Morean Arts Center**, which is perhaps best known for the Chihuly Collection **D** (720 Central Ave; tel: 727-822-7872; www.moreanartscenter.org/chihuly), which features a permanent collection of otherworldly glass creations by artist Dale Chihuly. Admission to the Collection also includes a free live local glassblowing demonstration

A docent demonstrates old-fashioned kitchen utensils at Heritage Village in Pinewood Cultural Park.

Morean Arts Center.

at the Morean Glass Studio & Hot Shop, plus visits to the nearby Morean Arts Center and the Morean Center for Clay (located in the Warehouse Arts District), featuring contemporary art by local, regional, and national artists

By far the most famous cultural attraction here is **The Dalí Museum** **E** (One Dali Blvd; tel: 727-823-3767; www.thedali.org; daily 10am–5pm, Thu until 8pm). This world-class institution may seem oddly out of place in this sun-loving vacationland, but it shows the more cultural side of Florida that often goes underappreciated. The gift of the Morse family, personal friends of Salvador and Gala Dalí, the collection features over 2,000 diverse works, including almost 100 oil paintings. The core of the collection is not the eight enormous masterworks, but rather the early Dalí landscapes of Spain, which are filled with lush Impressionist influences and are unexpectedly charming. To provide a deeper understanding of Dalí's paintings, the museum offers free docent and audio tours, audio-visual tours via a smartphone app, and Mustache Tour audio guides for children. The gift shop

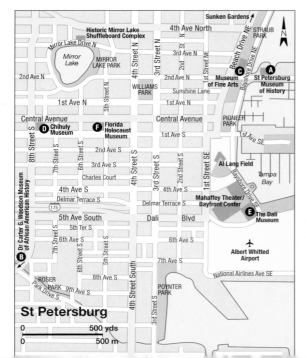

is a must for Dalí fans; 85 percent of the merchandise is exclusive to the museum.

A more somber experience is to be had at the **Florida Holocaust Museum** **F** (55 5th St South; tel: 727-820-0100; www.thefhm.org; daily 10am–5pm, last admission 4pm; docent-led tours Tue and Sat 1.30pm). This museum's central exhibit is a railroad car – Boxcart #113 069-5 – used to transport Jews and other prisoners to concentration camps. The boxcar sits on original tracks from the Treblinka Killing Center. Personal narratives, photographs, documents, and artifacts are also on display.

DUNEDIN

The historic communities of Pinellas Peninsula are just a short drive away from St Petersburg. If you're feeling ambitious, you can bike, jog, or hike the popular **Pinellas Trail**, a paved north–south urban trail on the former railroad tracks that starts in St Petersburg and ends 37 miles (60km) away in the Greek fishing community of Tarpon Springs.

North of Clearwater, on US 19, **Dunedin** **9**, famous for its March Celtic Music & Craft Beer Festival (www.dunedincelticmusicfestival.com) and Highland Games Festival, owes its name to Scottish merchants who arrived with the railroad in 1889. This pretty waterfront town is a great place to stroll or bicycle and visit unique boutiques and homespun galleries. Time your visit to coincide with the Friday or Saturday morning **Downtown Market** (Nov–June) and mingle with residents buying fruits and vegetables, home-made bread, Caribbean foods, organic coffee, local honey, organic salsa, cheese, and other goodies. These make great gifts or picnic fixings if you decide to head over the causeway to **Honeymoon Island State Park** **10** (1 Causeway Blvd; tel: 727-469-5942; www.floridastateparks.org/park/honeymoon-island; daily 8am–sunset), where rustic cabins became popular among honeymooners in the 1940s and '50s.

Tiny **Dunedin History Museum** (349 Main St; tel: 727-736-1176; www.dunedinmuseum.org; Tue–Sat 10am–4pm, also Jan–Mar Sun 11am–3pm), in the former railroad station, offers historic walking tours and an exhibit

The collection at the Museum of Fine Arts ranges from Greek and Roman antiquities to 19th- and 20th-century European and American paintings.

A Roman statue of Aphrodite at the Museum of Fine Arts.

⊘ ST PETE SHUFFLE

Shuffleboard is popular in Florida, where shuffleboard courts are found at many vintage motels. Players use cues to push weighted pucks down a narrow elongated court, with the aim of positioning them in a marked scoring area. The game, reputedly invented in England and played at the court of Henry VIII, is related to bowling, croquet, billiards, and shove ha'penny, a table-top pub version using coins. Organized in 1924, the **St Petersburg Shuffleboard Club** (559 Mirror Lake Dr North; tel: 727-822-2083) in downtown St Petersburg gained fame as the world's largest shuffleboard club in its postwar heyday, with a membership of 5,000 using 110 courts. Today, there are only 65 courts, but the historic shuffleboard complex is still going strong.

Salvador Dalí's Nature Morte Vivante is on display at The Dalí Museum in St Petersburg.

Though the sponge industry has declined, some sponges are still processed in Tarpon Springs and sold as luxury items.

of souvenirs from couples who vacationed on Honeymoon Island. To fulfill your own desert-island fantasies, hop aboard a ferry from Honeymoon Island, the only way to reach **Caladesi Island State Park** (tel: 727-460-5942; daily 8am–sunset).

TARPON SPRINGS

Celtic influences give way to Greek ones in **Tarpon Springs** , which sprang up on the banks of the Anclote River with the railroad. Key West "Conchs" cornered the sponge business in the late 1800s, but around 1900, with Key West's sponge beds dwindling, businessman John Corcoris summoned family and friends from the Aegean Islands to test the beds around Tarpon Springs. They found them rich in sponges, including grade A wool types and decorative finger sponges.

Corcoris pioneered the use of copper-helmeted diving suits for sponging in deeper waters, replacing the old-time "hookers" who rowed out to shallow waters, locating sponges by looking through a glass-bottomed bucket and hooking them with a hooked rod. Weighing up to 200lb (90kg), diving suits were frequently death traps for the young Greeks who wore them, as they dived deeper and suffered the fatal effects of nitrous-oxide build-up, commonly known as the bends.

The multimillion-dollar sponge industry began to ebb in the 1940s, when a disastrous episode of red tide disease killed off the sponges. The introduction of inexpensive, synthetic sponges virtually shut down the industry. The modern sponge market has since faded, but the epic story of Tarpon Springs' sponge divers lives on, kept alive by community pride, business know-how, and tourists eager to experience something real amid Florida's artifice.

In Tarpon Springs, you'll hear Greek spoken everywhere, see knots of older men passing the time on street corners, and enjoy moussaka, kebabs, baklava, and other Greek delicacies in family-run, Mediterranean-tiled cafés like **Mykonos** and **Hellas**. Tourism is

concentrated along the sponge docks on whitewashed **Dodecanese Boulevard**, now sadly devoid of its piles of sponges and savvy buyers. Nearby are warehouses where sponges are still washed, dried, hand-trimmed, and sold to luxury bath stores and home improvement centers for use in faux paint effects.

SPONGE DIVERS

Numerous cruises to beaches on Anclote Key depart from the docks, but only a few old-time spongers like George Billiris of **St Nicholas Boat Lines** (tel: 727-942-6425; www.stnicholas boatline.com) still demonstrate sponge-diving on a real sponge boat. The 1907 **Sponge Exchange** (www.thesponge exchange.com) is now a shopping arcade, where you can buy sponges in cool, dark shops smelling of the ocean. Tarpon's history is told on a plaque outside the Exchange and at **Spongearama** (tel: 727-942-3771), which has items and photos from earlier sponging days. On the dock is a statue of a sponge diver – a heroic, Adonis-like figure

gazing back to a glorious past, helmet in hand.

Greek youths in Tarpon still have their rites of passage. On the Feast of Epiphany in January, the Greek Orthodox archbishop blesses local waters and tosses a crucifix into **Spring Bayou**. Boys aged 16 to 18 dive into the chilly waters to retrieve it and earn extra blessings for themselves and their families. A white dove, symbolizing the Holy Spirit, is released to begin a glendi, or festival, with Greek food, music, and dance. **St Nicholas Greek Orthodox Cathedral** (36 N. Pinellas Ave; www.stnicholasarpon.org), built in 1943 in downtown Tarpon, is a replica of St Sofia Cathedral in Constantinople. Its neo-Byzantine walls are full of icons. One – a statue of the Blessed Mother – is said to shed tears.

MERMAIDS AND MANATEES

North of Tarpon Springs is another remnant of a glorious past: the 1940s roadside attraction known as **Weeki Wachee Springs State Park ⑫** (6131 Commercial Way, Spring Hill; tel: 352-592-5656;

A sponge diver in Tarpon Springs shows off an old deep-water diving suit.

In many parts of the Cedar Keys, boats are more common than cars.

⊘ SUNKEN GARDENS

Plumber George Turner, Sr, an avid gardener, created the 6-acre (2-hectare) **Sunken Gardens** (1825 4th Street North; tel: 727-551-3102; www.stpete.org/sunken; Mon–Sat 10am–4.30pm, Sun noon–4.30pm) in St Petersburg in 1903 by draining a lake and using the resulting fertile muck as the foundation for waterfalls, lush tropical plantings, and hundreds of vibrant plants lining tranquil walkways. The gardens became so popular that Turner began charging admission. Three generations tended the gardens before they were sold in 1999 to the City of St Petersburg, which now offers daily admission, horticultural workshops, and a wedding venue. The children's science museum Great Explorations occupies the restored 1926 Mediterranean Revival building next door, making this a popular family destination.

A Cedar Key gallery features the work of local artists.

Snorkelers can get a close-up view of manatees in the Crystal River.

www.weekiwachee.com; daily in summer 9am–5.30pm). Weeki Wachee had waters so clear that Navy frogman Newton Perry used them to stage underwater shows. He dressed young women in mermaid suits and taught then to breathe through hoses so they could remain below the surface for long periods of time. Today the mermaids perform strenuous acrobatics about 16ft (5 meters) underwater while visitors watch through plate-glass windows.

You can swim with manatees at the **Crystal River National Wildlife Refuge** (temporary office: 871 N. Suncoast Blvd, Crystal River; tel: 352-563-2088; www.fws.gov/crystalriver; daily) through local dive shops with special permits. The refuge is located in Kings Bay, where more than 70 local springs feed the Crystal River, providing a thermal refuge for more than 700 Florida manatees each winter. Some visitors prefer to use a boardwalk at Three Sister Springs that's accessed via a trolley, or a nature trail around restored wetlands that's rich with bird, fish, and snail sitings.

CEDAR KEY

A 25-mile (40km) drive on SR 24 crosses several bridges to reach the quiet fishing resort of **Cedar Key** ⑬, known for bird rookeries on surrounding **Cedar Keys National Wildlife Refuge** (SR 24; tel: 352-493-0238; www.fws.gov/cedarkeys) and as a weekend getaway for seafood-lovers. **Cedar Key Museum State Park** (12231 SW 166th Court; tel: 352-543-5350; Thu–Mon 10am–5pm) documents the port's short-lived prominence and displays an incredible collection of seashells.

Cedar Key Historical Society Museum (609 2nd Street; tel: 352-543-5549; www.cedarkeyhistoricalmuseum.org; Sun–Fri 1–4pm, Sat 11am–5pm) displays historical artifacts from the town, including the original heart-cedar Andrews Home and fiber brush factory. There is an exhibit on famed naturalist John Muir, who recuperated in Cedar Key in 1867, at the end of his 1,000-mile (1,600km) walk from Wisconsin.

Unique art galleries and boutiques occupy historic buildings on 2nd Street. Cedar Key's oldest and most famous building is the 1859 **Island Hotel** (372 2nd St; tel: 352-543-5111; www.islandhotel-cedarkey.com), a moody hostelry that has suitably creaky floorboards and is rumored to be haunted by spirits.

Local oysters, clams, and stone crab are reliably delicious when caught off the shores near Cedar Key. With the 1995 ban on gill nets, local fishermen began hatching clams and oysters in the shallow gulf waters around the salt marshes, aided by marine specialists from the University of Florida in Gainesville. This innovative thinking has invigorated the local fishing community. **Southern Cross Sea Farms** (12170 SR 24; tel: 352-543-5980; http://clambiz.com) offers daily tours of a clam hatchery. The **Cedar Key Seafood Festival** attracts thousands of seafood-lovers each October.

📷 BEAUTIFUL BEACHES

Beaches account for more than 1,300 miles (2,080km) of Florida's Atlantic and Gulf coastlines and are among the best in the continental US.

Broad ones, narrow ones, busy ones, quiet ones: beaches in Florida come in all shapes and sizes, and wherever you are in the state you should find one to suit your tastes. Even if you're not staying on the coast, the sea is never far away.

The Atlantic Coast has the best waves, while the water in the Gulf of Mexico is warmer and calmer. Many beaches lie on barrier islands, which ring much of the Florida peninsula, and an impressive number of beaches are protected as state or federal parks.

Florida's beaches, along with those of Hawaii, dominate lists of the top US beaches, which take into account everything from the softness of the sand to ease of access. Many of the best are on the Gulf Coast, where gorgeous sunsets are an added bonus. Everyone has his or her favorite beach, but below is a list of the beaches that are consistently praised. They are suitable for families and chosen from all areas. Even those within protected areas offer facilities.

Southeast: Crandon Park, Bill Baggs, South Beach (Greater Miami); Bahia Honda State Park (Keys).
Atlantic Coast: John Lloyd Beach State Recreation Area (Dania); Anastasia Beach (St Augustine).
Gulf Coast: Caladesi Island State Park (Dunedin); Siesta Beach (Sarasota); Fort de Soto Park (St Petersburg).
Panhandle: St George Island (Apalachicola); St Andrews (Panama City Beach); Grayton Beach; Port St Joe.

Before hitting the beach, check the UV forecast which is often broadcast on local news programs and published in local papers. The general rule is: The higher the UV Index, the higher the SPF needed in your sunscreen if you want to avoid a painful burn.

Florida beaches can be the best place to try your hand at flying a kite. There is almost always a breeze coming off the water, and plenty of open space to avoid tangling the line.

Florida has a number of rural trails that are suitable for inline skating, with compact or paved surfaces; there are also many beach boardwalks that are the perfect place to practice dodging the crowds.

All popular beaches have lifeguards, who can advise on local conditions.

Safety by the Seaside

Most people will enjoy a completely trouble-free time on the beach, but there are dangers to be aware of:

Sunburn: this tops the danger list; you should use plenty of sunscreen, wear a broad-brimmed hat, and stay out of the midday sun.

Sea currents: the waters off Florida are not generally dangerous, but you can encounter rough surf and strong currents, particularly along the Atlantic Coast. Most deaths occur when exhausted swimmers drown after trying to swim against a riptide or undertow. Riptides are the cause of 80 percent of lifeguard rescues in the US. If caught in either, do not panic! Swim across the current rather than against it.

Marine life: if you brush against a jellyfish in the water, you will receive only a short-lived sting; but stingrays, which move close to shore in August and September to mate, can deliver a very nasty sting. Seek medical help if the barb stays in the skin. Sharks nip at swimmers on occasion, especially at Central Florida beaches like New Smyrna and Cocoa. To stay safe, swim near others and near lifeguards, close to shore and in the daytime.

There is a warning system of color-coded flags at popular beaches:

Green: good swimming conditions

Yellow: caution

Red: danger from currents, winds, or lightning

Blue: hazardous marine life (eg jellyfish)

A large percent of Florida's beaches are privately owned, but only above the high tide mark. According to the Florida Constitution, any beach below the high tide mark is publicly owned, although frequently these areas are out of reach because private homes block the only access routes.

Tourists started coming to Florida in the late 1800s, but it was only after the 1920s that swimming in the sea and sun-bathing became popular, and visitors today can't get enough.

Gopher tortoises sometimes nest in sand dunes and should not be mistaken for sea turtles

GOPHER TORTOISE XING

The beautiful estate of Cà d'Zan.

SARASOTA TO NAPLES

Wonders abound on this stretch of the Gulf Coast, ranging from the extravagant winter home of circus magnate John Ringling to the sugar sand beaches and abundant bird-life on the barrier islands.

Southwest Florida's natural beauty remains unrivaled in this corner of the United States. But don't look for a desert island atmosphere if you visit between January and May; instead you should expect high prices. Many hotels are sold out months in advance for the peak season. Anticipate narrow highways crammed with cars, traffic gridlock in the city centers, and beaches packed with sunbathers.

Consider vacationing here from May through June (although it's hot and rainy) or October through December (with beautiful weather), when things are a little quieter. You could also stay on one of the islands that are accessible only by boat or floatplane, such as Cabbage Key or Cayo Costa Island. Boating is the most relaxed way to get an intimate look at this watery region, whether you're paddling a kayak on an estuary blue highway or steering a cabin cruiser on the famous Intracoastal Waterway.

ACROSS THE BRIDGE

Drive south on I-275 over Tampa Bay, passing through St Petersburg, and continue south into Manatee County via the Bob Graham **Sunshine Skyway Bridge** ❶ ($1.25 toll). South of the bridge, I-275 joins I-75 and historic Tamiami Trail (US 41). Head west on SR 64 to the relaxed Gulf island of **Anna Maria Key** ❷, an ideal place for weary visitors to decompress.

A Sanibel Island sunbather.

Just beyond **Bradenton** ❸, at the mouth of the Manatee River, lovely Anna Maria Key is one of the least developed Gulf islands. The gorgeous white-sand beaches of Anna Maria, Holmes, Bradenton, and Coquina line the narrow Gulf Drive, which has a good choice of beachfront retreats. Fine dining is excellent on this island, but you'll also find seafood shacks and beach cafés serving fantastic food. Islanders are involved in conservation efforts to protect endangered sea turtles, which crawl ashore nightly from May through

Main Attractions
Anna Maria Key
South Florida Museum
St Armands Circle
Mote Marine Laboratory and Aquarium
Marie Selby Botanical Gardens
John and Mable Ringling Museum of Art
Myakka River State Park
J.N. "Ding" Darling National Wildlife Refuge

Map on page 278

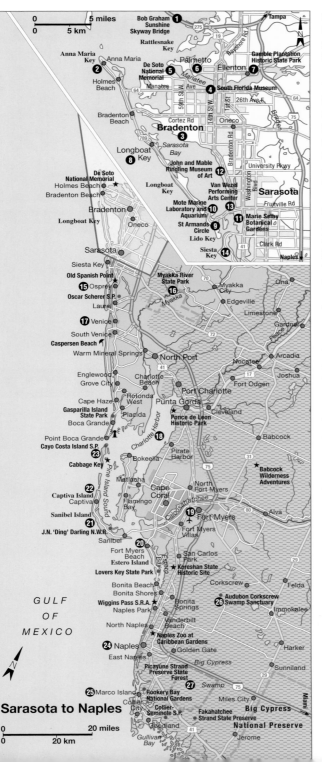

Sarasota to Naples

October to lay eggs on the beaches. Guided tours of nesting sites are available, call 941-778-5638 or visit www. islandturtles.com for detailed information.

The **South Florida Museum** ❹ (201 10th St W; tel: 941-746-4131; www.south floridamuseum.org; Tue–Sat 10am–5pm, Sun noon–5pm) in Bradenton is a well-interpreted museum that is renowned among aficionados for its Tallant Collection of more than 15,000 Native American artifacts that date from between AD 300 and 1725.

Snooty, the oldest manatee in captivity, shares living space with other injured manatees at the museum's **Parker Manatee Aquarium**. Daily shows about Snooty and his friends are a big draw for families and youngsters interested in ecology and the environment. The Bishop Planetarium uses a dual projection system to help visitors explore space.

The **De Soto National Memorial** ❺ (8300 De Soto Memorial Hwy, Bradenton; tel: 941-792-0458; www.nps.gov/ deso; visitor center: daily 9am–5pm; free) commemorates the spot where Spanish conquistador Hernando de Soto came ashore in 1539. This site has a visitor center, exhibits, live re-creations and demonstrations, as well as a small beach, nature trail, and picnic area.

Another popular local hangout is **Emerson Point Preserve** (5801 17th St West; www.mymanatee.org; free) in nearby **Palmetto** ❻. This bayfront archeological site preserves the area's largest shell mound. The **Gamble Plantation Historic State Park** ❼ (3708 Patten Ave; tel: 941-723-4536; www.floridastateparks. org/park/gamble-plantation; daily 8am–sunset; free) in **Ellenton** preserves an antebellum home on a mid-1800s sugar plantation that was used as a refuge by Confederate official Judah P. Benjamin (he later escaped to England).

SARASOTA'S ISLANDS

Returning to the barrier islands west of Bradenton, Gulf Drive meanders through well-heeled **Longboat Key** ❽ to **St Armand's Key**. Laid out around a central plaza, **St Armands Circle** ❾ (300 Madison Dr; tel: 941-388-1554; www.starmandscircleassoc.com) offers a pleasant retail experience with boutiques specializing in fashion, footwear, and local art and sidewalk cafés offering everything from crab cakes to home-made ice cream and both hot and cold lattes.

A few minutes away, **Mote Marine Laboratory and Aquarium** ❿ (1600 Ken Thompson Pkwy; tel: 941-388-4441; www.mote.org; daily 10am–5pm) was founded in 1955 by shark researcher Dr Eugenie Clark. Mote's main lab and public aquarium are located on a 10-acre (4-hectare) campus. The aquarium displays more than 100 marine species in exhibits showcasing the Lab's cutting-edge research. Learn about Mote's efforts to track sharks and other species, see real sharks in a 135,000-gallon (511,000-liter) tank, and view a wide variety of fish and invertebrates along with sea turtles, manatees, otters, alligators, and other reptiles. Touch tanks allow kids to pet rays, wriggly horseshoe crabs, and other sea life.

Near the main Mote Aquarium building is the excellent **Ann and Alfred Goldstein Marine Mammal Rehabilitation Center** (1703 Ken Thompson Parkway; free with Mote ticket). Exhibits contain resident sea turtles that need a lifelong home due to injuries or other issues, manatees including Hugh and Buffet, and exhibits featuring watershed animals including North American river otters, American alligators, and related reptiles.

Behind the scenes, Mote's adjoining **Dolphin and Whale** Hospital and Sea Turtle Rehabilitation Hospital rehabilitate sick, injured, and stranded marine animals with the goal of returning them to the wild. Since 1992, Mote's animal caregivers have worked to provide humane vetinary treatment while gaining scientific data to help benefit wild populations of marine animals.

THE UPPER CRUST

Like Dunedin to the north, **Sarasota** was pioneered by a Scottish immigrant businessman in the 1880s. John Hamilton Gillespie, an aristocratic lawyer and businessman, built historic

Folks gather on the pier at Anna Maria Key for a sunset view of the Gulf of Mexico.

A mastodon fossil at the South Florida Museum.

More than 20 large-scale artworks are on display along Sarasota's bayfront.

Desoto Hotel on Main Street and was named Sarasota's first mayor in 1902. Soon afterwards, wealthy Northerners started to settle in town.

Marie Selby Botanical Gardens (900 S. Palm Ave; tel: 941-366-5731; www.selby.org; daily 10am–5pm), south of downtown, was the home of Marie and Bill Selby. Voted one of Florida's top botanical gardens, it has a peaceful Zen theme, with plaques featuring Asian brush paintings and quotes, Buddha statues, and koi ponds amid peaceful pathways. There are native and seasonal plantings, spectacular banyan trees, a bamboo grove that Marie planted to screen out Sarasota's high-rises, and a popular gift shop and nursery. The greenhouse has many examples of the hothouse orchids and bromeliads (air plants) for which the gardens are known. The Selbys' former home is now a café.

THREE-RING CIRCUS

Sarasota's star attraction is, of course, the **John and Mable Ringling Museum of Art** (5401 Bayshore Rd; tel: 941-359-5700; www.ringling.org; daily 10am–5pm,

Mote Marine Laboratory and Aquarium.

Thu until 8pm), north of downtown. Devote a whole day to this attraction, as it's well worth the time. As well as the art museum, the estate includes historic Asolo Theater, the Ringling winter home, the circus museum, landscaped grounds, and a nice restaurant serving light Italian and American fare. Docent-led tours take place hourly.

Flush with profits from his Greatest Show on Earth and lucrative investments in oil, railroads, and real estate, John Ringling was a modest man with a grand vision. He brought artisans, red tile, stone, and artworks from around the world to create his estate. **Cà d'Zan** (House of John) was inspired by the Doge's Palace in Venice and was completed in 1926. You can tour the inside, where rooms feature tapestries and antiques, but it is the exterior, with its intricate terra-cotta decoration and boat landing, that makes this a unique American dream home.

John and Mable loved to travel and collect art. Their personal art museum, built in 1931 and now the state art museum, contains one of the most

important collections of works by the Flemish painter Peter Paul Rubens (1577–1640). Along with exceptional Baroque art, the museum displays Asian and American works and a magnificent replica of Michelangelo's *David*, which dominates a formal courtyard of allées lined with topiaries.

The 18th-century **Asolo Theater** (tel: 941-360-7399), built in Italy, sits near Cà d'Zan. The interior was dismantled piece by piece at a castle in Asolo, then shipped to Sarasota in 1950 and reassembled. The theater is host to a year-round roster of events, including dance and theatrical performances, chamber music concerts, art lectures, and a film series.

A less imposing building houses the **Ringling Museum of the American Circus**. The collection includes memorabilia, including rare posters and props, from Ringling's three-ring circus extravaganza. Don't miss the 3,800-sq-ft (350-sq-meter) miniature replica of Ringling Circus. It took model-maker Howard Tibbals 50 years to complete.

Another venue for dance and music is the **Van Wezel Performing Arts Hall** ⓭ (777 N. Tamiami Trail; tel: 800-826-9303; www.vanwezel.org), a purple shell-shaped building on the waterfront just south of Ringling Museum. Broadways shows, orchestra performances, plus comedy and dance are among the scheduled events.

South of Sarasota, **Siesta Key** ⓮ is renowned for its pretty sandy beaches (Dr. Beach rated them No. 1 in the country in 2017), low-rise development, and quiet, old-fashioned resorts. Just past Siesta Key, **Osprey** ⓯ is the location of the Blackburn Point Bridge, a one-lane bridge over the Intracoastal Waterway. **Myakka River State Park** ⓰ 13208 SR 72; tel: 941-361-6511; daily 8am–sunset) is Florida's largest state park and a good place to enjoy kayaking, hiking, and camping. The rustic cabins make a great alternative to busy beach hotels for those who love the outdoors and those on a restrictive budget. The park is used

by local schools as an archeological and environmental education center. It has an interesting exhibit called *Window to the Past*, which allows you to look inside an excavated Indian shell midden.

For immersion into nature and history with a touch of pampering, sign up for an ecotour with **((ecko))** (tel: 844-299-3493; www.ecktours.com; schedules vary). Expert scientists share their knowledge during hikes, bike rides, and kayak excursions to a Sarasota's waters and backwoods and to historical landmarks – locales you wouldn't find (or fully appreciate) on your own. The tours are sustainable and all-inclusive.

FROM VENICE TO FORT MYERS

Sarasota's circus legacy spilled over into **Venice** ⓱, a seaside community 20 miles (32km) south along US 41, which served as home to the Ringling Clown College until the 1990s. Venice's main claim to fame is as the Sharktooth Capital of the World. Tiny fossilized sharks' teeth wash up on undeveloped **Caspersen Beach**, the longest beach in Sarasota County. The teeth lure fossil collectors

Asian art is displayed throughout the Marie Selby Botanical Gardens.

The Ringling Museum is filled with art gathered during the Ringlings' visits to Europe in search of new circus acts.

A roller rink lights up the night at St Armands Circle.

The Selby mansion houses exhibits botanical art and photography.

to an annual Shark's Tooth Festival (www.sharkstoothfest.com) every April, the highlight of which is a popular seafood contest among local restaurants.

Things are quieter in the retirement communities around **Charlotte Harbor** , where the Peace River opens into an enormous bay. Although they have little in the way of attractions, **Punta Gorda** and **Port Charlotte** provide a change of pace from the rapid growth to the north and south. Legends of pirates and explorers are rife along the coast, culminating on Gasparilla Island, the so-called kingdom of the colorful but imaginary José Gaspar, who is celebrated in Tampa's annual Gasparilla Festival. **Boca Grande**, mid-island, offers a peek at the lifestyles of the rich and famous at an historic resort.

PARADISE COAST

Farther south, in **Fort Myers** ⑲, the **Edison and Ford Winter Estates** (2350 McGregor Blvd; tel: 239-334-7419; www.efwefla.org; daily 9am–5.30pm) spans both sides of McGregor Boulevard, the moneyed avenue leading into

downtown. After moving here for his health at the age of 39, Thomas Edison lived to the age of 84. He produced some of his greatest inventions in his Florida laboratory, including phonographs and motion pictures. After his death, Edison's widow bequeathed the estate to the city, as a shrine to her husband and his accomplishments.

Overlooking the broad Caloosahatchee River, Edison's Seminole Lodge was among the first prefabricated buildings in the US, constructed in Maine and brought to Fort Myers by schooner. Tropical gardens engulf the homes. Native Florida palms, satin leaf figs, calabash trees from South America, cinnamon trees from India and Malaysia, and the largest banyan tree in Florida – some 6,000 species were collected by Edison at a cost of $100,000. In this idyllic setting, he entertained famous friends such as President Herbert Hoover, Harvey Firestone, and automaker Henry Ford, whose modest vacation bungalow, **The Mangoes**, is part of the tour. Edison offered to light up his new town with

electric installations, but the townspeople famously refused for fear the lights would keep their cattle awake at night.

Visitors peer through Plexiglas into the furnished rooms of Edison's **Seminole Lodge**. You can also visit Edison's **Little Office**, the **Caretaker's House**, the **Moonlight Garden**, the **Rock Fountain**, and the **Swimming Pool Complex**. Edison's 1928 Botanic Research Corporation Laboratory, adjoining the visitor museum, gift store, café, and research garden across the street, is worth the wait to get in: it looks like the great man has just popped out for lunch, mid-experiment.

Fort Myers Beach ㉒, the lively resort town on **Estero Island**, attracts families in the high season. During the rest of the year, it reverts to being an attractive, old-fashioned, sleepy island community, where locals can stroll at sunset in undeveloped **Lovers Key State Park**, on the south end of the island.

SANIBEL AND CAPTIVA

Just west of Fort Myers Beach, a toll bridge leads to two exclusive island retreats – **Sanibel ㉑** and **Captiva ㉒** – where you can commune with nature and still buy a deli sandwich for lunch. The main attractions are the beaches and the millions of sea shells that turn up on the sands, luring thousands of collectors from all over the world.

Just about everything related to mollusks – from classification to artistic illustrations to medicine – is covered in the **Bailey-Matthews National Shell Museum** (3075 Sanibel-Captiva Rd; tel: 239-395-2233; www.shellmuseum. org; daily 10am–5pm), a good place to spend an hour figuring out your *murexes* from your *junonias*.

In 1974, Sanibel seceded from Lee County, set up its own city government, and put a near halt to the runaway development threatening to ruin its beautiful environment. By law, buildings here may not rise higher than a palm tree and must blend with the scenery. Even though the island is amply supplied with lovely homes, pricey hotels and restaurants, shopping centers, schools, and the like, natural beauty dominates the landscape.

Visitors take in the view from the top of Cà d'Zan.

Gasparilla Island golf course.

⊙ Quote

"There is only one Fort Myers, and 90 million people are going to find it out."

Thomas Edison, 1914

Less regulated than Sanibel, the island of Captiva is undergoing a construction boom and, sad to say, mini-mansions are gradually creeping in, threatening the quiet island ambience. Gift shops, island-style cafés, and vacation rentals are crammed into a village on the far end, close to a popular public beach.

Sanibel has many protected areas, the most notable being the outstanding **J.N. "Ding" Darling National Wildlife Refuge** (off Sanibel-Captiva Rd; tel: 239-472-1100; www.fws.gov/ding-darling; daily, hours vary, see website for details, Wildlife Drive closed Fri), named for the famous cartoonist and conservationist who made his home on Sanibel and helped develop the National Wildlife Refuge system.

These are some of the most productive wetlands for wildlife in Florida. The best birding is in winter, when early-morning low tides lure huge numbers of birds to the mudflats. At the entrance to the 5-mile (8km) **Wildlife Drive**, look for roseate spoonbills (the only naturally pink-hued birds; flamingos turn pink because of the crustaceans

they eat); several species of herons, including little and great blues and tricoloreds; white and brown pelicans; curve-billed ibis; long-necked anhinga "snake" birds; and other wading birds. The most eco-friendly way to see the refuge is to take one of the excellent tram tours with a trained naturalist, ride a bicycle or walk through the refuge, or paddle a kayak with concessionaire **Tarpon Bay Explorers** (tel: 239-472-8900; www.tarponbayexplorers. com). Binoculars come in handy.

Cayo Costa Island State Park ㉓, north of Captiva, is one of Florida's most unspoiled barrier islands. It has terrific birding and 9 miles (14km) of dune-backed beaches, and you can spend the night in one of the island's rustic cabins or camp out beneath the stars. You'll need to come by boat and bring in your own supplies. Expect only basic facilities; there's no hot water or electricity.

Another option is to take a boat or floatplane to the **Cabbage Key Inn and Restaurant** (tel: 239-283-2278; www. cabbagekey.com) from Captiva Island, Pine Island, or Punta Gorda. Historic Cabbage

The J. N. "Ding" Darling National Wildlife Refuge.

Key was built in the 1930s by the famous publishing family of author Mary Holt Rinehart. Today, it's a rustic island getaway, with cabins in the woods. Atop a shell mound perches an inn whose funky bar is papered with dollar bills. Things get lively when boaters tie up for hearty meals in the restaurant. Make your reservations well ahead.

NAPLES AND ENVIRONS

The pretty resort town of **Naples ㉔**, at the edge of the Everglades, is easy on the eyes but hard on the purse.

Naples revels in its outstanding natural beauty while, behind the beautiful facade, a long history of real estate speculation threatens the delicate balance of its fragile Everglades ecosystem. The infamous Golden Gate Estates boondoggle took place here in the 1960s, when crooked real-estate agents sold 29,000 lots to out-of-state buyers who had no idea they were purchasing unusable swampland. Progress has moved on, however, and today you'll find elegant seafront resorts, an emphasis on the arts and fine living, and abundant outdoor activities. These are a powerful lure for tourists and residents alike.

Naples has become a haven of wealth. It boasts the largest number of billionaires and golf courses (more than 80) in the country; overscaled mega-resorts along the beaches of Naples and nearby **Marco Island ㉕** continue to spring up; and every month new roads, strip malls, and residential areas are carved out of the swamp. In a sad irony, the names of these Las Vegas-style gated communities seek to celebrate the very threatened flora and fauna they are supplanting: Florida panthers, big cypress, and other disappearing Everglades species.

Extensive development is especially evident on Marco Island, which has little of the charm of the Gulf Coast's other islands. The northernmost and largest of the Ten Thousand Islands, Marco became a popular tourist destination when Captain William Collier moved his family to the north end of the island in 1871 and offered guests rooms in his home for $2 a night. It's

Birdwatchers flock to the J.N. "Ding" Darling National Wildlife Refuge on Sanibel Island.

A Marco Island marina.

Fishing is excellent in the Gulf Coast's many bays and inlets.

Luxury condos overlook the Gordon River in Naples.

said that the enterprising Collier was responsible for the persistent rumors of pirates on the Gulf Coast.

Sadly, most of Marco Island was sold for development during the real-estate boom of the 1960s. Today, after you cross the bridge to the island via North Collier Boulevard from Naples, you run slap-bang into anonymous beachfront high-rise resorts, restaurants, condo complexes, and a few residential areas.

For a fun twist on a history lesson, sign up for the seasonal Marco Murder and Mayhem tour (www.marcomurderand mayhem.com). It can be campy, but it's a light-hearted way to learn about the coastal community.

For casual visitors, Marco's attractions are all nature-oriented. Six miles (10km) north of Marco Island, **Rookery Bay National Estuarine Research Reserve** (300 Tower Rd; tel: 239-530-5940; www. rookerybay.org; daily), located at Collier Boulevard between Naples and Marco Island, interprets wildlife from Naples Bay to Everglades National Park. It has a popular **Southwest Florida Nature Festival** in January and offers guided birding tours to many locations, including **Tigertail Beach Park** (tel: 239-642-8414; parking fee) at the end of Hernando Drive on Marco Island, prime viewing for both shoreline and wetland birds.

For curiosity value alone, consider visiting **Goodland**, a funky little fishing village on the island's east side, where you'll find **Stan's Idle Hour Seafood Restaurant** (221 Goodland Dr West; tel: 239-394-304; www.stansidlehour.net; closed in summer) on the waterfront. Every Sunday afternoon during the cooler months, Stan's is the site of a raucous outdoor dance party and features seafood, lots of alcohol, and a lively band.

Naples is much more sedate. The historic old town, a few blocks from the beach, has been thoughtfully preserved and is a wonderful place to linger. **Third Street South** has many historic Craftsman bungalows, more than 100 distinctive shops, galleries, and restaurants, and free entertainment on Thursdays. **Fifth Street South** is a pedestrian-friendly hangout with a dynamic mix of theater, boutique hotels, shops, and restaurants.

The popular **Naples National Art Festival** takes place here in February, around the corner from the **Von Liebig Art Center**, home of the Naples Art Center (585 Park St; tel: 239-262-6517). There is plenty of parking near beach access points. A small historic complex includes the 1895 **Palm Cottage** (137 12th St South), which has exhibits on local history. It sits at the foot of **Naples Pier**, a small fishing pier that once served as Naples' only transportation access.

ZOO WITH A MISSION

For evidence of strong community spirit in Naples, look no farther than **Naples Zoo at Caribbean Gardens** (1590 Goodlette-Frank Rd; tel: 239-262-5409; http://napleszoo.org; daily 9am–5pm, last admission 4pm), set amid 45 acres (18 hectares) of historic botanical gardens. It started as a family operation in 1919, when botanist Dr Henry Nehrling acquired the land for his plant collection. In 1952, Julius Fleischmann (heir to the vast yeast empire) and his family restored the grounds and renamed them Caribbean Gardens. Then, in

1969, the Fleischmans invited "Jungle Larry" Tetzlaff and his family to join them from Ohio along with their collection of rare animals.

Parlaying a passion for wildlife into a job with animal collector Frank Buck, Tetzlaff and his wife, Nancy, offered more than merely a typical zoo. They emphasized wildlife conservation by using live animal shows as teaching tools. In 2004, Collier County voters opted for the jurisdiction to purchase the zoo and are now offered free visits on the first Saturday of every month

Naples Zoo is renowned for exhibiting exotic animals, including striped hyenas, honey badgers, giraffes, zebras, African lion, coyotes, and Malaysian tigers. The zoo regularly donates to various wildlife conservation organizations.

Among the ventures personally overseen by Conservation Director Tim Tetzlaff is a lemur project in Madagascar that involves local people in conserving the animal habitats around them. At Naples Zoo, Lake Victoria hosts a Primate Expedition Cruise that takes guests through islands of lemurs,

Stan's Idle Hour is a tiny slice of Old Florida on Marco Island, now largely given over to condos and commercial development.

Naples' Third Street shopping district.

Naples Pier was originally built in 1888 as a passenger dock and is now a popular gathering spot for viewing the sunset.

Naples Zoo at Caribbean Gardens.

monkeys, and gibbons. Alligator Bay is home to 16 American alligators.

Naples Zoo has five cat exhibits. With only a thick glass barrier as protection, the Leopard Rock exhibit allows you to sit inches from curious clouded leopards. You can also see a real, endangered Florida panther; it's rare to spot one in the wild. Two retired cheetah sisters inhabit their own exhibit. The zoo's Black Bear exhibit houses Florida black bears in a replica of an Old Florida homestead. Fosas, cotton-top tamarins, and Patagonian cavies are among the other animals on display.

NATURAL WONDERS

Nearly 80 percent of Collier County has been officially designated as protected land, and it's a primary habitat for endangered species including the wood stork and the Florida panther. Twelve sites are part of the south section of the Great Florida Birding Trail, where you can see some of the unique birdlife that calls Florida home. At the top of every birder's list is **Audubon's Corkscrew Swamp Sanctuary** ㉖

(375 Sanctuary Rd; tel: 239-348-9151; http://corkscrew.audubon.org; daily 7am–5.30pm, extended hours Apr–Sept), northeast of Naples in the western Everglades. This sanctuary is home to barred owls, egrets, roseate spoonbills, painted buntings, and a couple hundred more species. The sanctuary has a 2.25-mile (3.6km) boardwalk through an ancient bald cypress forest; daily walking tours are free with the price of admission. Also on the 13,000 acres (5,260 hectares) are a visitor center, a nature store with free-trade and artisan merchandise, a science and research center, an art gallery, and a café.

Less well known is **Picayune Strand Preserve State Forest** ㉗ (www.freshfromflorida.com; tel: 239-348-7557), where, directed by new laws to manage water for more natural, slow sheet flows for the Everglades wildlife and habitat, the South Florida Water Management District is removing decades-old canals, ditches, and roads, and is improving culverts through US 41 at the south end of the preserve. One of the first such projects, the Picayune Preserve, is worth visiting for its environmental and educational value. The site is still a bit rough, and the only visitor services are a developed equestrian campground and a trail at the main entrance on the north side. Drive east from Naples and cross I-75 to enter the preserve.

The roads and canals within the forest were built as part of that 1960s land scam. Today, horseback riders can use the 22-mile (35km) Belle Meade Tract. Walkers might prefer the Sabal Palm Hiking Trail, a 3.2-mile (5km) road that meanders among cypress trees that were too small to harvest in the 1940s and '50s. Some of these cypress trees are now over 100 years old, and they attract birds including hairy and red-cockaded woodpeckers. Old trams and trails are great for cycling expeditions.

The Renaissance-style gardens of the Ringling Museum of Art are filled with fountains and statues.

📷 SPRING TRAINING

The joys of summer come early in Florida, where baseball fans watch their favorite players and teams getting in shape for the upcoming season.

Balmy temperatures and friendly crowds are two great reasons to travel to Florida in late February, March, and early April for a late winter vacation. Another is to get a preview of the upcoming Major League Baseball season during spring training. Spring training in Florida is now a century-old ritual that offers relaxed practice time for players, tryouts for new recruits, and professional-level games at a low cost. You might even see a game between big-league teams like the Boston Red Sox and Minnesota Twins. More than 1.5 million people attended games during 2017's 37-day season.

Fifteen teams play in 13 venues throughout Florida in what's been dubbed the Grapefruit League. Most begin their workouts in mid-February, then play a series of games against other spring-training teams. Most competitors are other Major League teams, with an occasional foray against a local college team. They play daily during the month of March. Games are held at popular venues like the George M. Steinbrenner Field in Tampa and Roger Dean Stadium in Jupiter, which also offer special events such as bat and T-shirt giveaways. The athletes often come over and meet fans during pre-game workouts and after the games – an extra thrill for autograph-seeking kids.

Tickets go on sale as early as December with some as low as $5 for lawn seats. Ticket information can be obtained by calling the team's Florida box office or toll-free number. Learn more at www.floridagrapefruitleague.com.

The NY Mets do their spring training in Port Lucie, Florida.

Mookie Betts of the Boston Red Sox signs a baseball for a fan prior to a game against the Washington Nationals at JetBlu Park in Fort Myers.

A Phillies fan watches his favorite team take the field. Spring training is especially fun for kids, who often have a chance to meet their heroes up close.

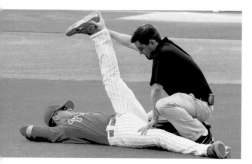

A trainer helps a ballplayer work out his winter kinks. Spring training gives veterans an opportunity to shape up for the regular season.

Peanuts, popcorn, and Cracker Jacks are perennial favorites, though some stadiums offer more ambitious fare.

Lou Gehrig (left) and Bob Shawkey with a mess of trout that Shawkey caught and brought to show his team-mates at the Yankees' training camp at St Petersburg in 1927.

The Birth of a Tradition

Spring training in Florida traces its origins to 1913, when player-manager Johnny Evers brought the Chicago Cubs to Tampa for training, after the team slid to a disappointing third place in the league. In February, the Cubs played the first of a three-game series against the Havana Athletics, a team of Cuban hotshots, most of whom had played American college baseball. Some 6,000 fans packed Plant Field – many of them Cuban cigar factory workers from Ybor City and West Tampa whose employers let them out early from work to attend the games. The Chicago Cubs trounced the Athletics in all three matches, then played several intra-team games and even a local team on Egmont Key. Tampa fell in love with baseball.

By 1914, other Florida towns were working hard to attract major-league baseball teams. Among them was Jacksonville, which hosted the league champions, the Philadelphia Athletics, in 1914. Their manager was Connie Mack, grandfather of Florida Senator Connie Mack III, who had played for the Washington Senators in 1888 and had been the first to skipper the Athletics for an entire season in Jacksonville in 1903. Over the years, improved train and auto connections brought more players to the Sunshine State, and, with the exception of the World War II years, when trains were commandeered for troops, spring training has been an annual ritual in Florida ever since.

The Grapefruit League encompasses 15 major league teams who play more than 30 games each. The spring training season usually lasts for six weeks, from mid-February to April.

A back-porch view of the Gulf of Mexico from a Seaside beach house.

NORTH FLORIDA

In this lightly-traveled corner of the Sunshine State are historic cities, pristine beaches, colorful seaside villages, and a vast inland wilderness.

A docent in period costume at Historic Pensacola.

In the middle of a sprawling expanse of pine forest in North Florida, a billboard long told the story of this largely undeveloped region. "Florida's Last Frontier," said the sign, put there by a real-estate agent eager to sell land to modern pioneers. The billboard is long gone, yet if it gave the impression that the northern reaches of the Sunshine State were a little old-fashioned and moved at a slower pace than the rest of Florida, perhaps it was correct – and still would be today. And if the sign meant that some of the state's hidden treasures – unsullied beaches, meandering rivers, and inland wilderness – still awaited discovery, that was true as well.

It is these piney woods that attracted Florida's first Spanish settlers, that resounded with gunfire during colonial and Indian conflicts and the American Civil War, and that helped some men amass fabulous wealth but seldom allowed them to keep it.

Pensacola is now a thriving metropolis, but the city over the years has been the possession of five different nations. There were places like Magnolia and Saint Joseph and New Port, once prosperous communities with fancy hotels and lavish mansions, now greatly diminished by disaster, disease, or economic downturns. Madison's Southern charm and Gainesville's air of academia have roots dating back before the Civil War. Indeed, the heritage of this entire region is written in overnight success – in booms of lumber, cotton, and citrus, followed by busts so total that little remains of the glory days.

Saint Mark's National Wildlife Refuge.

And what of North Florida today? It is a land of contrasts, cosmopolitan in the cities of Pensacola and Tallahassee but overwhelmingly rural in the spaces that stretch between them. Like the rest of the state, it has vibrant seaside communities. But there are fewer of them here than elsewhere, and many more stretches of pristine beach – known collectively as the Forgotten Coast, white and powdery as sugar, without a hint of a high-rise building in sight.

GAINESVILLE AND NORTH CENTRAL FLORIDA

Miles of scenic horse country, several historic waterways, and the quiet Nature Coast make this one of Florida's best-kept secrets.

For 50 years, zoology professor Archie Carr commuted from his home in Micanopy to the University of Florida campus in Gainesville via **Paynes Prairie Preserve State Park**, a 50-sq-mile (130-sq-km) limestone sinkhole reminiscent of the Everglades, with its changing wetlands, luxuriant sea of grasses, and extraordinary wildlife. "To a taste not too dependent upon towns, there is always something," marveled Carr in his 1964 essay *The Bird and the Behemoth*. "If only a new set of shades in the grass and sky or a round-tail muskrat bouncing across the blacktop or a string of teal running low with the clouds in the twilight in front of a winter wind. The prairie is a solid thing to hold to in a world all broken out with man."

GREEN AT HEART

Thanks to the efforts of Carr and wife, Marjorie, Paynes Prairie (named after Seminole chief King Payne) was recognized in 1971 as Florida's first state preserve. Today, it's one of Florida's most important natural resources: A major recharge for the Floridian Aquifer, which provides drinking water for millions; a sanctuary for wildlife such as wild horses, bison, cattle, alligators, and Florida's largest population of sand hill cranes; and a beloved greenbelt for Gainesville residents, who flock to its eight trails.

Florida Museum of Natural History.

Naturalist William Bartram traveled here by steamboat in 1774 and wrote so inspiringly about Paynes Prairie that poet Samuel Taylor Coleridge used the descriptions in his poem *Kubla Khan*. In 1928, writer Marjorie Kinnan Rawlings moved to an old home amid the citrus groves on Orange Lake. Kinnan Rawlings' stories about life among the fish camps of Cross Creek brought worldwide attention to this Florida backwater and won her a Pulitzer Prize for the classic tale of a boy and his fawn, *The Yearling*. The sleepy homestead

Map cn page 298

she restored, now a beautifully tended state park, is a symbol of Old Florida.

GATORS IN THE SWAMP

North-central Florida is huge, encompassing Alachua and neighboring counties between the hill country around Ocala to the south; the spring-fed Santa Fe River to the north; the St John's River, Lake George, and Ocala National Forest to the east; and the Suwannee River to the west. Consider basing yourself in Gainesville and then make day or weekend trips to surrounding sights.

An interesting cultural mix of city and country, rich and poor, brainy and brawny, **Gainesville** ❶ grew up around the citrus, turpentine, phosphate, and cattle industries in the mid-1800s, when the Cedar Key–Fernandina railroad opened East Coast markets. In 1906 a public university was founded in Gainesville, merging a seminary and agricultural college. A century later, 52,000 students attend the **University of Florida** Ⓐ, the country's fifth largest. Famous for its Gators football team, which plays in a stadium dubbed the Swamp, this public university excels as a research institution, with regular breakthroughs in food science (Gatorade

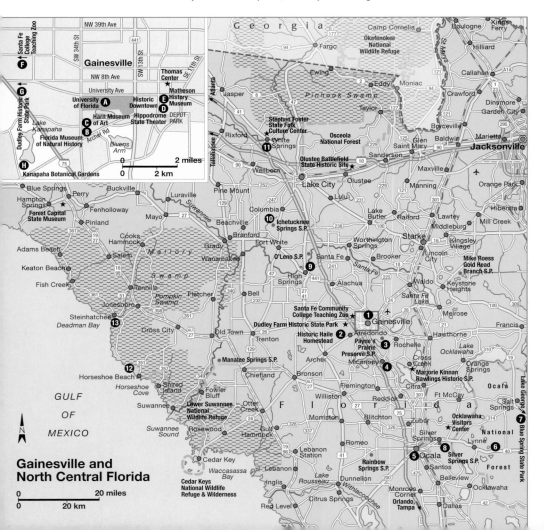

Gainesville and North Central Florida

and other commercial products were developed here), neurology, and agriculture. Archie Carr was one of UF's most popular professors until his death in 1987. To honor Carr's lifetime research and restoration work with endangered sea turtles, the Archie Carr Center for Sea Turtle Research was founded in 1986 to continue his conservation work.

NATURAL HISTORY

The best way to learn about the state's cultural and natural history is to visit the **Florida Museum of Natural History** Ⓑ (SW 34th St and Hull Rd; tel: 352-846-2000; www.flmnh.ufl.edu; Mon–Sat 10am–5pm, Sun 1–5pm), which shares information on about the state's history and landscape in an airy modern building in the UF Cultural Plaza. Kid-friendly, intelligent exhibits include fossils from the last 65 million years and the role of water as it flows through a hardwood hammock, bog, limestone cave, and other habitats. Florida's first peoples are well interpreted, with walk-through exhibits that include a replica Calusa Indian hut.

The hottest ticket at the Museum is the **Butterfly Rainforest**, a 6,400-sq-ft (600-sq-meter) screened vivarium filled with tropical plants and living butterflies. A Wall of Wings displays thousands of stunningly beautiful butterfly specimens.

Crisp, flowing water and Zen-like tranquility greet visitors to the **Harn Museum of Art** Ⓒ (3259 Hull Rd; tel: 352-392-9826; www.harn.ufl.edu; Tue–Fri 11am–5pm, Sat 10am–5pm, Sun 1–5pm; free). This teaching museum contains more than 7,000 examples of world-class art, from traditional Asian and African crafts to a large collection of modern masterpieces, including works paintings by Claude Monet and photographs by Ansel Adams. Downstairs, the chic **Camellia Court Café** is a lunch spot offering light entrées, fresh roasted coffee, and free Wi-fi. It's

open until 9pm on the second Thursday of each month for **Museum Night**, so if you're attending a performance at the Curtis M. **Phillips Center for the Performing Arts** (tel: 352-392-1900; http://performingarts.ufl.edu) across the plaza, you're in luck.

East of the university, the **Historic Downtown** is regenerating. Neighborhoods here are a mix of converted warehouses, turn-of-the-20th-century brick buildings, shotgun shacks, and Victorian mansions reviving as bed-and-breakfasts, restaurants, boutiques, and professional and government offices.

You can't miss the **Hippodrome State Theater** Ⓓ (25 SE 2nd Pl; tel: 352-375-4477; www.thehipp.org) in the former Federal Building, a glorious 1911 Beaux Arts building with Corinthian columns. A local favorite, the Hippo has stage performances and movies every night of the week. On Wednesday afternoons, the **Union Street Farmers' Market** in downtown's Bo Diddley Community Plaza is a good place to mingle with residents, listen to live music, and buy organic produce,

Century Tower rises 157ft (48 meters) above the University of Florida campus.

An Asian butterfly alights on a flower in an indoor rainforest at the Florida Museum of Natural History.

Exhibits at the Samuel P. Harn Museum of Art range from ancient to modern.

An old Micanopy inn.

dairy products, free-range meat, coffee beans, and European bakery items.

On the edge of Sweetwater Park, just east of downtown, is the **Matheson History Museum** (13 E. University Ave; tel: 352-378-2280; www.matheson museum.org; Mon–Thu 9.30am–3.30pm), where you can learn about Alachua County and tour the elegant 1863 **Matheson House**, the second-oldest home in Gainesville.

Among the family-friendly attractions on the rural outskirts of Gainesville are the **Santa Fe College Teaching Zoo** (3000 NW 83rd St; tel: 352-395-5604; www.sfcollege.edu/zoo; daily 9am–2pm, call for appointment), a unique and small zoo that teaches zookeeping skills; **The Thomas Center** (302 Northeast 6th Ave; tel: 352-334-5067; www. gvlculturalaffairs.org; Mon–Fri 8am–5pm, Sat 1–4pm; free), listed on the National Register of Historic Places, is a restored Mediterranean Revival-style hotel. It features two art galleries which include 1920 period rooms, local artist exhibits, and beautiful gardens. A free historical smartphone tour about the property

and the Thomas family is available. The **Dudley Farm Historic State Park** (18730 W. Newberry Rd; tel: 352-472-1142; www.floridastateparks.org/park/ Dudley-Farm; Wed–Sun 9am–5pm) is in Newberry, where costumed interpreters demonstrate pioneer life on a working family farm. Activities in the 18 historic buildings include tending heritage variety crops and livestock and cane grinding for a functioning cane syrup facility.

Kanapaha Botanical Gardens (4700 SW 58th Dr; tel: 352-372-4981; www.kanapaha.org; Mon–Wed, Fri 9am–5pm, Sat–Sun until 7pm or dusk, whichever is earlier) is the second-largest botanical garden in Florida. Named for the adjoining Kanapaha Lake (*Kanapaha* is a Timucua Indian word meaning "palmetto leaf house"), this 62-acre (25-hectare) garden features 1.5 miles (2.5km) of trails that meander through 20 plant collections. Highlights include Florida's largest bamboo collection, the largest herb garden in the Southeast, and a water garden. There's also a terrific gift shop, which sells unique nature-themed items.

☉ PAYNES PRAIRIE PARK

This park has the distinction of being Florida's first state preserve, and was established in 1971. It is named for the eldest nephew of Seminole chief Ahaya (the Cowkeeper). In the past, the prairie has flooded to create a lake (Lake Alachua). The last occurrence was from 1871 through 1886, during which time steamboats would cruise the waters of the temporary lake. Today the park is home to some 270 species of birds. It's the gateway site for the Florida Bird Watching Trail. Within the preserve you can find American alligators and Florida cracker horses and cattle, which were once herded by Seminole Indians. In addition, the preserve is home to a herd of plains bison. Although it is rare to see the bison, the most frequent sightings usually occur at Cone's Dike Trail.

The **Historic Haile Homestead** ❷ (8500 Archer Rd; tel: 352-336-9096; www.hailehomestead.org; Sat 10am–2pm, Sun noon–4pm) on the former Kanapa Plantation southwest of town, was a working farm of a different order. A cotton plantation and an antebellum home were built in 1854 by slaves who accompanied the Haile family from South Carolina. One feature of the homestead is its Talking Walls, unpainted surfaces where the Hailes recorded reflections on their lives.

If you have kids in tow, visit Depot Park (200 SE Depot Ave; www.depotpark. org). In addition to a Florida-themed playground, it has a waterfront promenade, a splash pad, and is home to the Cade Museum of Discovery + Invention (www.cademuseum.org) with displays that encourage visitors to think like an inventor and entrepreneur.

To tour the area leisurely, use your mobile/cellphone to learn as you drive through the Old Florida Heritage Highway. To use it, print out a guide at www. visitgainsville.com/dial-and-discover-cell-phone-tour) or pick one up at a visitor center. Then, as you drive along 48 miles (77km) of scenic Old Florida expanse, dial 352-327-9005# whenever you reach a tour stop to listen to recorded information. Of course, you may be distracted by horseback riding, canoeing, birding, and other opportunities.

ACROSS THE PRAIRIE

Sweetwater Branch Creek, on Gainesville's southeast side, drains into **Paynes Prairie Preserve State Park** ❸ (100 Savannah Blvd, Micanopy; tel: 352-466-3397; www.floridastateparks.org/park/paynes-prairie; daily 8am–sunset). Trails leave from the 15th Street preserve entrance. The 3-mile (5km) **La Chua Trail** begins at 4270 SE 15th St and brings you to the historic La Chua cattle ranch, passes Alachua Sink, where giant alligators loll menacingly below, and continues to an observation deck. Binoculars are helpful if you want to glimpse some of the 800 species of plants, 271 species of birds, and 430 species of vertebrates living in 25 diverse natural communities. The

A boardwalk leads visitors into Payne's Prairie Preserve State Park.

Park rangers in period costume illustrate life in the 1880s at Dudley Farm Historic State Park.

trail overlaps with the Gainsville-Hawthorne Trail – 16 paved miles (26km) which are great for cycling. To reach the main visitor center, drive south on US 441 and watch for signs. The center offers an interpretive film, exhibits, a bookstore, and ranger talks, and a trail leads to an observation tower. There's also a good observation platform on the east side of US 441.

Continue south to reach **Micanopy** ❹, founded as a fort during the Seminole Wars and the oldest inland town in the state. Stop at the former warehouse that houses the **Micanopy Historical Society Museum** (tel: 352-466-3200; http://micanopyhistoricalsociety.com; daily 1–4pm) to view exhibits and pick up a historic walking-tour booklet for the quiet main street. Many buildings house bed-and-breakfasts, antique shops, cafés, and unique stores like Mosswood, a purveyor of back-to-the-land goods.

Marjorie Kinnan Rawlings Historic State Park (18700 South County Road; tel: 352-466-3672; www.floridastateparks.org/park/,arjorie-kinnan-rawlings; grounds daily 9am–5pm, see website for details of house tours) is southeast of US 441, off CR 325. You can self-tour the sleepy farmyard, where chickens peck around the barn, oranges ripen on trees, and a vintage car awaits its former owner under an awning. Female rangers, dressed in 1940s house dresses, give tours of the home, a classic dog-trot building designed to maximize breezes in the days before air conditioning. Bring a picnic – there's a pleasant park next door.

THE GREAT OUTDOORS

Heading south to **Ocala** ❺, the landscape shifts to a pastoral scene of rolling hills, grazing horses, and picturesque barns. No surprise, then, that Ocala is the Horse Capital of the US, with more than 1,200 horse farms. A few stables offer tours, and there are horse-themed events throughout the year, including the Ocala Shrine Rodeo in August. Just east of the historic downtown is the **Appleton Museum of Art** (4333 NE Silver Springs Blvd; tel: 352-291-4455; www.appletonmuseum.org; Tue–Sat 10am–5pm, Sun

Marjorie Kinnan Rawlings Historic State Park preserves the author's humble homestead.

noon–5pm), a neoclassical building housing a wide-ranging collection and traveling exhibitions.

Ocala National Forest ❻ abounds with hiking trails and opportunities for camping, boating, and birdwatching on adjoining **Lake George**. Lake George is fed by the **St John's River**, an important travel corridor for Florida's earliest canoe cultures and later steamboat travelers. The location of the St John's River, flowing north to meet the Atlantic at Jacksonville, led to the development of riverbank communities such as **Enterprise** and **Palatka**. Thriving tourist centers during the Victorian period, they are now mere shadows of their former selves.

Your best bets for canoeing or tubing are **Alexander and Juniper Springs**. It's better to come on weekdays when attendance is light. The largest recreation area in the forest is **Salt Springs** on SR 40 and 314, with a canoe path from **Lake George** to the St John's River.

Snorkeling in crystal springs at **Blue Spring State Park** ❼ (2100 W. French Ave, Orange City; tel: 386-775-3663; www.floridastateparks.org/park/blue-spring; daily 8am–dusk) and **Lower Wekiva River Preserve State Park** (1800 Wekiwa Cir, Apopka; tel: 407-884-2008; www.floridastateparks.org/park/lower-wekiva-river; daily 8am–dusk) is also popular.

Silver Springs State Park ❽, just east of Ocala, harkens back to the steamboat era on the Ocklawaha River. It has wonderful old glass-bottom paddleboats that allow you to look down into Florida's deepest natural springs. The animals along these riverbanks live protected lives.

SPRINGS ETERNAL

"Springs are bowls of liquid light," wrote famed conservationist Marjorie Stoneman Douglas. That's certainly true of the hundreds of springs that percolate through Florida's underlying limestone. North of Gainesville, they feed the Santa Fe River and its tributaries, then merge with the Suwannee River. The farther north you drive toward the Georgia border on US 441, the more "southern" it gets. Historic towns like **Alachua** and **High Springs** ❾, which grew up with the railroad, have reinvented themselves as genteel rural villages, complete with historic bed-and-breakfasts, antique shops, and restaurants serving field-fresh greens. Canoeing and tubing are the preferred ways to beat hot summers in this neck of the woods, where almost every household has a boat in its yard.

At **Ichetucknee Springs State Park** ❿ (12087 SW US Hwy 27; tel: 386-497-4690; www.floridastateparks.org/park/ichetucknee-springs; daily 8am–sunset), 4 miles (6.5km) northwest of Fort White, rent a tube or canoe, park your car at the south entrance, board a tram to the north entrance, and float back down the crystalline Ichetucknee River to the parking lot at a leisurely pace (allow 2–3 hours). There are no alligators in the 72°F (22°C) water but plenty of basking turtles on logs

Daphnis and Chloe (1882) by Elizabeth Jane Gardner at Ocala's Appleton Museum of Art.

Silver Springs has an assortment of exotic wildlife.

Pointy roots grow from the cypress trees in river wetlands.

Steinhatchee is a remote fishing village at the mouth of the Steinhatchee River.

(laughingly referred to as "shell stations" by a ranger). Small fish among the eel grass form the main diet of the elegant snowy egrets and beady-eyed herons that stand motionless in the shallows, waiting to pounce. Park authorities protect water quality by banning water, food, and tobacco on the river, so eat a hearty meal and hydrate beforehand. Life doesn't get better than a canoe ride on the Ichetucknee in winter. Temperatures are pleasant and tubing is restricted to the south entrance, so you'll have the river to yourself.

The Santa Fe River joins the **Suwannee River** near Branford. The Suwannee rises in Georgia and meanders across northern Florida. Stephen Foster, composer of the 1851 song *Old Folks at Home*, never saw the Suwannee, but his lyrics evoked the way of life here so well that Florida adopted the tune as its state song in 1935. You can learn more at **Stephen Foster State Folk Culture Center** (US 41; tel: 386-397-2733; www.floridastateparks.org/park/stephen-foster; daily 9am–5pm) in

White Springs **⓫**, north of Lake City. Among the attractions are rides on a riverboat and a carillon that rings out Foster favorites like *Oh! Susannah* and *Camptown Races*. There's a **Florida Folk Festival** (www.floridastateparks.org/folkfest) here every May, and you'll see baptisms in the river, eat black-eyed peas, and hear storytellers and folk singers perform.

NATURE COAST

West of Chiefland, the Suwannee loses energy and meanders into Gulf waters in one of the largest undeveloped river delta-estuary systems. Protected as the 52,935-acre (21,422-hectare) **Lower Suwannee National Wildlife Refuge** (SR 347; tel: 352-493-0238; www.fws.gov/refuge/lower_suwannee), this area of scenic tidal marshes, coastal islands, and cypress groves is variously called the Big Bend, Hidden Coast, or Nature Coast. The refuge fronts 26 miles (42km) of Gulf coastline and protects 250 bird species. There are 40 miles (64km) of trails and 50 miles (80km) of forested back roads, but it's easiest to travel by boat. Kayakers can put in at **Shell Mound** and paddle the estuary or do three different river loops from the town of **Suwannee**.

North of Suwannee is **Horseshoe Beach ⓬**, a retirement community so remote it feels like you're on an island. Most popular is **Steinhatchee ⓭**, a fishing village that attracts retirees and tourists. **Steinhatchee Landing Resort** (www.steinhatcheelanding.com) offers activities for the whole family, and the pleasant waterfront has boat rentals, gift shops, and restaurants. Nearby **Keaton Beach** is one of the few settlements with a tiny patch of sand and slides for the kids.

The Nature Coast is Florida's most unspoiled region. Sunsets are extraordinary. For anyone looking to retreat from the modern world, a vacation cottage on stilts overlooking the Gulf may be your ticket to paradise.

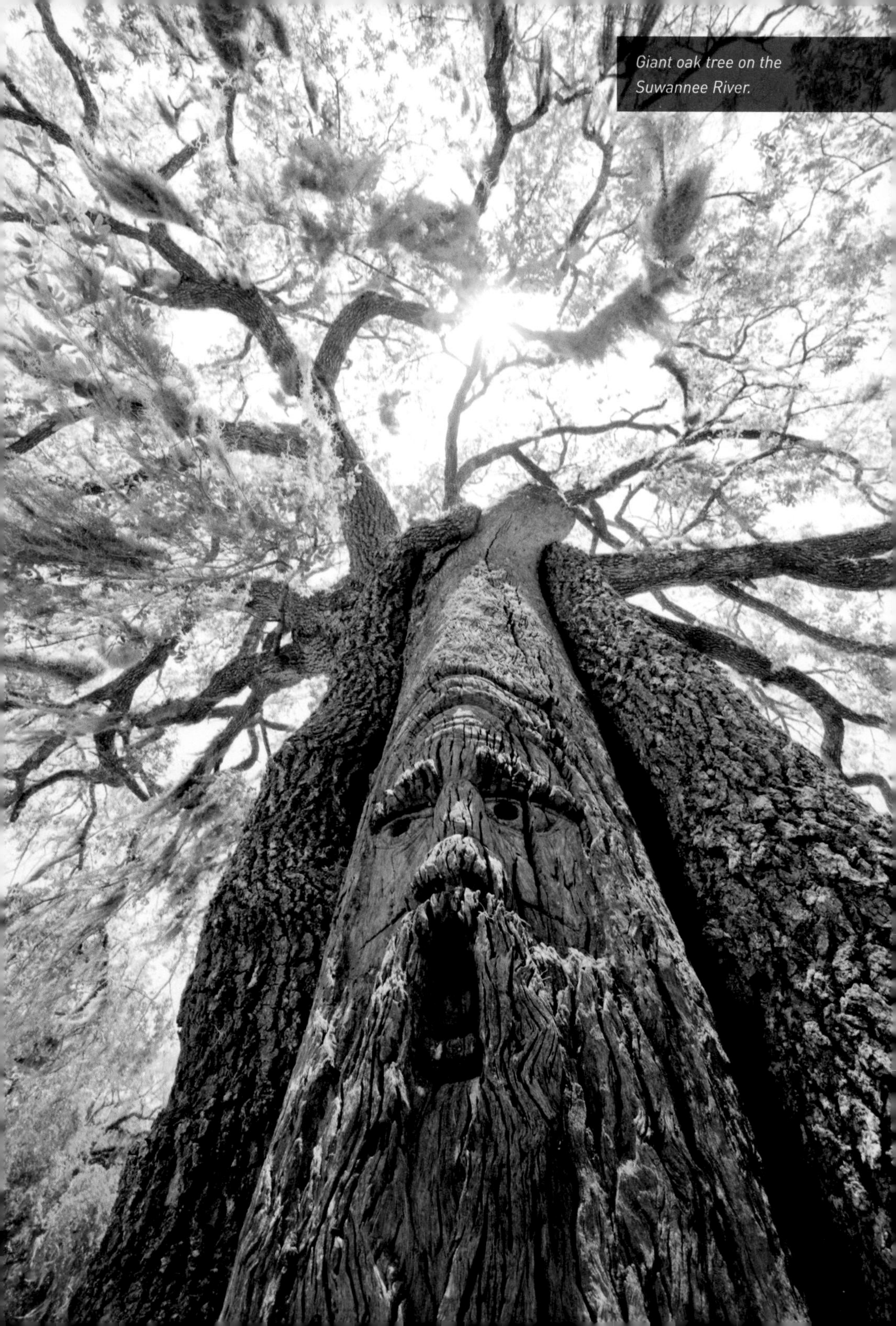

Giant oak tree on the Suwannee River.

A classic Panhandle beach.

TALLAHASSEE AND THE PANHANDLE

The capital is a gateway to a "Forgotten Coast" of gleaming white beaches, turquoise waters, and sleepy seaside villages.

in the early 19th century, most of Florida was a thick jungle. Settlement was concentrated in the northern tier, and Pensacola and St Augustine were the largest communities. Travel between these two territorial capitals was daunting and slow; trails through the interior were poorly marked, and pirates and storms plagued the ocean route. Each wanted to be the seat of territorial government, but the Territorial Legislative Council quickly realized that a more central location was necessary.

In 1823 two members of a site selection committee – one from Pensacola, the other from St Augustine – met at St Marks on Apalachee Bay to inspect the region selected by the council. This area was located between the Suwannee and Ochlockonee rivers and not far from a village that the Creek and Seminole Indians called "Tallahassee," meaning "old town" or "old fields." Both men were enamored with the hills and orchards of the area. One feature in particular seemed especially charming: a waterfall that graced a prominent hillside. The settlement that grew here kept the Indian name.

GOVERNMENT TOWN

Tallahassee ❶ has undergone many changes since then, but it's still a government town. The skyline is dominated by the high-rise capitol soaring 22 stories above a steep hill, but high-rise

residential condos are beginning to challenge the capitol's dominance.

Of those employed in the city, almost half work for local, state, or federal government. But don't let visions of boring bureaucrats frighten you. Tallahassee is one of the best-kept secrets in Florida. A friendly community, the city has done an excellent job of preserving its landmarks, its natural beauty, and a small-town flavor that belies its burgeoning growth rate.

All this adds up to a metro-area population of about 378,000 who live amid

Maps on pages 308, 310

⊙ Main Attractions
Old Capitol
Museum of Florida History
Tallahassee Museum
Wakulla Springs State
  Park
Apalachicola National
  Forest
Apalachicola
Panama City Beach
Pensacola
Historic Pensacola Village

Florida Supreme Court.

A satellite map gives visitors to Tallahassee a detailed overview of the state.

The Old Capitol.

a pleasing blend of old and new. It is a city rich in Old South town houses and plantation mansions that have been restored to their former grandeur. Oaks dripping with gray moss line picturesque streets, and dogwoods and azaleas bloom with vibrant spring color.

An elevator ride to the 22nd-floor observation deck of the **Florida State Capitol Ⓐ** (S. Monroe St and Apalachee Pkwy; tel: 850-488-6167; www.florida capitol.myflorida.com; Mon–Fri 8am–5pm) will give you a bird's-eye view of the city, awash in a sea of trees. The **Old Capitol**, restored to its 1902 condition, is a museum piece that sits at the foot of its high-rise successor. The state legislature sits for just 60 days a year. If you visit in April or May, you can watch representatives and senators in action.

For some background, visit the **Museum of Florida History Ⓑ** (500 S. Bronough St; tel: 850-245-6400; www. museumoffloridahistory.com; Mon–Fri 9am–4.30pm, Sat 10am–4.30pm, Sun noon–4.30pm; free). This fine museum provides an overview of Florida's history, with exhibits ranging from a 12ft (4-meter) -tall mastodon to Spanish treasure and war relics.

IN THE BEGINNING

In 1539, Spanish conquistador Hernando de Soto came to this area in search of the gold that he never found. While wintering here he celebrated the first Christmas in America. He explored the area around **Lake Jackson** north of town, but remains of his main camp were found at a site near downtown. Today, Lake Jackson is a favorite fishing spot, but it's known as the "disappearing lake" because of a sinkhole that periodically empties the lake in dramatic fashion.

In the 17th century, Tallahassee became the western capital of Spanish colonial Florida. A string of Franciscan missions ran between St Augustine and Tallahassee; the largest and most important of these was **Mission San Luis, billed as Florida's Apalachee-Spanish Living History Museum Ⓒ** (2100 West Tennessee St; tel: 850-245-6186; www. missionsanluis.org; tours Tue–Sun 10am–4pm), which today is re-created on the original site and is an archeological park.

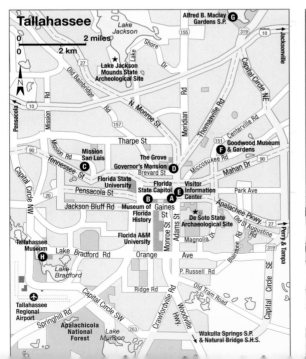

MAGNIFICENT MANSIONS

Wealth isn't new to the city, which has an array of restored homes built by prominent citizens in the years immediately before and after the Civil War. The most outstanding of these is **The Grove** (N. Adams Street), former home of territorial governor Richard Keith Call. Next door, at No. 700, is the more ornate **Governor's Mansion D** (tel: 850-488-4661; www.floridagovernorsmansion.com; see website for tour schedules; free), which was modeled on General Andrew Jackson's plantation home in Tennessee. Access to the governor's house is limited, but tours are available by appointment. Other historic residences can be seen on guided tours arranged through local hotels or the city's **Visitor Information Center E** (106 E. Jefferson St; tel: 850-606-2305; www.visittallahassee.com).

The real wealth, however, sparkles north of town in the form of 71 former plantations and 300,000 acres (120,000 hectares) that now serve as exclusive hunting preserves. In fact, the Tallahassee area boasts the largest concentration of plantations in America. Some of these estates are held by private owners, but there are a couple of exceptions. **Goodwood Museum and Gardens F** (1600 Miccosukee Rd; tel: 850-877-4202; www.goodwoodmuseum.org; gardens: Mon–Fri 9am–5pm, Sat 10am–2pm, main house: Tue–Sat, see website for guided tour times; free) is a replica of the plantation's 1911 Carriage House. You can explore the gardens and take tours inside the main house, which has original features such as marble fireplaces and a mahogany staircase.

You can also visit **Alfred B. Maclay Gardens State Park G** (3540 Thomasville Rd; tel: 850-487-4556; www.floridastateparks.com/park/maclay-gardens; park: daily 8am–sunset, gardens: 9am–5pm). New York financier Alfred B. Maclay fashioned a garden of camellias, azaleas, palmettos, and other native and exotic plants around a tiny lake. Guided tours are available, and you can swim, fish, picnic, and go boating.

Tallahassee retained its rural Southern flavor longer than many other Florida communities of its size. The **Tallahassee Museum H** (3945 Museum

Tallahassee's Kleman Plaza serves as a civic hub near the state capitol.

A lighthouse in St Marks National Wildlife Refuge guides ships in Apalachee Bay.

Shoppers will find a mix of treasures and tchotchkes at antique shops and knick-knack stores throughout the region.

Dr; tel: 850-576-1636; www.tallahassee-museum.org; Mon–Sat 9am–5pm, Sun 11am–5pm) pays homage to its not-so-distant past. Here a wonderful working farm depicts Florida pioneer life in the late 19th century, and nature trails wind through the grounds, where bears, bobcats, and alligators reside. Other exhibits include the restored home of Napoleon's nephew, Prince Achille Murat; a one-room schoolhouse; and a grist mill. The museum is on the shores of Lake Bradford near Tallahassee Regional Airport, 4 miles (6km) southwest of downtown Tallahassee.

MEMORIES OF WAR

Although Florida's role in the Civil War was mainly to supply men and food for battles raging farther north, it did not completely miss the action. As the war entered its final month, Union troops landed near St Marks intending to take the fort there as well as Tallahassee itself. But attempts to cross the St Marks River were met with disaster at Natural Bridge, a spot southeast of Tallahassee where the river

dips underground for 50 yards before resurfacing. Strongly entrenched Confederates – militia, old men, and teens – were ready for them. The Confederates inflicted heavy casualties on the Union soldiers and beat them back, making Tallahassee the only Confederate capital east of the Mississippi to resist capture.

The battlefield is preserved as the **Natural Bridge Battlefield State Historic Site** (7502 Natural Bridge Rd; tel: 850-922-6007; www.floridastateparks.org/park/natural-bridge; daily 8am–sunset), about 10 miles (16km) southeast of the city. There is an annual re-enactment of the famous battle on or about March 6.

THE REAL BLACK LAGOON

From Natural Bridge, backtrack to Route 363 and head south to SR 267. Proceed west to Edward Ball **Wakulla Springs State Park 2** (550 Wakulla Park Dr; tel: 850-926-0700; www.floridastateparks.org/park/wakulla-springs; daily 8am–sunset). The park encompasses a large virgin hardwood and pine forest, but the main attraction is the spring for which the

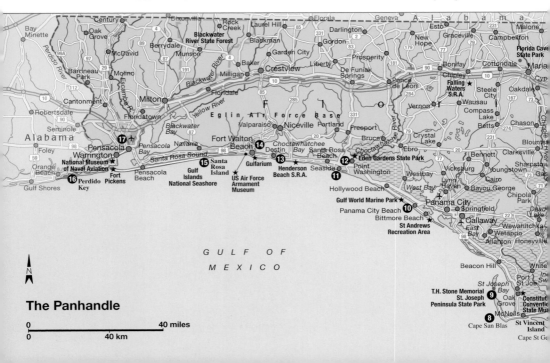

The Panhandle

0   40 miles
0   40 km

park is named, one of the largest in the world, pumping more than 687,000 gallons (2.6 million liters) of water a minute into a vast pool. You can swim in the clear spring waters or take a ride on a glass-bottomed boat. There are boat trips upriver, where alligators laze on the shores and anhinga birds dry their wings on cypress branches. The classic 1954 horror movie *The Creature from the Black Lagoon* was filmed here.

If you want to dig in for a longer stay, consider booking a room at the gracious **Lodge at Wakulla Springs** (550 Wakulla Park Dr, Wakulla Springs; tel: 850-926-0700; www.wakullaspringslodge.com), with its rare Spanish tiles adorning the Moorish-style doorways. Note the ceiling beams in the lobby. They were etched with Aztec and Toltec Indian designs by a German immigrant reputed to have once painted castles for Kaiser Wilhelm.

THE PANHANDLE

The Florida Panhandle is a world apart. In contrast to the theme parks, crowds, and craziness of the I-4 corridor in central Florida, the Panhandle is laid-back, shady, and more of what Old Florida used to be like. Still, tourism officials balk at the old-time moniker and prefer the region be referred to as Northwest Florida.

West of Tallahassee, the inland areas are covered in vast tracts of forest that hark back to the days when lumbermen and turpentine folks eked out a sparse living in the sandy woods. Wander through the **Apalachicola National Forest ❸** (tel: 850-643-2282; www.fs.usda.gov/apalachicola) just west of Tallahassee and **Tate's Hell State Forest** (290 Airport Rd, Carrabelle; tel: 850-697-3734) near Carrabelle and you'll see how wild Old Florida used to be.

Ecotourism has taken root in this region, which is rich in opportunities for hiking, biking, fishing, kayaking, and canoeing. Birdwatching is especially popular. Birders come from far and wide to see the birdlife of **St Marks National Wildlife Refuge ❹** (1200 Lighthouse Rd, St Marks; tel: 850-925-6121; www.fws.gov/refuge/st_marks; visitor center Mon–Fri 8am–4pm, Sat–Sun 10am–5pm, park daylight hours), a salt

The Panhandle has miles of undeveloped coastline and quiet fishing towns.

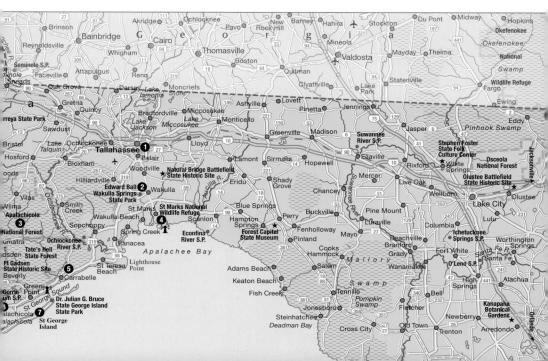

marsh that attracts some 300 bird species, including elegant, watchful hawks, noisy ducks, and numerous shorebirds.

BIG BEND

There are a couple of ways to explore the Panhandle. If you are in a hurry to get to Pensacola, take I-10 west from Tallahassee. You'll get there in less than four hours but miss a scenic drive along the **Big Bend**, where the Panhandle dips into the peninsula. While it makes for a longer drive, US 98 and its side roads are the only way to experience the essence of the region. Several roads in Leon, Wakulla, and Franklin counties are part of what is called the **Big Bend Scenic Highway**, 200 miles (320km) of scenic roads that lead motorists around Apalachicola National Forest to St George Island State Park.

South of Tallahassee, US 98 leads past a string of small fishing towns. Among the most prominent is **Carrabelle ⑤**. During the post-Civil War years it was a booming place, when lumber and turpentine were king, and stately schooners carried goods up

Historic inns throughout the Big Bend region preserve the spirit of Florida.

An exhibit at the Museum of Florida History traces the development of the Spanish colony.

north. The railroad also brought industry to Carrabelle and allowed salted mullet to be shipped north.

World War II brought another boom in the form of Camp Gordon Johnston, a gigantic training base for amphibious soldiers bound for Europe and the Pacific. Carrabelle later became a commercial fishing port, and, in recent years, a sportsman's paradise. What makes Carrabelle different from other coastal areas in this part of the Big Bend is its "true" beach – a rare commodity in a region noted more for its estuaries, tidal creeks, and rivers.

TO HELL AND BACK

Carrabelle is set near Tate's Hell Swamp, which sprawls over most of Franklin County. The name is connected to the legend of Cebe Tate, a hunter who vanished into the swamp almost a century ago. According to local lore, he entered the wilderness in search of a panther that had been killing his livestock. It took him a week to find his way out, but not before suffering a snakebite that ultimately proved to be fatal.

Tate's Hell drains into another vast domain with remote nooks and crannies of its own, Apalachicola National Forest. Covering 557,000 acres (225,400 hectares), this is the largest of Florida's three national forests. It encompasses pine forest, swamps, and rivers, and has numerous recreational facilities.

The lower end of the Ochlockonee River meanders through Apalachicola National Forest, providing canoeists with pristine rowing through woodlands rife with wildlife. A canoe trail begins 20 miles (32km) west of Tallahassee and continues downriver for 67 miles (108km) to **Ochlockonee River State Park**, south of **Sopchoppy**.

FLORIDA'S OYSTER CAPITAL

Twenty miles (32km) west of Carrabelle is the old cotton port of **Apalachicola ⑥**. Oystermen from this area provide the majority of Florida's oysters, which

are cultivated in the shallow waters of Apalachicola Bay.

Oysters aren't Apalachicola's only claim to fame: the area is also well known for its rich estuaries. The Apalachicola River and Bay are home to the Gulf striped bass, a native fish which has been known to reach weights of more than 50lbs (23kg). The Big Bend area offers some of Florida's best fishing, including the opportunity to catch tarpon and bull redfish. There are many charter fishing boats that will help you catch the fish of a lifetime. Offshore fishing offers the opportunity to land such big game fish as tarpon, cobia, and grouper. These giants can reach weights in excess of 200lbs (90kg). For those who prefer to catch something a little more manageable, try inshore fishing, where fish such as Spanish mackerel, redfish, pompano, or speckled trout are likely to dangle from your hook. Many of these fish will be under 15lbs (6.8kg).

During scallop season, which runs from July through early September, many charter companies offer scalloping trips. Catch them and cook them in the same afternoon. For a lovely evening on the water without the rod and reel, choose one of the local sunset cruises.

Apalachicola is famous as the birthplace of the world's favorite modern convenience, especially in places such as Florida. One of the city's early physicians made the world more bearable by inventing refrigeration and air conditioning. While trying to control malaria in the region in the late 1840s, Dr. John Gorrie succeeded in building an ice machine that kept his patients' rooms cool. Gorrie got a patent for the machine, but no credit for his work until long after his death in 1851. The **John Gorrie Museum State Park** (6th St and Ave D; tel: 850-653-9347; www.floridastateparks.org/park/john-gorrie-,useum; Thu–Mon 9am–5pm) has a replica of the very first ice machine (the original machine is in the Smithsonian Institution in Washington, DC).

CALM BEFORE THE STORM

Connected by a toll bridge to US 98 is **St George Island** ⑦, part of which is protected as **Dr. Julian G. Bruce St George Island State Park** (1900 E. Gulf Beach Dr,

Panhandle beaches are known for fine white sand and clear, blue water.

Nautical paraphernalia fill roadside shops near the Big Bend Scenic Highway.

A recreational boat is equipped for a day of fishing on the Gulf.

St George Island; tel: 850-927-2111; www.floridastateparks.org/park/st-george-island; daily 8am–sunset), with 9 miles (14km) of undeveloped beach and woods that are a favorite nesting place for ospreys.

One of the most anticipated events here is the annual St George Mullet Toss, which is held at the Blue Parrot Ocean Front Café on West Gorie Drive. Visitors from miles around make pilgrimages to participate in this annual June event. There are events held for men, women, and children, and prizes are handed out to the winners in each category.

Next door, but accessible only by boat from Apalachicola, is St Vincent Island, a nirvana for wildlife enthusiasts, who come to see loggerhead turtles, wild turkeys, and non-native sambar deer, originally from India.

Back on the mainland, you can detour along SR 30E to sample the magnificence of **Cape San Blas ❽**. Sunset is a particularly moody time to sit on the sand dunes and gaze out over the Gulf of Mexico, but be sure to take insect repellent. To the north is **T.H. Stone Memorial St Joseph Peninsula State Park ❾** (8899 Cape San

The calm waters of the Gulf of Mexico are excellent for kayaking.

Blas Rd; tel: 850-227-1327; www.floridastateparks.org/park/st-joseph; daily 8am–sunset), with miles of beautiful beaches and an excellent hiking trail, plus rental cabins and a basic campground.

Heading north on the mainland, you'll find **Port St Joe**, which burst into existence in the 1820s. In those days it was a major cotton-shipping port replete with warehouses, casinos, and sprawling mansions. Yellow fever swept the town in the early 1840s, killing more than two-thirds of the population. The town boomed again in the early 20th century due to the expanding railroad and export lumber business.

NOT JUST FOR SPRING BREAK

To the northwest is **Panama City Beach ❿**, where the 27 pristine miles (44km) of white beach sparkle and the water is emerald green. In fact, this part of the Gulf Coast has some of the world's most beautiful beaches.

Long known as the Spring Break Capital of the South, the destination has invested in getting classier. New museums, galleries, parks, and homes have

replaced dated ones, which has led to an increase in visitors. **St. Andrews Park** (46-7 State Park Ln; tel: 850-708-6100; www.floridastateparks.org/park/st-andrews; daily 8am–sundown) is a former military reservation. In addition to 1.5 miles (2.4km) of beachfront on the Grand Lagoon and Gulf of Mexico, it offers diving, snorkeling, kayaking, fishing from two piers, a jetty, and a boat ramp; no wonder it is the most-visited state park in the system. Visit **Gulf World Marine Park** (15412 Front Beach Rd; tel: 850-234-5271; www.gulfworldmarinepark.com; daily 7.30am–4.30pm) to watch performances by, or even interact with, dolphins, sea lions, and reptiles.

AN ARCHITECTURAL INTERLUDE

Between Seagrove Beach and Grayton Beach is **Seaside ⑪**, (www.seasidefl.com), one of the state's most unusual communities. Built in the 1980s, this experiment in urban planning attempts to re-create a Victorian resort. It has tidy streets lined with quaint wooden cottages complete with gingerbread detailing and picket fences. Seaside is worth a peek (and there's a beach, of course), but, as with many modern planned communities, there is a sense of surreal conformity. Little wonder that it was chosen as the setting for *The Truman Show*, the 1998 movie starring Jim Carrey.

Your main destination here is **South Walton** (www.visitsouthwalton.com), where 26 miles (42km) of sugar-white sand attracts those looking for magnificent shoreline without the crowds. You'll find all the basics including golf, paddle boarding, sunset cruises, charter fishing, even horseback tours through native foliage.

You'll find rather more authentic grace inland at **Eden Gardens State Park** and the **Wesley House** (off US 98 and CR 295 in **Point Washington ⑫**; tel: 850-231-4214; www.floridastateparks.org/park/eden-gardens; park open daily 8am–sunset, house tours hourly Thu–Mon 10am–3pm), where a stately old Southern mansion is set in the ornamental gardens. The white-columned home was built of heart-pine and cypress in the late 1800s by a local lumber baron.

⊙ Tip

Test your fish-flinging skills at the annual St George Island Mullet Toss in June.

Bikes at the beach.

⊙ Fact

An air base at Tyndall, east of Panama City, provides basic and advanced flight training for Air Force personnel. Tyndall opened on the morning that the US entered World War II and counted actor Clark Gable among its first graduates.

THE EMERALD COAST

Next on US 98 is **Destin ⑬**, the heart of the Emerald Coast area (www.emerald-coastfl.com) where the Gulf water is just as green and clear as the day it was created. Here, dozens of charter boat captains begin their day at 5am loading barrels of ice in anticipation of the day's catch. In fact, Destin has the largest fleet of fishing boats in the country. Coined "The World's Luckiest Fishing Village" in 1956 by the governor at the time, the area now encourages not only fishing but having local chefs cook your catch for dinner. It's called "You Catch It – We'll Cook It" and many restaurants participate.

In addition to the Boardwalk in Oka-loose Island, sand volleyball, golf courses, and paddleboard rentals, visitors often seek out the Destin Fishing Rodeo (www.destinfishingrodeo.com), a month-long tradition that has been held annually in October for over 70 years. The dolphin-watching is grand at the Okaloosa Pier.

At the **Destin History & Fishing Museum** (108 Stahlman Ave; tel: 850-837-6611; www.destinhistoryandfishingmuseum.org; Tue–Sat 10am–4pm), you can learn all about this fishing community's past. Highlights are more than 75 mounts of fish caught in local waters, an explanation on why the area's sand is so white, and an outdoor Museum Historic Park Complex with a historic seine boat, a mullet boat, and the original Old Post Office.

Just across from Destin is **Fort Walton Beach ⑭** and **Niceville**, home to the vast **Eglin Air Force Base**. Eglin is the largest base of its kind in the US, encompassing some 724 sq miles (1,875 sq km) of land and more than 97,000 sq miles (250,000 sq km) of airspace. The base employs some 20,000 people who contribute considerably to the local economy. The **US Air Force Armament Museum** (100 Museum Dr; tel: 850-651-1808; www.afarmamentmuseum.com; Mon–Sat 9.30am–4.30pm; free), just outside Eglin near Valparaiso, will interest fans of military aviation. The gift shop is full of models and other curiosities.

GULF ISLANDS

There are numerous small beach communities west along US 98, but the best route is SR 399, which veers south at Navarre onto **Santa Rosa Island ⑮**. Here you can revel in miles of billowing dunes topped by miniature magnolias. The strip's promoters claim the sands are the whitest in the world.

This part of the coast is all part of **Gulf Islands National Seashore (www.nps. gov)**, which protects 150 miles (240km) of pristine coastline that runs west as far as Gulfport in Mississippi. Visitors can stop at park sites and enjoy a day in the sun. There are campsites and nature trails as well as picnic areas and other facilities. Another gorgeous section of the National Seashore is on **Perdido Key ⑯**, a 30-minute drive southwest of Pensacola, with charming beaches and salt marshes rich in birdlife.

PENSACOLA

Finally, more than 200 miles (320km) from Tallahassee, is **Pensacola ⑰** (www.visitpensacola.com), a coastal city that is

Seaside is a planned community modeled after a Victorian-era resort.

a mixture of Old South charm, Spanish heritage, and Navy bravado. The city has taken steps to preserve its 400-year-old heritage in two historic districts near downtown as well as in museums, battle sites, and forts. And it isn't just in museum pieces that the city's history lives. It's in streets with names such as Palafox, Intendencia, Zaragoza, and Cervantes, and it moves in the wind at St Michael's Cemetery, where tombstones bearing Spanish inscriptions date back to the 1700s. The area also has beautiful beaches – miles and miles of undeveloped coast where sand dunes (not condominiums) rise high above blue seas.

CONTESTED TERRITORY

Don Tristan de Luna was the first to attempt establishing a settlement in the area in 1559, six years before St Augustine. But de Luna and the 1,500 colonists who came with him abandoned the settlement two years later due to a massive storm. It wasn't until 1752 that a permanent settlement was established at Pensacola, though the Spaniards had tried again in 1698 and 1722. Since its founding, Pensacola has flown the flags of five countries in Plaza Ferdinand VII. The city celebrates its proud history each spring with the **Fiesta of Five Flags**. There are parades, art shows, and a re-enactment of de Luna's landing in 1559.

The British occupied Pensacola during the Revolutionary War but lost the city to the Spanish in 1781 after a month-long siege. The victory cut off British access to the fledgling American states and buoyed the hopes of colonists fighting for independence.

Four decades later, Andrew Jackson marched into Pensacola to claim Florida for the United States. Jackson, the first territorial governor of Florida, tried to convince the Spaniards to clean up streets he found "filthy and disgusting." Fed up, he packed up and went home after two months.

HISTORIC PENSACOLA VILLAGE

Today, the original town square near Pensacola Bay is the centerpiece of the **Seville District**, a 37-block section of restored homes, shops, and old-time eateries that is Pensacola's crowning

A dolphin trainer works with one of her pupils at Gulf World Marine Park in Panama City Beach.

Fort Walton Beach.

Architectural details add charm and character to Pensacola's historic downtown.

The Gulf Islands National Seashore as seen from a Pensacola resort.

achievement in historic preservation. The square and nearby streets are a pleasant place to spend an afternoon strolling around.

Several museums and some lovely restored homes in this district have been gathered together under the name **Historic Pensacola** (www.historic pensacola.org; complex open Tue–Sat 10am–4pm, museum hours vary, tours daily 11am, 1pm, and 2.30pm). Guides in period dress share tales of the area, where British and Spanish forts once stood. **Tivoli House** (205 E. Zaragoza St; tel: 850-595-5985), which serves as a ticket center, is a reconstructed tavern, and gaming and boarding house.

One of the most notable restored houses in the neighborhood is "the Oldest House" on Church Street, known as the **Lavalle House**. The exact construction date of Lavalle House c.1805, but historians consider it typical of the French Creole cottages of the 19th century. Other fine houses are the nearby **Dorr House**, on the corner of Church and Adams streets, and the so-called **Steamboat House**, on Government Street.

Several good museums are part of Historic Pensacola. On Zaragoza Street are the **Museum of Commerce** and **Museum of Industry.** The nearby **T.T. Wentworth Jr. Florida State Museum** (330 S. Jefferson St; tel: 850-595-5990) is a fine Spanish Renaissance Revival building with a fascinating collection of Florida memorabilia. Other old houses host assorted tourist-oriented businesses. The **Pensacola Museum of Art** (407 S. Jefferson St; tel: 850-432-6247; www.pensacolamuseum. org; Tue–Sat 10am–5pm) has an eclectic array of artworks ranging from pre-Columbian pottery to modern painting.

Seville Quarter (www.sevillequarter.com), billed as Pensacola's premier entertainment and dining complex, is in a restored 19th-century building on Government Street, on the fringe of Seville Square. It's a good place for a night out, with a wide range of bars and restaurants.

The city's third historic district takes you back to the days of Pensacola's lumber boom. Residents built big houses and made big money. Today, dozens of houses from the era still stand in a 50-block area called the **North Hill**

Preservation District, north of Wright Street. Thanks to preservationists who set out to save the decaying neighborhood, many of the handsome homes have been restored. Visitors must content themselves with a view from outside, as most are private residences.

DEFENDING PENSACOLA

Across the bay, **Fort Pickens** (tel: 850-934-2635; daily), a pentagonal stronghold with a bastion at each corner, took five years to build and accommodated as many as 600 men.

In the early days of the Civil War, Union soldiers at Fort Pickens on the western tip of Santa Rosa Island engaged Confederate troops at **Fort Barrancas** (Pensacola Naval Air Station; tel: 850-455-5167; www.nps.gov/guis/planyourvisit/fort-barrancas.htm) on the mainland. Pickens guarded the harbor entrance and prevented the Confederates from using the shipyard and adjacent railyard. Some historians believe the first shots of the tragic conflict may have actually been fired here, not at Fort Sumter in South Carolina. In the end, the Yankee invasion of Tennessee in 1862 forced Confederate leaders to move their manpower north, and Pensacola was abandoned. The town stayed in Union hands for the rest of the war. In the 1880s the fortress was famous for its imprisonment of Apache chief Geronimo. Both forts can be toured; Fort Pickens has a campground.

HIGH FLYING

The panhandle is also home to the **Pensacola Naval Air Station**, the nation's largest, founded in 1914. All Navy training for land and sea is headquartered at the base, and it is the center for advanced training for Naval flight officers. It is also home of the renowned Blue Angels, who perform astounding flight shows.

The **National Museum of Naval Aviation** (1750 Radford Blvd; tel: 850-452-3604; daily 9am–5pm; free) exhibits more than 150 restored aircraft, ranging from a World War II airship to four former Blue Angels Skyhawks. There is also an IMAX theater and flight simulators for those who need a little more speed and excitement in their entertainment.

⊘ Fact

Pensacola is a sizable city, with a metropolitan population of almost half a million, six colleges and universities, an international airport, a distinctive downtown, an educated workforce, fine hospitals, and centers of research and technology.

⊘ INLAND EMPIRE

Most tourists in the Panhandle focus on the coastal region, but lovers of nature will find the interior equally enticing. In an isolated spot on the Apalachicola River just south of I-10 is Torreya State Park (tel: 850-643-2674). The park encompasses more than 13,000 acres (5,200 hectares) of the state's most diverse geography and is home to a rare species of the Torreya tree. To the west, 3 miles (5km) north of Marianna off SR 167, is Florida Caverns State Park (tel: 850-482-9598; daily 8am–sunset), one of a few parks with air-filled caves, replete with spellbinding limestone formations. On the surface are trails for hiking and horseback riding. A canoe trail runs 52 miles (84km) south to Dead Lakes, north of Wewahitchka on SR 71. See www.floridastateparks.org for more information.

Historic Pensacola.

Gasparilla Island.

FLORIDA

TRAVEL TIPS

TRANSPORTATION

GETTING THERE

By Air

Most major US and international carriers serve Florida. Shop around before buying a ticket; also, a variety of discount fares and "package deals," which can significantly cut round-trip rates to and from Florida, are available. Last-minute online deals can be found, and budget airlines such as Allegiant offer no-frills travel – with no presence on traditional fare-search websites.

Florida has 10 international airports, but the state's major hubs are Miami, Orlando, Fort Lauderdale, and Tampa. The others are in Fort Myers, Jacksonville, Sanford, Palm Beach, Sarasota, and St Petersburg-Clearwater. Miami International Airport is the state's largest. It is also a major jumping-off point for flights into the Caribbean and Latin America. In addition, there are connections to regional airports, such as Daytona Beach, Fort Myers, Jacksonville, Key West, Marathon, Melbourne, Naples, Palm Beach, Panama City, Pensacola, St Petersburg-Clearwater, Sarasota-Bradenton, and Tallahassee. Orlando International is the state's second-largest, and a third wing is under construction.

Scheduled services are supplemented by charter flights. Many of these land at Orlando-Sanford Airport, 30 miles (48km) north of Orlando. In summer, this small airport is jammed with tourists, and lines at immigration can be long. Furthermore, the extra distance can be costly, especially if you plan to use public transportation to reach Orlando. A rental car is essential if you arrive at a distant airport.

Leave extra time to go through security checks at all airports due to Homeland Security anti-terrorism rules. Domestic travelers who buy TSA Precheck, Clear, or Nexus may get through quickly. Either way, pack items in both carry-on and checked luggage in clear bags and leave gifts unwrapped.

The contact details for the main airports are:
Miami International Airport (MIA), tel: 305-876-7000, www.miami-airport.com
Fort Lauderdale/Hollywood International Airport (FLL), tel: 866-435-9355; www.fll.net
Orlando International Airport (MCO), tel: 407-825-2001; www.orlandoairports.net
Orlando-Sanford International Airport (SFB), tel: 407-585-4000; www.orlandosanfordairport.com
Tampa International Airport (TPA), tel: 813-870-8700; www.tampaairport.com

International and Domestic Airlines

Airlines serving Florida include:
Allegiant: tel: 702-505-8888; www.allegiantair.com
American: tel: 800-433-7300; www.aa.com
British Airways: tel: 800-247-9297; www.britishairways.com
Delta: tel: 800-221-1212; www.ddeelta.com
Frontier: tel: 801-401-9000; www.flyfrontier.com
JetBlue: tel: 800-538-2583; www.jetblue.com
Silver Airways: tel: 801-401-9100south; www.silverairways.com
Southwest: tel: 800-435-9792; www.southwest.com
Spirit: tel: 801-401-2222; www.spirit.com
United Airlines: tel: 800-864-8331; www.united.com
US Airways: tel: 800-433-7300; www.usairways.com
Virgin Atlantic: tel: 800-862-8621; www.virginatlantic.com

By Boat

Surrounded by water, Florida is easy to travel to or from by sea, and cruises into the Atlantic, Gulf of Mexico, and Caribbean depart year-round. Packages vary, with cruises lasting from a few hours or a day to over two weeks. Three-day jaunts to the Bahamas are popular. So, too, are the one-day or one-night coast-hugging trips, which, for some people, are just an opportunity to gamble. Casinos are illegal in Florida, except on the Seminole reservation, but the law does not apply in international waters.

For a complete overview, ask a travel agent, check the travel ads in any Sunday newspaper, or check online at sites like www.cruise.com.

By Rail

Amtrak (tel: 800-872-7245; www.amtrak.com) offers leisurely service from the Midwest, Northeast, and South – and connecting service to points west – to numerous Florida cities. The Silver Service routes between New York City and Florida have major stops in Jacksonville, Orlando, Tampa, and Miami. For those who want to take their car, the Auto Train from Lorton, Virginia, near Washington DC, to Sanford, north of Orlando, is an option. All Aboard Florida's Brightline (http://gobrightline.com) express service in South Florida travels to Miami, Fort Lauderdale, and West Palm Beach. A line connecting Miami with Orlando is under construction.

By Bus

Greyhound (tel: 214-849-8966; www.greyhound.com) provides bus services all over the state. Intercity service includes many out-of-the-way stops en route and can be slow; try to use "Express" buses, which stop in fewer places. Bus terminals are often in run-down areas of town, so take care when traveling to or from stations. Private bus companies offer alternatives, often with TVs and Wi-fi. One example is Red Coach USA (www.redcoachusa.com), with stops in about a dozen cities.

GETTING AROUND

Public Transportation

Cities with walkable historic downtowns, such as Tampa, Key West, St Augustine, and St Petersburg, encourage visitors and residents to use inexpensive trams and light rail to get around. Florida's abandoned railway beds have found new life as trails linking historic communities under the Rails-to-Trails program. For information on public transportation in Florida, visit www.floridatransit.org.

By Bus

Greyhound bus service links cities throughout Florida. Once there, city bus lines can be an excellent and inexpensive way of getting around.

By Rail

Amtrak serves several cities in Florida. The commuter Tri-Rail service (tel: 800-874-7245; www.tri-rail.com) links Miami and West Palm Beach and can be useful for reaching places like Fort Lauderdale and Boca Raton. Trains run at least once per hour, with reduced weekend service. Several cities, including Tampa and Orlando, have light rail service throughout the downtown and adjoining tourist areas.

⊘ Safety Tips for Motorists

Get advice from the car rental agent about the best route from the airport to your hotel. Better still, arrange to pick up your rental car from an agency near your hotel on the morning after you arrive, rather than tackle unfamiliar routes when very tired. Many car rental agencies will deliver your car to your hotel at no (or only a small) extra charge. If you have Internet services, a GPS app will be of help. If not, rent a GPS with your car, and a Sunpass, so you don't need to pay every toll with coins.

Ignore pedestrians or motorists who try to stop you. If you develop engine trouble, call the local police or state police for assistance. Always keep your car doors locked, windows closed, and valuables out of sight. Avoid taking short cuts in urban areas. If you get lost, drive to a well-lit and preferably busy area before stopping to look at your map.

By Taxi

Taxis are available in all the main tourist centers. They tend to be expensive, and you usually have to telephone for pick-up. Your hotel can call for you, otherwise numbers are listed in the Yellow Pages and online. Don't stand by the side of the road, even in Miami, and expect to hail a passing cab. Water taxis – a fun way to sightsee – are available on the Intracoastal Waterway in Fort Lauderdale. App-based transporters such as Uber and Lyft offer an alternative on some markets, generally costing less than taxis.

Private Transportation

Boat Rental

Floridians have an intimate relationship with water and many can park a boat right next to their house; in some places such as the Keys, a boat is almost a necessity. Guided sightseeing, fishing, and diving cruises are available in many areas, along with boat rentals. Don't leave Florida without getting out on its sparkling waters at least once.

Car Rental

Most rental agencies require you to be at least 25 years old and have a valid driver's license and a major credit card. Many take debit cards, too, and some will take cash in lieu of a credit card, but this might be as high as $500. Foreign travelers will need to produce a driver's license from their own country.

You will find rental car companies in most cities and airports; vehicles range from modest economy cars to luxury convertibles, vans, and 4WD vehicles. Rates are cheap both by US and international standards, but you should still shop around, preferably online, for the best rates and features. Smaller local rental firms outside the airports are often less expensive than the large national companies because they don't charge high airport fees. When choosing a vehicle, take into account gas prices, which, although cheap by European standards, add up on long-distance drives.

It's cheaper to arrange car rental in advance. Check with your airline, bus, or rental agent, travel agent, or the Internet for special package deals that include a car: rental rates can be reduced by up to 50 percent if you buy a so-called "fly-drive" deal. Be wary of offers of "free" car rental: such cars do not include extras like tax and insurance.

Go over the insurance coverage provisions carefully with the agent before signing the rental agreement. Loss Damage Waiver (LDW), or Collision Damage Waiver (CDW), is essential. Without it, you'll be liable for any damage done to your vehicle in the event of an accident, regardless of whether or not you are to blame. You are advised to pay for supplementary liability insurance on top of standard third-party insurance. Insurance and tax charges can add a lot to an otherwise inexpensive rental, so take it into account in your budgeting. Also, be sure to check your rental car carefully for existing damage, and make a careful note of any dents or dings before leaving the lot.

Driving

Of Florida's 112.3 million annual visitors, more than 57 million enter the Sunshine State by car. Bus, train, and taxi services within Florida are irregular, unreliable, and slow to cover the state's vast distances. A car is the most convenient way to travel around Florida.

Traffic has grown exceptionally dense on Florida's highways, reflecting the large numbers of new residents and growing tourism. Speed limits are strictly enforced. Drive with care and allow plenty of time to get to your destination. Avoid rush hour while traveling in metro areas. It's quickest to drive on interstates, the largest and fastest of the highways.

I-75 connects northern Florida with Gulf of Mexico cities and Miami; I-95 is the main east-coast route. I-10 is an east-west route across the Panhandle, and I-4 links Tampa to Daytona Beach. Toll roads include the Florida Turnpike across central Florida between the I-75 near Wildwood and Florida City, and the Beachline Expressway between Orlando and the Space Coast. Carry plenty of quarters and dollar bills if your car does not have a Sunpass or Epass; some highways do not have manned toll booths to give change.

US highways are not fast throughroutes; they are heavily trafficked and often lined with stores and interrupted by traffic lights. State routes are usually similar in size. County roads are secondary roads that are better for enjoying the scenery. Blue signs on the side of the road say "in case of emergency dial FHP". It is just another way to call 911, Florida's Highway Patrol or Emergency Services.

A

Accommodations

Accommodations in Florida range from luxury resorts, which cater to your every last need, to modest mom-and-pop motels; cozy, antiques-filled bed-and-breakfasts and small historic inns; and budget lodgings in youth hostels and campgrounds beside the ocean or in the forest.

Although rather anonymous, chain motels and hotels are usually reliable and in some places, such as Gainesville, are your main option if you don't want to go the bed-and-breakfast route. Family-owned motels, many built close to popular roadside attractions of the 1940s and 1950s, are usually acceptable if you're on a budget; a quick check online for photos and reader reviews can sometimes head off problems. In major tourist areas like Orlando, Tampa, and Miami Beach, the quality and variety of tourist accommodations is particularly good. Bedrooms are often large and normally come with two double or queen-sized beds.

Florida's beach communities and theme-park destinations like Orlando and Kissimmee also have a huge selection of self-catering vacation rentals, an often-over-looked option. Most are either in modern housing estates called "subdivisions," or in self-catering complexes, consisting of privately owned individual properties, or condominiums. The former, though usually in residential areas, are generally the best choice: homes are often large and have a pool and excellent facilities. Major tour operators offer self-catering accommodations. If you don't want to go completely self-catering, consider staying in one of the excellent all-suites hotel chains or in a motel room with a kitchenette, known as an efficiency.

Beachfront vacation rentals offer the best of both worlds. Many are right on the beach within small resort complexes that have swimming pools, laundry, barbecue grills, and gear for beach activities. In remote undeveloped areas along the Gulf, vacation rentals predominate.

Reservations and Prices

Reservations are generally required in advance. If you are traveling in the high season, book several months in advance if you have your heart set on a particular hotel – or if you want to stay inside Walt Disney World. Room rates vary enormously between the high tourist season in the winter months and the off-season months of January through mid-February and September through December (except Thanksgiving and Christmas weeks); the cost can rise by 30 percent or more during peak tourist months. Ask for a discount if you are staying for a week or more, or if you are visiting during the off season, which for many hotel proprietors is an extremely lean time. Florida imposes a resort tax in addition to the usual sales tax, which is added to the price of the rooms. It varies from county to county and ranges from 6 to 7 percent.

Chain Hotels and Motels

These are ubiquitous throughout the United States. Some people dislike chains because they offer no variety, lack a personal touch, and are often located in the most commercial, nondescript areas of town next to busy highways. The advantage is that once you've been to a hotel run by a particular chain, even though these are usually a franchise, you can bank on certain facilities and a standard of service wherever you are in the US. For travelers wanting to focus on their vacation, this can be a boon. Many of the chains offer free buffet breakfasts that are far from gourmet but do help offset costs, especially for a family.

Bed and Breakfasts

Bed-and-breakfasts vary greatly in terms of price and quality, but the one thing they have in common is that they are almost invariably in a private and/or historic home. Old towns such as Key West, St Augustine, Mount Dora, and Gainesville are known for their historic bed-and-breakfast accommodations; in outlying rural areas, bed-and-breakfast might be offered in a modern private home on several acres. Few have restaurants, and facilities will not be as extensive as in a regular hotel. Privacy can be an issue in older inns, but some have separate cottages with self-catering facilities, allowing you to come and go as you please. Hosts are usually a mine of information about local sights, and this can be a great way to make lifelong friends. For those travelers who enjoy the personal ambience – not to mention the afternoon teas, wine and cheese happy hours, and wonderful home-cooked breakfasts found in such places – bed-and-breakfasts are a great choice.

Camping

Over 100,000 campsites at some 700 campgrounds all over Florida offer ample choice of outdoors accommodations – from simple areas for tents and sleeping bags to elaborate villages with utility hook-ups for recreational vehicles (RVs), restaurants, pools, mini-golf courses, and planned activities.

Private Campgrounds

These have blossomed around popular tourist attractions, with the majority in Central Florida to accommodate the droves of Disney tourists. Walt Disney World is southwest of Orlando, and south of that, in Kissimmee, are many areas that are surprisingly rural and densely forested. If you avoid the main commercial strip, which is noisy and heavily trafficked, camping can be a good option.

A nationwide network of private campgrounds, called Kampgrounds of America (KOA, tel: 888-562-0558; www.koa.com), has around 30 members in Florida. They offer good-quality facilities, including swimming pool, restaurant, laundry, etc. Most accept reservations. Contact KOA at PO Box 30558, Billings, MT 59114-0558; tel: 888-562-0000; www.koa.com.

To obtain information about private campgrounds in Florida, contact Florida Association of RV Parks and Campgrounds' Camp Florida arm (tel: 850-562-7151; www.campflorida.com). The association will send you the Camp Florida Directory, which lists hundreds of campgrounds (representing nearly 50,000 campsites in Florida divided by region and with details of amenities. You can also see the properties online and download a digital copy of the book. You can make reservations using toll-free numbers listed in the brochure.

Camping in State Parks

Florida's state parks are blessed with incredibly scenic settings such as barrier-island beaches, natural springs, and inland forests. Many have campgrounds where campsites can be rented for up to 14 days and excellent, clean facilities, including showers, laundry, etc. They are hugely popular, especially among Florida residents, so book well in advance to avoid disappointment. For those who prefer a total nature experience, Primitive Camping is another option, and so is boat camping and equestrian camping. In general, reservations are accepted up to 11 months in advance of check-in: call the park where you plan to camp or the statewide number, 800-326-3521. You can also make a reservation online at http://floridastateparks.reserveamerica.com/welcome.do. In addition, parks normally hold back some spaces for people who arrive on the day. For more information, visit www.floridastateparks.org/things-to-do/stay-the-night.

Arrive early morning in the most popular areas to get a site. For traditional campsites, the base fee, usually $16–42, depending on location,

covers up to four people; up to eight people may stay at any site. At least one person, 18 years or older, must be in each group. There is a small charge for extra cars and electricity. Only pets on handheld leashes are allowed in state park picnic areas; no pets are allowed in the campgrounds or on public beaches. Fees tend to be higher in the Florida Keys, and only Florida residents may obtain an annual camping permit. Most state park campsites are booked solid in the busy late winter and early spring seasons. Cabins run $30 to $160 (less for seniors).

Camping with Mickey

Walt Disney World's Fort Wilderness Resort, located amid 650 acres (263 hectares) of woods and streams on Bay Lake, east of the Magic Kingdom, has 799 campsites. You can also rent trailers, which have air conditioning, color TV, radio, cookware, and linens, and sleep up to six people. It also has 409 Wilderness Cabins.

For information and reservations, contact Walt Disney World Central Reservations, PO Box 10,000, Lake Buena Vista, FL 32830; tel: 407-934-7639; http://bookwdw.reservations.disney.go.com.

Admission Charges

Admission is usually charged at both private and public museums and attractions, and national and state parks. As a rule, entrance fees vary widely, from $10 or under per person to $25 for special traveling exhibits at nationally known museums. Museums often offer free or reduced entrance fees certain days or evenings.

Consider buying multi-site passes for attractions in Orlando and Miami, if available. Local visitor centers and state welcome centers can assist you with planning, and many also offer discount coupons, with excellent deals on local attractions, hotels, and dining.

Budgeting for Your Trip

Allow $100–125 a night for decent-quality hotels for two people, although really memorable hotels

and bed-and-breakfasts tend to run closer to $200 or more a night – higher in hotspots like Miami Beach. At the other end of the spectrum, Florida has many gorgeous oceanside and forested campgrounds with full facilities for about $20 and up a night, and hostels and barebones motel lodgings can be found for less than $75.

You can probably get away with $30–40 a day per person for basic meals if you stick to diners, cafés, markets, and inexpensive restaurants and don't drink alcohol. Meals in better restaurants cost a lot more, but if you're determined to visit that famous high-end establishment and don't have the cash, one insider trick is to eat lunch there: you'll find many of the items on the dinner menu at much lower prices and still get to say you've eaten at a hip eatery.

Budget $2–3 per gallon for fuel for your rental car, though prices have been fluctuating wildly in recent years; most economy vehicles get over 30 miles per gallon. Trams, light rail, buses, and other public transportation in cities like Tampa and Miami are just a few dollars per ride, allowing you to get around for much less.

Children

Two things about traveling with children: First, be prepared, and second, don't expect to cover too much ground. Take everything you need, along with a general first-aid kit and those wonderful all-purpose traveler's aids: wet wipes and Ziploc baggies. If you need baby formula, special foods, diapers, or medication, carry them with you.

Although Florida is known for its theme parks (some of which which are geared toward children), much of the rest of the state can be an exciting destination for children of all ages. The many coastal towns offer beach opportunities, and exploring the Everglades can be an adventurous excursion. Make sure you have the appropriate gear whatever your destination. An extra bottle of water is always a good idea in the heat, and a wide-brimmed hat and high-factor sunscreen is essential with Florida's sunny weather.

Climate

Hurricanes

The hurricane season in Florida usually runs from June 1 through November 30. The number of Atlantic hurricanes in a given year can range from 2 to 20; on average one strikes Florida every two years. Still, the National Hurricane Center in Miami tracks each tropical storm very carefully, ready to issue evacuation orders if a hurricane is headed for the mainland.

Needless to say, tourists caught in Florida during an impending hurricane should immediately drop their plans and follow the National Weather Service bulletins on radio and television. A hurricane warning is usually issued 36 hours prior to predicted landfall; during this time high water and storm surges are highly possible. If warnings identify coastal areas where you are staying, be ready to evacuate to a designated shelter. Follow the blue road signs for your designated evacuation route.

Lightning

Florida is unofficially dubbed the "lightning capital of the country." The worst-hit area is by the central Gulf coast, but all of Florida receives its abundant share. The state recorded 52 deaths from 2007 to 2017. In just 1/1000th of a second, a bolt of lightning delivers a shock of 6,000–10,000 amps that can paralyze all body functions. If you see dark clouds and lightning nearby, take cover; many lightning victims are killed when getting in or out of cars. Do not use an umbrella during a lightning storm. Boaters should head for the nearest place they can tie up and evacuate their vessel.

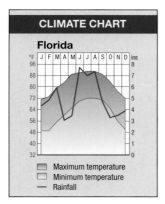

CLIMATE CHART

Florida

☐ Maximum temperature
☐ Minimum temperature
— Rainfall

Rainfall

Florida's hottest months are also the rainiest. Thunderstorms occur with such regularity each day that you can set your watch by them. South and Central Florida get rain almost daily in June and July. The Everglades soak up nearly 9ins (23cm) on average in June. In contrast with other parts of the US, there is little rain in November and December: only 2ins (5cm) falls on average across the whole state.

Temperature

Average summer temperatures range from 86–91°F (30–33°C), with little variation from north to south. Due to the relatively mild winters, many South Florida homes have meager heating systems that are tied into the air-conditioning systems, and erratic winter weather in recent years (including occasional snow flurries in Miami) has caught residents unprepared. At night, temperatures "cool off" to between 70°F (21°C) and 80°F (26°C), which usually means you'll need to use air conditioning or a fan to sleep in comfort.

Sea breezes along the coast and daily thunderstorms can create more bearable temperatures in north Florida cities in summer. Having said that, Florida is equally well known for oppressive heat and humidity and extreme weather conditions, arising from its location in Hurricane Alley, the path of hurricanes forming in the Caribbean.

Crime and Safety

Florida doesn't have a squeaky-clean reputation when it comes to crime, and attacks committed against tourists ruin the state's idyllic vacation-in-the-sun image periodically. The authorities have come up with various safeguards designed to protect visitors. Many of these are aimed at motorists, particularly in Miami. Road signs have been improved and orange sunburst signs help guide visiting drivers along the main routes to and from the airport.

A little common sense goes a long way: Don't carry large sums of money or expensive video/camera equipment. Walk purposefully and don't make eye contact with unwelcome strangers or respond to come-ons. Don't travel alone at night. Ask the staff in your hotel for advice about areas that should be avoided.

Customs Regulations

You can bring into the US the following duty-free items: 1 liter of alcohol, if over 21 years of age; 200 cigarettes, 50 cigars (not Cuban) or 2kg of tobacco, if you're over 18; and gifts worth up to $100 ($800 for US citizens). Travelers with more than $10,000 in US or foreign currency, travelers checks, or money orders must declare these upon entry. Meats, fruits, vegetables, seeds, or plants (and many prepared foods made from them) cannot be brought in to the country and must be disposed of in the bins provided before entering. For more information, contact US Customs & Border Protection (tel: 877-227-5511; www.cbp.gov).

Disabled Travelers

Florida accommodations, attractions, restaurants, and parks welcome visitors with physical disabilities and impairments. From ADA-compliant hotels to on-loan beach chairs and even mobility-assisted snorkeling and hang-gliding, visitor services throughout Florida go to great lengths to make sure everyone enjoys barrier-free access to sun and fun.

Under the Americans with Disabilities Act (ADA), accommodations built after January 26, 1995, and containing more than five rooms, must be usable by persons with disabilities. Older and smaller inns and lodges are often wheelchair-accessible. For the sight-impaired, many hotels provide special alarm clocks, captioned television services, and security measures. To comply with ADA hearing-impaired requirements, hotels have begun to follow special procedures; local agencies may provide TTY and interpretation services. Check with the front desk when you make reservations to ascertain to what degree the hotel complies with ADA guidelines. Ask specific questions regarding bathroom facilities, bed height, wheelchair space, and availability of services.

Restaurants and attractions are required to build ramps for those with limited mobility. Many major attractions have wheelchairs for loan or rent. Some provide menus, visitor guides, and interpreters for hearing- and seeing-impaired guests.

Visitors from out of the country can obtain the special parking permit by bringing a copy of their handicapped parking permit from home, photographic ID such as a passport, and $15 to a Florida vehicle licensing bureau. Visit www.flhsmv.gov to find a location.

For disability resources in Florida, contact the National Clearinghouse on Disability & Exchange (tel: 542-343-1283; www.miusas.org/ncde). The Society for the Advancement of Travel for the Handicapped (tel: 212-447-7284; www.sath.org) publishes a quarterly magazine on travel for the disabled.

Eating Out

As with everywhere else in the United States, you could travel from one side of Florida to the other and only ever eat in fast food restaurants. You'd never know there were gourmet meals to be had, or even excellent-quality casual meals, as sometimes even high-end restaurants hide behind unpretentious exteriors. But with its abundance of sunshine – and rain – it's a state where good, fresh produce is readily available, and chefs in restaurants of all levels – from counter-service to fine dining – are using locally raised fruits, vegetables, eggs, meat and fish in their kitchens. In fact, some culinary leaders have day-boat fishermen from both coasts text photos of their bounty so the chefs can choose which items to buy for that night's dinner service.

What to Eat

Florida has a very varied cuisine, with influences from lots of different places. Northern Florida is more like the rest of the southern USA, with plenty of barbecue, fried chicken, and grits, plus Louisiana-style Creole and Cajun flavors. Further south the Caribbean influences from places like Cuba and the Bahamas come into play, producing both authentic reproductions and hybrid style they call Floribbean. This is heavy on tropical tastes, from the many exotic fruits that grow here, including bananas, coconuts, mangoes, and papayas. Be sure to try a Cuban sandwich, too.

⊙ What to Do if a Hurricane Hits

During the storm

Stay indoors once the hurricane is buffeting your area. When the eye (the low-pressure area at the center of a hurricane) passes over, there will be a temporary lull in wind and rain for 30 minutes or more. Don't think it's over. When the eye has passed overhead, the storm will, in fact, resume – possibly with even greater force – from the opposite direction (hurricane weather systems rotate counterclockwise). Wait for word from the authorities before venturing out of your shelter.

If ordered to evacuate

Most coastal communities have detailed evacuation procedures in place. Evacuation route signs are permanently located along highways in many of these areas. Follow instructions and designated routes as quickly as possible. Take blankets, flashlights, extra clothing, food, water, and medications. Leave behind pets (which are not allowed inside public shelters).

After the storm passes

Drive with caution when told to return home. Debris in streets can be a hazard. Roads in coastal areas may collapse if soil has been washed from beneath them. Steer clear of downed or dangling utility wires. Stay tuned to radio stations for news of emergency medical, food, housing, and other assistance. If you have been staying in a rented home, re-enter the building with caution and make temporary repairs to correct hazards and minimize further damage. Open windows and doors to air and dry the house. Be careful when dealing with matches or fires in case of gas leaks.

Seafood abounds, of course, and you'll want to try local specialties like conch fritters, ceviche, and grits and grunts: southern grits served with grunt fish. You can indulge yourself with crabs and lobsters, which are both fresh and affordable, and try the novelty of gator tails. You'll also want to savor a key lime pie made with fresh key limes, whether you actually go to the Florida Keys or not.

Local entrepreneurs are starting to create local foods that are new to Florida. To point: In Ocala, Clear Creek Farm (www.clearcreekfarm.com) planted an olive grove and now produces flavored boutique olive oils and soaps. Artisan foods from jams to jerkies can be found in farmers markets and food halls throughout the state.

Theme Parks

For the most part, the theme parks are thought of, food-wise, as only fast food providers, but in certain cases that's not true. You can get a burger-fries-cola combo at any major park, but the biggies such as Walt Disney World and Universal Orlando Resort offer excellent full-service experiences within their parks and in the hotels and dining/shopping/entertainment complexes on campus – and they have tempting, healthful options on quick-service menus too.

The Mythos Restaurant at Universal's Islands of Adventure, for example, has been voted the World's Best Theme Park Restaurant, and offers dishes like Cranberry Blue Cheese Crusted Pork alongside hamburgers and grilled chicken. Lombard's Seafood Grille, also at Universal, gets rated highly too and provides a ringside seat at the evening lagoon show.

Disney World offers quality places such as The Hollywood Brown Derby, and Be Our Guest, with three dining rooms inspired by *Beauty and the Beast*. At the Animal Kingdom Lodge, the African-inspired restaurant Jiko (upmarket, table service) and Boma (buffet, but don't let that scare you in this case) offer top-of-the-line meals with a touch of exotica, plus South African wines.

What to Drink

Classic Florida drinks reflect the food, with a more southern US influence in the north – mint juleps – and a Caribbean influence in the south – mojitos and cuba libres. You'll find margaritas north, south, east, and west, as although the drink wasn't invented here, Jimmy Buffet finished writing his hit song 'Margaritaville' while in Key West and you'll hear it everywhere you go. Craft cocktails are all the rage in the more trend-forward restaurants and lounges, so you can get a cocktail made with fresh herbs and boutique spirits if you'd like. If you prefer non-alcoholic drinks, seek out a farm stand that sells fresh citrus juices. Boba teas are also popular in the larger markets.

You might think that beer would be popular in a hot state like Florida, and while Florida was late to the craft-brewing trend, it is game-on now from Pensacola to the Florida Keys. From Tampa's Angry Chair (http://angrychair-brewing.com) to Longwood's Hourglass Brewing (http://hourglassbrewing.com/), from Key West's Waterfront Brewery (www.thewaterfrontbrewery.com) to Santa Rosa's Ye Olde Brothers Brewery (www.yeoldebrothersbrewery.com), you can enjoy lovingly crafted ales, IPAs, lagers, ciders, and meads throughout the state. The website http://beerinflorida.com will match you up with breweries near your lodgings.

You can also enjoy good wine in Florida... if you order a bottle of Californian wine. The Florida climate doesn't lend itself to viniculture, but some people are experimenting with making wine from the state's tropical fruit. The results are, shall we say, variable. Some entrepreneurial oenophiles are taking a combo approach: They're producing wine in Florida using grapes imported from California. In the Orlando area, both Quantum Leap (www.quantumleapwinery.com) and Snowbirds Vintners (www.snowbirdsvintners.com) are leaders in this arena and their wines are quite respectable. Check their websites to see where you can find their wines in restaurants and retail stores.

Spirits are produced here now more than ever, too. In Central Florida, Winter Park Distilling Company (https://wpdistilling.com/) cooks up bourbon, rum, and more in a distillery open for visits. Palm Ridge Reserve (http://palmridgereserve.com/home.html) makes a whisky you may seek out once you try it. Also look to Alchemist Distilleries (http://alchemistdistillery.com/) in Miami, Fish Hawk Spirits (http://fishhawkspirits.com/home.html)in Ocala, and Cotherman Distilling (www.cothermandistilling.com) in Dunedin. For a full list, contact the Florida Distillers Guild.

Electricity

The United States uses 110–120 volts AC (60 cycles). US sockets take flat two-pronged plugs, sometimes with a third round prong. If visiting from outside North America, you may require an electrical adapter and a voltage transformer for any electronics or appliances you want to bring.

Embassies and Consulates

Foreign embassies are located in Washington, DC, several with outposts in Florida or New York.
These are the nearest consulates for English-speaking countries:
Australia: (Honorary Consul, by appointment only) Law Offices of Slesnick and Casey, LLP, 2701 Ponce de Leon Boulevard, Suite 20, Coral Gables, FL 33134; tel: 786-505-6802.
Canada: 200 South Biscayne Boulevard, Suite 1600, Miami, Florida 33131; tel: 305-579-1600.
New Zealand: 37 Observatory Circle, NW, Washington DC 20008; tel: 202-328-4800.
Republic of Ireland: Suite 260, Monarch Plaza, 3414 Peachtree Road, Atlanta, GA 30326; tel: 404-554-4980
South Africa: 333 East 38th Street, 9th Floor, New York, NY 10016; tel: 212-213-4880.
UK: 1001 Brickell Bay Drive, Miami, FL 33131; tel: 305-400-6400.

Emergencies

Wherever you are in Florida, in case of emergency, dial 911 to contact the local police, fire, or ambulance service.

H

Health and Medical Care

Most visitors to Florida will encounter no health problems during their stay: sunburn and mosquito bites in summer are the main nuisance. If you need medical assistance, ask the reception staff at your hotel, consult the Yellow Pages, or a Web search for the physician or pharmacist nearest you (in large cities, there is usually a physician's referral service number listed). The larger hotels may have a resident doctor.

If you need immediate attention, go to a hospital emergency room (ER). Walk-in medical clinics are much cheaper than hospital emergency rooms for minor ailments. Throughout the state, "urgent care" clinics welcome visitors with no appointment; without insurance patients pay a set price for each service. For small medical issues, many CVS (www.cvs.com/minuteclinic) and Walgreen's (www.walgreens.com/topic/pharmacy/healthcare-clinic.jsp) pharmacies have clinics, as well.

There is nothing cheap about being sick in the US – whether it involves a simple visit to the doctor or a spell in a hospital. The initial fee charged by a good hospital might be exorbitant on its own, and that's before the additional cost of x-rays, medicines, examinations, and treatments have been added. Foreign visitors are strongly advised to purchase travel insurance before leaving to avoid high urgent-care costs; a minimum coverage of $1 million unlimited medical cover is strongly recommended. Be sure you're covered for accidental death, emergency medical care, trip cancellation, and baggage or document loss.

Pharmacies: Always bring enough prescription medicines from home to cover the length of your trip. The cost of prescription medicine in the US is extremely high, and the same drugs may not be available.

For over-the-counter medicines, look for branches of Walgreens or CVS; many are open 24 hours. Wal-Mart, Target, Publix, and other grocery retailers also have pharmacy sections.

Health Hazards

Insects
People aren't the only creatures attracted to Florida's sun and sand. The state has many different types of insect.
Cockroaches or Palmetto Bugs: These pests grow to sizes unheard of in colder climates and usually steer clear of people.
Fire ants: Another Florida nuisance, fire ants can deliver a painful bite feeling like a stinging sensation. Some people suffer allergic reactions (dizziness and/or nausea) from fire ant bites and should seek immediate medical attention.
Love Bugs (Bibinoid Flies): These insects are sometimes called "love bugs" because you usually find them "flying united" into your hair, face, or car's windshield. They don't bite and are considered harmless, although they can be annoying.
Mosquitoes and Sand Flies: Are notorious for ruining outdoor

gatherings, especially at sunrise and sunset. The best combatant is repellent, lightweight clothing, and a thick skin.

Sunburn

One of the most common sights in Florida is that of the over-baked tourist painfully trying to sit or walk without rubbing against anything. If you are determined to get a suntan, do so gradually. Always wear a broad-brimmed hat and good-quality sunglasses, and use a high-factor sunscreen (40 plus) to protect your skin. Even on overcast days the sun's ultraviolet rays penetrate the clouds, giving you a false sense of safety. Dehydration and salt deficiency can lead to heat exhaustion, especially if taking medications or drinking alcohol or strong coffee. It's important to moderate these, drink plenty of water, and take time to acclimate to the heat and humidity if you aren't accustomed to it.

Heatstroke is a common problem for those from northern climates and is a potentially serious condition, so don't ignore the telltale signs. Long, uninterrupted periods of exposure to high temperatures can lead to heatstroke, which means that the body's core temperature rises to dangerous levels, and its normal cooling system – reddening and sweating – is overwhelmed. If you feel dizzy and fuzzy-brained, feel muscle weakness and start to stumble, and your skin has become pale and dry rather than red and sweaty, immediately begin spraying yourself with water or, better yet, pour it on. To head off problems, keep major arteries in your neck cool by wearing a wet bandanna or cotton shirt with a collar.

Internet

Most hotels offer complimentary high-speed internet access in their rooms and public areas. Many theme parks have Wi-fi too. Wireless access is often available in coffee bars such as Starbucks, restaurants including Panera, and fast food spots such as McDonald's. You'll have fewer options in rural areas, but most lodgings offer at least weak Wi-fi. Public libraries often offer free Wi-fi. Many large business-oriented hotels charge for internet access, though

free internet is increasingly becoming the norm.

LGBTQ Travelers

Parts of Florida are as conservative as the Bible Belt, and rural destinations away from the cities may be less welcoming of gay travelers. Keep a low profile in such areas to avoid any problems. Gay travelers receive a huge welcome in gay-friendly locales like South Beach (Miami), Fort Lauderdale, Key West, and downtown Orlando, where the annual Gay Days (www.gaydays.com) event at and away from theme parks attracts thousands of LGBT visitors every year. For more information, contact The Hub in Miami (tel: 305-397-8914; www.gogaymiami.com; at Equality Park of South Florida in Fort Lauderdale (tel: 954-463-9005; www.pridecenterflorida.org), the Gay and Lesbian Community Center in Key West (tel: 305-292-3223; www.glcckeywest.org), and The Center in Orlando (tel: 407-228-8272).

The Gay and Lesbian Yellow Pages (tel: 800-697-2812; www.glyp.com) offers regional information on GLBT activities in Florida. The Damron Company (www.damron.com) publishes guides aimed at lesbians and gay men and lists gay-owned and gay-friendly accommodations nationwide.

Media

Newspapers

Daily newspapers roll off the presses in every large Florida city. The most widely the *Orlando Sentinel* also have a reasonably wide circulation. There are several Spanish-language newspapers, and *The Miami Herald* has a very popular Spanish language sister paper, *El Nuevo Herald*. You can usually pick up *USA Today* from newspaper dispensers in the street or receive a free copy at certain hotel chains. Other national newspapers available in dispensers or good newsstands and bookstores include *The New York Times*, *The Washington Post*, and *The Wall Street Journal*. If you are planning on staying in a

particular area, check out the local newspaper ahead of time for advance information. All major newspapers today have online equivalents.

Television

All major cities have stations affiliated with major networks, local stations, and a vast number of cable hookups and satellite dish offerings. Hotel rooms usually have cable television, but you often have to pay to watch movies (Pay Per View). Newspapers give daily and weekly information on TV and radio programs, and you can view an on-screen program guide for TV.

Money

American dollars come in bills of $1, $5, $10, $20, $50, and $100, all the same size. The dollar is divided into 100 cents. Coins come in 1 cent (penny), 5 cents (nickel), 10 cents (dime), 25 cents (quarter), 50 cents (half-dollar), and $1 denominations. There is no Value Added Tax (VAT) in the US, but cities charge a sales tax, usually around 7–8 percent of the sale. Car rental companies charge both sales tax and service fees.

Nearly every tourist-oriented business in Florida accepts credit cards, but foreign visitors who prefer to use cash are advised to take US dollar travelers' checks, since exchanging foreign currency – whether as cash or checks – can prove problematic. You can seek out currency exchange facilities at busy centers like retail malls, but overall they're hard to find.

The easiest way to take out money is from an ATM (automatic teller machine) with a debit or credit card using your PIN. ATMs are readily available in the state, including at most supermarkets. The most widely accepted cards are Visa, American Express, MasterCard, Diners Club, and Discover. Maestro cards are often not accepted.

Be sure to check the rate of exchange and any other charges your bank may levy before using your card abroad. Some charge prohibitive rates. The ATM operators will usually apply a charge as well, though you will be notified of this on-screen before you complete the transaction.

Credit Cards are very much part of life in Florida, as in other parts of the US. They can be used to pay for just about anything. It is very common for car rental firms and hotels to take an imprint of your card as a deposit. If you rent beach equipment or bicycles you man have to leave your card at the counter. Car rental companies may oblige you to pay a large deposit in cash if you do not have a credit card.

If visiting Florida from another part of the USA or another country, make sure you tell your bank or credit card company that you'll be using your card out-of-state.

Opening Hours

Stores are often open seven days a week and tend to stay open into the evening, especially in tourist areas. Government offices are usually open only on weekdays from 8am or 9am to 5pm or 6pm.

Postal Services

The opening hours of federal post offices vary between central, big-city branches, and those in smaller towns or suburbs, but all are open Monday to Friday and some are also open on Saturday mornings. Drugstores, supermarkets, and hotels usually have a small selection of stamps. There are stamp-vending machines in the lobbies of most post offices as well as Automated Postal Centers that allow you to use a credit card to ship mail.

Large envelopes over 13oz must now be sent by two- to three-day Priority Mail in the US, or Media Mail if the envelope contains printed materials. The fastest service offered by the post office is Express Mail, which guarantees next-day delivery to most destinations within the US, and delivery within two to three days to foreign destinations by Global Express Mail. Private courier services offering overnight and two-day delivery are usually the most reliable, although more expensive than the US Post Office. Ground delivery, taking an average of five days, is very popular. Contact information for the main courier services are:

US Postal Service: 800-275-8777; www.usps.com

FedEx: 800-463-3339; www.fedex.com/us

DHL: 800-225-5435; www.dhl-usa.com
UPS: 800-742-5877; www.ups.com

Public Holidays

Public holidays in the US include: New Year's Day (January 1), Martin Luther King's Birthday (January 15), President's Day (third Monday in February), Memorial Day (last Monday in May), Independence Day (July 4), Labor Day (first Monday in September), Columbus Day (second Monday in October), Veteran's Day (November 11), Thanksgiving (fourth Thursday in November), and Christmas Day (December 25).

Telephones

In this era of mobile/cell phones, you'll find fewer public telephones in hotel lobbies, restaurants, drugstores, garages, roadside kiosks, convenience stores, and other locations throughout the state. To make a long-distance call from a payphone, use either a prepaid calling card, available in airports, post offices, and a few other outlets, or your credit card, which you can use at any phone. Watch out for in-room connection charges in the more upscale hotels: it's cheaper to use a payphone in the lobby. Many travelers use smartphone apps to call family and friends for free rather than making traditional calls. WhatsApp, Skype, and Facetime are all popular. Be aware that you probably won't be able to pick up a signal in remote rural areas, such as the Everglades and more remote Keys in South Florida. Check the coverage before starting out.

Time Zone

The continental US is divided into four time zones. From east to west, later to earlier, they are Eastern Standard Time, Central Standard Time, Mountain Standard Time, and Pacific Standard Time, each separated by one hour. Florida is on Eastern Standard Time (EST), five hours behind Greenwich Mean Time. On the first Sunday in April, Floridians set the clock ahead one hour in observation of daylight saving time. On the last Sunday in

October, the clock is moved back one hour to return to standard time.

Tipping

Service personnel expect tips in Florida. The accepted rate for baggage handlers is $2 per bag. For others, including taxi drivers and waiters, 15–20 percent is the going rate, depending on the level and quality of service. Sometimes tips are automatically included in restaurant bills when dining in groups of six or more. In high tourism areas 15–20 percent may be automatically added to any restaurant bill. In a hotel, count on around $2 per bag or suitcase handled by porters and bellboys, and 15–20 percent for room service. You should tip a doorman if he holds your car or performs other services. It is not necessary to tip chambermaids unless you stay several days, then budget about $2 a day. Some resorts include a mandatory "resort fee" that covers the service for the duration of your stay, regardless of your use of the various resort amenities.

Tourist Information

Information is available from various outlets in Florida, including www.visitflorida.com. Most cities have a Convention and Visitors Bureau (CVB) with a wealth of information on its website. State and national parks normally have excellent visitor centers, which dispense information and maps and offer ranger-guided talks and walks. Below is a list of some of the main tourist information offices in Florida:

Daytona Beach Area Convention and Visitors Bureau
Welcome Center: 616 S. Atlantic Avenue, Ormond Beach 32176
Office: 126 E. Orange Avenue, Daytona Beach 32114
Tel: 386-677-3308
www.daytonabeach.com

Greater Fort Lauderdale Convention and Visitors Bureau
101 NE Third Avenue, Suite 100
Tel: 954-765-4466 or 800-227-8669
www.sunny.org

Greater Fort Myers Chamber of Commerce Visitor Center
2310 Edwards Drive, PO Box 9289
Tel: 239-332-3624 or 800-366-3622
www.fortmyers.org

Visit Jacksonville and the Beaches
208 N Laura Street, Suite 102
Tel: 800-733-2668
www.jaxcvb.com

Florida Keys and Key West: Monroe County Tourism Development Council
510 Greene Street, Key West
Tel: 305-296-1552 or 800-771-5397
www.fla-keys.com

Miami Convention and Visitors Bureau
701 Brickell Avenue, Suite 2700
Tel: 305-539-3000 or 800-933-8448
www.miamiandbeaches.com

Art Deco Welcome Center
1001 Ocean Drive, Miami Beach
Tel: 305-531-3484
www.mdpl.org

Naples, Marco Island, Everglades Convention and Visitors Bureau
2660 North Horseshoe Drive, Naples
Tel: 800-688-3600
www.paradisecoast.com

Visit Orlando
Visitor Center: 8102 International Drive
Tel: 407-363-5872
www.visitorlando.com

Discover The Palm Beaches
1555 Palm Beach Lakes Boulevard, Suite 800
Tel: 800-554-7256
www.thepalmbeaches.com

Panama City Convention and Visitors Bureau
17001 Panama City Beach Parkway, Panama City
Tel: 850-233-5071
www.visitpanamacitybeach.com

Visit Pensacola
1401 E. Gregory Street, Pensacola
Tel: 850-434-1234 or 800-874-1234
www.visitpensacola.com

St. Augustine, Ponte Vedra, & The Beaches Visitors and Convention Bureau
29 Old Mission Avenue, St. Augustine
Tel: 904-209-4422
www.floridashistoriccoast.com

St Petersburg/Clearwater Area Convention and Visitors Bureau
8200 Bryan Dairy Road, Suite 200, Largo
Tel: 727-464-7200 or 877-352-3224
www.visitstpeteclearwater.com

Visit Sarasota County
1710 Main Street, Sarasota
Tel: 941-706-1253
www.visitsarasota.com

Visit Tallahassee
106 E. Jefferson Street, Tallahassee
Tel: 850-606-2305 or 800-628-2866
www.visittallahassee.com

Visit Tampa Bay
Visitor Center: 615 Channelside Drive, Suite 101A
Tel: 813-223-2752
www.visittampabay.com

Visas and Passports

Most foreign visitors need a machine-readable passport (which should be valid for at least six months longer than their intended stay) and a visa to enter the US. You should also be able to provide evidence that you intend to leave the US after your visit is over (usually in the form of a return or onward ticket), and visitors from some countries need an international vaccination certificate.

Certain foreign nationals are exempt from the normal visa requirements. Canadian citizens with a valid Canadian passport need no visa. Nor do Mexican citizens provided they have a Mexican passport as well as a US Border Crossing Card (Form I-186 or I-586), and as long as they are residents of Mexico.

Under the visa-waiver program (https://travel.state.gov/content/visas/en/visit/visa-waiver-program.html), citizens of 38 countries do not require a visa if they are staying for less than 90 days and have a round-trip or onward ticket. These include the UK, Ireland, Australia, New Zealand, Japan, France, and Germany. If you travel under this program, you will need to present an e-passport if your passport was assigned on or after 26 October 2006.

Mistakes are not accepted on immigration forms you fill in during the flight. So don't cross anything out – ask for a new form.

Those requiring a visa or visa information can apply by mail or by personal application to their local US Embassy or Consulate.

As of 2018, domestic travelers from Kentucky, Maine, Minnesota, Missouri, Montana, Oklahoma, Pennsylvania, South Carolina, and Washington will need not only a state driver's license to fly, but also another form of ID such as a passport, military ID, or permanent resident card.

Weights and Measures

Despite efforts to convert to metric, the US still uses the Imperial System of weights and measures.

A Miccosukee Indian family in the Everglades.

FICTION

Carl Hiassen: a *Miami Herald* journalist, Hiassen writes excellent comic thrillers set in Florida. They include: *Native Tongue*, which pokes fun at theme parks, and *Lucky You*, a twisted, wacky look at lottery winners.

Ernest Hemingway: many of "Papa's" novels and short stories were written in the 10 years he lived in Key West, but *To Have and Have Not* is the only one set in the town.

James W. Hall: the author of excellent Florida-based thrillers, including *Tropical Freeze*, *Bones of Coral*, *Hard Aground*, and *Mean Tide*.

James Weldon Johnson: raised in Jacksonville, son of Florida's first black female teacher, Johnson was part of the Harlem Renaissance. His *Autobiography of an Ex-Colored Man*, a fictional account of a biracial man, was originally published anonymously.

John D. MacDonald: one of Florida's most prolific novelists, MacDonald wrote many color-themed yarns about his detective Travis McGee, including *The Deep Blue Goodbye*, *The Dreadful Lemon Sky*, and *Dress Her in Indigo*.

Marjorie Kinnan Rawlings: the former New Yorker's 1942 work *Cross Creek* celebrates her colorful neighbors in the eponymous backcountry hamlet. *The Yearling*, the story of a boy and his fawn, won her a Pulitzer Prize.

Frank Slaughter: *Storm Haven, East Side General*, and *In a Dark Garden* are all novels with a Florida backdrop from another of the state's tale-spinners.

Harriet Beecher Stowe: The famed author of the 1851 antislavery serial novel *Uncle Tom's Cabin* also wrote travel essays that boosted Florida tourism in the Victorian steamboat era.

Zora Neale Hurston: one of Florida's leading black authors, Hurston is best known for *Their Eyes were Watching God*, about the devastating 1928 hurricane.

NATURAL AND CULTURAL HISTORY

Birds of Florida by Frances W. Hall. The definitive guide to Florida's feathered inhabitants.

Diving Guide to Underwater Florida by Ned DeLoach. An excellent guide to Florida's underwater world.

Dream State: Eight Generations of Swamp Lawyers, Conquistadors, Confederate Daughters, Banana Republicans, and other Florida Wildlife by Diane Roberts. The title of this engaging book by a Florida native says it all!

Everglades: River of Grass by Marjorie Stoneman Douglas. This seminal work describing the magic of the Everglades contributed to the creation of Everglades National Park.

The Florida Keys: A History and Guide by Joy Williams and Robert Carawan. This book provides a good introduction to the history of the islands.

Life on Mars: Gangsters, Runaways, Exiles, Drag Queens and Other Aliens in Florida by Alexander Stuart. An entertaining look at Florida, giving an insight into the motley bunch of people who live there.

The Magic Kingdom: Walt Disney and the American Way of Life by Steven Watt. A highly readable account of Walt's life and analysis of his huge influence on US – and world – culture.

Miami Then and Now by Carolyn Klepser and Arva Moore Parks. A look at the historical and contemporary development of Florida's famous city.

The Tropic of Cracker by Al Burt. An insightful and diverting look at past and future Florida.

Kerouac in Florida: Where the Road Ends by Bob Kealing. A well-written account of the famed writer's secretive Florida life.

A Naturalist in Florida: A Celebration of Eden by Archie Carr. Poetic essays about Florida's extraordinary natural history by the famed UF professor.

The Hiking Trails of Florida's National Forests by Johnny Molloy. A vividly descriptive guide to Florida's hiking trails, filled with facts and tidbits.

Some Kind of Paradise: A Chronicle of Man and the Land in Florida by Mark Derr. A fascinating history, with an emphasis on the impact of human society on the environment.

Team Rodent by Carl Hiassen. A scathing rant against all things Disney.

Visiting Small-Town Florida by Bruce Hunt. An insightful and interesting look into small-town Florida.

☉ Send Us Your Thoughts

We do our best to ensure the information in our books is as accurate and up-to-date as possible. The books are updated on a regular basis using local contacts, who painstakingly add, amend and correct as required. However, some details (such as telephone numbers and opening times) are liable to change, and we are ultimately reliant on our readers to put us in the picture.

We welcome your feedback, especially your experience of using the book "on the road". Maybe you came across a great bar or new attraction we missed. We will acknowledge all contributions, and we'll offer an Insight Guide to the best letters received.

Please write to us at:
Insight Guides
PO Box 7910
London SE1 1WE

Or email us at:
hello@insightguides.com

OTHER INSIGHT GUIDES

Insight Guide titles cover every major travel destination in North America, from Alaska to Arizona. City titles include *Boston, New York, Chicago, Las Vegas*, and *San Francisco*. Regional and state titles include *Colorado, USA on the Road, Arizona and the Grand Canyon, California, New England, Texas*, and *Alaska*.

CREDITS

4Corners Images 90
Alamy 79, 220, 236, 243B, 250
AWL Images 18, 126BL, 127BL, 160/161
Baltimore Orioles 291BR
Busch Entertainment Corp 54
Busch Gardens 262, 263
Charles E. Bennett 26, 28, 39
Corbis 46L, 55, 115ML, 164, 291TR
Delaware North 86/87, 163B
Discover Dominica Authority 71
Fotolia 150/151T, 151TR
Gaston de Cardenas 102T
Getty Images 7TR, 7TL, 8R, 14/15, 16, 53, 64/65T, 64BR, 64BL, 82, 88/89, 98, 111B, 124, 126/127T, 139, 141TR, 142, 175B, 181, 182, 183, 244B, 290/291T, 290BL, 305
Greater Miami Convention & Visitors Bureau 27, 102B
Gregory Wrona/Apa Publications 322
Henry Morrison Flagler Museum 46R
Historical Association of Southern Florida 127TR
iStock 1, 7ML, 9T, 17T, 65BR, 91T, 107T, 127BR, 129, 131B, 140/141T, 140BR, 141BL, 149, 150BR, 150BL, 151BL, 151BR, 153, 173, 175T, 176B, 190T, 191, 198, 275TR, 332
Jason Collier/SeaWorld 237B
Julie Fletcher/Visit Florida 207T, 230, 241, 242, 243T, 246
LEGOLAND Resort Florida 247, 248B
Library of Congress 31, 37, 40, 41, 42, 43R, 43L, 44, 45, 48/49, 51
Maitland House 245
Manuela Davies 83

Mark Read/Apa Publications 65ML
MOca/Steven Brooke 105B
NASA 7BL, 185T, 185B, 186B, 187
NOAA 65TR
Nowitz Photography/Apa Publications 6MR, 6BL, 6MR, 7BR, 10/11, 17B, 19, 20, 21, 22, 23, 24, 25, 29, 30, 32, 36R, 50, 58, 59, 60, 61, 62, 63, 65BL, 66, 67, 68R, 68L, 69, 70, 77R, 80, 81, 94, 95T, 95B, 96/97, 99, 101, 104T, 104B, 106, 108B, 109B, 109T, 110T, 110B, 111T, 112, 113, 114/115T, 114BR, 116, 117, 119T, 119B, 120B, 120T, 121B, 121T, 122, 123B, 123T, 128, 130, 131T, 132T, 133, 134T, 134B, 135T, 135B, 136, 137T, 137B, 138, 140MR, 141ML, 141BR, 143, 145, 146, 147B, 147T, 148, 152, 155T, 155B, 156, 157T, 157B, 158T, 158B, 159T, 159B, 162, 163B, 165, 167, 168, 169, 170T, 170B, 171, 172, 174, 176T, 177T, 177B, 178B, 178T, 179, 186T, 188, 189, 190B, 193T, 193B, 194T, 194B, 195B, 195T, 196T, 196B, 197B, 197T, 199T, 199B, 200T, 200B, 201T, 201B, 202T, 202B, 203B, 203T, 244T, 248T, 252/253, 254, 255T, 255B, 256, 257, 258, 259T, 259B, 260, 261T, 261B, 264, 265, 266, 267B, 267T, 268T, 268B, 269T, 269B, 270B, 271T, 271B, 272T, 272B, 273, 274/275T, 274BR, 274BL, 275ML, 275BL, 275BR, 276, 277, 279T, 279B, 280T, 280B, 281T, 281B, 282T, 282B, 283B, 283T, 284, 285B, 285T, 286T, 286B, 287B, 287T, 288T, 288B, 289, 290BR, 291ML, 291BL, 292/293, 294, 295T, 295B, 296, 297, 299T, 299B, 300T, 300B, 301T, 301B, 302, 303T, 303B, 304T, 304B, 306, 307, 308T, 308B, 309T, 309B,

310, 311, 312T, 312B, 313T, 313B, 314T, 314B, 315, 316, 317T, 317B, 318T, 318B, 319, 320, 324, 331
Patrick Farrell/Visit Florida 91B
Public domain 33, 34, 36L, 47, 52
Rey Villavicencio 56/57
Robert Harding 4, 12/13, 115BL
Rubell Family Collection, Miami 103T, 103B
Salvador Dalí Museum 270T
© Salvador Dalí. Fundación Gala-Salvador Dalí, (Artist Rights Society), 2014 / Collection of the Salvador Dalí Museum, Inc., St. Petersburg, FL, 2014. 7MR
Scott Audette/Visit Florida 75
SeaWorld 8L, 76, 238T, 238B
Shutterstock 9B, 35, 108T, 125, 126BR, 180, 184, 204/205, 206, 239
State Library and Archives of Florida 38
Steven Brooke/Museum of Contemporary Art, North Miami 105T
Stock Connection/REX/Shutterstock 132B
SuperStock 107B, 114BL
Universal Orlando Resort 6ML, 72, 77L, 231, 233, 235, 237T
Visit Florida 74, 84/85, 115TR, 115BR, 213, 249
Walt Disney World Resort 73, 207B, 208, 209, 211, 214, 215, 216T, 216B, 217, 218, 219, 222T, 222B, 223T, 223B, 224T, 224B, 225, 226, 227T, 227B, 229
Wheninusa 212
Willie J. Allen Jr/Visit Florida 240T, 240B

Front cover: Miami South Beach *iStock*
Back cover: Ripsaw Falls ride at Universal Studios *Shutterstock*
Front flap: (from top) Miami Beach *iStock*; Sloppy Joes, Key West

Shutterstock; Miami's Little Havana Calle Ocho Festival. *iStock*; Airboat in the Everglades *Shutterstock*
Back flap: The Hulk coaster at Universal Studios *iStock*

INSIGHT GUIDE CREDITS

Distribution
UK, Ireland and Europe
Apa Publications (UK) Ltd;
sales@insightguides.com
United States and Canada
Ingram Publisher Services;
ips@ingramcontent.com
Australia and New Zealand
Woodslane; info@woodslane.com.au
Southeast Asia
Apa Publications (SN) Pte;
singaporeoffice@insightguides.com
Worldwide
Apa Publications (UK) Ltd;
sales@insightguides.com
Special Sales, Content Licensing and CoPublishing
Insight Guides can be purchased in bulk quantities at discounted prices. We can create special editions, personalised jackets and corporate imprints tailored to your needs.
sales@insightguides.com
www.insightguides.biz

Printed in China by CTPS

First Edition 1982
Fourteenth Edition 2018

Every effort has been made to provide accurate information in this publication, but changes are inevitable. The publisher cannot be responsible for any resulting loss, inconvenience or injury. We would appreciate it if readers would call our attention to any errors or outdated information. We also welcome your suggestions; please contact us at:
hello@insightguides.com

www.insightguides.com

Editor: Rachel Lawrence
Author: Rona Gindin
Head of Production: Rebeka Davies
Update Production: Apa Digital
Picture Editor: Tom Smyth
Cartography: original cartography Berndtson & Berndtson, updated by Carte

CONTRIBUTORS

This new edition of Insight Guide Florida was commissioned by **Rachel Lawrence**, Insight Guides' North America editor. It was updated by **Rona Gindin**, an award-winning travel writer based in Orlando, who travels all over the USA and abroad. She loves Florida for the range of its activities, from the thrill of seeing manatees and 'gators in the wild, to cultural highlights like the Dalí Museum, and the fun of places like the Space Coast and of course the theme parks. This edition builds on earlier editions produced by **Mike Gerrard**, **Martha Bayne**, **Joann Biondi**, **Jason Dehart**, **Nicky Leach**, **Kay Scheller**, **William Scheller**, **Elana Schor**, and **Christina Tourigny**. The text was indexed by **Penny Phenix**. Most of the spectacular photography is the work of **Richard** and **Abraham Nowitz**.

ABOUT INSIGHT GUIDES

Insight Guides have more than 45 years' experience of publishing high-quality, visual travel guides. We produce 400 full-colour titles, in both print and digital form, covering more than 200 destinations across the globe, in a variety of formats to meet your different needs.

Insight Guides are written by local authors, whose expertise is evident in the extensive historical and cultural background features. Each destination is carefully researched by regional experts to ensure our guides provide the very latest information. All the reviews in **Insight Guides** are independent; we strive to maintain an impartial view. Our reviews are carefully selected to guide you to the best places to eat, go out and shop, so you can be confident that when we say a place is special, we really mean it.

Legend

City maps

	Freeway/Highway/Motorway
	Divided Highway
	Main Roads
	Minor Roads
	Pedestrian Roads
	Steps
	Footpath
	Railway
	Funicular Railway
	Cable Car
	Tunnel
	City Wall
	Important Building
	Built Up Area
	Other Land
	Transport Hub
	Park
	Pedestrian Area
	Bus Station
	Tourist Information
	Main Post Office
	Cathedral/Church
	Mosque
	Synagogue
	Statue/Monument
	Beach
	Airport

Regional maps

	Freeway/Highway/Motorway (with junction)
	Freeway/Highway/Motorway (under construction)
	Divided Highway
	Main Road
	Secondary Road
	Minor Road
	Track
	Footpath
	International Boundary
	State/Province Boundary
	National Park/Reserve
	Marine Park
	Ferry Route
	Marshland/Swamp
	Glacier Salt Lake
	Airport/Airfield
	Ancient Site
	Border Control
	Cable Car
	Castle/Castle Ruins
	Cave
	Chateau/Stately Home
	Church/Church Ruins
	Crater
	Lighthouse
	Mountain Peak
	Place of Interest
	Viewpoint

INDEX

MAIN REFERENCES ARE IN BOLD TYPE

INSIGHT ⦿ GUIDES

OFF THE SHELF

Since 1970, **INSIGHT GUIDES** has provided a unique perspective on the world's best travel destinations by using specially commissioned photography and illuminating text written by local authors.

Whether you're planning a city break, a walking tour or the journey of a lifetime, our superb range of guidebooks and phrasebooks will inspire you to discover more about your chosen destination.

INSIGHT GUIDES

offer a unique combination of stunning photos, absorbing narrative and detailed maps, providing all the inspiration and information you need.

PHRASEBOOKS & DICTIONARIES

help users to feel at home, when away. Pocket-sized with a free app to download, they go where you do.

CITY GUIDES

pack hundreds of great photos into a smaller format with detailed practical information, so you can navigate the world's top cities with confidence.

EXPLORE GUIDES

feature easy-to-follow walks and itineraries in the world's most exciting destinations, with our choice of the best places to eat and drink along the way.

POCKET GUIDES

combine concise information on where to go and what to do in a handy compact format, ideal on the ground. Includes a full-colour, fold-out map.

EXPERIENCE GUIDES

feature offbeat perspectives and secret gems for experienced travellers, with a collection of over 100 ideas for a memorable stay in a city.

www.insightguides.com

Islands of Adventure

Universal Studios
Florida

Men In Black

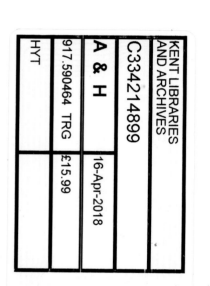

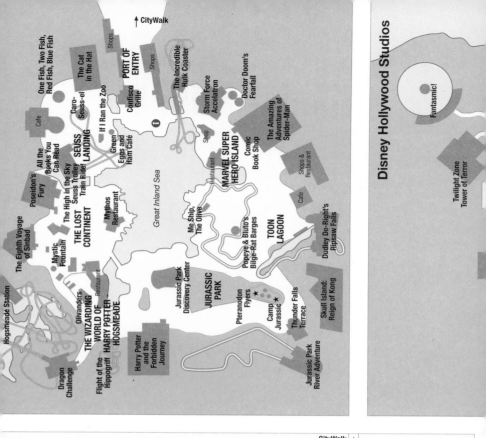

↑ CityWalk

PORT OF ENTRY

Shops

One Fish, Two Fish, Red Fish, Blue Fish

The Cat in the Hat

Caro-Seuss-el

Confisco Grille

If I Ran the Zoo

Cafe

SEUSS LANDING

All the Books You Can Read

Poseidon's Fury

Green Eggs and Ham Café

The High in the Sky Seuss Trolley Train Ride!

The Incredible Hulk Coaster

Storm Force Accelatron

Doctor Doom's Fearfall

The Amazing Adventures of Spider-Man

MARVEL SUPER HERO ISLAND

Comic Book Shop

THE LOST CONTINENT

Mythos Restaurant

Restaurant

Shop

Great Inland Sea

Me Ship, The Olive

Popeye & Bluto's Bilge-Rat Barges

Cafe

Shops & Restaurant

TOON LAGOON

Dudley Do-Right's Ripsaw Falls

The Eighth Voyage of Sinbad

Mystic Fountain

Olivanders

Restaurant

THE WIZARDING WORLD OF HARRY POTTER - HOGSMEADE

Hogsmeade Station

Jurassic Park Discovery Center

JURASSIC PARK

Pteranodon Flyers

Camp Jurassic ★ ★

Thunder Falls Terrace

Skull Island: Reign of Kong

Dragon Challenge

Flight of the Hippogriff

Harry Potter and the Forbidden Journey

Jurassic Park River Adventure

Disney Hollywood Studios

Fantasmic!

Twilight Zone Tower of Terror

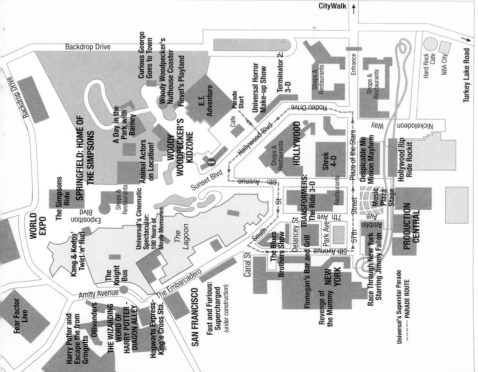

↑ CityWalk

Backdrop Drive

Backdrop Drive

Curious George Goes to Town

Woody Woodpecker's Nuthouse Coaster

WORLD EXPO

A Day in the Park with Barney

Fievel's Playland

Parade Start

Terminator 2: 3-D

The Simpsons Ride

SPRINGFIELD: HOME OF THE SIMPSONS

Animal Actors on Location!

WOODY WOODPECKER'S KIDZONE

E.T. Adventure

Cafe

Universal Horror Make-up Show

Hollywood Blvd

Exposition Blvd

Shop & Restaurants

Sunset Blvd

Universal's Cinematic Spectacular: 100 Years of Movie Memories

The Lagoon

5th Avenue

8th Avenue

Rodeo Drive

HOLLYWOOD

Shops & Restaurants

Shops & Restaurants

Shrek 4-D

Entrance

Shops & Restaurants

Kang & Kodos' Twirl-'n'-Hurl

The Knight Bus

South St

Canal St

Delancey St

TRANSFORMERS: The Ride 3-D

7th Ave

Restaurants

Plaza-of-the-Stars

Despicable Me Minion Mayhem

Nickelodeon Way

Shops & Restaurants

Hard Rock Cafe

NBA City

SAN FRANCISCO

The Embarcadero

The Blues Brothers Show

Park Ave

57th Street

Music Plaza Stage

Hollywood Rip Ride Rockit

Fear Factor Live

Amity Avenue

Harry Potter and the Escape the from Gringotts

Olivanders

THE WIZARDING WORD OF HARRY POTTER - DIAGON ALLEY

Hogwarts Express - King's Cross Sta.

Fast and Furious: Supercharged (under construction)

Revenge of the Mummy

NEW YORK

Finnegan's Bar and Grill

Race Through New York Starring Jimmy Fallon

5th Avenue

Amblin Ave

PRODUCTION CENTRAL

Turkey Lake Road

Universal's Superstar Parade
- - - PARADE ROUTE